Archival Afterlives

Archival Afterlives

Cixous, Derrida, and the Matter of Friendship

Laura Hughes

NORTHWESTERN UNIVERSITY PRESS
EVANSTON, ILLINOIS

Northwestern University Press
www.nupress.northwestern.edu

Printed in the United States of America

10 9 8 7 6 5 4 3 2 1

Library of Congress Cataloging-in-Publication Data

Names: Hughes, Laura (Laura Elspeth Neeley), author.
Title: Archival afterlives : Cixous, Derrida, and the matter of friendship / Laura Hughes.
Description: Evanston, Illinois : Northwestern University Press, 2023. | Includes bibliographical references and index.
Identifiers: LCCN 2023017337 | ISBN 9780810146273 (paperback) | ISBN 9780810146280 (cloth) | ISBN 9780810146297 (ebook)
Subjects: LCSH: Cixous, Hélène, 1937—-Criticism and interpretation. | Cixous, Hélène, 1937—-Friends and associates. | Derrida, Jacques—Friends and associates. | Authors, French—20th century—Archival resources. | Critics—France—Archival resources.
Classification: LCC PQ2663.I9 Z745 2023 | DDC 848.91409—dc23/eng/20230418
LC record available at https://lccn.loc.gov/2023017337

To my parents

CONTENTS

ACKNOWLEDGMENTS

The great joy of this project has been to experience the archival communities and ensembles that give life to literary artifacts. I am grateful to all of the archivists, librarians, staff, and researchers for their work and for our interactions, however brief.

Work for this project began in 2008 at the Bibliothèque nationale de France, to which I returned many times over the next ten years. It was an ongoing honor to bear witness to Marie-Odile Germain's craft in the *fonds* Cixous, and a treasure to experience her generous hospitality and patient, thorough explanations of the collection over the course of many years as this project attempted to keep pace with those growing, morphing archives. The close readings of Cixous's manuscripts, and of her writing process, in what follows are an homage to Germain's work. At the IMEC, which I visited in 2012, 2013, and 2015, I came to understand the vibrant intellectual life of archival communities—especially the dialogues across multiple *fonds*. The enchantment of research at the IMEC arises not only from the site itself but from conversations with the archivists, specialists, and scholars in residence there, all of whom I thank, and particularly André Derval, for his support at the beginning stages of this research. I am grateful for the assistance of archivists at the Special Collections & Archives at the University of California, Irvine's Langson Library in 2012, 2014, and 2018, and for exchanges with Christine Kim, Steve MacLeod, and especially Alex Bisio in the reading room there and through e-mail, which illuminated the inner workings of archival science, method, and innovation. My research in the Department of Special Collections at Princeton's Firestone Library in 2016 was guided and facilitated by archivists and librarians: it was there that I came to physically feel the power of eclecticism and asynchrony in archival assemblages. My very first taste of "archival afterlives" was in the Harry Ransom Center (at the University of Texas at Austin), where Charles Rossman introduced me to the James Joyce manuscripts, and where I also consulted the manuscripts of Beckett and Kerouac with delight and awe. I thank the archivists there for their indulgence.

Without Hélène Cixous's generosity of mind and spirit, this book would certainly have been meager: she answered questions and granted access to her materials in her role as author, and my conversations with the virtuosic thinker and teacher that she is helped me to develop essential aspects of this project. Her seminar, freely given, continuously, has been an internal intellectual workshop for this project at many points along the way. I thank Benjamin Gregg at the University of Texas, Austin, for pointing me in that direction. My gratitude is also extended to Jacques Derrida's heirs for granting permission to access and include materials from the Derrida collections in this book.

A preliminary version of this project was shepherded by Anne Emmanuelle Berger, who guided a "remedial Derrida" workshop in 2008 that planted the seeds of crossover between Cixous and Derrida. In my mind, there has never been a textual Derrida without Cixous, and for that I have Anne Berger to thank. I also thank Marie-Dominique Garnier and Tiphaine Samoyault at the Université Paris 8 (Vincennes/Saint-Denis) and the Centre d'études de genre for thinking through early iterations of this project with me.

I thank Manuel Irniger and Claudia Simma, the best kind of *archontes à domicile*, for their hospitality and archival tour. I am grateful to Marta Segarra for convening Cixous and Derrida scholars for many crucial conversations at conferences through Paris 8 and the CNRS group LEGS. Thank you to Peggy Kamuf for delightful, inspiring conversations and crucial support of this project. I am grateful to Laurent Milesi for his reading and his decisive comments.

The encouragement, persistence, patience, and labor of Faith Wilson Stein, Anne Gendler, and Trevor Perri at Northwestern University Press deserve immense thanks. I also extend my gratitude to the anonymous readers for the press, whose comments honed the shape and argument of this book.

I am fortunate to have been part of an intellectual community at New York University that gave continued life and support, as well as much-needed critical resistance, to this project as it took shape. Much of this research was made possible by fellowships and grants from the Institute for Citizens & Scholars (formerly the Woodrow Wilson Foundation) and from New York University and its Department of French, as well as the NYU Paris Global Research Institute. Emily Apter's guidance as thesis advisor both sharpened and broadened the project as she lent her critical verve to the aesthetic and political implications of my ideas. Denis Hollier, Richard Sieburth, Geoffrey Bennington, Avital Ronell, Judith Miller, Phillip Usher, Lucien Nouis, and Cécile Bishop lent critical weight with their readings and discussions. Lisa Darms's work on ephemera at the Fales Library blew my mind. I owe a huge debt of gratitude to Sarah Kay for forever changing the way I think about manuscripts: the inspiration of her work and the generosity of her repeated readings and conversations widened the scope of this project both theoretically and methodologically.

For friendship and intellectual life, I thank Anne Brancky, Youna Kwak, and Katie LaPorta, who were there for the most chaotic moments, helping me to refine my ideas and prose. For intellectual companionship, I thank yasser elhariry, Raphaël Sigal, Fredrik Rönnbäck, Matt Amos, Niamh Duggan, Iris Brey, Virginie Lauret, Manoah Finston, Michelle Lanchart, Andrew

Dubrov, Dan Benson, Suzy Cater, Chris Bonner, Downing Bray, Rachel Watson, and Nazanin Yvonne Sullivan; and Ophélie Chavaroche and Jennifer Row. Gratitude for widening my writing lens: Katherine Herman, Sarah Labrie, Stephanie Staab. For hospitality: Anna Shoemaker, Marie Lesbats, Emilie Bannwarth, and Maria Pisciotta Ito. For Sappho, at a crucial moment: Stephanie again, Anna bis, Eiren Shea, and Emily Thetford-Smith.

Immense gratitude is due to Patricia Hughes and Daniel Hughes, and to Corinne Tassin, for life itself, and for unflinching material and emotional support throughout the years, for not only encouraging me to continue this work, but also for sharing my enthusiasm, and letting me work out some of my ideas; for example, in salvaging and restoring hundreds of my grandmothers' recipe cards, soaked through by the floodwaters of Hurricane Harvey. The ones written in pencil survived.

I cannot adequately express my gratitude for the incalculable influence and support of my partner in life and in making of all kinds: thank you, Edwin. And to Dot, whose arrival motivated me to see this through.

Archival Afterlives

Introduction

✦

An Archived Friendship

puissant *l'esprit de* *la lettre*	*je mourrai de mon* *vivant*
mighty *the spirit of* *the letter*	*I will die* *living*

The black ink is crisp against the tan background: a heavy-weight *chemise* folder, cut imprecisely along the crease, stabilizing the thick sheaf of papers. These two morsels of text bracket a central annotation, in blunted blue pencil slanting diagonally across the surface. Reoriented, it reads:

Aucun mort
n'a jamais dit
son dernier mort.

None of the dead
has ever said
their last word.

Mort . . . or is it *mot*? The pencil marks bear down hard, but I can barely make out the annotation as it runs on, nearly indecipherable, into the mottled surface of sturdy paper stock. Its corners are bent, curving around the papers it supports: loose-leaf, photocopied pages of a long, handwritten manuscript. The manuscript and the annotations are written by two different hands. The ink and pencil annotations resonate with an aphoristic ambiguity in their archival context. The life and death of this artifact are entangled in disparate moments of reading and writing.

I am consulting one of Hélène Cixous's manuscripts in Jacques Derrida's library, very likely a version of *OR: Les Lettres de mon père*.[1] The manuscripts are drafts of works in their final stages that Cixous had sent to her friend, whose annotations leave a record of reading on the documents: some handwritten and photocopied, some typed up and printed out, with notes to the recipient explaining their provisional state. In fact, I am not in Derrida's library, which occupied his home outside of Paris, but in Princeton, New Jersey, where the contents of his library have been transferred and conserved. The finding aid for this collection, which lists items in their original shelving order, "allows the virtual reconstruction of the contextual placement of works on his Studio shelves," prompting the researcher to envision the space and imagine the logic of Derrida's idiosyncratic filing system. At Princeton University's Firestone Library, this order has been disturbed as the materials have been sorted and stored according to their value and fragility: books with handwritten annotations and interleaved artifacts are stored off-site in order to preserve the delicate content. I have requested several boxes of these materials—books and "documents" by Cixous—looking for traces of Cixous and Derrida's friendship that connect the two writers beyond their publication record.

Acquired in 2015, nearly a decade after his death, the Jacques Derrida Library at Princeton is the third and most recent archival collection of Derrida's oeuvre. Along with the *fonds* Cixous,[2] it is the fourth collection to contain documents of friendship between the two writers. Other friends are present in these collections, too, in correspondence and in manuscripts. But Cixous and Derrida's friendship was exceptional: it spanned four decades, generated a wealth of texts, and left traces in their archival collections both in France and in the United States. Their publications about each other and about their friendship increased in the 1990s and early 2000s, and at the same time the two authors were setting up separate archival collections, indicating that for both authors friendship and archiving are interrelated. As both authors envisioned an afterlife for their writing in material, institutional form, their friendship became a venue for experimenting with the legacy of their writing. In parallel, the archive—both the theme and the thing—bears dynamic traces of their vital friendship, a dialogue that continues in the archival collections. This book takes the "matter" of their friendship, in both senses of the word, as grounds for living on in the archive.

Cixous's and Derrida's four archival collections contain work spanning seven decades, in a wide variety of materials on paper and digital supports, in four separate institutions both public and private, on two continents. In 1990, Derrida's papers inaugurated the Critical Theory Archive at the University of California, Irvine, which had welcomed Derrida as a professor and thinker for over twenty years. The interest in Derrida's work at UC Irvine and other American universities contrasted with the lukewarm and even skeptical attention his writing received in France.[3] Yet Derrida's donation to UC Irvine was not exhaustive, and later in the decade he began to envision and then to set up a second collection at the Institut Mémoires de l'édition contemporaine (IMEC) in Normandy, France. His manuscripts and course materials are spread across the two institutions; the IMEC holds his correspondence and other documents and continues to receive materials from Derrida's estate. When Princeton acquired his personal library in 2015, the goal was to transfer the entirety of his bookshelves' contents and preserve their original order, though some materials were diverted to the collection at the IMEC. The relationships between the three sites of Derrida's archives—in California, New Jersey, and Normandy—indicate diverging institutional archival paradigms, as well as challenges to preservation and accessibility at the material level of individual documents.

Cixous's archives further complicate this constellation. Having considered placing her papers in the IMEC around the same time that Derrida's collection was being established there, she decided instead to donate the entirety of her work to the Bibliothèque nationale de France (BNF), where an archivist had expressed particular interest in and knowledge of her writing.[4] The *fonds* Cixous there, inaugurated in 2003, continues to grow as the writer releases new and newly discovered material to the BNF. It also awaits a significant amount of correspondence between Cixous and Derrida, stored at Cixous's home, calling attention to other extra-institutional, personal archives holding materials such as Cixous's seminar recordings, which were only recently transferred to the BNF.

As it makes its way into their published texts, their personal correspondence, and other archival artifacts, Cixous and Derrida's friendship causes overlaps and echoes in the archival records, often couched materially in evocative groupings. For example, the first text Derrida wrote about Cixous, in the fervor of his initial discovery of her writing, is stored at Princeton. The yellowing typescript is paper-clipped to several other papers, folded in half, and interleaved in Derrida's copy of Cixous's first book, *Le Prénom de Dieu* (1967). This artifact—the book and its contents—illustrates Derrida's "use of the library as an ad-hoc filing system" (as Princeton's finding aid describes it), as well as Derrida's practice of reading and rereading Cixous over several decades. The text is attached to a schedule for the 1998 conference "Hélène Cixous, Croisées d'une Œuvre," where Derrida presented his long essay *H. C. pour la vie, c'est à dire. . . .* In this lecture, Derrida sets for himself the impossible task of distilling Cixous's writing into its most elemental form and of putting words to the force he perceives in her work. He describes his first encounter with Cixous's writing as "un mélange de révélation et d'incompréhension" (126; "a mixture of revelation and incomprehension," 147), and describes the manuscript of *Le Prénom de Dieu* as "un objet littéraire non identifiable" (14; "an unidentifiable letter and literary object," 7). As if to prove his long-standing readership dating back to *Le Prénom de Dieu*, he turns to the archive: "J'ai même écrit le 'quatrième de couverture' du livre dont l'éditeur n'a retenu que quelques lignes mais dont je viens de retrouver l'original dans mes papiers. Je l'ai là, je le trouve en souriant, quant à elle ou quant à moi, d'une pré-voyance quasi somnambulique"

(127; "I even wrote the 'blurb' on the back cover of the book, from which the publisher only kept a few lines but whose original I have just found again among my papers. I have got it here; I find it with a smile, concerning her or myself, almost somnambulistic in its foresight," 148). Here it is, he says at the conference; and here it is in the Derrida Library, clipped to the conference schedule and tucked into the book it was meant to accompany: *Le Prénom de Dieu*. At the conference, Derrida refers to the typescript of his first critical text on Cixous with an ambiguous agency that goes beyond simple personification: he finds it smiling. It could be Derrida who is smiling here—*je le trouve en souriant*—but this ascription must be revised when "elle" (Cixous) and "moi" (Derrida) become the objects of the smiling gaze conferred by the typescript, in a state of consciousness somewhere between sleeping and waking: an otherworldly vigilance that suggests a slip in identity and temporality. The "pré-voyance" of the typescript measures the duration between Derrida's first and his later reading. These two texts are joined in the archive. Encountering this typescript and the book that encloses it at the Firestone Library relaunches Derrida's readings of Cixous, as the artifact becomes an *objet littéraire non identifiable* akin to Cixous's first texts.

The artifact is further emblematic of the general principle of archival instability, as it is linked to Cixous's rediscovery of her manuscript of *Le Prénom de Dieu*. Cixous had long considered the manuscript lost, but it reappeared in 2009, bearing handwritten marks Cixous recognized as Derrida's. The manuscript's rediscovery is the subject of *Double Oubli de l'Orang-Outang* (2010). At the BNF, the dossier of *Double Oubli* includes a fragment of an unidentified typescript claiming to quote from "le premier texte que Jacques Derrida ait jamais tourné vers le texte d'Hélène Cixous" ("the first text Jacques Derrida ever turned towards Hélène Cixous's texts"), in late-1960s Derridean style, though it includes nothing to confirm its author.[5] But the fragment does not correlate to the text at Princeton. Derrida's doubled "first" readings call into question the notion of an archival original through the typescripts that circulate in and around *Le Prénom de Dieu* at the BNF and at Princeton.

These documents are important not only as evidence of Derrida's first encounter with Cixous's writing, and as precious originals giving rise to published texts, but also for the way these textual objects circulate between the two writers and their archival collections. Marking a crossover between Derrida's and Cixous's archives, the two typescripts and Derrida's copy of Cixous's book are emblematic of their literary friendship, both at its beginnings and as it spans time. The contingencies of their preservation and rediscovery make for a dynamic experience of consultation. The idiosyncrasies of the artifact's physical makeup encourage conservation and contemplation: the marks left by a rusty paper clip, simultaneously corroding the papers and branding their point of contact, the tears and folds, the insertions and retractions, even the weight of the paper and its porosity to ink and stains. The artifact's material fragility signifies beyond its textual content. Derrida stored manuscripts, notes, and other documents between, in, and around his copies of Cixous's books on the shelves of his attic workroom, and his personal storage system offers a virtual connection between institutions. His copy of *Le Prénom de Dieu* and the draft of his first short text on Cixous link up with the manuscript of *H. C. pour la vie* at the IMEC, with the dossier of *Le Prénom de Dieu* at the BNF's *fonds* Cixous, and with the former site of Derrida's library in his home. The material, temporal, and geographic circumstances of these objects are themselves capable of producing networks of meaning and communication. They illustrate the open-endedness of Cixous's and Derrida's archival collections and the circulation of materials after the writer's death, like a sleepwalking presence, or a revenant.

What kind of afterlife is this? What kind of *mort*, *esprit*, or *vivant* (word, spirit, living) is at work in Derrida's blue pencil marks on the yellow backing of Cixous's manuscript? The annotations reconfigure the relationship between life and death, between animate and inanimate. Resonating in their archival context, these words evoke uncanny possibilities of survival, legacy, and transmission from the perspective of the document. "*Puissant / l'esprit / de la lettre*" ("mighty / the spirit / of the letter"), the manuscript affirms.[6] The afterlives of Cixous's and Derrida's literary artifacts posthumously extend the dialogue between friends. Their overlapping collections suggest that the two authors saw archives as a way of prolonging and expanding the scope of their friendship and of anticipating what comes after death. In the archive, sharing and influence between friends corrode rigid notions of identity and ownership. The archive becomes a venue for creative conversation, enduring across time periods and materials.

In the pages that follow, I describe an archival theory inspired by these two authors' attitudes toward archives. Two major axes traverse Cixous's and Derrida's archives: the notion of a shared, dynamic archive; and the practice of closely reading literary artifacts that their dynamism demands. This archival theory emerges through a heightened material attention stoked by the challenges of resistant artifacts and institutions. The result is an approach that remains close to the materials and simultaneously takes an expansive view of what constitutes a literary artifact. Through a hybrid methodology drawing from archive studies across disciplines, I consider what it means to closely read a textual object, expanding the scope of literary criticism's mainstay. In what follows, readings of Cixous and Derrida offer an archival approach to the study of manuscripts and literary artifacts, investing the material artifact with affect—including dreams, haunting, and desire—which are crucial to maintaining its afterlife. For the two writers, archiving and friendship are intertwined. Throughout their lifetimes, their friendship is inflected with questions of legacy and transmission. They explore mourning—and its corollaries, such as *survie* (living on)—as a source that imbues the archive with creative potential. The archive opens up the dyadic partnership of Cixous and Derrida, and of manuscript and author, to other terms: researchers, archivists, and connected collections comprise an ever-expanding network. With recent developments in archival studies, foregrounding in particular affect and materiality, the network can be further expanded to include archival artifacts as well.

Two Insisters

The story of Cixous and Derrida's friendship develops in published texts between 1990 and 2004, in parallel with the creation of their archival collections. In retelling and reaffirming their relationship, they invent a mode of relationality particular to their persistent writing *à deux*, eminently aware of the implications for the legacy of their writing inflected by sexual difference, yet beyond traditionally gendered intellectual partnerships. Establishing the legend of their friendship is one way Cixous and Derrida seek to control the record of their conversation and ensure its continuation. Their first encounters can be recounted in a handful of dated events described repeatedly in published texts: in 1956, Cixous attended Derrida's *agrégation* defense unbeknownst to him ("je l'ai vu de dos," "I saw him from the back");[7] eight years later, in 1964, they met in Paris to discuss her work on Joyce and his on Husserl; and around 1965, he read drafts of her first poetic texts that would later be published as *Le Prénom de Dieu*. Their first meetings have interested many scholars for their symbolic resonance, highlighting both the affective charge of the meetings as "scènes primitives" and their ambiguity (was their first meeting really in 1956 if Derrida did not see her?).[8] Following their initial encounters, the two writers were linked in their involvement with the *Tel Quel* group;[9] the founding and subsequent intertwining of two educational institutions, the Collège international de philosophie (by Derrida and others in 1984) and the doctoral program in women's studies at the Université Paris 8 (by Cixous in 1974);[10] and political activism such as the anti-apartheid movement in support of Nelson Mandela.[11] Derrida and Cixous also shared earlier intersections, unknown to both writers at the time: growing up Jewish in Algeria under the Vichy régime; and consulting manuscripts, of Husserl and Joyce respectively, as young scholars in the United States.[12] These and other nodes of their decades-long friendship are linked up in the repetition of essential dates, anecdotes, and phrases throughout the published record of Cixous and Derrida's friendship, sketched out primarily in the 1990s in a series of talks and published texts which inscribe their friendship within a tradition of intimate exchange between thinkers and writers. The fabular form of these anecdotes, strewn through "Contes de la différence sexuelle," "Fourmis," *H. C. pour la vie*, *Portrait de Jacques Derrida en Jeune Saint Juif*, and other texts, sheds the precision of verifiable dates and places, establishing a mythological status through repetition. This corpus publicly solidifies the literary friendship between the two writers, constituting a semi-biographical foundation on which Cixous and Derrida build their concatenation of correspondences, leaving a "legend" of traces to be read and interpreted, an autobiography *à deux*.[13]

That their rhythm of exchange would indeed seem to be one of crossing, a back-and-forth in which each takes a turn to offer a reading of the other's work. A public reading in 1990 sets this off: at the conference "Lectures de la différence sexuelle," Cixous's text "Contes de la Différence Sexuelle" is immediately followed by Derrida's "Fourmis." Then at the Décade de Cerisy on Derrida's work in 1992, Cixous presented "Quelle heure est-il, ou La porte (celle qu'on ne passe pas)." Their coauthored *Voiles* (1998) features Cixous's text "Savoir" and Derrida's commentary on it in "Un ver à soie"—an anagrammatic rewriting of Cixous's title. Derrida follows with *H. C. pour la vie* (1998), and Cixous answers with "Ce corps étranjuif" (2000), which would later become *Portrait de Jacques Derrida en Jeune Saint Juif* (2001). Derrida's *Genèses, généalogies, genres . . . et le génie* (2003), written the year before his death, would be his final contribution, to which Cixous responds in *Insister à Jacques Derrida* (2006). But the apparent regularity of these texts, each figured as a response to the last, is complicated by several factors. Within the tradition of intellectual and artistic exchange in and out of the archive, Derrida and Cixous use their friendship as a critical lever to work through themes of legacy, loyalty, and sexual difference.

The notion of exchange is complicated from the beginning of Cixous and Derrida's dialogue. In their essays presented at the conference "Lectures de la différence sexuelle" and published in its proceedings, the writers question the order of "coming before" and "coming after," of preceding and following, of origins and originality. Cixous opens her talk with a "scène" between two unnamed characters debating who will begin: "—Tu commences et . . .—Pourquoi moi ? . . .—Tu me précèdes . . .—Non, c'est toi qui m'as toujours . . .—Toi aussi tu me précèdes" ("—You go first and . . .—Why me? . . .—You go before me . . .—No, you're the one who has always . . .—You also go before me").[14] Derrida's talk begins by highlighting their exchange before going on to query the expression and gesture of letting someone speak: "Hélène me laisse, comme on dit, la parole" ("Hélène leaves me, as one says, *la parole*").[15] Their friendship provides the specific context for this interrogation: because they suggest it is impossible to say who came first, the two seem inextricably linked, joined, twinned.

But what kind of duo are they? It is tempting to see Cixous and Derrida as partners in a kind of productive, *generative* textual relationship, one that continues to engender—and perhaps gender—text upon text, each one representing a crossing point, an event, a *point de rencontre*, a meeting point. When applied to a literary partnership that plays out over time (several decades in this case), the narrative of exchange produces a chronological bio-bibliography that most scholars of Derrida and Cixous use to introduce their close readings, similar to the one I have just given. Derrida and Cixous seem to encourage the repetition of their friendship story over many texts, creating a corpus of relationality and the impression of ongoing exchange.[16] In one example, Laurent Milesi's essay "Portraits of H. C. as J. D. and Back" includes a section titled "Bibliographical Crossings," which is meant to give a sense of the depth and breadth of Cixous and Derrida's joint prolificity or fecundity.[17] And although Ginette Michaud admits that "il n'est pas si simple de départager de quel côté l'un(e) et l'autre se retrouvent" ("it is not so simple to parse out on which side the one and the other find themselves," my translation), she returns repeatedly to the metaphor of the "couple."[18] The figure of the chiasmus is, according to Michaud, "particulièrement apte à pouvoir à la fois annuler et renouveler dans ses anneaux la contradiction et à tenir sans les opposer des termes supposés contraires, tels la vie la mort, dans une structure d'altération réciproque" ("particularly capable of simultaneously canceling and renewing contradiction in its rings and of holding without opposing them two supposedly contrary terms, such as life and death, in a structure of reciprocal alteration").[19]

Yet the notion of chiasmus warrants closer consideration, especially as it relates to exchange dependent on the figure of the couple. The chiasmus requires two terms, which remain separate on either end of the figure. The two terms cross exclusively in the middle, regaining opposite camps on the other side, to create an X. This deeply dialectical figure privileges the singular event, the intersection, geometrically: one point replicates the moment of copulation and conception, favoring a narrative of climax and engendering. In fact, in genetics, "chiasma" names the moment in meiosis (the type of cell division that occurs during sexual reproduction) where genetic material is exchanged during chromosomal crossover. But this kind of structural dichotomy facilitates a relationship that hinges upon the heteronormative sexual politics of biological sex and, by false extension, gender and sexuality. The notion of chiasmatic equilibrium between male and female relies on binary opposition for (sexual) productivity. This structure of generative reciprocity has implications for transmission and legacy within the context of intellectual partnership.The history of twentieth-century European thought provides a lineage of intellectual couples in which the woman outlives her masculine counterpart: Arendt after Heidegger, Beauvoir after Sartre.[20] Even these couples were fraught with dispute and eschew the paradigm of a conventional heterosexual relationship; yet in both cases the woman takes on—or is saddled with—the mantle of intellectual executrix, figuratively if not legally. Setting aside the notable difference between platonic and romantic relationships, it could be tempting to use a similar model to frame Cixous and Derrida's literary partnership as a joint effort to ensure the legacy of deconstruction, as though deconstruction relies on Cixous's continued writing in order to extend its relevance. Laurent Dubreuil has suggested, for example, that Cixous's writing "transposes," "transfers," "transforms . . . and evolves"

Derrida's thought from the philosophical to the literary realm; and their friendship "explains Cixous's recourse to the position of Derridean deconstruction" and her "deconstruction of deconstruction."[21] This view of their friendship risks shoring up perceptions of Cixous as a student or follower of Derrida, an agent and executor of Derridean readings and concepts. The danger is that this understanding of transmission minimizes Cixous's influence on Derrida's writing and his thought. Derrida's *H. C. pour la vie*, for example, is an extended theorization of temporality, virtuality, and necessity, and his *Genèses, généalogies, genres . . . et le génie: Les Secrets de l'archive* provides a coda to his archival theory laid out in *Mal d'archive*. Both of these texts are based on intricate analyses of Cixous's writing and demonstrate the centrality of Cixous's work, friendship, and collaboration in Derrida's thought and writing.[22]

Derrida and Cixous explicitly and implicitly play with the conventionally assigned roles of masculine and feminine writers, illustrating a view of sexual difference beyond binary essentialism: the roles are not fixed and are subject to interpretative fictions. This is especially overt in the dialogue that opens Cixous's "Contes de la différence sexuelle," quoted above, which declines to grammatically gender either conversant, as well as in Derrida's "Fourmis," staged as a rejoinder to "Contes":

> Si Hélène et moi étions ici . . . comme une figure accouplée de la différence sexuelle *elle-même*, si nous jouions ici le rôle mis en scène de la différence sexuelle à la tribune, . . . nous pouvons encore et toujours nous tromper de place en jouant, faire semblant de jouer à nous tromper de place sans faire exprès, interpréter le rôle de l'autre et franchir à chaque instant la ligne de la partition assignée.
>
> If Hélène and I were here to *figure* and, God forbid, if we appeared then as a mated figure of sexual difference *itself*, if we played the staged role of sexual difference here from the platform, . . . we could still and we could always take the wrong place in play/by playing, pretend to play at mistaking our place without meaning to, interpret the role of the other and at every instant cross the line of the assigned partition.[23]

In their self-conscious performance of a heterosexual couple, Cixous and Derrida present a duo that runs on resistance, not on symmetry, and on the continuous potential for overlap, not on discrete points of contact. As Derrida writes of sexual difference in "Fourmis," the legend of their friendship must be *read* and interpreted, taken as a figure of exceptional friendship, all while interrogating the commonplaces of friendship's embroilment in sexual difference, heterosexual coupling, inheritance and transmission, fidelity and betrayal, and the exclusion of women.[24] In Cixous's and Derrida's repetition of their friendship's legend, each becomes a figure for the other: the poet-philosopher, the thinker of the future, the ideal reader. Indeed, most of the texts in their shared bibliography are based on readings of unpublished manuscripts, further contributing to the sense that each writer is a privileged reader—the first reader, in many cases.

But within this idealized figuration of the other, Cixous and Derrida also problematize friendship, complicating their proximity with a feedback loop of magnetisms and antagonisms. Insisting above all on their divergences, difference becomes a refrain in their work in common, as they carve out a "partage" in writing, thinking, and teaching. They even dream differently.[25] For Derrida, an essential difference separates the two: that between "death or life," on the side of fathers or mothers.[26] Of course, Cixous will resist being characterized this way, and Derrida will himself work to diffuse this dichotomy. Their conversation could alternately be framed as a disciplinary entanglement: Cixous's and Derrida's writing and thinking exist at the limits of philosophy and literature. But it would be a mistake to say that each falls into one camp, and equally a mistake to say that they neatly converge. Cixous's work, pushing the limits of fictional and autobiographical writing to explore the potential of writing in French (with echoes of English and German), is in dialogue with a plurilinguistic personal canon of writers across centuries. Derrida likewise engages in intimate conversation with a Western philosophical heritage; and though his project involves a rigorous attention to writing, his method is fundamentally concerned with displacing and renewing a conceptual framework. Above all, the nuanced distinctions between their writing and their intellectual projects constitute an oppositional tension that further fuels their conversation. Difference becomes the operative term of their friendship, as they present it.

Through their dialogue, the two writers evoke alternate forms of bonding and kinship: in the role of the *insister*, Cixous problematizes the trope of "the daughter of deconstruction," of Derrida's handmaiden or intellectual heir. For example, when she writes: "Tu es *my insister*, me dit-il. . . . Toi aussi tu es *my insister. Mon insister. Mon insisteur*" ("You are *my insister*, he says to me. . . . You too you are *my insister. My insisting*").[27] Derrida and Cixous: two insisters. The insister is not exclusive, nor is it gendered. It is not limited to Cixous, who shares the term with Derrida, calling him her insister. Not quite the friend or lover of philosophy that figures in Deleuze and Guattari's dialogue,[28] and unlike the mother or daughter of philosophy that Derrida imagined in the 2002 film *Derrida*, the *insister* indicates an alternate way of naming and disrupting kinship, of thinking about legacy and afterlife: not a vertical genealogical inheritance, but a horizontal transmission.[29] Furthermore, their insisterly bond contributes to a rewriting of the privileged fraternal relation and its political implications. In *Politiques de l'amitié*, Derrida exposes democracy's foundational concept of fraternity as an essentially masculine friendship, restrictive in its "double exclusion" of women from friendship between women and with men.[30] Fraternity is debunked as a "condition *rêvée*" (a "*dreamt* condition").[31] In its place, Derrida dreams of an alternative form of friendship: "Pourquoi l'ami serait-il *comme* un frère? Rêvons d'une amitié qui se porte au-delà de cette proximité du double congénère" ("Why would the friend be *like* a brother? Let us dream of a friendship which goes beyond this proximity of the congeneric double").[32] The dream, shared between two writers, is a place out of which a newly imagined relationality can emerge. *Insister* is one such text that traffics in dreams, a meeting ground for the two writers, and a trope spooled out in textual dialogue.

As insisters, Derrida and Cixous encourage new models of partnership and exchange to emerge. The trope of doubled writing, with which Derrida and Cixous alternately experiment and disavow, counters the idea of a harmonious binary that would drive a productive, conventional heterosexual writing relationship. The theme of simultaneous, telepathic, and excessive writing further challenges the volley of exchange served and returned in a gift-style economy. Their decade of writing friendship is set off by the simultaneous, separate publication in 1990 of two books: Derrida's *Mémoires d'aveugles: L'Autoportrait en ruines*, and Cixous's *Jours de l'an*, which contains the section "Autoportrait d'une aveugle." Despite the overlapping themes of blindness and life writing in these two texts, both writers have claimed they wrote in ignorance of the other's project. Shared themes and topics across this decade—language, animality, the secret, autobiography, Algeria, dreams—ricochet between both writers. The theme of telepathy is further deployed by Cixous after Derrida's death, in *Philippines*, where she explores twinning and doubling in her reading of Derrida's essay "Télépathie."

Cixous and Derrida's friendship, as presented in their writing, goes beyond reciprocal exchange, providing a critique of the chiasmatic model of sexual difference in presumed heterosexual literary partnerships. This kind of kinship depends on a biological understanding of partnership whose successful outcome is a matter of hybridization, copulation, and exchange. But what is also at stake in the figure of reciprocal exchange, especially after Derrida's death, is the issue of how to maintain the rhythm of production in this contretemps where exchange seems to break down. How can writing between friends go on after death? How is reciprocal exchange to address questions of legacy and inheritance? In this book, the archive emerges as a field of potential, an alternative to the chiasmatic model. The archive and those who engage with it lend a promiscuity to the couple's dyad, opening up the strictures of balanced equality to a heterogeneous dissymmetry that can proliferate beyond the bounds of the pair.[33]

Approaching the friendship between Cixous and Derrida from the perspective of the archive illuminates connections beyond what is conventionally expected of literary exchange. Because it is written, their friendship is archivable—especially since the two writers' archival awareness contributes to their writing with, for, and about each other during this period. The objects, documents, and artifacts in the *fonds* Derrida and Cixous link up the two writers' collections, bringing into view degrees of commingling and overlap instead of crossing points or nodes, or the directional traces of exchange. But the archive is not to be taken at face value to corroborate, supplement, or flesh out a factual biographical record: it is saddled with imbalances and dissymmetries of its own. Instead, Derrida and Cixous use the archive as an additional venue for complicating and enriching timelines and chronologies of life writing.

Living on in the Archive

Particularly because the subjects of death and mourning find important echoes between Cixous's and Derrida's writing and their archives, the collections offer rich venues for exploring the afterlives of writing. The circulation of their work, so publicly intense from 1990 on, was constricted by Derrida's death in 2004 and by the institutional separation of their archives. Cixous's work after his death is full of sorrow, especially as his absence overlaps with the impending loss of her mother. She mourns her friend again and again as she discovers traces of him in manuscripts he had given her, stashed away and forgotten in desk drawers, and in dreams, another viaduct through which he flowed into her writing. Derrida's continuing presence in Cixous's writing after 2004 maintains the dialogue between friends (especially in *Hyperrêve*, *Double Oubli*, and several essays and talks in the immediate aftermath of Derrida's death). The concentration of published writing from the early 1990s until Derrida's death does not preclude friendship before and after this span of time. The portrait of the surviving friend (Cixous) as mourning and tending to the absence of her deceased friend is amended with vibrant memory in the archival overlaps that stitch together their decades-long friendship, from its beginnings in Paris in the early 1960s, to their affinities in thinking and reading, and their shared experience of growing up Jewish in Algeria. The archive allows for an expansive view of their friendship beyond the time frame of the two decades of concentrated writing together, for, and about each other.

After a friend's death, how does the one who goes on living continue an intellectual dialogue? If philosophy is about learning how to die, to paraphrase Montaigne, it is also about living on, learning to negotiate the continuation of writing and thinking through loss. Cixous's and Derrida's attention to questions of mourning and inheritance in their textual conversation places their friendship within a Western philosophical and literary tradition from Plato writing after Socrates, and Montaigne after La Boétie, as well as Madame de Sévigné, Engels, Scholem, and Deleuze.[34] In each case, mourning and writing are foundational and inextricably linked, the one fueling the other, contributing to what Derrida referred to as the "structure testamentaire" ("testamentary structure") of friendship itself.[35] Through writings, teachings, correspondence, and in living memory, the friend becomes a figure of the deceased writer's connection to posterity, embodying the transmission of thought in the Western philosophical and literary tradition. Because Derrida's death does not preclude the continuation of his friendship with Cixous, and because he continues to be present in her writing after his death, the absence left in the wake of his death is an opportunity for Cixous's *survie* to intensify their friendship, to render it just as potent as it is prolific.

For both writers, mourning is a creative act.[36] Cixous's focus on mourning as a subject in her writing after Derrida's death reveals an ethical, metaphysical, and aesthetic concern: mourning is not only the means by which to endure and come to terms with loss, but is also a source of creative and philosophical stimulus. Her writing mourning Derrida (*Insister* and *Double Oubli* most notably) establishes a through-line to earlier work engaging the subject of her father's death from tuberculosis when she was eleven: especially *Dedans* (1969), *Le Troisième corps* (1970), and *Les Commencements* (1970), as well as, later on, *OR: Les Lettres de mon père* (1997). The connection between mourning and writing is made in these works as well as in essays such as the autobiographical interview *Photos de racines* (with Mireille Calle-Gruber, 1994) and Cixous's Welleck lecture *Three Steps on the Ladder of Writing* (given in 1990 in English, published in 1993). In the latter, Cixous describes "the School of the Dead" as one of the driving forces of her writing, along with "the School of Roots" and "the School of Dreams." Death's pedagogical function has a philosophical precedent, though Cixous's apprenticeship reverses Montaigne's famous claim, echoing Plato, that "philosopher c'est apprendre à mourir" ("to philosophize is to learn to die"), making death the source of knowledge and of creativity. Claiming that "the first book I wrote rose from my father's tomb," Cixous reinvests her father's death not as a symbolically liberating event casting off the confining shackles of patriarchy, but as a gift or an inheritance: "I wouldn't have had death, if my father had lived. . . . he gave me death. . . . Each of us, individually and freely, must do the work that consists of rethinking what is your death and my death, which are inseparable. Writing originates in this relationship."[37] Cixous's formulation echoes in the title of Derrida's *Donner la mort* (*The Gift of Death*), a first version of which was given in 1990 at the Colloque de Royaumont, making both essays contemporaneous texts in dialogue. In *Donner la mort*, Derrida stresses the impossibility of completely incorporating the other, who remains irrevocably singular: "tout autre est tout autre" ("every other [one] is every [bit] other").[38] He points to another limitation of the tradition of death-giving: its patriarchal genealogy, suggesting that it depends, like friendship traditionally conceived, on the exclusion of women. Derrida asks : "Le système de cette responsabilité sacrificielle et du double 'donner la mort' est-il au plus profond de lui une exclusion ou un sacrifice de la femme?" though he does not expand on this, proposing to "Laiss[er] ici la question suspendue" ("Does the system of this sacrificial responsibility and of the double 'gift of death' imply at its very basis an exclusion or sacrifice of woman? Let us leave the question in suspense").[39] Cixous takes up this question of exclusion, inserting herself into a patriarchal genealogy of death-giving. By accepting her father's death as her inheritance and the fuel for her writing practice, Cixous proposes that the transformation (or translation) of the death of the other is a creative act.

Other deaths and losses haunt and fuel Cixous's writing: her first child, born with Down syndrome, who died in his first year (the focus of *Le Jour où je n'étais pas là*, 2000); ties with Algeria, the country of her birth, and Germany, where her mother was born (especially in *Osnabrück* [1999] and *Gare d'Osnabrück à Jerusalem* [2016]); and finally her mother, Ève, who has long been a presence in Cixous's autobiographical fictions and essays. The symbolic implications of her mother's career as a midwife in Algeria dovetail in Cixous's writing with the significance of the end of Ève's life. One series within her work anticipates her mother's death—*Hyperrêve* (2006), *Si près* (2007), *Ciguë: Vieilles femmes en fleurs* (2008), *Ève s'évade* (2009), *Revirements* (2011)—and another deals with the aftermath of her death—*Homère est morte* (2014), *Le Détronement de la mort* (2014), *Gare d'Osnabrück à Jerusalem* (2016), and *Une autobiographie allemande* (2016).[40] Here too her mother's death is transformed into written matter, as Frédérique Chevillot remarks: "Elle rend organique l'anticipation de la douleur du traumatisme de la perte: elle la sculpte dans ce que l'écriture a de plus sensuel et de plus ressenti" ("She turns the anticipation of pain and the trauma of loss into something organic: she sculpts it into the most sensual and the most felt parts of writing").[41] Whether in a position of anticipatory mourning or of post hoc grief, the intertwining of Ève's life and death into Cixous's life and writing is a constant from the late 1990s onward. Cixous's concern is to integrate her mother into the present moment of her writing (as Mairéad Hanrahan has suggested)[42] so that writing would be capable of safeguarding all the beloved details of her mother's life *and* simultaneously capable of sustaining Cixous's own vitality in the present. Writing serves as an automatic archive of her mother's life in the face of death, and a means of living on. Cixous's friendship with Derrida and her texts mourning his death develop in parallel with this broader arc in her oeuvre, and many of her reflections on archiving from 2000 onward arise from her life with her mother.

Derrida's focus on mourning and spectrality in the 1990s and early 2000s indicates an interest in alternate forms of existence beyond death. His conception of *survie* characterizes the surviving friend as well as a state of existential intensity that overrides a clear distinction between life and death. Elaborated in *Spectres de Marx* and "Survivre," the focus on *survie* heightens the ethical component of his later work on mourning and spectrality and, as we will see, informs our understanding of archival temporality. Yet the idea of *survie* is also foundational to Derrida's theory of writing and the trace from *De la grammatologie* and *L'Écriture et la différence* onward. The trace indicates the impossibility of marking a set point of origin or a stable presence in the signifier, launching in a violent passion the perpetual projection of meaning in *différance*.[43] This would seem to focus Derrida's theory of writing around absence and death. But if writing is barred from establishing a unity of being or coalescing into meaning, this condition of *différance* indicates that writing is not simply embroiled in the constant risk of death and finitude, but is subject to an infinitely transforming *survie* that takes writing beyond itself. The conjunction of trace, writing, and *survie* calls into question the status of writing and of death as well, broadening both beyond their everyday meaning. This is the aim of grammatology as elaborated in Derrida's earlier work.

The enfolding of writing and *survie* extends throughout Derrida's work and informs comments on his own practice of "everyday writing." In the last text published before his death, an interview with Jean Birnbaum for *Le Monde* (first titled "Je suis en guerre contre moi-même," and then *Apprendre à vivre enfin* when published soon after by Galilée), Derrida describes how writing is intimately, and inevitably, linked to death, life, and living on: "La trace que je laisse signifie à la fois ma mort, à venir ou déjà advenue, et l'espérance qu'elle me survive. . . . Je laisse là un bout de papier, je pars, je meurs: impossible de sortir de cette structure, elle est la forme constante de ma vie" ("The trace I leave signifies to me at once my death, either to come or already come upon me, and the hope that this trace survives me. . . . I leave a piece of paper behind, I go away, I die: it is impossible to escape this structure, it is the unchanging form of my life").[44] Moving from a generalized notion of "la trace" that does not necessarily entail graphic notation to the specific material reference of "un bout de papier," Derrida gives both a particular and a broad sense of what writing is and can do. Furthermore, the *survie* of writing toggles between the personal and the social, situated in a specific historical moment.

Derrida's texts collected in *The Work of Mourning* in 2001, and then in *Chaque fois unique, la fin du monde* in 2003, were written in homage to friends and colleagues following their deaths—from Roland Barthes's in 1980 to Maurice Blanchot's in 2003. In the collected volume, they come to resemble "un cimetière où quelques-uns des noms sont encore déchiffrables grâce à ces actes de deuil et d'amitié," according to Pascale-Anne Brault and Michael Naas, echoing Proust, in their introduction to the 2003 edition ("a cemetery where some of the names are nonetheless still legible because of these acts of mourning and friendship").[45] Many of these texts highlight questions of responsibility and faithfulness toward a deceased friend, and the possibility of orchestrating a means for these friends to live on in some form after death. The project of gathering these texts is itself a collective act of friendship, as the volume was conceived not by Derrida himself but by

Brault and Naas.[46] Yet as Derrida remarks in his preface to the text, "ce que nous publions ici est donc un étrange artefact" ("what we are publishing here is therefore a strange artifact"), highlighting the potential dissonance of collecting under the theme of mourning that which, Derrida argues, necessarily remains unique.[47] The published artifact is a "cemetery," yet the work of mourning must take place on a different plane: individual, intimate, and discrete.

In his "Avant-propos" to *Chaque fois unique*, Derrida directs the reader to *Béliers* as an introduction to his work on mourning. Published in 2003 (and therefore separately from *Chaque fois unique*), *Béliers* was written in the wake of Hans-Georg Gadamer's death, and the book's subtitle, "Le Dialogue ininterrompu: Entre deux infinis, le poème," suggests the possibility of maintaining a conversation through writing. Yet the death of each "unique vivant" marks "la fin de l'unique monde"—a finitude that the surviving friend must bear and repair: "Alors le survivant reste seul. . . . Il se sent du moins seul responsable, assigné à porter et l'autre et *son* monde, l'autre et *le* monde disparus" ("The survivor, then, remains alone. . . . At the least, he feels solely responsible, assigned to carry both the other and *his* world, the other and *the* world that have disappeared").[48] In *Béliers* Derrida considers how this act of carrying the other can take place: "Je dois alors le porter, *te* porter là où le monde se dérobe, c'est là ma responsabilité. Mais je ne peux plus porter l'autre, ni toi, si *porter* veut dire inclure en soi-même, dans l'intuition de sa propre conscience égologique. Il s'agit de porter sans s'approprier" ("I must then carry it, carry *you*, there where the world gives way: that is my responsibility. But I can no longer carry the other or you, if *to carry* means to include in oneself, in the intuition of one's own egological consciousness. It's a question of carrying without appropriating to oneself").[49] What form does this relationship take, if not an appropriation or an incorporation? In *Béliers*, as in the individual texts in *Chaque fois unique*, Derrida attempts a form of writing that would allow for an unheard-of and perhaps impossible conversation beyond death. These texts offer the possibility of imagining new relationships in the afterlife.

Derrida borrows the verb "to carry" from a poem in Paul Celan's collection *Atemwende* (*Breathturn*) whose line "Die Welt ist fort, ich muß dich tragen" ("The world is gone, I must carry you") inspires Derrida's reflection on the responsibilities of the survivor towards the lost world. The call to carry the other and their world after their death evokes a corporeal act. The psychic weight of mourning becomes physical. In this relationship, the two parties depend on each other: the one who survives is interpellated by the responsibility to maintain the uniqueness of the dead friend in order to keep each of them intact and, therefore, to keep the relationship going. In her assessment of Derrida and Cixous's friendship, Claire Colebrook writes that "Derrida's Cixous and Cixous's Derrida archive each other as vehicles through which they came to be what they ought to be."[50] Colebrook uses the verb "archive" here figuratively, evoking a textual relation infiltrated by otherness, to suggest that both Derrida and Cixous are deeply imbricated in one another's writing. This touches on what Derrida means by taking up Celan's "to carry." Faced with the unique difference of the other's text, the survivor serves as an archive that will maintain the ethos of the friend's writing. What's more, the friend can become an archive of friendship, actively sustaining a dialogue beyond death. And when we consider the corporeality of Derrida's call to carry the other, as well as the physical archival collections that Derrida and Cixous developed throughout the last decade of their worldly friendship, the notion of the friend as an archive takes on a material resonance.

The friend must "porter l'autre" ("carry the other"), as Derrida says in *Béliers*, acting as a kind of archive of the other. But the goal of archiving is also to lay the groundwork for what Frédéric Regard calls "faulty burials," which would allow for surprising encounters to take place.[51] In the position of the *insister*, Cixous's at times excessive, incommensurable intimacy is met with a Derridean haunting—*his* insistence—in the form of unexpected returns or rediscoveries of certain manuscripts and dreams that form the fabric of their exchange. *Their* insistence: Derrida's annotated copy of Cixous's first text resurfaces in a box in her closet; the manuscript of their co-written *Voiles* "fait revenance" in a desk drawer. But this *revenance*, linked to the materiality of writing, is not limited to one kind of media. Cixous's and Derrida's archival afterlives take place in the form of paper scraps, hard drives, film, dream-texts, and seminar notes and recordings, all of which participate in the process of mourning and multiply the potential for living on through the archive.

Institutional "Incorruptibility" and *Incomplétude*

The writer's archive is an expanded network that fosters the continued afterlife of the work. It also opens up the friendship between Cixous and Derrida to others through whom the work can proliferate, independently of the authors' intentions. Derrida's comments on writing and the trace in *Apprendre à vivre enfin* suggest that in the months before his death, he considered the survival of his work to be dependent on its archival status, and on the safeguarding of its reputation by surviving friends. This afterlife is not assured: material integrity is threatened by "l'accélération des modalités de l'archivation, mais aussi l'usure et la destruction" ("the acceleration in the forms of archivization, though also use and destruction").[52] Yet this archival risk is one he is willing to take, as he explains: "J'ai . . . le *double sentiment* que, d'un côté . . . on n'a pas commencé à me lire . . . mais aussi bien que, d'un autre côté, simultanément donc, quinze jours ou un an après ma mort, *il ne restera plus rien*." Derrida continues, qualifying the apocalyptic *plus rien* with an archival addendum: "Sauf ce qui est gardé par le dépôt légal en bibliothèque" ("I have simultaneously . . . the *double feeling* that, on the one hand . . . one has not yet begun to read me . . . but also, on the other hand, and thus simultaneously, I have the feeling that two weeks or a month after my death *there will be nothing left*. Nothing except what has been copyrighted and deposited in libraries").[53] Although the "sauf" of the library's safeguarding cannot, by nature, encompass the totality of Derrida's writing, it entails a necessary compromise. Derrida concedes the survival of his work to the library's unknown future and its inevitable incompleteness.

The combination of material concern and recognition of the role of the other in maintaining a legacy of writing is at work elsewhere in *Apprendre à vivre enfin*, when Derrida discusses the grouping of thinkers with whom he is often associated—"de Lacan à Althusser, en passant par Lévinas, Foucault, Barthes, Deleuze, Blanchot, Lyotard, Sarah Kofman . . . je pourrais citer des dizaines de noms ici"—and decries the tendency of critics to gloss over the fault lines and disagreements within this group and create a false amalgam.[54] But Derrida ultimately settles on a commonality among them: "Hélène Cixous nous surnomme les incorruptibles" ("Hélène Cixous calls us the 'incorruptibles' ").[55] Riffing on the moral rigor of Robespierre, nicknamed "l'Incorruptible," the term here designates, Derrida explains, a common ethos of stylistic and intellectual integrity or "severity" that refuses to be cowed by public opinion into distilling complexity and nuance, but instead maintains an attitude of critical "resistance."[56] Cixous's nickname for a generation of thinkers, as related by Derrida, links the project of archiving to the ability to ensure the legacy of thought and its spiritual *survie*. In the archive, the "thought" would maintain its critical attitude of resisting a reductive status quo and maintaining complexity. This complexity relates both to the integrity of a group of people (a "generation") and to the material traces included in an archive. Cixous's term "incorruptible" highlights the extent to which the survival, or *survie*, of writing depends on difference: the ever-morphing differential of *différance*, the movement of the trace escaping any claim to presence, as well as an alterity that is ethical at its core, dependent on others. Yet this alterity is not clear-cut: the ambiguous "nous" to which Cixous could or could not belong suggests that she is neither fully part of the fold, nor completely external to it. As the figure of the surviving friend, her name takes on the responsibility of continuing to name and maintain the incorruptibility of this grouping, and contributing to the *survie* of a whole ethos of writing and thinking.

If the individual friend can serve as an archive, can this "archival friendship" be extended to a larger network of friends, a community or a generation, or an institution? What is the role of the archivist and the institution in maintaining the "incorruptibility" of intellectual dialogue, and the dynamic *survie* of the archive? How does this responsibility square with the charge to preserve and conserve the physical artifacts from their own material corruptibility? There is an irony in the use of "incorruptibility" called up in

Apprendre à vivre enfin: archiving is both a threat to writing's material integrity *and* its saving grace. Derrida recognizes that his writing will be subject to "l'usure et la destruction" as well as simply being forgotten; the archive is offered as writing's only hope, but can guard against corruptibility only to a certain extent. Derrida imagines the "incorruptibility" of his writing—and that of his peers—in the face of inevitable material and social dissipation. Yet the line between dissipation and *différance* leaves some space for a potential *survie*. In this study I develop the ironic designation "incorruptible" to consider the role of the institution in facilitating the *survie* of writing, and to investigate what is potentially "incorruptible" about the material artifacts consigned to archives.

Archival institutions have of course been sites and even actors of violence and exclusion. The outsized authority of the archive underscores its potential to impact the afterlife of a literary work, insofar as the institution is devoted to maintaining the ethos of a network of writers as well as the material integrity of their work. Nowhere is the role of the institution as friend more intensely embodied than in the archivists in charge of processing, maintaining, and granting access to archival materials in these collections. The risk of this role lies in the potential for exclusion, control, and manipulation. At their etymological origin, Derrida explains, the *archontes* are guardians of the archives "dans ce *lieu* qu'est leur maison" ("in that *place* which is their house"); they grant entrance while maintaining "la sécurité physique du dépôt et du support" ("the physical security of what is deposited and of the substrate"), but their role has hermeneutic implications as well.[57] The archive thus orchestrates a complex relationship of hospitality (or as Derrida called it, "*hosti*-pitalité")[58] underwritten by the risk of exposure between researchers and archivists, underscoring the contingencies of human interaction on which archival work depends, and which contribute to the archive's afterlife, its vibrancy and dynamism. A knowing, generous archivist is crucial to the fate of the collection: "Une telle avant-gardienne est vitale . . . elle assure la vie et la survie," Derrida wrote of Marie-Odile Germain, the archivist in charge of the BNF's Cixous collection ("Such an avant-guardian is vital for the Omnipotence-other of literature . . . she ensures life and living on").[59] The nickname "avant-gardienne," which was taken up by Cixous in *Tours promises*, the book that immediately followed the conference inaugurating her archives at the BNF, and again six years later in *Double Oubli de l'Orang-Outang*, confers institutional authority and critical, even tactical foresight on the archivist, as well as an affectionate intimacy with the materials she is tasked with protecting.[60]

Each of the four archival institutions that currently house Cixous's and Derrida's collections, and all of the archivists that have contributed to the keeping of these collections, contribute to the network that enables the artifacts' *survie*. An overview of the contents of each collection highlights the particular context of each institution and serves to acknowledge the work of the archivists, whose intimate relationship with the collections is not always apparent. Each collection's guide, called a finding aid or a *plan de classement*, describes the collection's contents and indicates the organizing system best suited to conserving the materials and providing access to them. Authored by the archivists, the guide indicates the priorities of archival conservation and access, as determined by the archivists themselves and by the institution more broadly. The collection guides for the Derrida collections at the IMEC and UC Irvine, and the Cixous collection at the BNF, illustrate how the desire for the "incorruptibility" of writing to which Derrida alluded plays out in archival practice.[61] Are the priorities of archivists and archival institutions regarding material preservation at odds with the intellectual "incorruptibility" Derrida calls for? Which materials pose the greatest challenge to the goal of incorruptibility—in the sense of conservation—in the archive by their fragility? Which materials are best suited for critical "resistance," or for participating in a continuing intellectual "champ de tensions"—another kind of incorruptibility?

The IMEC is particularly capable of highlighting the interconnections that indicate the critical rigor and dynamism of intellectual exchange: its collections include individual *fonds* such as those of Derrida, Guattari, Althusser, and Kofman, as well as the archives of organizations in which these thinkers participated, such as the Collège international de philosophie, the Groupe d'information sur les prisons, and the Parlement international des écrivains. Benoît Peeters, Derrida's biographer, characterizes the IMEC's holdings as archives of "la vie intellectuelle" ("intellectual life"), representing "un champ de tensions" ("a field of tensions") that refuses to coalesce into a single school of thought—the idea of a unified generation that Derrida also rejected. Peeters describes this network further: "une série de relations, c'est une série de croisements, c'est une série permanente d'alliances et de conflits" ("a series of relations, a series of crossings, an unending series of alliances and conflicts"). The institution can work to draw out "croisements" of various kinds between and within collections, a potential latent in the IMEC website's lists of "renvois vers d'autres fonds de l'IMEC," pointing the researcher toward other individual collections.[62] Alongside Cixous's and Derrida's published writings and their public delivery of written texts, their collections serve as sites for convergence, overlap, and dialogue between the two writers and others—as well as the institutions, archivists, and researchers implicated in their collections.

The potential for the IMEC to harness the dynamic tension of "la vie intellectuelle" across time and spatial history—including the site's former use as an abbey and monastery—is offset by a commitment to the principles of privacy and confidentiality that underwrite the IMEC's rigorous *respect de fonds*, as seen in the respect for the estate, and the relationship with researchers. In this case, the effort to protect delicate content is connected to a desire to control access and maintain the private nature of personal archival collections, which might be corrupted in the hands of an undiscerning public. The IMEC's discretion pervades the institution's role as well: it takes seriously its role as guardian of its collection's contents—as *archonte*—respecting the ultimate authority of Derrida's estate, whose approval is necessary to gain information about the slightest detail concerning the material contents and their processing. The following distilled version of the Derrida collection's "Plan de classement," having for several years only been available to consult on-site, is now accessible on the IMEC website:

1. Activité philosophique
2. Universités: Archives administratives et suivi des étudiants
3. Engagement politique et activité associative
4. Correspondance
5. Gestion de l'œuvre par l'auteur
6. Dossier biographique
7. Iconographie
8. Dossier critique et réception de l'œuvre
9. Mémoires et textes reçus
10. Archives audiovisuelles[63]

1. Philosophical activity
2. Universities: Administrative archives and student advising
3. Political work, activism and collective work
4. Correspondence
5. Maintenance of the work by the author
6. Biographical dossier
7. Iconography
8. Critical dossier and reception of the work
9. Dissertations and texts received
10. Audiovisual archives

This inventory gives a general sense of the collection's content, moving from the most solitary authorship to more collaborative work, and ending with the work's reception and texts written by others. Individual work is foregrounded, following archival conventions, leaving any connections across collections in a virtual state, unaccounted for in this administrative documentation.

But this archival document also demonstrates that the collection is in flux. Over the past decade, archivists at the IMEC have been working to reorganize the papers as new materials have been added to the collection since the transfer of Derrida's personal library to Princeton. Indeed, the IMEC's *fonds* Derrida has been an open, shifting collection from the beginning. In the mid-1990s, Derrida had already donated his papers to the Critical Theory Archive at UC Irvine's Langson Library. Around 1999, he was contemplating the creation of a second archive at the IMEC in France. This collection was conceived of as a virtual counterpart to UC Irvine's: materials were to be shared between the two institutions, first relying on existing facsimile technologies, and later, Derrida hoped, using more sophisticated, virtual platforms to increase access over great distances.[64] Tensions between the two institutions grew, however, and eventually reached a breaking point when Derrida threatened to withdraw access to his collection at UC Irvine in response to an investigation of his friend and colleague, Dragan Kujundzic, who had been accused of sexual harassment and coercion. Problems increased after 2004, when UC Irvine sued Marguerite Derrida and her sons for withholding materials after Derrida's death; his estate claimed he had never intended to give these materials to Irvine. The lawsuit was dropped in 2007.[65] The struggle over the Derrida papers demonstrates how literary archives participate in the circulation and accumulation of valuable cultural capital by conferring prestige on institutions, and the history of the Derrida collections shows the power of archival institutions to determine the scope and access of the materials they house.

The organization of the Jacques Derrida papers at UC Irvine further illustrates the close connection between archivists and the writings they process and conserve: an intimacy that destabilizes the insularity of the Derrida-Cixous couple, opening up their dyad to other friendships, beyond their lifetimes. Thomas Dutoit, Jeffrey Atteberry, and other scholars completed the initial processing of Derrida's papers at Irvine in 1998. Equipped with an intimate knowledge of Derrida's writings, they were attuned to the thematic and theoretical resonance of the materials, which allowed them to devise archival strategies that other archivists might consider unconventional.[66] These scholars faced the challenge of whether, and how, to extrapolate Derrida's early theorizations of writing and trace to the materiality of his papers—a topic Derrida himself would address explicitly in his writing of the mid-1990s, as he reflected on the development of archival collections of his own writings and of institutions he was involved in creating. In accordance with archival standards, the following overview of the UC Irvine collection's organization specifies the quantity of papers contained in each series and suggests that the series were established based partly on material differentiation (seen in the separation of photographs and recordings, and press clippings) and partly on content (creating a subset of files relating to the de Man controversy, for example).

Series 1. Student work, 1946–ca. 1960. 1 linear ft.
Series 2. Teaching and seminars, 1959–1996. 8.3 linear ft.
Series 3. Publication and conference activities, ca. 1960–ca. 1998. 32.3 linear ft.
Series 4. Audio and video recordings, 1987–1999. 2.4 linear ft.
Series 5. Photographs, ca. 1970–2000. 0.3 linear ft.
Series 6. De Man controversy files, 1940–1989 (bulk 1988). 1.7 linear ft.
Series 7. Argus de la Presse clippings, 1969–2002. 8 linear ft.

The full guide, accessible online, gives a thorough explanation at the subseries level of the reasoning behind the detailed, item-level processing that sought to anticipate the links between the content of writing and the archival material and to highlight the materiality of the writing process. Envelopes and folders whose creases were deemed too delicate to be handled by the many researchers expected to open and close them were removed from access and carefully conserved apart from their contents. The notecards that Derrida used to jot down ideas, shuffled together in stacks, are also preserved in their original orientation: the archivist's numbering at the bottom right corner of each card reaffirms how the artifact was found, whether upside-down or backwards. These details demonstrate the intricate involvement of archivists concerned with preserving the potential significance of materials for future researchers who might expect to be able to re-create Derrida's own thinking in his writing process.

Similarly, Marie-Odile Germain's extensive knowledge of Cixous's work as well as her writing process characterizes her involvement with the materials in the BNF's *fonds* Cixous, and informs their arrangement in the archive. Because Cixous's output is continuous, the collection grows annually, and the loose organization of the *fonds* accommodates an ever-growing corpus:

I.	1–42	Fictions
II.	1–61	Théâtre
III.	1–5	Essais
IV.	1–10	Articles, comptes rendus, entretiens, préfaces
V.	1–33	Cours, séminaires
VI.	1	Correspondance
VII.	1–4	Varia

The materials in the categories "Fictions" (the term that appears on many of Cixous's texts published by Galilée), "Essais," and the open-ended "Varia" chiefly consist of thin, unlined sheets of paper on which Cixous has written in ink: preparatory notepads, photocopies of notebooks or other texts; handwritten manuscripts on loose-leaf paper, reordered and renumbered multiple times; typescripts prepared by an assistant (Fatima Zenati is credited with this work in *Rêve je te dis*), and amended and corrected until the text is finalized.[67] Although each page bears Germain's light-handed penciled pagination and the red oval stamps marking the BNF's ownership of the material, the categories of the *fonds* Cixous evince a generalized series-level processing. New materials are easily integrated into this broad organizational schema. The various elements of Cixous's archive intersect and feed each other, indicating the protean quality of Cixous's writing process. There is no clear progression or hierarchy between categories: collaborative work is woven throughout, including the vast category "Théâtre," comprising documents associated with Cixous's involvement with the Théâtre du Soleil, and "Cours, séminaires," which includes bureaucratic, institutional documents related to the creation of the Centre d'études féminines in addition to limited transcriptions of Cixous's seminars.

The diverse material forms of Cixous's seminars pose distinct challenges to archival preservation: along with questions about how to conserve new media such as fragile tape recordings, the seminar material extends far beyond the reaches of any single institution. Furthermore, what is held at the BNF is spread across multiple departments and locations due to the seminars' varying material supports. Held continuously since 1969, the seminars' institutional aegis has passed from the Université expérimentale de Vincennes to the Centre d'études féminines et d'études de genre (within the Université de Vincennes) to the Collège international de philosophie. The BNF's *fonds* Cixous contains twenty boxes of transcriptions made by Marguerite Sandré, a longtime participant in Cixous's seminars; but the cassette tapes she reused from one session to the next are not held there. Other audio and video recordings are kept at the private homes of Cixous's colleagues, friends, and students, awaiting institutional support that would allow them to be digitized and accessible.[68] One such technological model for the consultation of digitized materials has been realized at UC Irvine, where a virtual reading room provides access to a selection of digitized manuscripts and seminar recordings.[69] All three institutions—UC Irvine, the IMEC, and the BNF—face the challenges of ordering and classifying a hybrid, multimedia writing process, making use of printouts and handwritten notes as well as typewritten documents, floppy disks, and recordings. Derrida's hard drive, held at the IMEC, is another challenge to conservation and access, but it is not impossible that, like the hard drive of writers such as Susan Sontag and Salman Rushdie, Derrida's will one day be available for consultation.[70]

This is one example of how media provokes new connections within and between archives. The separation of archives, whether of a single author or of many writers or thinkers in close contact, is being rethought in a new digital age. Applying new technologies and techniques of archiving and preserving materials to these collections can enhance the sense of openness and dynamism that Benoît Peeters describes as a permanent chain of interconnections. The addition of new materials likewise gives the sense of a continuously changing archival landscape. This is particularly striking at the BNF, which receives new material from Cixous with each new publication or discovery of manuscript files, and at the IMEC, which received several major *versements* (deposits) of new material from Derrida and his estate, most recently in 2014 when Princeton's Firestone Library acquired the contents of Derrida's own library, including books as well as other materials, some of which were rerouted to the IMEC. As more documents are processed and become accessible (or inaccessible) to researchers through different platforms, the archive's openness shifts. Material reconfigurations create new possibilities for "champs de tension" between writers, documents, archivists, and researchers, contributing to a material sense of the institutional particularities that contextualize and contexturize the experience of consulting materials in each collection.

Archivists and archival institutions play a major role in preserving the dynamism of materials within a wider archival network. Archived artifacts are preserved to maintain their material integrity, despite the inevitability of eventual material corruptibility, bit rot, and decay. The tension of "incorruptibility" rides between an archival desire for preservation and the artifact's potential for *survie*. Yet the artifact's inherent fragility and ephemerality in fact participate in its *survie*: its inevitable transformation enables it to resist the archival impetus to stabilize and fix. What's more, the necessary gaps, absences, and silences—that which remains outside the purview of the institution—are a source of resistance to the totalizing archival impulse that seeks to contain all.

For Derrida, the question of absence is central to the functioning of the archive, in particular its relationship to the future and therefore to the survival of the material it claims to protect. He characterizes archival time as inherently futural, and links the archive with *le futur antérieur*, the "future perfect." At a conference titled "Questions d'archives," concerning the archives of the Collège international de philosophie at the IMEC, he explained: "Le concept d'archive n'est pas tourné vers le passé . . . La mémoire, c'est la question de l'avenir, et pour l'archive, c'est toujours le futur antérieur qui . . . décide de son sens, de son existence. C'est toujours dans cette temporalité-là que les archives se constituent" ("The archival concept is not turned towards the past . . . Memory is a question of the future, and the future perfect is what always determines the meaning, the existence of the archive. Archives are always established within this temporality").[71] It is a question of what, in the future, will have happened to the materials being archived: the constitutive present moment in which archives are created is in service of an imagined retrospective moment that takes place in the future. Derrida's archival temporality is akin to the spectral temporality of hauntology described in *Spectres de Marx*. Just as the specter scrambles linear time with its atemporal and asynchronic haunting, the archive unsettles the primacy of the present moment, the here-and-now, and its role within a teleological timeline.[72]

Moreover, the archive's temporality is active. It calls into question the future, and in particular whether the future will come to be. This is made clear in *Mal d'archive*: "Autant et plus qu'une chose du passé, avant elle, l'archive devrait *mettre en cause* la venue de l'avenir" ("As much as and more than a thing of the past, before such a thing, the archive should *call into question* the coming of the future").[73] In doing so, the archive leaves open the possibility for ongoing transformation. Recalling Derrida's hopeful statement in *Apprendre à vivre enfin* that "la trace que je laisse signifie à la fois ma mort, à venir ou déjà advenue, et l'espérance qu'elle me survive" ("the trace I leave signifies to me at once my death, either to come or already come upon me, and the hope that this trace survives me"), the archive maintains the constant deferral of the future, and thus the potential for the survival of the trace.[74] The archive's modality as future perfect is represented in the lag of survival or anticipatory haunting. In a way, the archival imperative to "mettre en cause" ("call into qustion") is inherently critical, unrelentingly problematizing, and is akin to the "incorruptibility" that characterizes Derrida and Cixous's peers. The archive resists: it consists of "le survivre d'un excès de vie qui résiste à l'anéantissement" ("the surviving of an excess of life which resists annihilation").[75] This resistant excess is that which cannot be contained, a necessary "incomplétude" (incompleteness) that leaves the archive open to what is to come.[76]

Archival *incomplétude* and its potential for ensuring the ongoing vitality of the archive as it confronts the future is illustrated by a scene in Safaa Fathy's documentary, *D'ailleurs, Derrida*. The film gives an intimate view of the writer at home and of his writing process, emphasizing the individual humanness of this distinguished intellectual figure. In one scene, the camera pans across stacks of books and papers that slouch into disarray, threatening chaos, as Derrida glosses his nickname for his workspace, which is situated in the attic of the house: *mon sublime*. "Je me retire en m'élevant à peu de frais, c'est une cachette sublime," Derrida explains ("I retreat by rising up with no trouble, it's a sublime hideaway"). The nickname, somewhat ironic, contributes to a romanticized portrait of the writer at work, an effect that is heightened by the visit to the dark garden shed in the scene that follows. Fathy presents the shed as a kind of ancillary archive and a counterpoint to Derrida's attic. In contrast to the light-filled *sublime*, the contents of the shed cannot be rendered on camera because it is too dark inside. "Là ce sont des papiers . . . Je ne sais pas si vous voulez rentrer là . . ." ("Those are papers there . . . I don't know if you want to go in . . ."), Derrida says, lingering with Fathy at the threshold. The filmmaker declines the half-invitation to come inside: "Non, c'est trop sombre" ("No, it's too dark"). Meanwhile Derrida is pulling out various papers, showing off his wares with familiarity and a wry sense of humor. "Je ne jette à peu près rien. Comme il n'y a plus de place dans la maison, je . . ." he trails off ("I barely throw anything away. Since there's no more space in the house, I . . ."). Shaking his head as if to recognize the absurdity of his archival tendencies, he exits the shed and closes the door. Perhaps unwittingly, Fathy seems to highlight Derrida's awareness of his own archival anxieties, his penchant for what some might call hoarding, and the idiosyncrasy of one writer's relationship to the materials of his own process. In Fathy's portrait of Derrida, whether up high or down below, the ruins of writing are paper and ink, loose or bound, torn and mildewed, stacked, boxed, and sometimes forgotten: materials that accumulate in visible heaps, even if they are merely alluded to. These are traditional materials representing a writer's archive: materials that visually evoke the fragility of the artifacts, their need for protection. What registers on camera is the presence of vulnerable artifacts of writing, as well as the archive's tendency to overtake, to overwhelm, in its demand for totality. The archive will always demand more, because the archive will always be incomplete.

But what is invisible or illegible in this portrait, what it leaves out and what remains hidden, "en cachette," is just as crucial to Derrida's writing process, as well as to the archival experience. His personal computer, the machine with which he composed the vast majority of his work from the 1990s onward, is absent from Fathy's portrait. Its absence weighs equally heavily across the Derrida collections at Irvine, Princeton, and the IMEC. Yet this artifact is perhaps the most vulnerable of all: subject to obsolescence and bit rot, Derrida's hard drive presents a challenge to the archival desire for incorruptibility and its inevitable *incomplétude*. Situated just beyond the archival frame, this type of material represents the horizon of preservation and access. Like Cixous's seminar recordings, or the correspondence between Derrida and Cixous, or the materials that continue to shift between institutions, to be unearthed in personal archives, or penned in an ongoing writing process, the archive will continue to shift in the face of its own *incomplétude*. Part of this shift involves recalibrating the frame to rethink what counts as an archival artifact: what registers on camera, and what is "trop sombre" to be included.

As it orders and presents textual objects and literary artifacts, the archive subverts the causal chronology of dialogic exchange. A publication record shows one version of intellectual exchange taking place, with texts plotted along a timeline, appearing as responses sent between writers one after another. But this is not what the archival record shows. Archives seem to step in to supplement the publication record, though with their own gaps and lapses: Cixous's correspondence with Derrida at the IMEC indicates that the two writers maintained a friendly correspondence—invitations to visit Algeria, requests for advice—throughout the 1970s, despite the absence of published texts for or about each other during that time. Yet the IMEC holds only a small portion of their correspondence, according to Cixous, who has the bulk of their letters at her home, Derrida having given back her letters to him before his death so that the two sides of the correspondence would be preserved together.[77] Derrida's hard drive, another silent artifact, is held at the IMEC but without the appropriate technology and legal protocol necessary for it to be accessible. The inventory of Derrida's collection at Irvine abruptly ends in 2000, and is silent on the status of the writer's output in the last, prolific years of his life.[78] The IMEC guide refers to a "supplemental collection" of Derrida's work, which it must do in order to explain the fact that most of its holdings are photocopies of the material housed at Irvine—even photocopies of annotated photocopies or typescripts.[79] The gaps and lapses that occur in processing decisions or inconsistencies, in willful withholding or the accidental disappearance of documents; even the inclusion of items that appear out of order or irrelevant introduce much more uncertainty, irregularity, and imbalance into what otherwise would seem to be a reciprocal economy of exchange. Alternating moments of synchronicity with delay and disjointedness, the intersections of Cixous's and Derrida's lives and writing appear in moments of untimely discovery, missed connections, and quirks of coincidence.

This is not at all uncommon in writers' archives, and it might be expected that the sense of *incomplétude* would be exacerbated when working between two or more collections. By considering *incomplétude* and the *incorruptibles* as archival principles drawn from Cixous's and Derrida's reflections on archiving in community, we can reconsider supposedly obvious characteristics of archiving—materials will always be missing and will inevitably deteriorate—for renewed critical significance. The artifact's apparent corrosion is what contributes to its ironic incorruptibility, in the sense of Cixous's nickname: resistant, future-leaning, and fleeting. It outpaces the institution's attempts to contain and make sense of it. It demands new methods of conserving and interpreting. It calls for new ways of doing research into literary archives. Incorruptibility paired with *incomplétude* is key to understanding the power of archives.

Derrida and Cixous conceived of their own *fonds d'auteur* as a place where writing could live on—especially when it is reactivated by readers. We can consider their collections as invitations to witness and even participate in Cixous and Derrida's archived friendship. Taking up a manuscript and turning its pages, or following along with a seminar recording, the researcher in the archive contributes to the work of writing's *survie*. In a sense, the researcher becomes a friend to archived materials, shouldering the task of carrying the other, as Derrida says in *Béliers*. The literary archive can be understood as a coauthored product that combines the work of writers, archivists, and researchers, all of whom contribute to an archive's form, creating content and meaning in the processing, preservation, and presentation of archival materials.

The principles of incorruptibility and *incomplétude* help us think about the silences and absences inherent in the archival record. Furthermore, these ideas characterize the archive's dynamism and vitality, the possibility of artifacts living on. They do so in part because they involve a larger network of "friends," whether a community or generation, or an institution, and because they allow for an understanding of artifacts as participants as well. This book explores how Derrida and Cixous adopt the role of *incorruptible* and *insister* to incorporate and preserve each other's work: by enfolding one text into another, for example, or by stapling parts of a text back together to approximate its manuscript form. But material artifacts can also act as *insisters* or *incorruptible* things, indicating a broad idea of archival friendship that implies an ethics of archival practice.

Method and Matter

How should a record riddled with silences and absences be read? How should an archive that is obscure, withheld, or in pieces be consulted? Although archives are by nature incomplete, archival research has long held that materials can and should be accessible and readable, and that they contain unearthed truths awaiting perceptible discovery. Archival theory over the past few decades, and most notably coinciding with the development of new materialisms and affect theory, has challenged this understanding of archival research as a process of revelation or resurrection. In place of findings, results, and discovery, archival studies have come to focus on practices of storing, ordering, and consulting archives—what Ann Laura Stoler described as a shift "from archives-as-source to archives-as-subject."[80] I situate *Archival Afterlives* within this framework of archival study: the methodology of archival research is just as important, if not more so, than what it finds in the archives. Put differently, in a play on current standards of archival science, this book's concerns are more process, less product.[81]

Like Ann Laura Stoler in *Along the Archival Grain*, I look beyond what appears clearly and visibly as the surface of the archival record. Stoler's attention to traces of archival processes highlights colonial anxieties and the failings of a dominating system. When the researcher follows the logic and the "sensibilities" of the archival documents, as Stoler suggests, artifacts become "active, generative substances with histories, as documents with itineraries of their own."[82] By lingering over these substances in Cixous's and Derrida's archives, I discern moments of sharing that do not readily appear in the publication record, but are instead glimpsed in the archive, or in relation to it. The archive contextualizes Cixous and Derrida's lived friendship by putting texts together in conversation, sometimes unexpectedly, *con-texturizing* as it lends a depth of sensory richness to the accumulation of materials. Reading the archive along the grain also considers the gaps in the record to be just as meaningful as the overflowing dossiers. The supposedly "empty parts" of an archive can in fact "be full," to quote Anjali Arondekar.[83] Arlette Farge's *Le Goût de l'archive* emphasizes that physical contact with materials allows the artifacts themselves to dictate the pace and objectives of research. Through this intuitive, adaptable, creative approach ("créatrice"), "a new object is created, a new form of knowledge takes shape, and a new 'archive' emerges" ("se fabrique un objet nouveau, se constitue une autre forme de savoir, s'écrit une nouvelle 'archive' ").[84] Noting the importance of affective and sensory attention in archival research implicates the researcher in the archives.

Yet Farge cautions against an over-identification with materials and their imagined human creators, pointing to one pitfall of a hyper-attentive approach to archival research. Other dangers of narrativizing research include a potentially anthropocentric focus that verges on heroicizing the researcher, on a quest for hidden truths or a search to resurrect lost voices of the past. Motivated by the warnings of Farge and others, in this study I situate descriptions of the artifacts and my encounters with them within a broader ensemble, an archival ecosystem that includes other artifacts, architecture, atmosphere, archivists, archival principles, and researchers, all of which contribute to the archive's contingent, dynamic nature. Foregrounding them in the present moment of their archival state shakes off the romanticism of an imagined attachment to the scene of writing. The artifacts are not physical extensions of Cixous and Derrida, and by consulting them I am not, by extension, any closer to the people who created them. When I touch a manuscript, I am not under the illusion that I am touching Cixous or Derrida, or some trace of them. The manuscript is not an intermediary through which to access the writer. If anything, interacting with the artifacts can destabilize any imagined auratic connections between the author and the manuscript.

This study is based in a form of close reading that entails an intimacy with the archival arrangements at hand. It is philological work, in the broadest sense.[85] Engaging with archival materials is, I demonstrate in what follows, a matter of proximity, an "involved reading," borrowing from Martha Rust's study of bibliophilic sensibility in the manuscript matrix. The engaged approach I adopt here is inspired by new philologies, medieval manuscript study, as well as by recent work in archive studies foregrounding affective methodologies. Feeling is central to archives, in their formation, their preservation, and their consultation: archival practices harness fantasy, imagination, provocation, passion, and *jouissance*. Derrida's "mal d'archive," translated as "archive fever," is the symptom of the missing archive: a desire, yearning, or longing, akin to nostalgia. At its core, *mal d'archive* highlights the affective, sensorial aspect of archives. Especially when the materials in consideration are unconventional, it is necessary to invent what Kate Eichhorn has called "dirty methods."[86] Across disciplines, the critique of hegemonic authority in archives has led to the development of new methods and paradigms, including the impulse to save the archives of marginalized groups, collective and community archives, through reconstructive and restorative archival practices. Ann Cvetkovich underscores the importance of alternative archival materials and the range of emotions they provoke. By widening the archival net in *The Archive of Feelings* to a variety of objects, Cvetkovich brings in a catch that is more materially diverse and more emotionally charged than conventional studies of archives. She writes in particular about how archives of lesbian public culture destabilize traditional archival methods with alternative notions of kinship, body, community, and time. Affect, along with "ephemeral evidence, spaces that are maintained by volunteer labors of love rather than state funding, challenges to cataloging, [and] archives that represent lost histories," confirm for Cvetkovich "the status of the archive as a practice of fantasy made material."[87] Her approach draws on collections such as the Lesbian Herstory Archives, which themselves "propose that affects—associated with nostalgia, personal memory, fantasy, and trauma—make a document significant" through their collecting and processing practices.[88] While the Cixous and Derrida collections are relatively conventional literary archives with ordinary, everyday materials, the work of scholars like Eichhorn and Cvetkovich has enabled me to perceive the idiosyncrasies of these two archives and to discern their critical significance: the range of media included; the networks of people, institutions, and contexts involved in the archives; the intricacies of the two writers' archival practices and writing processes; and the system of sharing and saving manuscripts, correspondence, and other ephemera. Overall, affective archives prompt a shift beyond the manuscript as the central artifact in literary archival criticism, toward a more expansive view of what counts as an object of literary study in the archive.

The vibrancy of archival afterlives that expand beyond the singular author is underscored in Joan W. Scott's *Fantasy of Feminist History*, which concludes by imagining the archive as a utopian space of possibility. Scott's focus is the Feminist Theory Archive at Brown University's Pembroke Center, newly created at the time of Scott's writing, and by 2018 the largest and most comprehensive archive of critical theory in the world.[89] Scott posits the archive as "a living reminder [that] marks not the exhaustion or the death of feminist theory, but its continuing vitality."[90] She suggests that the space of a collective theory archive in particular proposes a form of critique that foregrounds the interaction between people and artifacts. Archival interaction thus has the potential to reactivate an archival *jouissance* that could "issue forth without end."[91] This reactivating work is the driving force of archival vibrancy, of critique, and of theory. Scott's claim rightfully suggests that the archive offers an ideal venue for continuously renewed critical thought, especially as the archive's material dynamism counters any facile characterization of theory or of literature as abstract, idealizing, or impractical. Shared archives sharpen the lens of contemporary thought by animating a constellation of critical discourse on text, body, subject, and matter. In *Archival Afterlives*, I expand on Scott's notion of "continuing ramifications" that "open the space in which critique can flourish" by thinking about archival space beyond what is geographically localized, toggling instead across institutions, countries, and archival traditions.[92] The Cixous and Derrida collections invite this kind of movement and multiplicity.

The methodology of close archival reading developed in this book is based on the ontological understanding that literary artifacts, texts, things, and matter amount to forms of being. Active, volatile materials become animated in assemblage, as Jane Bennett describes it: "Assemblages are ad hoc groupings of diverse elements, of vibrant materials of all sorts. Assemblages are living, throbbing confederations that are able to function despite the persistent presence of energies that confound them from within."[93] The concept of the assemblage, which Bennett traces through Deleuze and Spinoza, contributes to the notion of vitality that I employ in this book to describe literary artifacts. I understand artifacts to be "agentic" not because they have a life of their own, but because they participate in assemblages, where agency is "distributed across an ontologically heterogeneous field, rather than being a capacity localized in a human body or in a collective body produced (only) by human efforts."[94] The artifact, the history of its creation, and the archival environment surrounding it, including the archivists and researchers who encounter it, together form a dynamic ensemble. The "life" of writing, lodged in or on the text, is refracted into countless forms by new technologies. The human researcher, re-situated in a network of potentialities that reaches across conventional hierarchies of time, matter, and life, no longer occupies a position of privilege.

Manuscripts have long been seen as sites of this kind of dynamism and fluidity: shifting, virtual spaces that draw together elements of reading from physical and social conditions and encounters with readers individually and in community. Thanks to the work of book historians and new philologists, the literary artifact can be understood within in an expanded field of creation and of being.[95] Martha Dana Rust "assumes an ontological continuity across categories—the text and the book, words and things" in her development of the concept of the manuscript matrix in the context of the medieval period.[96] This focus on ontological fluidity destabilizes the binary of life and matter, allowing for two important shifts in thinking about literary artifacts. First, it loosens the creative fastenings that bind an artifact to an author—bonds that encourage fetishizations of the literary artifact as a metonymic extension or prosthesis. And second, it encourages a holistic consideration of the artifact, indicating modes of reading and interpretation beyond hermeneutic conventions of truth hidden beneath a dissimulating surface, waiting to be uncovered, like a nut whose hull is to be cracked and discarded. This does not require us to choose between reading textual content on the one hand and physical form on the other. Instead, negotiating between form and content in the present moment of reading enables the researcher to discern new relationships in and around the artifact, beyond the purview of the writer.

The vitality of literary artifacts, so crucial to Derrida's and Cixous's interest in the *survie* of their own writing in archival afterlives, is apparent in their materiality. The artifacts' material endurance depends on their ability to stand up to disintegration and destruction. Even as they struggle with the material problem of maintaining their own integrity, their materiality is also what allows them to reappear, to insist, to come again in scenes of doubling, multiplying, and other forms of intensification. Cixous is often interested in what happens "before the book," in what she calls "l'ère qui bouillonne avant le livre" ("the seething era before the book"), and her confidence in the power of everyday materials such as paper and pencil to endure increases in her writing after Derrida's death in 2004, anticipating her mother's illness and eventual death a decade later. In her 2010 book *Double Oubli de l'Orang-Outang*, a box and its contents—including the typescript of her first text, *Le Prénom de Dieu*, annotated in pencil by Jacques Derrida—proves to be miraculously resistant to the ravages of time and physical decay, forty years on. The narrator is amazed by its "endurance," describing the box as "léger, résistant, solide comme un roc, marginal, un peu surhumain comme un cercueil portable" ("light, sturdy, solid as a rock, marginal, somewhat superhuman like a portable coffin"), noting its durability as well as an unidentifiable strangeness.[97] Elsewhere, in Cixous's *Hyperrêve*, pencil and Post-it notes are designated as privileged materials because of their "vie dure," their "endurance": "ils n'ont l'air de rien et ils traversent les années" ("these post-its are tough, they look like nothing and go on for years").[98] The dynamism of textual objects is linked to their materiality, which is integral to their resilience and their incorruptibility.

Considering "incorruptibles" to include archived materials opens up new horizons for thinking about the legacy and survival of writing, its relationship to the writer, and the ontological status of both. What kind of life is possible for writing in the archive? How does "survie" apply in this case? Does it offer extended creative potential beyond the "life" of the writer? If so, what kinds of connections exist between writers and the artifacts they leave behind? How does the material resilience of the textual object, its incorruptibility, square with the ephemerality of other forms of writing and recording? And with a Derridean theorization of the trace as non-presence? Can the trace and writing, understood broadly, indicate alternate modes of living and being? If we do consider these traces to be part of a kind of "life," albeit a different kind than the "life" of the writers who made them, what are the implications for literary criticism attuned to life writing, autobiographical writing, and biographical concerns more broadly?

Reading Derrida's and Cixous's literary archives in a materially oriented vein allows for a reconsideration of the role of ontology and agency in Derrida's theorization of the trace in a post-human context. For Christopher Johnson, the post-human is embedded in Derrida's theory of writing from its beginning. Particularly in "Freud et la scène de l'écriture," Derrida's understanding of cybernetics underwrites his rereading of Freud's Mystic Writing Pad, his *Wunderblock*: whereas Freud understands this technology's agency to be limited as a machine and not a living thing, Derrida recognizes a false supplementarity in this view, questioning the limits between "living and mechanical systems," between humans and machines.[99]

From *De la grammatologie* to *Mal d'archive* to *Genèses, généalogies, genres . . . et le génie*, Derrida's theory of *écriture* and of the trace encourages a wide view of what writing is. Beyond "writing in the narrowest sense" (as Juliet Fleming puts it), writing includes other modes and techniques, including speech and experience.[100] This necessarily impacts what we are looking for and at in the archives. While it may appear that by focusing on the material form of writing I am restricting my study to the "narrow" sense of writing as Derrida understands it, my search for dynamic literary objects is motivated by an expansive view of writing: a reconsideration of what counts as the marks, scraps, substrates, objects, and textual bodies of writing. What is the impact of the Derridean notion of grammatology as the "effacement of the trace" on the material form of writing? My wager is that the archived artifact shows the effacement of the trace at work: not caught between a dichotomy of presence and absence, of life and death, but demonstrating an ongoing transformation.

Derrida would seem to occupy an unsettling position vis-à-vis new materialisms, whose thinkers have also inspired much of my thinking about literary objects and how to interact with them. In *Cultural Graphology*, Juliet Fleming emphasizes Derrida's distance from the concept of matter: "Derrida's concerns are semiotic; even when they are focused on the plastic properties of language (e.g., its extension, location, or duration), they are predicated on the assumption that information resides not in matter itself but in the differences that may be perceived between quantities and qualities within a given context."[101] In this regard, Fleming differs from Christopher Johnson, who seeks in *System and Writing* to recontextualize the "visible links with the 'atomist' or 'materialist' side of Derrida's philosophy," although Johnson stops short of characterizing Derrida as a materialist.[102] Even when Derrida focuses on "the wax, resin and celluloid of the Mystic Pad," Johnson explains, it is to demonstrate that "signification does not reside in an other-worldly, inner palace of faculties, but requires the passage through, that is, a passion *in*, the world. . . . Psychical processes are dependent on a material support, but they are at the same time neither substantial nor localizable."[103] Johnson insists on the "dynamism and autonomy" that pervade Derrida's descriptions of the trace, working directly against "a conventional conception of the psychic script as a lifeless, petrified archive"; in Derrida's words, "[la] présence impassable d'une statue, d'une pierre écrite ou d'une archive" ("the serene presence of a statue, of a written stone or archive").[104] I have found a similar tendency towards dynamism and vitality at work in Derrida's writing about writing and in the archival documents I have consulted, which has led me to emphasize the association of trace and writing with *survie*. It is this aspect of Derrida's theory of writing that Catherine Malabou finds provocative and perturbing in her exploration of plasticity: if "the trace forms no body," then how can we make sense of a "plasticity of presence" that Malabou finds most apt to describe the contemporary philosophical trajectory?[105] I ultimately align myself with Malabou's view that Derrida's call for a "modification" and an "enlargement" of writing beyond its "everyday meaning" implies "the plasticity of the concept of writing."[106] It is my goal in this book to demonstrate the unfixity, the malleability, and thus the dynamism of matter, as we see it in writing in the archive.

A focus on archived artifacts and archival practices highlights the complexity of matter, materiality, and materialism in Derrida's theory of writing. The conceptual basis of Derrida's understanding of writing, as spelled out in *De la grammatologie*, for example, is refracted through his archivally minded corpus, between published texts, the archival projects he conceived of in at least two institutions, and the documents and objects that made their way into those and other collections. Bringing literary and manuscript studies to bear on Derrida's archives and his writing about archives, which is often literary in style and form ("Circonfession" and *La Carte postale* are two examples), widens the perspective on Derrida's writing via two avenues: through its intersections with disciplines such as literary studies and archive studies; and in its dialogue with Cixous's writing. One outcome of this approach is a strengthened relationship between trace, *écriture*, and *survie*. Another outcome is a broadened view of what is understood to be writing, the textual object, and the literary artifact, heightened by evolving techniques and technologies of writing and archival preservation that are not separate from Derridean thought but are anticipated by his work.

In this book, I situate archival materials within a broad landscape of the writing process, which is characterized by invention, illusion, and interpretation.[107] Instead of simply presenting a faithful, realistic portrait, archival materials are taken as the matter of legend and fiction, channeling desires, riddling the archival record with silences and gaps that seem to invite speculation. The "life" of writing, in its archived state, does not correlate to lived experience or a publication record, but exists instead in a liminal space between life and work. *Archival Afterlives* seeks to expand a model of the archive as biographical material, of the use of archives to tap into or re-create a life, of the faith in archives as evidence or the revelation of truth. Archiving is a kind of autobiographical writing: a life writing, or *live* writing.

This is the second meaning of "afterlife": the afterlife of the writer and the afterlife of the artifact are not one and the same, though their imbricated relationship is the subject of this study. The afterlife of the writer and their work is often informed by the writer's archival presence, as the documents they leave behind are mined for biographical information, unpublished material, and alternative critical interpretations. Expanding the scope of archival attention within a study of writers' archives entails a reconfiguration of the relationships between writer and artifact, document and researcher, eschewing hierarchies of knowledge, attention, and ways of being. Such an approach has advanced the study of literary figures with controversial or materially intriguing archives. Emily Dickinson scholarship has transformed in the past decades as attention to the material aspects of her manuscripts contributed to a revised understanding of the poet's relationship with her own output and her intentions for her oeuvre on a broad scale, as well as to the material culture that surrounded the creation and circulation of much of Dickinson's writing. A return to Sylvia Plath's archives has revealed the ways her work was edited and shaped by her estate immediately following her death, and in the decades that followed.[108] These approaches to literary artifacts enrich the study of the *avant-texte*, the realm of genetic criticism and its interest in what creates a published work.[109] Inspired by genetic criticism's *avant-texte* and other approaches to manuscript study, I propose to consider the archive not as an *avant* that prefigures a more finished, polished product, but as material that accompanies and embodies a working process; a process that is aware of its own ability to be shared and sustained.

Unlike an analytical mode of differential comparison or a linear plotting of intersections, a focus on the material afterlives of literary artifacts, broadly understood, illuminates what happens *between* Derrida and Cixous. Moments of overlap between Cixous and Derrida, and between the text and the archive, include manuscripts exchanged, stashed away, and rediscovered; dreams told on the telephone or briefly jotted down; the seemingly simultaneous, unplanned, quasi-telepathic writing about uncannily similar subjects; their enigmatic correspondence, which is largely absent from institutional collections; and the rituals of reading and guest appearances in the space of the seminar. These moments, described in interviews, conference asides, seminar transcriptions, and a variety of other published and paraliterary texts, combine to form a portrait of the archives that relies just as much on what is imagined, ideal, and fictional as on what is physically present. Archival absences have a generative potential, animating archival impulses, prompting anticipatory speculation and imagination.

This approach brings out connections between Cixous and Derrida beyond what is available in their published bibliography: connections that are not always tangible, sometimes withheld, and that consist of silences, lapses, and imbalances as well as talismanic artifacts, but that together combine to form a map of archival impulses, desires, experiments, and placeholders. This map charts a multisensory and even supersensory experience of the archive, invoking touch, sight, sound, and taste, linking up with affective and psychic overlays. Its vulnerability exposes it to collapse, yet its sensitivity allows it to shift and morph. Cixous's and Derrida's approaches to archives in their published texts have implications for ways of doing archival research, and their archival writing informs an archival approach. Reflected back on to their archival materials, their writing draws out the artifacts' potential for *survie*, for living on in the archive.

The Shape of This Book

The first half of this book, "Live Materials," features volatile and dynamic archival materials, presenting the archives as a place of potential and future renewals. In these chapters I offer a portrait of Cixous's and Derrida's writing processes, showing how the idiosyncrasies of material and practice suggest an archival awareness that informs how their collections are set up. The relationship between materiality and virtuality forms a main thread of this investigation: rather than opposing material and virtual, or digital and physical, I show how attending to the intersection of these terms invigorates the afterlife of writing. It is not virtuality that invests matter with meaning or vitality and transcends it into a future state; rather, materiality contributes to the artifact's potential to have continued vitality and continued effects. To demonstrate how the "life" of writing is located in the material, I first argue that manuscript objects must be dissociated from their creator in chapter 1. I then show how this independent material operates, unexpectedly and uncontrollably, in chapters 2 and 3.

Throughout this book, the chapter titles indicate a particular strategy that Derrida and Cixous essay, each in their own ways, though sometimes together and with others, in order to explore how writing can live on in the archive. Grounding the study in the physical aspects of writing and archiving, the first chapter, "Write in Pencil: Material Endurance from Cixous's First to Derrida's Last Work," shows how Cixous and Derrida experimented with the durability of materials as a venue for living on in the archive. Cixous's love of the "avant" or preliminary stages of writing, as well as her concern for the manuscripts she consults at the BNF, leads her to develop an understanding of the "other life" of literary artifacts. In *Double Oubli de l'Orang-Outang* (2010), Cixous marvels over the "endurance" of pencil markings and paper, notably on the manuscript of her first text, *Le Prénom de Dieu* (1967), which was annotated by Derrida. Though written in pencil, these marks prove to be surprisingly fresh and steadfast—paradoxically so, because of their exposure and vulnerability to chance. Writing's vitality is channeled through its materiality, a principle at work in Derrida's "Circonfession," and in *Genèses, généalogies, genres . . . et le génie*, his last analysis of Cixous's writing. In both texts, the embodiment of the writing process sidesteps an equivalency between writer and writing. Finally, Derrida's last "work in progress," an envelope of intriguing scraps held at the IMEC, serves as a counterpoint to Cixous's first work. Through close readings of these documents' tangible, physical aspects, I demonstrate the potential for a non-fetishistic approach to writers' papers after their death. Caught in a tension between the desire for mark-making and the risk of material breakdown, the documents featured in this chapter are imbued with a vibrancy that stems from their materiality.

The second chapter, "Allow for Change: Material Contingencies on Free-Floating Ephemera," builds on the advantageous instability of archival materials. Following material endurance in chapter 1, I turn in chapter 2 to the ephemerality of certain artifacts in readings that highlight the dynamic potential of archives. Materials have a symbolic and practical resonance in Cixous's *Manhattan* (2002) and *Tours promises* (2004), books that feature the scene of writing: easily reused and rearranged, Post-it notes and loose-leaf pages reinforce the potentiality of the work in process in the archive. Ephemera found in Derrida's library at Princeton University are similarly unstable: as they were processed, the scraps, notes, and letters Derrida had interleaved in books were returned to the IMEC; Cixous's correspondence there was amended to include some of these artifacts. Shifting between collections, these materials run the risk of getting out of order or being lost, but it is in this danger that I locate their particular force. Illustrating a kind of *destinerrance*, a term which Derrida developed in *La Carte postale* through a one-sided correspondence with Lacan, the contingency of archived materials poses challenges to archival conservation and consultation. This plays out in notecards and materials in the dossier of *La Carte postale* at UC Irvine, where reactive materials destabilize archival principles of original order and provenance, slipping out of sequence and eschewing linear progression. They encourage the archivist and researcher to rethink their influence in the afterlives of these materials and account for the role of chance in archival practices.

I continue to consider archived materials in their own right, independent from their creator, in the third chapter, "Create a Copy: Accumulations of Derrida's Facsimile Drafts and Cixous's 'Book I Do Not Write.' " Cixous and Derrida forego the trope of the unique, original copy, turning instead to doubled or twinned archives that may better preserve their writing despite their perceived absence. The double harnesses the potential of the simulacrum to evoke a virtual archive. The Derrida collections at UC Irvine and IMEC make use of facsimiles to approximate the shared archive that Derrida imagined in *Mal d'archive* and other texts. The "double" archive that Cixous dreams of echoes Derrida's concerns for a "virtual archive" shared across institutions, attempting to account for what an archive cannot contain. Derrida's hard drive poses a particular challenge both to technologies of archival preservation and to understandings of virtualization and digitalization as abstract and immaterial. Cixous's "Book I Do Not Write," a recurring figure in her work around the time of her archives' creation, speaks to the impossibility of a wholly inclusive collection. But these impossible doubles also show that the simulacrum is in fact a rich model for Cixous's and Derrida's archival projects. Both authors' desire for multiple, divergent archives destabilizes the limits of what is considered material and virtual in archival science.

The first half of this book foregrounds the material form of literary artifacts and their role in the preservation of the life of writing. In the second half of the book, titled "Live Transmission," I focus on how materiality impacts forms of circulation and exchange, and how readers interacting with this material contribute to the continued life of writing. While the first half of the book considers the separate relationships Cixous and Derrida foster with their own writing, the second half is mostly concerned with how Cixous and Derrida read each other and invite the participation of other, unknown readers. Chapters 4, 5, and 6 continue to reinforce the notion that literary artifacts are not extensions of their creators, but instead make critical inroads into conceptions of authorship and property. The chapters in this section move through three venues for communication: the surface of the manuscript page, shared dreams, and seminars. These all create affective networks that contribute to the afterlives of artifacts and of Cixous and Derrida's friendship.

In chapter 4, "Share with Others: Handling Manuscripts between Friends," I turn from materials that appear imbued with vitality to the ways Cixous and Derrida interact with each other's manuscripts. The practice of sharing works in progress, I argue, extends the life of writing through points of contact on the manuscript page, which allows for an expansive view of the manuscript surface and the connections possible there. Cixous's experience of consulting manuscripts at the BNF (in *Brouillons d'écrivains*) informs her attempts to reconstitute the manuscript of Derrida's "Circonfession" in *Portrait de Jacques Derrida en Jeune Saint Juif*. Cixous's practice finds a parallel in Derrida's "Un ver à soie," which I analyze as a close, even tactile reading of Cixous's short text "Savoir." In both cases, I argue that Cixous and Derrida practice a form of reparative reading, taking Eve Kosovsky Sedgwick's concept literally to analyze marks of friendship shared between Cixous and Derrida. Drawing the two writers together through material artifacts demonstrates that their methods of reparative reading also destabilize conceptions of autobiographical writing, especially since handling the manuscript forms a counterpoint to traditional views of a manuscript as being handwritten by a single author. Furthermore, the manuscripts' tactile transmission carries the risk of loss at the hands of the other, bringing ethical considerations to bear on literary artifacts, especially in the gendered dynamics of inheritance, identity, and embodiment.

Continuing to explore the friend's contribution to a writer's legacy, in chapter 5, "Dream On: Other Conversations," I turn from the physical handling of manuscripts to the psychic realm of dreams, which for both writers were a venue for continued encounters and cultivating new writing. Unconventional forms of transmission such as telephone calls and dream texts challenge the limits of what an archive can store and who can consult it. I read Cixous's *Hyperrêve* and *Insister*, both written after Derrida's death, for the importance of dream-texts (written on manuscripts, Post-it notes, and letters), alongside Derrida's study of Cixous's archive at the BNF, *Genèses, généalogies, genres . . . et le génie: Les Secrets de l'archive*. Dream-texts make unexpected, phantomatic appearances, as in Derrida's *Fichus*, or in Cixous's reinterpretation of *Fichus* and telepathy in *Philippines*. The two writers' shared interest in dreams unsettles the archival quest for knowledge, complicating the distinction between *avant-texte* and finished product, and countering the stabilizing force of the archival institution.

The fifth and sixth chapters test the limits of what is archivable: first in dreams shared between friends, and then in the seminar. In the sixth and final chapter, "Return to the Scene: The Seminar as Virtual Archive," I consider the place of seminar recordings in the archives of two writers for whom teaching was an integral part of their life work, and a form of co-creation with a small community. Both Derrida and Cixous developed teaching styles that countered notions of masterful transmission of knowledge from pedagogue to student. Moreover, they staged this performance of unmastery through readings of each other in seminars and lectures. Documentation—whether in the form of digital recordings or students' notes—is particularly important for Cixous's improvised seminars. Using a photographic archive of the Université Paris 8 (Vincennes/Saint-Denis) and my own seminar notes, I interrogate the potential of documentation as a means of accessing the history and memory of an intellectual community: Cixous's long-running seminar, and through it, the Université expérimentale de Vincennes. The seminar is analogous to the concept and form of the archive, suggesting that the archive is a virtual and a collective enterprise.

This book can be read in a linear progression from the first to the last chapter, but reading across the book's two halves, between "Live Materials" and "Live Transmission," highlights particular approaches to archives. The interrogation of authorship and autobiography in chapter 1 continues in chapter 4. Read in sequence, chapters 2 and 5 widen the scope of what is considered to be a literary artifact by taking an expansive view of manuscripts and their materiality. Readings of Derrida's "Circonfession" in chapters 1, 3, and 4 explore the relationship between body and writing. Concepts of virtuality and the digital tie chapters 3 and 6 together in a media studies perspective. Readers looking for close readings of materials found in Cixous's and Derrida's archival collections will find them interspersed throughout.

In the book's conclusion, "Les Incorruptibles," I return to the nicknames Cixous coined—*incorruptibles* and *insister*—which are evocative both of Cixous and Derrida's friendship and of archived artifacts, and their contributions to the afterlives of writing. I consider the advantages and challenges presented by archives shared between intellectual and artistic communities, and articulate the stakes of literary studies within the growing field of critical archiving. Cixous's and Derrida's collections participate in a larger archival network of thinkers and writers: an affinity for other writers (in the case of Cixous), for an institutional ethos (for Derrida), and for literary and philosophical contemporaries (for both) motivated their choices of where and with whom to be archived. In these cross-generational configurations, Cixous and Derrida bypass the designation of "Critical Theory," allowing their writing to emerge and circulate within other, continuously shifting networks. These networks suggest new directions in archival studies, as advancing technologies manage conservation and access in order to promote the discovery of connections, affinities, and encounters across archival materials. Collective archiving dislodges theory from its perceived intellectual place of privilege, re-situating it within the tangle of conversation and debate that is so vital for Cixous and Derrida.

Part I

Live Materials

Chapter 1

✦

Write in Pencil

Material Endurance from Cixous's First to Derrida's Last Work

"Je veux l'avant d'un livre" ("I want the beforehand of a book"), Hélène Cixous writes in 1991, describing her writing process: not the progress toward a finished product, but the book's continual becoming.[1] Cixous's desire for and interest in preliminary, provisional writing becomes increasingly present in her writing throughout the 1990s. The *avant* is a lively place for Cixous, who explores the limits of that vitality as her relationship with the Bibliothèque nationale de France strengthens. What will happen to the life of artifacts in the archive? How will they endure? What will live on? The question of what is most alive about a manuscript, particularly concerning the relationship between a writer and their writing, imbues Jacques Derrida's explorations of writing and its materiality around the same time as he was conceiving of his own archival collections. Is the work's animating force linked to that of the writer? How might the answer inform archiving and research? Tracing Cixous's and Derrida's attitudes towards the materiality, vitality, and endurance of manuscripts through their archives prompts a reconsideration of the approach to archival preservation and consultation. From the drafts of Cixous's first book, rediscovered after several decades, to a dossier titled "Travaux en cours été 2004" ("Works in progress summer 2004") containing Derrida's unfinished work, material endurance demonstrates the potential for writing to live on in the archive. But in what way is this material "en cours," in progress? Is this posthumous state an *avant-texte*? How can the vitality Cixous cherishes in the "avant d'un livre" continue its creative work in the archive?

Cixous was invited to consult manuscripts at the Bibliothèque nationale de France before deciding to bequeath her own papers to that institution, and she was struck by the fragility of the artifacts she saw there. In her contribution to the exhibition catalog *Brouillons d'écrivains*, she describes her reaction: "L'effacement est là. À l'œuvre. Met à l'épreuve les matières. . . . C'est saisissant ce mourir lentement. Longue cérémonie. Décomposition de décomposition. Message secret de chaque manuscrit: Je suis fini" ("Erasure is there. At work. Tasking the matter. . . . This slow death is striking. Long ceremony. Decomposition of decomposition. Each manuscript's secret message: I am finished").[2] In the archive, the mortality of manuscript matter is put to the test: it will deteriorate, breaking down into an unrecognizable state—as will the body of the person who wrote on it. But the two deaths are not concomitant, for the manuscript dies much more slowly, in a "longue cérémonie." The lively struggle that took place before the book is subdued here, and writing is finished off, susceptible to its own impermanence. Is this the vibrant "avant d'un livre," or a declining *après*, the end of the manuscript?

As she consults these materials, perhaps imagining her own manuscripts in their place, Cixous's attitude towards the work of other writers lingers for a time in the morbid, and then surprisingly pivots to a fascination with, and even trust in, the endurance of matter: "Le papier garde. . . . Il reste dans le papier, dans l'entremêlement peint des caractères, du caressé, du touché, de l'odeur. On sent la mort—chanceler—la vie—continuer—longtemps après" ("Paper keeps. In the paper remains, in the painted intermixing characters, caressings, touchings, scent. The feeling of death—stumbling—life—continuing—long after").[3] Although manuscripts are not exempt from fragility and mortality, from the laws and limitations of the trace, Cixous sees both the finitude of manuscripts and their life: "Manuscripts are by no means dead things. An 'other-life' passes between the manuscript and whoever touches it."[4] Above all, the "germes," "restes," and "vestiges" of the writings in the BNF indicate life in the past and present: "Trace, preuve et visage qu'il y a vie, qu'il y a eu vie, trace toujours finie d'un être fini" ("Trace, proof and face that there is life, that there was life, trace always finite of a finite being").[5] In these essays, and as we will see in books such as *Manhattan*, *Tours promises*, and *Double Oubli*, Cixous understands the "trace" to be motivated by a physical encounter with a textual object, from which she gleans not a record of death but an indication of life, frequently finite and nonhuman.

What Cixous sees in the BNF's manuscript reading room is not simply the remains of work by writers such as Proust, Flaubert, and Pascal. Her visit is marked by tactile encounters with the material substrate of artifacts:

> J'allai m'approchant du biblique des livres, qui sont d'abord des objets magiques, des pâtes composées de peaux, de membranes d'arbre, de pellicules de roseaux d'Égypte, de peaux d'agneau de Pergame, de la peau des doigts humains. . . . Non, rien à voir avec ces lectures de textes extraits de leur couche matérielle, ces détachements de textes auxquels souvent je me livre pour me délecter de délectures savantes. Ici, dans la Librerie je palpais.
>
> I drew near to the biblical in books, which are above all magical objects, blendings of skins, of tree membranes, reels of Egyptian

> reeds, sheepskin from Pergamon, skin from human fingers. . . . No, nothing to do with readings of texts extracted from their material cover, these textual detachments which I often indulge in to reel in wise dereadings. Here, in the Bibliothèque I was palpating.[6]

Attention to material detail at the level of the physical surface leads to an awareness of its liveliness, and thus of kinds of life that are not human: skins, trees, reeds. This draws Cixous to the manuscripts housed at the BNF and informs her decision to house her own papers there: "I was won over in advance to the vital necessity of this sublime chemistry; and when the doors of the BN opened, I said yes," she explains.[7] The vital necessity she observes in her visit to the library does not allude to a mortal survival, a dream of immortality, or a writer's desire to live on in her work. The "other-life" of manuscripts is not guaranteed by a metonymic transfer of the writer's hand or body to the manuscript page; it is felt by the reader who touches them in this passage. For Cixous, the life of manuscripts is neither human nor mortal, neither a literary personification nor wishful thinking.

Cixous's attitude toward the endurance of manuscript materiality shifts throughout several books that feature the archiving of her papers: from *Manhattan* and *Tours promises*, both written around the time she donated her papers to the BNF, to *Double Oubli de l'Orang-Outang*, written nearly a decade later. All three books stage archival encounters in the narrator's own home, but in *Double Oubli* the discovery of the writer's first manuscripts in a linen closet is particularly striking. These artifacts appear to Cixous as a wholly other kind of textual creature, especially as they bear the marks, in pencil, of their first reader, whom the narrator identifies as her friend Jacques Derrida. At play is a hypersensitivity to the material makeup of artifacts on the move to the archive and an awareness of them as *other*.

Cixous's shifting attitude toward material endurance finds a parallel in Derrida's equivocal remarks on handwriting and the body throughout his oeuvre. His comments about the "decisive" effects of Cixous's handwriting for her archival collection in *Genèses, généalogies, genres . . . et le génie* (2003), read alongside his autobiographical essay "Circonfession" (1990), suggest a way of reading alterity and agency in the materials surrounding Derrida's writing process. We see through these works that Derrida's and Cixous's attitudes towards the potential of material endurance involve a crucial separation between the writer and what they have written. Breaking the metonymic chain that links a writer in life and in death to their manuscripts, Cixous and Derrida ultimately present manuscripts and other literary artifacts as independent, idiosyncratic beings, imbued with a kind of existence different from their own: what Cixous calls an "other-life." In examining the tension between their fragility and endurance, both writers suggest the possibility of new afterlives for artifacts in the archive. Close readings of Cixous's and Derrida's reflections on their own writing processes reveal that it is not institutionalization that confers an archival status on their writing; rather, their writing processes are archival from the start, in their *avant* state, their "beforehand." Their concern with and interest in the materiality of writing develops as an approach to archival survival, in the sense of a heightened living-on, a *sur-vie*.

"*Sur le vif*": The Life and Death of Cixous's Archived Manuscripts

Cixous's concern for the future survival of her own manuscripts is based on her awareness of their material vitality. In reading Cixous's descriptions of her writing process and in consulting archived materials, we see that she is invested in the physical as well as the psychical effects of writing. Books such as *Jours de l'an* (1990), *OR: Les Lettres de mon père* (1997), and *Le Jour où je n'étais pas là* (2000) are haunted by their own coming into being; they are strewn with descriptions of materials, methods of noting, storing, and ordering, and are tense with questions of whether and what to divulge, invent, or withhold.[8] Essays and short texts such as "Sans arrêt, non . . ." (1991), "Germes, gestes, restes" (2000), and "de main en main jusqu'à un maintenant éphémère" (in *Brouillons d'écrivains*, 1999) further develop the topic of Cixous's relationship with writing, a position of fascination and antagonism. The process is tumultuous, chaotic, dispersed: a "struggle," even "carnage," characterizes the scene of writing.[9]

A portrait of the writing process emerges as descriptions of materials pile up: blank pages torn from cheap notepads ("des blocs Leader Price"); notebooks of various sizes received as gifts; Post-it notes; and smaller and smaller scraps—"des dizaines de petits bouts de papiers . . . de petits carnets, je griffonne sur une serviette en papier" ("dozens of little pieces of paper . . . little notebooks, I scribble on a paper napkin").[10] In an interview with Susan Sellers published in *Hélène Cixous: The Writing Notebooks*, Cixous explains how her writing emerges from the accumulation of materials:

> When I start writing, that is when I engage myself on the way of what is going to be a book, I have all types of material, from large notebooks, to small ones, to all kinds of pages, because I need . . . it's as if they were pieces of ground, but pieces of living ground: screens. . . . When, suddenly, a light flashes, I have to note down extremely quickly, because it disappears as fast as it appears.[11]

Writing directly from life or from nature, as close as possible to the source, and as faithfully as possible, Cixous's writing process proceeds as a kind of collection of materials taken from life—"sur le vif."[12] The expression *le vif* speaks to the urgency Cixous describes here, and alludes to that which is most animate about a living being, indicating for example the tender, sensitive flesh that can be cut to the quick. This vitality makes all the scraps that accumulate in the writing process worth keeping: "Tout ça je garde. J'ai une tendresse pour le germe" ("I keep all of it. I have a tenderness for the seed").[13] Beyond its liveliness, the "germe" elicits tenderness because it is incipient, because of its potential—this is the "avant d'un livre" that Cixous desires. But this is not the *avant-texte* of genetic criticism as defined by scholars such as Pierre-Marc de Biasi, the drafts gathered retrospectively by the critic working from the book as end point.[14] What compels Cixous is the *avant* of writing in its state of perpetual becoming, which contributes to the scraps' and seeds' vitality. The "gestes" included in this series—*germes, gestes, restes*—further suggest movement and dynamism in the signs or signals that constitute the beginnings of this gestation, an active state. When Cixous writes that she has "une tendresse pour le germe," her sensitivity indicates an expansive compassion for what she considers to be living.[15]

Written in the years following Cixous's decision to donate her papers to the BNF, *Manhattan: Lettres de la préhistoire* and *Tours promises* evoke the difficulties of that decision by describing the affective intensity of the materials to be archived. In *Manhattan*, the narrator reflects on the "prehistory" of her writing career, a period of time when she traveled to the United States to consult manuscripts. Her research is sidelined by a romantic encounter that leaves her heartbroken, and the emotional aftershocks of this experience resonate decades later when the writer sorts through boxes of papers from that time. Written in homage to the intensity of archival research, *Manhattan* has an indirect but significant relationship to Cixous's own incipient archives in their prehistory. *Tours promises* approaches the archival event more directly, with scenes of packing up and preparing boxes for transfer to the BNF. It includes segments of the essay Cixous presented at the conference inaugurating her archives. These books offer a view of Cixous's attitude towards the materiality of manuscripts around the time her archives were set up at the BNF. Their portrayal of *le vif* and of mortality illuminates the vitality of the manuscript so dear to Cixous in her desire for "l'avant d'un livre."

Manhattan explores both a fascination with the "avant d'un livre" and the dread of the "avant de l'archive." The narrator's house has been transformed: "des centaines des milliers de traces sont déposées comme dans une sorte de bibliothèque" ("hundreds of millions of traces are set down as in a kind of library").[16] In the section titled "Une chemise JAUNE" ("A Yellow FOLDER") she discovers, for example, "une sous-chemise dans laquelle je jette depuis des dizaines d'années les vestiges, déchets, restes membraneux, pellicules, empreintes, écailles de défaites. Collé au recto un post-it rose cru" (51; "a file into which I've been tossing vestiges, debris, scraps, hangnails, flakes, prints, chips of defeat for decades," 35). From what we have seen in Cixous's essays, we might expect that this kind of attention to *germes* and *restes*, enumerated to convey the eclecticism and fullness of the ensemble, would provoke a certain tenderness. But as she dredges up old boxes and sifts through their contents, the narrator becomes increasingly troubled by her encounters with her personal archives. Her anxiety issues from one room in particular: "il y a dans la petite pièce en forme de tunnel que nous appelons tantôt cave, tantôt grenier tantôt archive quelques cartons contenant les restes, vestiges, preuves pièces, cartons ayant contenu des bouteilles de vin pour commencer contenant pour finir de terribles secrets" (75; "in the little tunnel-shaped room that we sometimes call cellar, other times attic others archive are a few boxes that contain the remains, vestiges, exhibits, cartons having held bottles of wine in the beginning, containing dreadful secrets in the end," 56). What the boxes contain is not quite apparent and certainly not stable; neither is the room itself, which changes names and functions. The room and the boxes are a site of metamorphosis, transforming bottles into secrets: a troublesome prospect for this pre-archival state.

Described as "bêtes allégoriques" and as "des cercueils portables" (75; "allegorical beasts," "portable coffins," 56), the boxes stored in this room are terrifying. The narrator finds it "intolerable" to return to the box's potentially explosive, emotional contents, as she explains upon one such discovery, finding "un de ces trop nombreux cartons qui couvent leurs volcans dans le dos de ma vie et dans lesquels j'ai dans des paniques aux dates diverses jeté chaque fois un désordre de trésors et de déchets mêlés, rendant les fouilles ultérieures à jamais intolérables" (66; "one of those far too numerous boxes brooding on their volcanoes in the back of my life, into which at variously dated moments of panic I have tossed a hodgepodge of treasures and trash that render later excavations forever unbearable," 48). In a pre-archival state of chaos, the box and its contents are a heterogeneous, brewing or brooding amalgam; an impending natural disaster, like a dormant volcano—or, as she says in the *prière d'insérer* (request to publish) that accompanies the book *Manhattan*, "ceci n'est pas un objet mort mais une explosion souterraine" ("this is not a dead object but an underground explosion," vii). Clearly, the box and its contents are not dead, insensible matter, for they continue to transform. Their affective aftershocks are felt long after they have been buried in the back of a closet or of life. But neither do they belong fully to the realm of the living. They exist, doubly, in a liminal state: both as "l'avant d'un livre" that has already come to exist in published form, and as "l'avant de l'archive," waiting to be transferred over to the BNF.

Tours promises stages this transfer. Having agreed that she will give everything—" 'tout' donner"—to the library, the narrator finds herself living uneasily with boxes ready to be archived:[17]

> Ma maison s'était transformée en moins d'une semaine en cimetière de vampires sans que j'y puisse rien, il me semble que je marchais entre des tombes dans le couloir, toute la partie ouest où respiraient lourdement les caisses de carton qui n'avait pas fait le moindre signe auparavant était devenue lieu de répulsion pour moi. (15)

> My house had transformed in less than a week into a cemetery of vampires without my being able to do anything about it, I seemed to be walking between tombs in the hallway, the entire western part where the cardboard boxes breathed heavily having never before made the slightest motion had become a place of revulsion for me.

The problem is not that these boxes are dead: instead, it is their state of undead that is so revolting. These boxes move, breathe, and have the power to alter the entire atmosphere of the narrator's home. They are filled with "purée cadavérique," with "hontes et démons," with "de la momie et de la bouillie" (61–63; "cadaveresque goo," "shames and demons," "mummies and mush"). Yet the box, with its amorphous, viscous contents, "avait commencé à vibrer" (62; "had begun to vibrate"), as if compelled by the imminent force of the Bibliothèque to manifest the full force of their putrefaction. This mess is crawling with "des liasses d'enveloppes, des enveloppes guenilles pleines d'enveloppes vermines, des grouillances de sentiments flétris pourris" (62; "bundles of envelopes, ragged envelopes full of vermin envelopes, swarmings of wilted rotten feelings"). And although the narrator's mother encourages her to discard of all this ("Jette ça," "Enterre," 63; "Throw that out," "Bury"), the writer knows that the donation to the BNF will not entail a proper burial, or a renewed existence. Instead, the undead matter will continue its gruesome quasi-existence: "Morbidité d'une résurrection des morts morts par l'artifice des fouilles. Morts rappelés de force sans bénéfice de vie ni réparation ni joie. Comme une animation respiration artificielle de cadavres. Ouverture violente de tombes" (63; "Morbidness of a resurrection of the dead dead from the artifice of excavations. The dead called back by force without benefit of life nor reparation nor joy. Like an artificial respiration life support for cadavers. Violent opening of tombs"). The narrator has no illusion that her papers will come back to life in the library, and no hope that their decay will be stayed by some all-powerful technology of preservation. At best, the breath would be a weak imitation, the artifice of life. As Cixous saw in her visit to the BNF, what is exposed there is the "longue cérémonie" of decomposition. In *Tours promises*, this ceremony has already begun.

The narrator here shirks back, whereas the writer Cixous, desirous of "l'avant d'un livre," had looked on in fascination at the passionate melée taking place on the page, likened to a generative space: "la forge folle et tumultueuse, où l'Amour et la Haine embrassés, se roulent dans les convulsions qui déjouent tout calcul et toute espérance" ("the mad and tumultuous forge, where Love and Hate embrace, rolling around in convulsions which thwart all calculation and all hope").[18] In *Tours promises*, the narrator also vacillates between these two modalities, showing moments of "tendresse pour le germe" as well as revulsion. She admits a sense of obligation to an incalculable number of "secrets redoutables [qui] dorment dans des caisses bâillonnées" (99; "fearsome secrets sleeping in gagged cases"). The tenuousness of the secrets, "ces trésors du cœur humain," is materially apparent in their "structure fragile, concave, et sujette à frissons et tremblements" (100; "these treasures of the human heart," "fragile, concave structure, subject to shiverings and tremblings"). These secrets, and the life they convey, depend on their written form for survival. But even two Post-it notes bearing "les traces encore vivantes" of a lived moment will fade away: "Tout cela sera décoloré l'an prochain. Un livre non écrit ne dure pas" (173; "traces still living"; "All that will be discolored next year. A non-written book doesn't last"). With a kind of divine omniscience, the narrator is able to make out "le corps aux membres disjoints et à la tête étrange" among "les morceaux de phrases, les feuillets à demi calcinés, les pages maculées" (53; "bodies with separated limbs and strange head," "bits of phrases, pages half charred, pages stained"). Discerning a body and a life in what appeared to be a swarming, rotting mess, she is seized with compassion. Yet Cixous's descriptions of material disintegration and disjointedness never amount to a straightforward personification relying on human tropes. The embodied vitality of these bits and pieces of literary artifacts suggests that there is potential for living on in the archive, though the gruesome descriptions offset any facile comparisons with a humanesque existence.

Material "Endurance" in *Double Oubli* and *Le Prénom de Dieu*

Cixous's experience of archival animation continues in her discovery of one particular manuscript's surprising durability. After the first boxes of her papers were sent to the BNF, Cixous developed a rhythm of writing and archiving in the first decade of the collection—sending the manuscript to the BNF soon after a book was published. The archivist Marie-Odile Germain speaks of a "gradual transfer" that took place "in successive waves since the beginning of 2000."[19] The absence of earlier manuscripts stood out, including that of "Le Rire de la Méduse," widely considered to be a cornerstone of Cixous's work, and which to date has not been found. But then, manuscripts began to reappear. The manuscript of *Voiles*, cowritten with Derrida, was found in a drawer—an episode recounted in *Insister* (2006). And the manuscript of *Le Prénom de Dieu* joined the collection at the BNF in 2009. The discovery—and fictionalized disposal—of this manuscript is the subject of *Double Oubli de l'Orang-Outang* (2010). Focusing on the manuscript's materiality lays the groundwork for the significant impact these surprise encounters have on the friendship and communication between Cixous and Derrida, especially after the latter's death. Convinced of the vitality of the manuscript, the narrator grapples with the ethical implications of dealing with this "other-life," which prompts similar considerations in the reader. If these artifacts are, indeed, in some way living, they would require a carefully considered approach to archival preservation and consultation.

In what follows, I consider artifacts as they appear between published texts and the archive. The relationship between *Le Prénom de Dieu* and *Double Oubli de l'Orang-Outang* is significant for the author's archival practice, including the representation of archiving in her work. The manuscript of *Le Prénom de Dieu* is not a genetic predecessor to *Double Oubli*: the former does not contain material directly relating to the writing process of the latter. To a certain extent, it eschews classification as an *avant-texte*, as conventionally understood by genetic criticism, in which successive manuscript states constitute a path toward a final, published text and can be mined for clues as to the text's development and meaning. (Furthermore, a genetic reading of *Le Prénom de Dieu* through its manuscript is not my focus here: the textual content of the manuscript at the BNF, composed mainly of typescripts, presents minimal divergence from the final published text of *Le Prénom de Dieu*. More fruitful for the consideration of Cixous's writing process and archival practices in the present study is the relationship between the manuscript of *Le Prénom de Dieu* and *Double Oubli*.) The emotionally charged rediscovery and consultation of the manuscript, and the extensive descriptions of its material makeup, make it the central figure of *Double Oubli*. So while the manuscript of *Le Prénom de Dieu* does not properly constitute the genetic dossier of *Double Oubli*, and indeed has its own separate dossier in the chronology of manuscripts in the *fonds* Cixous, the treatment of the manuscript in *Double Oubli* is significant for understanding the relationship between the two texts in the archive. In a genetic reversal, it is *Double Oubli* (a published text) that sheds light on the manuscript of *Le Prénom de Dieu* and, further, on Cixous's archival practices. Extrapolating from Cixous's treatment of artifacts in *Double Oubli*, I show that the divergence of writing in the archive from the published text is key to the possibility of living on otherwise in an archival state.

But the narrator must first face a dilemma upon discovering a box containing the manuscript of her first work, long considered lost: to read or not to read this book, written "blindly," decades ago, in an era of harrowing personal upheaval? In *Double Oubli* the narrator grapples with this question as she slowly unpacks the box and examines its contents, many of which provoke intense emotion and further surprises. The final, most striking discovery comes at the end of the book, when the narrator realizes that some of the typescripts and manuscripts have been annotated in pencil by another reader, whose handwriting she recognizes as that of Jacques Derrida, who had died five years before. Faced with these manuscripts, she sees herself repeating identical gestures and emotions as in her 1964 consultation of Joyce's manuscripts in the United States for her dissertation. The box summons up the memory of archival research, the emotion she felt upon discovering "un trésor encore vierge, que me voilà, je me vois, en train de dévoiler vite et doucement, d'accueillir, de célébrer, me voilà en train de violer le plus tendrement" ("a yet unravished treasure, and there I am, I can see myself, quickly and gently unveiling, greeting, celebrating, there I am tenderly ravishing").[20] As she makes her way through the box, the narrator sorts through the tension between tender adoration and rapture—and violent metaphors of rape and uncovering—that underlie conventional methodologies of archival research.

In contrast to the morbid attitude towards material decline in *Manhattan* and *Tours promises*, the manuscript's fragility is not a matter of anxiety and concern in *Double Oubli*. Instead, an idiosyncratic, dynamic object is capable of preserving writing and eliciting strong emotion, to the point of seeming to be animated by an "other-life." Perhaps surprisingly, its vitality informs the narrator's decision to abandon the box and its contents at the end of the book, and although this does not correlate to the actual status of the manuscript, we will see that this seemingly alternate, fictional fate is not wholly at odds with its archival afterlife. The manuscript of *Le Prénom de Dieu* is preserved at the BNF, but it could have been otherwise. As an undercurrent to the encounter with this object and the descriptions of its makeup in *Double Oubli de l'Orang-Outang*, the material contingency of these papers reinforces their vibrant force. But the materials' contingent nature does not mean they are subject to passive decay and decomposition: in their liveliness, they resist.

The artifacts in *Double Oubli* are characterized by their material endurance. An entire box and its contents, including the manuscript of *Prénom de Dieu*, have miraculously resisted the ravages of time and physical decay. The narrator notes the box's durability as well as an unidentifiable strangeness, describing it as "léger, résistant, solide comme un roc, marginal, un peu surhumain comme un cercueil portable" (45; "light, sturdy, solid as a rock, marginal, somewhat superhuman like a portable coffin," 30). Attempts to pin the box down, to determine what kind of thing it is (rock? superhuman?), are qualified through metaphor and hedging. Its strangeness is linked to its material form: the box is "hermétiquement fermé par des bandes de papier scotch marron intactes. Inviolé" (41; "hermetically sealed by brown paper sticky-tape, unbroken. Inviolate," 27). Its resistance to destruction and decay, as well as desecration, seems miraculous to the narrator: "On ne s'étonnera jamais assez de son endurance: ces animaux ont une résistance extraordinaire. Ils ne se décomposent pas. Ils ne sont pas mangés par les vers et les mousses" (27; "There will never be astonishment enough at its endurance—these animals have extraordinary resistance. They do not decompose. They are not eaten by worms and moss," 16, translation slightly modified). Even when the box has been opened and unpacked, it continues to project the "force" of its being through "les émanations mortelles" ("mortal emanations," 43) and "une puissance propre" (62; "a power all its own," 43). This power is itself a form of resistance: "C'est étrange. Il ne se laisse pas faire" (61; "It's odd. It won't be pushed around," 43).

Ascribing a life, an *anima* to these "animals," Cixous sets up the ethical predicament that will take place at the end of *Double Oubli*—whether to discard or to keep the manuscript of *Le Prénom de Dieu*—as murder, saying "ils ne meurent que si on les tue" (27; "They only die if they are killed," 16). When the narrator decides to "détruire le Carton" ("destroy the Box," 171), she considers burning, burying, or drowning it, but rejects each of these methods because Le Carton is not inanimate: "Je ne peux pas vouer de l'âme au bûcher. Je n'y survivrais pas . . . comme il est lourd le corps d'un Carton auquel on a outrepensé" (218; "I can't condemn a soul to the stake. I wouldn't survive that. . . . you've no idea how heavy the body of a Box that's been outthought is," 172). As a conscious being, Le Carton even seems aware of its own impending demise: once the decision to abandon it has been made, the box gives its own death rattle, emitting "des grésillements d'insectes" (217; "an insect-like buzzing sound," 171) throughout the day.

The contents of the box are likewise fascinating in the vitality of their material endurance. In her first inventory, the narrator pulls out "des liasses de copies dactylographiées et copies carbone de textes . . . tapés à simple interligne en plusieurs exemplaires identiques . . . le désordre est la cause d'une rapide succession d'humeurs: une bourrasque d'excitation, de surprise, d'indifférence suivie de jubilation" (49–51; "bundles of typed and carbon copies of texts . . . typed single-spaced in several identical copies . . . whose disorder is the cause of a rapid succession of moods: a gale of excitement, surprise, of indifference followed by jubilation," 32–34). We are close to the scene of archival research and the taste for the heightened pitch of discovery that the box called up from 1964, especially when the narrator discovers her own handwritten manuscripts underneath the first layer of typewritten pages. The sight of "plusieurs nouvelles entièrement manuscrites recto verso" ("several stories, entirely handwritten on both sides of the paper," 36) sends the writer to "la pointe exquise de l'élévation" ("the exquisite heights of elevation," 36); she writes, "j'ai été enchantée" (53; "I have been enchanted," 36). Acknowledging the simplicity of her reaction, described as "émoi naïf d'un enfant qui se réjouit d'avoir trouvé dans le sable des verroteries somptueuses dont il fera don à sa mère allégorique à majuscules, la Grande Bibliothèque" (51; "the naive pleasure of a child jubilant at having found glass jewels buried in the sand that she will give to her allegorical mother in capital letters, the Great Library," 34), the discovery appears to her as a treasure, a gift that she can in turn pass on to the archive.

Though this naive joy will become more nuanced by the end of *Double Oubli*, the thrill of discovery in the moment has to do with reliving and reanimating, a kind of momentary eternal return: "Il n'est pas impossible que le souvenir de ces avant-traces soit ranimé s'il est donné à l'individu de l'espèce littéraire l'occasion, accidentelle, de vivre une autre fois dans un autre monde la même scène exactement" (52; "It is not impossible that the memory of these fore-traces would be revived were the individual of the literary species to be granted the accidental opportunity to live once again and in another world the exact same scene," 35). It's unclear whether the "individu de l'espèce littéraire" is the reader or the object, both of whom could be reliving the reanimated "souvenir." The text is in fact quite ambiguous as to what or who is living in this scene: Is the narrator's consultation a reliving made possible by the manuscript? Or is the manuscript itself brought back to life ("ranimé") by her consultation? The relationship between the narrator and the artifacts is not simply one of creator and creation, or of active researcher and passive document.

The notebooks themselves, in which the first drafts of these texts were written, are given a "visage" in this memory. Like each individual scrap of paper that the narrator discovers, "parcourant avec une délicate exaltation les centaines de visages de ces morceaux de manuscrits" (51; "rifling through with delicate jubilation the hundreds of faces of these pieces of manuscripts," 34), even the fragments of a manuscript come to have faces into which the researcher peers. But the "visage" does not correspond to any particular human face:

> Je me souvenais du visage de mes premiers textes, . . . les cahiers aux couvertures brunes, des cahiers de petit format, d'une peau épaisse, solide, aux pages cousues, desquels je m'attachais avec nervosité et confiance. . . . L'âme du livre qui se faisait avec l'esprit du cahier: sec musclé bref carré dru ferme. (64)

> I remembered the faces of my first texts, . . . the notebooks with brown covers—small ones, in thick, sturdy skin, the pages sewn together, by which I held myself together nervously, trustingly. . . . The soul of the book in the making had the notebook's spirit: lean sturdy brusque square thick-set staunch. (45)

The narrator gives the portrait of the notebooks through the details of their physical makeup. Although they have a face and skin, the texts described here cannot be explained by a trope of personification by which the physical qualities of the notebooks resemble those of the writer, since the notebooks' spirit, skin, musculature, and face are separate. Nor does the "attachment" that takes place in the first moments of writing metonymically imbue the material with the writer's affect. Instead, the steadfast character of the material replaces the writer's nervousness with confidence, and the "soul" of the book and the "spirit" of the notebook are dependent on the latter's material form.

The manuscripts' specific materiality points to a life that is distinctly not human: an "other-life." Cixous insists repeatedly on the conjunction of life and material in the perusal of these objects, highlighting the vitality of matter that overrides any material/immaterial binary. Time, life, and memory all take the material form of paper:

> Le Carton est plein de temps. Ce qu'il y a dans le Carton: un cube de temps, découpé dans la matière-histoire de ma vie, et structuré comme du carton ondulé: deux feuilles de papier, entre les deux une

> troisième feuille de papier maintenue ondulée. Il n'y a pas de matériau plus merveilleusement résistant que le temps en papier. . . . Je suis fascinée par les propriétés textuelles de la vie sur papier: que la mémoire ait trouvé à se protéger et à protéger la jeunesse de ses personnages dans les ondulations d'un tissu! (97)
>
> The Box is full of time. What is in the Box: a cube of time, carved up into the matter-history of my life, and structured like corrugated cardboard: two sheets of paper, with a third sheet—also corrugated—in between. There is no more wonderfully durable material than paper time. . . . I am fascinated by the textual properties of life on paper, by the fact that memory has found a way to protect itself and to protect the youth of its characters in the folds of a fabric! (71)

Cixous attempts here to describe the "propriétés" of "le temps en papier" and "la vie sur papier," fragile yet surprisingly steadfast, by mixing concrete and abstract references. Time takes the form of paper in this passage, while life alights on its surface. Memory becomes animated in its search for protection and perpetuity, which it finds in the roughness of textile, the "ondulations d'un tissu." The papers, which the writer finds miraculously well preserved within the box, become fantastical objects in this transformation. While they have a striking capacity for endurance, they are by no means inert or fixed; they are dynamic objects.

Significantly, *Le Prénom de Dieu* only appears in *Double Oubli* through the physical form of its manuscript and surrounding documents: its content is never discussed. If the manuscript of Cixous's first book can reanimate memory and provoke ethical recognition, it is as a collection of material "traces" and "avant-traces," to use Cixous's own terminology, that act in recombination, living or reanimated, and not as a singular, individual being that remains recognizably self-same and stable. Most of the documents that fill Le Carton are typed out on onionskin paper ("Le papier: pelure," 50) ("The paper: peel," 33), but the overall effect is of a heterogeneous mass: "un ensemble nombreux—des centaines peut-être—de feuillets, de différentes consistances et épaisseurs" (51; "a large collection—hundreds, maybe—of sheets of paper, of varying consistencies and thicknesses," 34). The narrator finds this unruly, chaotic assemblage stimulating, its variety a sensorial delight. The eclectic materiality of the ensemble is essential to its archival vitality.

Cixous's published, archivally minded writing is not just descriptive; it also suggests a theory and a method of archival practice that foreground the interplay between different kinds of artifacts, the varying endurance of materials, and the kinds of liveliness they convey. The dossier of *Prénom de Dieu* at the BNF offers an example of the dynamic interaction within an archival assemblage and illustrates the materially divergent yet harmonious relationship between archived artifacts and published texts. Two archival boxes contain notes, correspondence, and drafts of the short texts of *Le Prénom de Dieu*. This dossier differs from other, later manuscripts in the *fonds* Cixous, such as *Double Oubli* or *Tours promises*. Instead of handwritten pages rearranged, developed, and corrected by hand, followed by a typescript that closely resembles the final, published text, the documents in the *Prénom de Dieu* manuscript alternate between corrected typescripts and photocopies of handwritten pages for the same story. In Box II, two separate folders contain various stages of the *Prénom de Dieu* texts: a blue folder with "Nouvelles pour *Prénom de Dieu*, dactylographiées et manuscrites" ("Stories for *Prénom de Dieu*, typed and handwritten") and a beige folder with "Nouvelles publiées ou non dans *Prénom de Dieu*" ("Stories published or not in *Prénom de Dieu*") (according to the archivist's notes). The text "L'outre vide," for example, appears across both folders in manuscript and typescript form, here fragmented, there corrected, demonstrating the material variability of the text in multiple formats, with little textual divergence.

The onionskin typescripts and photocopied manuscript pages that compose this dossier exist as a heterogeneous assemblage more than as a composite entity, akin to Cixous's description of the manuscript in *Double Oubli*. In particular, onionskin paper's material makeup, on display in the archive, demonstrates the durability that captured the narrator's admiration in *Double Oubli* (though in this case the material is not foregrounded in the text). At first glance, the thin, nearly translucent onionskin gives the artifact a fragile appearance. But because of the high density of fibers and their composition, the paper is in fact very strong. It is thus the perfect archival document: low bulk, high endurance. Furthermore, its cockled finish, which gives a rustle when handled, prevents sheets from sticking to each other or to other surfaces. Each sheet can thus maintain its integrity as a singular artifact, while also contributing to the "différentes consistances et épaisseurs" of the "ensemble nombreux" that is the manuscript. The varied material makeup of the manuscript of *Le Prénom de Dieu*, as described in *Double Oubli* and observed in the archived dossier, is key to its archival existence. Onionskin paper engages hearing and touch in sensory play that is evocative of the manuscript's materiality. But the dossier also highlights the divergence from Cixous's description in the published text. Photocopies of the handwritten pages of *Le Prénom de Dieu* stand in for the manuscript, underscoring its absence. They cast into sharp relief the bent and torn edges of those manuscript pages, emphasizing their fragility. The awareness of fragility extends to the other components of the assemblage: several onionskin typescript pages have begun to show signs of wear, fraying along the edges. Although the account of the manuscript in *Double Oubli* is primarily concerned with its surprising durability, it promotes a heightened awareness of the artifact's physical makeup that opens up another possible viewing in the archive. Cixous's material attention keeps her first text in play beyond the textual content, activated in its provisional, archival condition. The archival and published states are intertwined, but not in a linear progression from the rough to the fair copy. The divergent fates of the manuscript in *Double Oubli* and the BNF coexist in the continuous present of the archive, allowing for a potential parallel afterlife for these texts.

Pencil, by Chance

Just as important as the "faces" of notebooks and papers in the Carton of *Double Oubli* are the penciled marks on the typewritten onionskin pages, which renew the artifact in the moment of consultation. In the top margin of the first page of four different *nouvelles*, the narrator of *Double Oubli* discovers four annotations: a title (*Le Lac*); a number (7); an unreadable phrase scribbled out; and another title (*La Baleine de Jonas*) whose ghostly gray marks peek out from under inked letters overlaying them. These annotations are all written in pencil and have an uncanny allographic quality to them; both of these qualities are essential to the endurance of the manuscript, for the narrator. Glancing over a heading, she has "le sentiment fugitif que le L majuscule première lettre du titre *La Baleine de Jonas* a quelque chose d'*autre*" (210; "the fleeting sense that the capital L that was the first letter of the title *La Baleine de Jonas* has something *other* about it," 165, translation slightly modified). The number 7 has its own agency, presiding over the top margin "entouré d'un fin halo, qui pour être plus accessible, comme s'effectuant dans un air plus pur, moins inquiet, n'en est pas moins émouvant" ("surrounded by a fine halo, which for all that it is more accessible, for taking place in a more rarefied, less turbulent air, is no less affecting," 118); the simple hooked numeral has an unexplained quality that makes it "ressemble à J. D." (157; "It looks like J. D." 118). The penciled title *Le Lac* "n'est pas de mes mains," the narrator notes, recognizing the handwriting as Jacques Derrida's (143; "*that Lac* is not by my hand," 107).

If these are Derrida's annotations, the narrator speculates, his reading could be interpreted as a conferral of authority: "c'est lui . . . qui aura *chiffré* les disloqués démembrés égardés, ramenés à la raison," the writer suggests, giving meaning to these texts through their first reading in which "l'objet a été décidé par lui: jugé, cousu, acquitté" (157; "it was he . . . who will have *ciphered* the dislocated dismembered mislaid, brought back to their senses"; "the object was decided by him: judged, sewn up, acquitted," 119). The numbers and titles index and order the texts with a legitimizing gesture, transforming the scraps of writing that the narrator calls "larves," "choses autres," and "restes" (153, 157, 219; "larvae," "things other," "remains," 115, 119, 172). The writer proclaims that "ces lettres [*Le Lac*] dessinées d'une main nette pour racheter le malheureux objet trouvé" (204; "the letters spelled out in a firm hand to redeem the unfortunate foundling," 160) effectively save the document, transforming it from a meaningless thing into a readable text. The economic echoes of *racheter* suggest an exchange, though another meaning slips alongside the transactional one: this simple handwritten phrase has a mystical, transformative potentiality that confers grace.[21]

Cixous's reading of the penciled annotations reverses the conventional trajectory of a text's progression towards publication: the "force" of handwriting, not the typewritten draft, is what transforms the texts that become *Le Prénom de Dieu* into a readable, published book. Whereas in some cases the manuscript appears to be reanimated on its own, as we will see with *Voiles*, in this case, according to Cixous, Derrida's reading saved the text twice over: first, in the original reading that legitimizes these preliminary drafts; and second, in the rediscovered pencil markings that bring the narrator back to the scene of Derrida's first reading, allowing her, as well as the manuscript, to relive its inchoate state. It would seem in this narrative that the text is a passive object to be saved heroically by the human reader. But in a closer look, the text's authoritative salvation is countered by the state of the pencil marks, which are much more equivocal, and yet more enduring.

Another annotation made on the manuscript of *Le Prénom de Dieu* illustrates the paradoxical force of the pencil marks and their power to preserve and be preserved. The narrator deciphers the phrase "On le garde" behind the screen of a tight scribbling, "un gribouillis serré," on the top margin of the first text, "Croisé." Although she contemplates erasing "la rature, au crayon" ("the crossing-out, in pencil") in order to see what it covers over, she is ultimately relieved not to destroy the "sacred" marks. Yet the annotation on the manuscript in the BNF does not correspond to the annotation described in *Double Oubli*. There is no "gribouillis" screening the phrase, which reads as *on la garde*, not *on le garde*. Rather than confirming Cixous's account of the manuscript in the published text, the direct relationship between the manuscript and the published text is severed. Of course, we are dealing with two texts here, *Le Prénom de Dieu* and *Double Oubli*. But the shift from the manuscript annotation to its fictional form establishes an alternative existence in the archival state. The pronoun (*le* or *la*) remains ambiguous, floating, in the gender shift from manuscript to published text, between masculine or feminine form, as if its meaning were screened, like the "gribouillis" Cixous describes. Without clear referents, the phrase could mean "we keep her/it" or "they keep her/it," and the verb tense vacillates from present to a close future. The phrase "on le garde" is especially significant on the first text of Cixous's first work: both an imposing incipit and a command to save, this penciled annotation ironically exemplifies the voice of the archive which, echoing Derrida's formulation in *Mal d'archive* (11; 1 in English translation), unites the principles of commencement and commandment.[22] But it is unclear who or what voices this command, especially since the author of these markings—whether Derrida or some other reader—is unverifiable.[23] The discrepancy between the published text and the draft is paralleled in the fate of the manuscript, whose fate in *Double Oubli* diverges from its archival status. These variations on the true status of the manuscript contribute to the archive's dynamic potentiality.

The phrase "on le garde" may imply an authorization of writing for the narrator of *Double Oubli*. Yet Cixous's book emphasizes the fact that these notes were written in pencil, and the most decisive annotation, "on le garde," is muddled and scratched out, according to the narrator; its ambiguity between archive and published book destabilizes the authority of both. "Hésitation du baptême?" the narrator wonders (154). Would ink have conferred a more assured legitimacy? Yet for the narrator, the inked pages she finds in Le Carton seem less forceful than the wayward pencil marks:

> Je note ici *l'endurance* du crayon. Le trait a gardé une fraîcheur qu'aucune encre n'aurait pu préserver. C'est peut-être cette jeunesse intacte qui me touche d'abord. Entre le Crayon et le Carton, un accord: une manière féerique de se passer du temps. De se maintenir épargnés. Alors que les pages de ma main sont embaumées, la forme forte ronde saisie et pâlie par les âges. (144)

> Here I note the pencil's *endurance*. Its stroke has kept a freshness that no ink could have preserved. Perhaps it is this untouched youth that touches me at first. Between the Pencil and the Box, a certain harmony—a magical way of dispensing with time. Of remaining spared. Whereas the pages of my handwriting are embalmed, the strong round form gripped and faded by ages. (108–9, translation slightly modified)

While ink appears to be affected by the years, aging and overdone, the pencil seems to have escaped time. The youthful freshness of the pencil markings is maintained on the page. The impermanence paradoxically works in the pencil's favor: it is not the "traits" themselves that are "intact," but rather their vibrancy. Writing by pencil is "une préparation qui laisse des caractères à la fois périssables et cependant aussi résistants que s'ils étaient tracés au safre" (154; "a preparation that leaves characters both perishable and yet as durable as if they were drawn in smalt," 116).

In fact, the "chance" and "hasard" of the pencil marks renders them powerful (154). The mark could have been easily erased ("Il aurait pu . . . etre aisément efface," 146; 109 in translation); its presence attests more to randomness than to the inherent endurance of the mark. The fate of the pencil marks, the papers, and even the box itself are precarious at every turn. Even the presence of the box seems indeterminate, not fixed in stone. Does it, should it even exist? Will it continue to exist? The narrator deliberates on the fate of this box and its contents: "J'aurais pu déménager. Je pourrais. Jeter ce Carton sans le regarder. . . . Tout peut encore être perdu" (57; "I could have moved away. I still could. Throw this Box away without looking at it. . . . All might yet be lost," 39). Contingency thus plays an important role in the narrator's decision to abandon the box, in the final scene of *Double Oubli*, to the garbage collectors passing through the neighborhood one morning. A literal reading of this book might balk at this ending, which seems to jar with the *actual* fate of the manuscript of *Le Prénom de Dieu*: it is safely stored at the BNF in the *fonds* Cixous. But the simple distinction between fact and fiction does not suffice: in *Double Oubli*, the contingency of the manuscript emerges as a crucial aspect of its archival modality.

The continuing vitality of the manuscript depends on contingency: it is alive because it could be otherwise. Cixous acknowledges that the Box's contents are strange embodiments, mangled forms: "des choses autres, des corps, dont les têtes et les sexes ou bien n'étaient pas encore formés, ou bien étaient séparés" (157; "things other, bodies, whose heads and sexes were either not yet formed, or else separated," 119). But even if they are not exactly alive, they can still suffer some kind of death: "Ils ne meurent que si on les tue" (27; "They only die if they are killed," 16). The narrator's decision not to burn, drown, or bury the box is based on the Carton's status as living: the narrator remembers its body, and its soul, for which she is ethically responsible: "Je ne peux pas vouer de l'âme au bûcher. Je n'y survivrais pas." (218; "I can't condemn a soul to the stake. I wouldn't survive that," 172). Although she abandons the box, she does not kill it; therefore, it does not die. The manuscript can survive, entering the archive following the logic of the text.

Moreover, the fate of Le Carton reveals that decisions to abandon, destroy, or conserve are not as final as they would seem. The writer cannot reliably carry through an intentional act, deciding whether to keep the manuscript or to give it over to the Bibliothèque. "Dès qu'on met 'en carton,' on a déjà abandonné ce que l'on a mis en garde. Ce qui est beau c'est qu'on croit *sincèrement* garder ce que l'on vient de condamner," the narrator admits from the beginning of *Double Oubli* (26; "From the moment of 'boxing up,' what has been entrusted for safe-keeping is already abandoned. What is beautiful is that we *sincerely* think we are saving what we have just condemned," 15, translation slightly modified). She likewise comes to realize the complexity of having given these texts to their first reader decades before: "H. C. . . . a dû 'donner' (ce mot peut être remplacé: déposer, abandonner, fuir, confier, etc.) à J. D. des choses autres" (157; "HC . . . must have 'given' [this word may be replaced: deposited, abandoned, fled, entrusted, etc.] J. D. things other," 118–19). Throughout much of the book, abandonment and destruction hide behind the act of keeping or giving, but in the final scene, as the garbage trucks arrive to take the Carton away, the narrator amends the term "les bennes" (garbage truck) to pun, ironically, "une bénédiction" (219), a blessing. Her wordplay suggests that discarding the material can be an affirming act, a saving grace. The book ends by evoking the "chances" the Carton still has as it embarks on its new path: "Le Destin décidera de ce Reste, arrive que pourra" (219; "Destiny will decide for this Remainder, what will be will be,"

172). Fate is the ultimate force in determining the continuing existence of the manuscript.

In particular, the artifact's material contingency—the fragility of its material makeup, its potential for destruction or decay in many forms—is what ensures its animate dynamism. For Cixous, the manuscript materials found in Le Carton constitute an "other-life" because of their surprising endurance. This "other-life," in turn, manifests in the archive through its divergence from the published text that catalogs its reemergence and material specificity. In light of the manuscript's archival presence, *Double Oubli*'s subtle refusal to fix the manuscript's physical form amounts to a strategy for the preservation and continuation of writing. *Le Prénom de Dieu* lives on in an archival state beyond Cixous's authorly purview, whether in the fictional "bennes" or in the BNF, a homophonic kin.

Writing with Derrida's Squirrels

For Derrida, too, the force of writing is not dependent on a human author and their intentions for the text. Throughout his work, he critiques the link between author and text, whether based on legal identity or a verifiable signature (in "Signéponge," for example). In several texts about Cixous's and his own writing, Derrida suggests that the vitality of writing consists of an elusive, idiosyncratic sexuality, animatedness, or animality, which he frequently locates in writing's material makeup. His interest in the materiality of writing contributes to a non-anthropocentric understanding of the trace and of mark-making. By taking an expansive view of the life of writing, Derrida frees the writer from the presumed superior position as individual and human. Divesting the writing from ontological hierarchies also liberates writing in its physical form, allowing it to continue on as lively and unpredictable.

Beginning with his first published texts on writing and the dissemination of the trace, a major through-line in Derrida's writing from the late 1960s through the early 2000s is an interest in the materiality of writing at different stages of the writing process and the resulting document's life span. His early work on *trace* and *écriture* develops through analyses of the mechanics of writing and thinking in writers such as Freud, Artaud, Mallarmé, Nietzsche, Heidegger, and Rousseau, whose encounters with writing surfaces and implements serve as a springboard for Derrida to counter a derogatory view of *technē* as being caught in a binary between speech and writing that, Derrida demonstrates, forms the logocentric basis of Western metaphysics.[24] Derrida sought to distance the trace and writing from a reliance on form and presence, giving an expansive view to his theory of writing. Yet his texts consistently reflect an experimentation with material, formal conventions, which are disrupted in order to better call attention to the theoretical seismic shifts at work. As Christopher Johnson points out in *System and Writing*, this does not indicate that Derrida has faith in the stability or unshakeability of matter: rather, it is precisely the volatility of matter and the material form that lends itself to Derrida's textual approach.[25] Derrida's abiding interest in the materiality of the book and *mise-en-page* is evident across decades of his writing, from "Tympan" and "La Fin du livre et le commencement de l'écriture," the first chapter of *De la grammatologie* (1967), to the typographical experimentation in *Glas* (1974) and *La Carte postale* (1980). In the latter text, as in "Circonfession," collections of papers, writing, and textual objects receive sustained theoretical and poetic attention; indeed, the materiality of writing is a structural condition of both texts' creation and their theoretical considerations. *La Carte postale*'s long opening section, "Envois," takes as its fictionalized premise the attempted incineration of a collection of love letters.[26] In "Circonfession," the writer draws from his own notebooks to formulate a resistant, unsystematizable (and therefore unarchivable) element of his work: the body.

In addition to the rigorous melding of theory and practice in Derrida's writing, this integrated approach cultivates an exploration of writing from an autobiographical perspective, gaining momentum in the 1990s with "Circonfession" and other texts. The autobiographical consideration of writing matters for Derrida's oeuvre as the latter comes into institutional and archival focus, prompting attempts at periodization that would distinguish between early and late work, with the earlier characterized by a denser style, and the later by a more overtly political or personal focus. It is not my intention here to reinforce this division in focusing on Derrida's writing about his own writing. Rather, I want to suggest that the autobiographical framework enables Derrida to explore the theory and practice of writing as interconnected. Derrida's interest in the materiality of writing, books, papers, and archives permeates his entire oeuvre, with a recognition of all that "writing" and "archive" have come to signify, including writers' papers stored in libraries and special collections, state archives, private archives, and the internet. This has implications for Derrida's theorization of writing, particularly as he considers the role of handwriting in Cixous's writing practice.

With its fraught relationship to and as *technē*, handwriting in particular illustrates the shifting place of the materiality of writing in Derrida's work over the decades. Perhaps because of his own writing practices, Derrida was particularly adamant that handwriting not be seen as an old-guard bastion linking the hand to an implement that graces a writing surface, but should include typewriters and other word-processing machines such as his Macintosh computer: he discusses his own use of these technologies in "La Machine à traitement de texte" (1996) and "Le Papier ou moi, vous savez . . ." (1997), two interviews published in the 2001 volume *Papier machine*, which also contains the essay "Le Ruban de machine à écrire," on the mechanization of writing. Techniques and technologies of writing form a major through-line in Derrida's theoretical work, from *De la grammatologie* to *Mal d'archive*, and beyond. In "La Main de Heidegger (Geschlecht II)," Heidegger's preference for writing by hand—"Heidegger, lui, ne pouvait écrire qu'à la plume, d'une main d'artisan et non de mécanicien" ("Heidegger himself could write only with the fountain pen, with the hand of a craftsman and not a machine")—is linked to a hierarchy of the artisanal over the machine, but also of the human over the nonhuman, reinforced by an insistence on the "rapport de la main à la parole et à la pensée" ("the hand's relation to word and to thought," my translation).[27] Having laid the groundwork for a deconstruction of these binaries in his examination of ontology and sexual difference in Heidegger's work ("Geschlecht I"), Derrida begins "Geschlecht II" with an apology for the writing machine Heidegger so reviles: "Ne l'oublions pas comme on le fait souvent, l'écriture de machine à écrire contre laquelle Heidegger va élever un réquisitoire implacable est aussi une écriture manuelle" ("Don't forget, the writing of the typewriter against which Heidegger is going to raise an implacable indictment is also a handwriting").[28] With the writing machine rehabilitated as another form of writing by hand, and not just a prosthesis that would act as a supplement to a more authentic body part, it becomes clear that the root of Heidegger's anxiety is that "[la] mécanisation typographique détruit cette unité du mot, cette identité intégrale, cette intégrité propre du mot parlé que la manuscripture, à la fois parce qu'elle paraît plus proche de la voix ou de corps propre et parce qu'elle lie les lettres, préserve et rassemble" ("Typographic mechanization destroys this unity of the word, this integral identity, this proper integrity of the spoken word that writing manuscripts, at once because it appears closer to the voice or body proper and because it ties together the letters, conserves and gathers together").[29] Associating Heidegger with logocentrism, as mobilized by the singular, masterful, unifying hand, Derrida himself shows a preference for writing with two hands, or more, opening writing as a technique to other modes of living, tracing, and making.

Given Derrida's decades-long problematization of what it means to write by hand, his veneration of Cixous's handwriting in *Genèses, généalogies, genres . . . et le génie* seems surprising:

> Elle écrit toujours à la main, quoi qu'il arrive, elle écrit à l'outil—crayon ou stylo—c'est-à-dire sans machine ni machine-outil ; sans machine à écrire ou machine à traitement de texte. Chose désormais assez rare et décisive pour l'immense archive dont nous parlons, et j'aurais aimé consacrer quelques réflexions . . . à la phénoménale manuscripture d'Hélène Cixous, à sa forme, à ses lignes, à son rythme et à l'économie de ses abréviations quasi sténotypiques, à son corps graphique et aux enjeux archivistiques qui s'y trouvent engagés.

> She always writes by hand, no matter what, she writes using a tool—pencil or pen—that is, without a machine or a machine-tool; without a typewriter or word processors. Something which is fairly unusual

> and of critical importance for the immense archives of which we speak, and I should have liked to have devoted some remarks . . . to Hélène Cixous's phenomenal handwriting, to its form, to its lines, to its rhythm and to the economy of its quasi-stenographic shorthand, to its graphic body and to the archival stakes in all that.[30]

Derrida foregrounds the handwrittenness of Cixous's oeuvre as a determining quality of the work's "génie" (genius), to echo the book's title—as well as of the archival project the BNF has taken on. Developing what he means by writing by hand, he describes Cixous's writing process by distinguishing between machine and tool, between machine and hand, seeming to contradict his previous work. Derrida's attempt to find the right terminology to describe Cixous's writing is complicated not only by a whole strain of his own work seeking to override these very binaries, but also by the nature of Cixous's writing process. If she writes "à la main" (by hand), she also writes, Derrida remarks, "au réveil" (on waking), drawing out the way in which waking contributes to writing, like a tool or fuel, a technique, technology, or a medium, just as one would say "elle écrit au crayon, elle écrit à l'encre, elle écrit à la main" (51; "she writes in pencil, in ink, by hand," 40). Furthermore, the state of the waking dream compels and commands Cixous's writing: "Le rêve assigne alors l'ordre d'écrire . . . il use sans mesure de ce pouvoir qu'il exerce sur elle, sur une écriture qui s'y livre à son corps consentant" (51; "The dream then gives the order to write down . . . it uses unstintingly of the power it has over her, over the writing that bends its willing body to it," 40). In this portrait of writing, the dream and waking are materialized as energy that fuels the writer, "comme on dirait d'une fusée qu'elle se propulse par exemple et se meut à l'énergie atomique" (51; "as one would say of a missile that it is propelled, for example, and driven by atomic energy," 40–41). Over the course of three pages in *Genèses*, Derrida draws out a relationship between writer and writing in which the writer is likened to a machine, a body whose materiality is on the same level as the materials it draws upon in order to write.

Cixous's handwriting interests Derrida because it is "rare" and "décisive," and because it destabilizes the notion of a non-passive, authoritative creator of an oeuvre. More than this, however, it contains within it a kind of life force so expansive that it shakes off the shackles of human-centered handwriting. Derrida insists further on this "essential" quality of her work:

> Qui n'a pas vu la ligne même de son écriture manuelle manquera quelque chose d'essentiel dans ce qui communique au corps du texte publié cette vie inspirée et cette *anima*lité, cette manualité souple de la plume, cette accélération patiente de la lettre, fine, vive, agile, sûre, économe, claire, lisible, emportée dans une cursivité ininterrompue et inimaginablement curieuse, c'est-à-dire soucieuse de trouver vite . . . Son écriture me rappelle tous les écureuils du monde. (my emphasis)

> Whoever has not set eyes on the lines of her handwriting will be missing something essential of the vivacity and animality they communicate to the body of the text, the supple handwriting of the pen, the patient acceleration of the letter: fine, lively, agile, sure, economical, clear, legible, running on in an uninterrupted and unimaginably curious cursiveness, careful that is, to find quickly . . . Her handwriting reminds me of all the squirrels in the world.[31]

Strikingly, for Derrida, the liveliness of Cixous's handwriting is strong enough to resonate in the published text. Indeed, this description is driven by a series of feminine nouns—*la ligne de son écriture*, *cette vie inspirée*, *cette animalité*, *cette manualité*, *cette accélération*, *la lettre*, *une cursivité*—that run together in an adjectival amalgam, through which this writing comes to resemble "tous les écureuils du monde" ("all the squirrels in the world"). Cixous's handwriting, taken on its own terms, runs on an energy source that is not a personalized, human genius but is, rather, an idiosyncratic "animalité."

In his reading of Cixous's handwriting and her writing process, Derrida suggests a relationship between hand, body, and manuscript that cuts across categories of living. Here, human hand and body do not imbue the passive textual object with genius or liveliness; the writing is animated, but its vitality is not necessarily human. Furthermore, Derrida's description of graphology reinforces a bond between the two writers. By evoking the squirrel, Derrida identifies himself as a close reader of Cixous's particular mythology, alluding to the motif of the half-buried squirrel that recurs in *Tombe* and *Manhattan*. The *éc-ureuil* of Cixous's *éc-riture* contains echoes of the phoneme *éc-* explored in Derrida's *Glas*, and animates not only Cixous's handwriting but also Derrida's own writing process, described in "Circonfession": in his writing and archiving, both on the computer and in the accumulation of paper in his attic writing room, Derrida compares himself to a squirrel unbounded by spatial constraints: "je n'ai ni haut ni bas, comme l'écureuil qui monte et descend à l'horizontale" ("I have neither up nor down, like the squirrel climbing up and down horizontally").[32] The squirrely nature of their writing—the one by hand, ink, and paper, the other with two hands on a keyboard—is not a factor of the individual, human author, or of their proclivities for certain writing practices. The squirrel links together their two writings as having a shared spirit, a kinship in common. Drawing the two oeuvres together, the squirrel constitutes one of the textual echoes Cixous later called "secrécitation."[33] These two very different *écureuils* offer a nonanthropocentric view of life, *anima*, and writing.

Derrida's identification with the squirrel aligns with his reflections on the trace in relation to nonhuman bodies and modes of living. From as early as his work on Husserl, Derrida sought to override the dialectic of speech and writing, insisting on the writtenness of all language and, later, all living activity. Motivated by a concern for the nonhuman and for questions of sexual difference, Derrida foregrounded writing as the main way to deconstruct phallogocentric and anthropocentric traditions of Western philosophy.[34] Cixous remarked on this aspect of Derrida's work in her essay "Corresponding Voix-You":

> Thus, with the first trance of the thinking of the trace in *Of Grammatology*, the whole machine that tends to replace the word "writing" in the ordinary sense by "trace" or the word "speech" by trace, had as its final purpose that writing, speech, trace are *not the proper characteristic of the human*. There is animal trace, animals write. (emphasis in original)[35]

Cixous's awareness of this animal aspect of Derrida's work and her attention to it strengthen the bond between their two bodies of writing. If Derrida's remarks on Cixous's handwriting serve as a link between the two writers via the squirrel, they also can be understood within the theme of trace and writing that carries over several decades, including Derrida's work on animals.[36] Beyond the handwritten quality of Cixous's manuscripts, Derrida emphasizes the "animalité" of writing, giving "le corps du texte" ("the body of the text") a vitality that animates Cixous's writing in the archive. As we will see, Derrida conceived of his "own" handwriting precisely by giving it a nonhuman and non-identitarian force, moving handwriting toward what he calls *skizzes* in the autobiographical text "Circonfession." Indeed, the text problematizes the very notions of one's "own" handwriting and of life writing.

The Surprise of *Skizzes*

Derrida uses the word *skizzes* to refer to his preliminary sketches or writings, his drafts, in notebooks he had been collecting for over a decade in his personal archives. The completed text of "Circonfession" consists of "cinquante-neuf périodes et périphrases écrites dans une sorte de marge intérieure, entre le livre de Geoffrey Bennington et un ouvrage en préparation" ("fifty-nine periods and periphrases written in a sort of internal margin, between Geoffrey Bennington's work and work in preparation").[37] The "ouvrage en préparation" is mentioned in the eleventh *période* (or "period") as a study of "les circoncisions dans le monde" ("circumcisions in the world") on which the writer is collecting research—"documents" that he is accumulating "au grenier" ("in the attic") but also in a series of "carnets de notes en vue d'un livre sur la circoncision, *Livre d'Élie*, projeté à partir de 1976" from which Derrida quotes ("notebooks preparatory to a book on circumcision, 'The Book of Elijah,' projected from 1976").[38] The cover of one of these notebooks is reproduced in the book *Derrida*: a medium-sized Canson brand "Album" whose decorative cover features the printed words CROQUIS KPOKI SCHIZZO

SKIZZE SKETCH SCHETS in a frame surrounding the brand label. The words SCHIZZO and SKIZZE are boxed in pen, and the Hebrew word *milah* (circumcision) is written twice in marker on the cover. The term *skizzes* and its counterparts, accumulating on the artifact, indicate an interest in the word to evoke the materiality of writing, from the beginnings of this text in the preparatory notebooks Derrida draws from in "Circonfession." The *skizzes* harness the intimacy and idiosyncrasy of writing.

Derrida's essay "Circonfession" runs along the bottom third of the pages of *Derrida*, underneath Geoffrey Bennington's text "Derridabase," which is presented as a description of Derrida's work to date: "sinon la totalité de la pensée de J. D., du moins le système général de cette pensée" ("if not the totality of J. D.'s thought, then at least the general system of that thought").[39] The danger of the "logique" that Bennington's "program" presents, if it succeeds, would be to establish, as Derrida explains, "la loi de production de tout énoncé passé, présent et pourquoi pas futur que je pourrai avoir signé, . . . si bien que me voilà privé d'avenir" ("the law of production of every past, present, and why not future statement that I might have signed . . . so that here I am deprived of a future").[40] Derrida suggests that the only hope of maintaining some kind of freedom for his future work is if he writes "des choses improbables qui déstabilisent, déconcertent, surprennent à leur tour le programme de G. . . . *unpredictable things* pour lui survivre" ("improbable things which destabilize, disconcert, surprise in their turn G's program . . . *unpredictable things* to survive him").[41] Derrida's *skizzes* constitute a surprise, drawn from his personal archives, for the "système général" that Bennington's "Derridabase" seeks to establish.

How does one write something so personal that it could be completely surprising to the work's critical reception, something written in a "marge intérieur" (an "internal margin") at work from within? How to represent the interiority of writing, the life of writing, "ce qu'il y aura eu de plus vivant en moi," as Derrida writes ("what will have been most alive in me")?[42] Derrida explores these questions in "Circonfession" through seemingly conventional metaphors of writing, which is figured as blood and breath throughout the text. But these metaphors come up against the technologies of writing Derrida juggles here: both the *skizzes* in notebooks (from 1976 onward) and the writing on his computer, composing "Circonfession." The computer, he explains, has in fact radically altered his handwriting, nearly beyond recognition: "voilà ce que les lecteurs n'auront pas connu de moi, la virgule de ma respiration désormais, sans continuité mais sans rupture, le temps changé de mon écriture, la graphique, pour avoir perdu sa verticalité interrompue, presque à chaque lettre, pour se lier de mieux en mieux mais se lire de plus en plus mal depuis près de vingt ans" ("that's what my readers won't have known about me, the comma of my breathing henceforward, without continuity but without a break, the changed time of my writing, graphic writing, through having lost its interrupted verticality, almost with every letter, to be bound better and better but be read less and less well over almost twenty years").[43] If the physical form of handwriting is unknowable to the reader, neither is it the intimate, personal property of an author, a stand-in for him, or a reliable signature. In this passage, the writer's breath takes shape in the commas that punctuate the text, with the period only used to mark the end of each section of the text, organizing it into fifty-nine "périodes." The comma does not represent the metaphorical breath of genius, but instead contributes to a dynamic shift towards illegibility over the years. This change is not easily ascribed to the vitality of writing, as the quotable "je posthume comme je respire" indicates ("I posthume as I breathe").[44] The breath of writing is thus not a clichéd breath of life animating the work.

But what of another potential cliché of writing? In "Circonfession," writing has a pulse. The movement of writing is echoed in "le pouls d'une phrase contournante, la pulsion du paragraphe" ("the pulse of an encircling phrase, the pulsion of the paragraph").[45] Figured as blood drawn, taken, or spilled, the circulation of blood is proof of life within:

> Le dedans de ma vie s'exhibant tout seul au-dehors, s'*exprimant* sous mes yeux, absous sans un geste, oserai-je dire d'écriture si je compare la plume à une seringue, et toujours je rêve d'une plume qui soit une seringue, une pointe aspirante plutôt que cette arme très dure avec laquelle il faut inscrire, inciser, choisir, calculer, prendre l'encre avant de filtrer l'inscriptible, jouer du clavier sur l'écran, tandis qu'ici, une fois trouvée la juste veine, plus aucun labeur, aucune responsabilité, aucun risque de mauvais goût ni de violence, le sang se livre seul. (emphasis in original)
>
> The inside of my life exhibiting itself outside, *expressing* itself before my eyes, absolved without a gesture, dare I say of writing if I compare the pen to a syringe, and I always dream of a pen that would be a syringe, a suction point rather than that very hard weapon with which one must inscribe, incise, choose, calculate, take ink before filtering the inscribable, playing the keyboard on the screen, whereas here, once the right vein has been found, no more toil, no responsibility, no risk of bad taste nor of violence, the blood delivers itself all alone.[46]

Derrida compares the pen to a syringe and his blood to writing in this scene of a "prise de sang" ("taking blood") that is also a bloodletting.[47] It is a release, a "glorieux apaisement" ("glorious appeasement") to give oneself over to the flow of blood or writing.[48] The blood "expresses" itself on its own: it is a self-expression that is independent from the author's named self. Rather than providing an identifiable link to the author—a DNA signature—the writer's body is freed in this form of expression. The "periods" of the text evoke menstruation, giving an expansive corporeal quality to the practice of writing, beyond the author's biological sex.[49] The author is eclipsed in this active passivity; the technology of writing within a circulatory system is here able to draw out the ink and then filter it, removing not the impurities but what is "inscriptible."

Imagining this technology and the interplay of writing technologies in "Circonfession," Derrida suggests that writing by hand is not at odds with the more technologically "advanced" computer. Indeed, his attack on this opposition roots out its dualistic, paternalistic perspective: "et si cette histoire ne ressemble à rien, c'est aussi par défi lancé à ces cons qui croient que l'ordinateur nuit à l'écriture, la bonne vieille à la plume Sergent-Major, l'écriture parentale, la plume de mon père, la plume de ma mère, et règle enfin le problème des doubles ou de l'archive, quelle naïveté, c'est parce qu'ils n'écrivent pas à l'ordinateur" ("and if the story doesn't look like anything, this is also by way of a challenge thrown out to those idiots who think that computers are harmful to writing, to the good old Sergeant-Major pen, parental writing, *la plume de mon père, la plume de ma mère*, and finally sorts out the problem of doubles or the archive, what naïveté, it's because they don't write on a computer").[50] The condemnation of an old-guard faction of pro-*plume* writing in this passage continues further into an explanation of Derrida's own preferred technique. If these old-fashioned writing snobs disdain "machine"-driven writing, "c'est parce qu'ils n'écrivent pas à l'ordinateur": it's because they don't practice this kind of writing and therefore don't understand the freedom it affords. The passage continues:

> Le mien [l'ordinateur] je l'ai surnommé *subjectile* comme j'avais baptisé mon grenier, là où je stocke les skizzes de ma circoncision, *mon sublime*, mes dessus dessous, car je n'ai ni haut ni bas, comme l'écureuil qui monte et descend à l'horizontale, la forme de mon monde, une littérature d'apparence, comme l'allure même de mon écriture, cosmonautique, flottante en apesanteur, marine et *high-tech*, plus nue, quoi qu'ils disent, grâce au simulacre.
>
> I've nicknamed mine [i.e., my computer] *subjectile*, like I'd baptized my attic, where I stock the skizzes of my circumcision, *my sublime*, my upside downs, for I have neither up nor down, like the squirrel climbing up and down horizontally, the form of my world, a literature that appears to be, like the very look of my writing, cosmonautical, floating in weightlessness, marine and *high-tech*, more naked, whatever they say, thanks to the simulacrum.[51]

Derrida's writing system, a combination of the *sublime* and the *subjectile*, can be read as a counterpoint to the "système général de cette pensée" that Bennington has prepared. The writer moves in all directions, on the vertical and horizontal axes, animal and free "comme l'écureuil qui monte et descend à l'horizontale," making for a personal and physical archival experience. Writing is figured as something alive yet not human: squirrely in one estimation; in another, "cosmonautique, flottante en apesanteur, marine et *high-tech*." Derrida's *skizzes* come to the fore as nonhuman, non-identitarian marks that are more naked, evoking a body. But whose body? What kind of body?

In a metaphor that runs through "Circonfession," the writer's body becomes a writing surface, cut and marked in the processes of circumcision and of the *prise de sang*. But this is not a simple reversal of the writing surface, of active and passive agents. Derrida's use of the term *subjectile* to name his computer complicates the notion of the materiality of the writing or written body. In fact, an image of Derrida's computer screen is reproduced in "Circonfession," a corollary to the reproduction of his circumcision notebook cover, indicating the multidirectionality of his *skizzes* across multiple formats and materials. In chapter 3, we will see how the conjunction of the intangible page on the screen and the hard drive's magnetized platter offer a doubling structure that is echoed in the pairing of *subjectile* and *sublime* in Derrida's writing process. We will also see (in chapter 4) how the liquid metaphors of Derrida's *skizzes* offer a type of materiality that is particularly suited to transmission, to circulation and communication with readers. In "Circonfession," Derrida offers a portrait of the materiality of writing that upends conventional metaphors of body and text that purport to connect *corps* and *corpus*.

Derrida's surprise for Bennington's *programme* arises from his own notebooks—handwritten in 1976, reread in 1989, and reintegrated into Derrida's word-processing software, on the eve of his papers' entry into UC Irvine's Critical Theory Archive. The *skizzes* are certainly an archival arrangement: they are "stocked" in the attic, they constitute "[un] corpus infini, ma skizzolâtrie en carnets" ("the infinite corpus, my skizzolatry in notebooks").[52] Once archived, do the *skizzes* resist being processed, identified, and cataloged by a totalizing archival impulse, continuing to destabilize any programmatic, absolute analysis of Derrida's work? As an "unpredictable thing," the *skizzes* suggest that the materiality of writing—intimately related to, though not replicating, the writer's body—is the key to keeping the work alive, squirrely, and free. In the archive, this prompts a heightened awareness of the nonhierarchical and unpredictable elements of the artifacts and the system being consulted.[53]

Derrida's "Travaux en cours été 2004" Still at Work

We have seen that Cixous's confrontation with material fragility in the BNF is echoed, in a more optimistic tone, as she recognizes the fragility and endurance of her own "unpredictable things": for instance, the manuscript of *Le Prénom de Dieu*. Derrida mobilizes his own notebooks as "unpredictable things" that offer a chance for writing to live on. Both writers read each other's mark-making as "décisive": Derrida's penciled annotations and Cixous's handwriting confer a certain force and vitality on the textual object. But if writing can live on in its physical form, how does this "vivant" ("living") fare in the archive? If archival practices are to account for the material endurance of artifacts, they must consider their continuing existence, their ability to remain "in process," independently from those who had a hand in their making. In this chapter I have considered Cixous's and Derrida's writing processes through the lens of their own published texts. One of Cixous's later works, *Double Oubli de l'Orang-Outang*, projected the manuscript of her first text, *Le Prénom de Dieu*, into a perpetual archival state by emphasizing both the durability and the contingency of the manuscript's physical makeup. How does this strategy apply to work suspended in progress, interrupted in the early stages with no publication in view? Can an artifact "en cours" retain its dynamism in archival suspension?

Three bulky boxes in the IMEC's Derrida collection are designated "Travaux en cours été 2004" ("Works in progress summer 2004") and are made up of work in progress in the months leading up to his death. Their contents have the look of an agitated assemblage: eight uneven folders, varied states of incompletion, and a diverse collection of media, including letters, articles, photocopied manuscripts, and floppy disks. The stacked folders sit awkwardly on the reading room table. Inside the first lumpy folder, a manila envelope—postmarked June 10, 2004—must be carefully opened and its contents delicately extracted so as not to disturb the order of the thick fistful of paper scraps that threaten to spill out.

Some of the notes in this folder are written in Derrida's recognizable, slanting handwriting, some in another hand. Many are illegible. Some are written on torn scraps of paper, others on Post-it notes, tiny notepads, hotel stationery, or the back of cardstock invitations, whose printed text is as contingent as the weight of the paper, its texture and dimensions:

> *Les Éditions Galilée—A Wonderful Life d'Alain Coulange—1996*
> *Istituto Italiano per gli studi filosofici, Napoli—Mal d'archivio—1996*
> *Chevalier de la Légion d'Honneur à Jacques Derrida—1992*

A floppy disk labeled "→ L'Herne. (20-4-2004)," a letter dated *17 déc. 1982*, and a Post-it note with a "Rêve" jotted down are lodged within the bundle. Turning over a Kanterbrau coaster, I can barely make out the following:

> *et prêts à tout*
> *toutes les grammaire de*
> *fl ∂¢o} fait d j'érαℑe*
> *†ß ⌠∝ςω dans l'air*
> *de ce syllabe; prêts*
> *demeure*[54]

and ready for anything
all the grammar of
ﬂ ∂¢ o} made o I αℑe
†ß ⌠∝ςω in the air
of this syllable; ready
stay

Particularly when the handwriting is indecipherable (hence my use of various symbols to transcribe my own reading experience), the material support becomes noticeable, rising up from the background: the pulpy, pressed board of the coaster, its rough, cream-colored thickness, marked with the half-sphere of a wet glass. Or the thin, hand-softened paper of a note folded and unfolded so many times that it is ripping along the creases, leaving segments dangling precariously. What stands out most in this cluster are the idiosyncratic material details of each scrap: a fragile, yellowing sheet of paper, creased. A notepad filled with page after page of tiny scribblings and page numbers. Hotel insignia. A business card for a pub called "The Hungry Monk." A tiny insect wing and other detritus caught on the sticky strip of a Post-it note.

My interest is compounded since these scraps are a rare find. Because Derrida worked on a computer, and on a typewriter before that, his archived manuscripts are rarely indicative of beginning stages of work, of the preparations, false starts, hesitations, and multiplied variants that represent the working stages of a published text. His collections, at the IMEC and at UC Irvine, consist mainly of successive versions of typed texts printed on white A4-size paper—final drafts, offprints, and proofs, with minor marginal handwritten corrections. Each detail of the materials labeled "Travaux en cours été 2004" thus seems important and precious, even the words that slip into illegibility, and the floppy disk that has been rendered obsolete by shifting technologies.

The materials in these folders appear to illustrate the provisional state to be smoothed over by the printed page. But what does "en cours" signify? If these materials consist of "works in progress," what kind of route or trajectory are these works progressing along? What kind of work is being done here? Indeed, what kind of process is still *en cours*, years after Derrida's death in 2004? Instead of preserving a moment in suspension—the originary moment of genius stirring, or the unfinished business of a life interrupted—these materials *en cours* represents the continuous and continuing activity of writing. The variety of material floating in a mostly unfixed archival treatment—contained in its original manila envelope as a cluster, not individually processed—contributes to the impression that work is still happening here: *en cours* as ongoing, open-ended.

In giving these scraps so much attention, my aim is not to seek out the personal in each physical artifact as a monument to the deceased, nor to conceive of the archive as a reliquary for what may have touched or belonged to the author. I read the scraps not as fetishes, but as objects that present a cacophony of details, ones of visual and tactile interest, independently of Derrida's authorial function. These details are just as important to the artifacts' potentiality as the writer's intention or the textual content. They contribute to an understanding of the archive not as a crypt but as a living space. Handling these notes triggers a hyperawareness of their materiality: each fold or fall changes the object minutely, though not imperceptibly, and registering these material changes creates a record of the transformation of the artifact. The fragile scraps are becoming something else, beyond any intention Derrida might have had for them. They are in process, not in progress: "en cours," not as *work* left undone, but as materials in transformation beyond the purview of any human attempt at conservation.

Yet the manila envelope of "Travaux en cours été 2004" also contains poignant traces of mortality, registering specific irony in the text written on a rectangular, light yellow Post-it note:

> *Jusqu'ici il ne pensait qu'à la*
> *mort et la voyait venir à chaque*
> *instant. Maintenant, il avait déjà, et*
> *ce fut tout autre chose, mais insensiblement,*
> *commencé à mourir.*
>
> *Up to this point he thought only of*
> *death and saw it coming at every*
> *instant. Now, he had already, and*
> *it was something entirely other, but imperceptibly,*
> *started to die.*

In the context of the archive, the note's evocation of mortality resonates beyond the fact of the author's passing, conferring a mournful sense on the artifact itself in its fragility. Written in pencil, the ephemerality of these enigmatic phrases is compounded by the absence of any indication of reference that would root the note as a citation. The third person places it at a further remove, opening the pronoun and the narrative voice up to include a variety of potential subjects—Derrida, the author, a character, the archive, or the artifact itself. To be clear, I am not suggesting that the note, personified, speaks "il" here in the third person. Instead, an attentiveness to the material makeup of this artifact and those that surround it can make the "il" vacillate—to detach it from the author Jacques Derrida, project it towards other potential subjects, and interrogate who or what the "il" is here, what kind of dying it is doing, and what "ici" and "maintenant" (here and now) the note might be referring to. Reading manuscripts—or here, archived ephemera—calls up a curious temporality, as the manuscript scholars Carolyn Dinshaw and Deborah McGrady have suggested: one that contributes "asynchrony" to the "complex and vascular" moment of archival experience, collapsing moments of writing, reading, and consultation.[55] The archival assemblage of this artifact enriches the note's significance, the "ici" and "maintenant" of the moment of writing converging with those of archival encounters. As it highlights the material context of this artifact beyond its textual content, the archive refocuses the reading experience, encouraging a consideration of the materiality and vitality of writing.

Though it refers to an anticipated demise, the temporality proposed by the note substitutes dying as a *process* for death as an *event*, shifting from the terminal ending to an unfinished, constantly beginning state, thus drawing attention to the material present. In this note, death is at work, *en cours*. But it, "il"—the note—is not already dead. The content of the note seems to refer to the writer's death in the present (Derrida as deceased), and yet through its presence in the archive, it indicates a way of living on in posthumous fragility. The things it has taken along with it in its sticky strip—a few hairs, some fuzz, three plant seeds, and the wing of a small insect—are reminders of the uncontrollable material life that surrounds the archive and infiltrates it.

Derrida's and Cixous's views of the materiality of writing and its vitality hone a sensitivity to various forms of living and dying. Instead of approaching the archive and its take on finitude "insensiblement," to echo the note above, their materials demand attention and reflection: Which writing methods can ensure the survival of the material artifact? Write in, on, and with what? Archival survival entails not simply the physical preservation of artifacts, but also, through preservation, the continuation of the work. An archival attention reveals that the content of the work is inseparable from its material form. Through its fragility and endurance, the artifact's materiality contributes to an afterlife or an "other life."

The "death" of the manuscript is not the "death of the author." The one is not a stand-in for the other. In order for the artifact to become an "unpredictable thing," it must be separate from the body of the writer, from their life and from their death. Detachment allows manuscripts to circulate, highlighting their dynamism and capacity for movement, allowing them to be shared more readily with readers. As we have begun to see with Cixous's treatment of the manuscript of *Le Prénom de Dieu*, found and then "abandoned," we will see in the next chapter that along with material endurance, which contributes to an artifact's liveliness, material contingency also allows the artifact to live on—though with risks.

Chapter 2

✦

Allow for Change

Material Contingencies on Free-Floating Ephemera

At the end of a day of research in the *fonds* Cixous at the Bibliothèque nationale de France, I wait at the central desk to return the manuscript I have been consulting. The desk's antique style fits in with the ornate décor that surrounds it: the wood-paneled walls, intricate chandeliers, and red carpet barely mask the creaking of wood floors in the Salle de Lecture of the Département des Manuscrits, part of the BNF's Richelieu site since 1875. The archivist has exchanged my seat number for the plaque to check out at the front desk, and has turned his attention elsewhere, shuffling materials around his workstation. Finally, he turns back to me, perplexed that I'm still there. "Is there anything else?" he asks. I tell him that I'd like to return the manuscript. He looks shocked. How could he have missed the manuscript? Is *that* the manuscript?? That stack of papers, in a bright green or orange paper sleeve, a *sous-chemise* that acts more as a dividing folder than a protective cover? Ah! But I thought those were *your* papers! I am relieved that his tone becomes more amused, nearly chuckling, as he realizes the confusion. The unassuming manuscript is quickly whisked away and nestled in its protective gray archival box.

The archivist's confusion points to the inconspicuous appearance of many documents in the *fonds* Cixous. The commonplace materials Hélène Cixous uses in her writing process take on a kind of camouflage in this sumptuous manuscript reading room, which would allow them to pass under the radar. Most of the manuscripts consulted in the BNF's Département des Manuscrits, medieval and modern, are bound in leather tomes. There are some exceptions: letters are often preserved unbound, and contemporary collections, such as Foucault's, include materials such as typed printouts.[1] In contrast to the majority of artifacts in the BNF reading room, most of Cixous's manuscripts consist of loose-leaf papers of varying sizes, unbound, torn from inexpensive white correspondence pads ("des blocs Leader-Price, les plus-moins-chers d'Europe," "Leader-Price-brand pads, the most-least-expensive in Europe")[2] or organized in ubiquitous, brightly colored *chemises* and *sous-chemises*, the standard array of folders found in French office supply stores and supermarkets. These have been annotated with highlighters and Post-it notes, and amended with staples and tape. But more than their ordinariness, these materials are significant because they can easily be rearranged, or even separated from one another. This may also be the case for other contemporary writers who make use of everyday supplies, which may be banal but contribute nonetheless to the writing process and the possibilities for conservation. Despite the relatively uncommon practice of continuing to compose manuscripts by longhand, as writers increasingly favor word-processing software, Cixous's use of materials is not exceptional, but bears consideration within the context of studies of her writing process. Attention has been given to her use of dream transcription and quasi-automatic writing, but the unfixed, changeable and material aspect of her process has not been explored.[3] This aspect of her writing is crucial to the experience of consulting Cixous's manuscripts in the BNF, and has implications for the archival preservation of her work and that of other contemporary writers who also make use of ordinary, seemingly unremarkable materials.

"*E pur si muove*"

It could have been otherwise: the published text could have turned out differently. It still can—and will—be otherwise. The material will degrade, erode, or disintegrate sooner or later, depending on its physical makeup and technologies of preservation. In addition to this kind of change, the material is susceptible to movement and reordering, reshuffling, slipping out of a file, falling out of sequence, in the archive as in the writing process. Volatile materials foil archival principles of original order and provenance, slipping out of sequence and eschewing linear progression.[4] I echo Elizabeth Grosz's use of "volatile" to reframe matter as dynamic, shaking off its conventional characterization in Western philosophy as passive and inert.[5] The more mobile the materials in question, the more the importance of change is illuminated. But by allowing for change, and for chance, I also mean to highlight the reactivity and instability of the archival materials at hand. This certainly contributes to their vibrancy or vitality, the sense that they are animated by some principle of movement or force: an impression that could be explained as a principle of matter itself, as Catherine Malabou's concept of plasticity suggests. Plasticity is matter's ability to both hold form and explode form; the idea of material volatility speaks to the risk involved when matter changes shape or place.[6] Yet this volatility also ensures that matter continues to exist. For the archived artifact, however ordinary or unconventional—manuscript, Post-it, loose-leaf, or flower—the possibility of change is crucial to its survival, even though it may transform beyond recognition.

As it weaves between materiality and temporality, contingency is an important idea for the study of literary archives, and in particular for genetic criticism. The focus on dynamism is especially prominent in "Drafts" (the 1996 special issue of *Yale French Studies* on genetic criticism), whose editors remark: "The textual *ne varietur* has been shaken up by an *e pur si muove*."[7] In this statement, a curious chronology is itself shaken up: the draft, associated with Galileo's insistent *e pur si muove* (and yet it moves), destabilizes the invariable printed text. This revises a conventional association of draft with a *before* to the published text's *after*, which we find in the terminology of genetic criticism's *avant-texte*. To study a draft is to overturn this chronological relationship and consider the literary artifact on its own terms, and in particular, its capacity for movement—and yet, undeniably, it moves—and thus its capacity for change. In *Logiques du brouillon*, Daniel Ferrer also highlights the *avant-texte* as a place of continuous creation: "pour le généticien il s'agit . . . de remettre l'œuvre *en mouvement*—ou peut-être de révéler *le mouvement* qui l'habite toujours secrètement" (emphasis mine; "for the genetic critic it is a question of putting the work back *in motion*—or perhaps to reveal the *motion* that always secretly inhabits it").[8] Ferrer sees textual creation as a "dynamic" and "projective" process; by exposing this process, the genetic critic can participate in it.[9] The *avant-texte* in flux contains all the possibilities and potentialities of a text in progress, making the reader constantly aware of what could have been otherwise. In contrast to the term *avant-texte*, the terms "drafts" and "brouillon" highlight the unfinishedness and unfixedness, the draftiness of materials that makes them lighter, easily ruffled by a breeze, swept across a work surface.

We have seen Cixous's interest in the *avant* as a material state invested with the potential to endure and live on. In this chapter, I explore the consequences of movement and change for the literary artifact. The draft's dynamism amounts to a kind of potential energy, one not yet fully realized, still capable of being deployed. Material contingencies—what could have been and what could still be—can be understood in this way as a virtual projection of the work in progress. If the *avant-texte* is the site of "le halo de virtualités qui entoure la création" ("the halo of virtualities that surrounds creation"), then the work of the genetic critic is to demonstrate "le rôle du possible dans les processus d'écriture" ("the role of the possible in writing processes"), to understand the writing process as a negotiation between all possible states of the text being written.[10] Crucially, this is not a matter of setting up the *avant-texte*'s virtuality against an actualized text, but a way of considering the draft material itself as powerful and projective. Much in the same way, the manuscript scholar Bernard Cerquiglini's concept of *variance* incorporates an understanding of the virtual as digital but also as potential, which does not place the virtual in opposition to the material but rather works with it. Cerquiglini emphasizes that this is the case both in medieval manuscripts and in born-digital materials stemming from recent technological developments.[11]

In chapter 3, we will see how the digital entails an understanding of virtuality rooted in the present moment, as is especially apparent in copies and doubling that Hélène Cixous and Jacques Derrida explore. Foregrounding this view of virtuality at play in both writers' archives, I explore in this chapter how virtuality contributes to writing and archived artifacts' potentiality. The artifact's dynamism, its capacity for change, impacts its survival.

If the dynamism of archival materials counters notions of inert matter, it also destabilizes a reliance on linear time and necessity. This chapter considers artifacts at the conjunction of matter and time: their material contingency has a temporal aspect. The artifacts conserved and consulted in the archive are not irrevocably linked to the finalized, published text, nor are they the faithful portrait of the author at the scene of creation. Each moment of consultation takes stock of the artifact in the present, juxtaposing discrete moments in the varied existence of the manuscript: a unique temporal constellation that points up intervals, interrupting a sense of continuous time. Yet this momentary temporal coincidence cannot quite override the gnawing archival feeling of belatedness. In the archive, the researcher and artifact stage a contretemps, an encounter that is out of step and rhythm.[12]

In a sense, the archival encounter could be understood as an *après-coup*, or as *destinerrance*, two terms that Derrida explores in relation to potentiality: a temporal lag calls into question the actualization of a signifying trauma (in the *après-coup*) and of arriving at a destination (*destinerrance*).[13] To describe the temporality of the archive, Derrida suggested the future perfect tense, *le futur antérieur*: what will have happened, what will have taken place. Derrida's *futur antérieur* is above all a way of understanding the institutional foundation of the archive: "Le concept d'archive n'est pas tourné vers le passé . . . La mémoire, c'est la question de l'avenir, et pour l'archive, c'est toujours le futur antérieur qui . . . décide de son sens, de son existence. C'est toujours dans cette temporalité-là que les archives se constituent" ("The archival concept is not turned towards the past . . . Memory is a question of the future, and the future perfect is what always determines the meaning, the existence of the archive. Archives are always established within this temporality").[14] The *futur antérieur* situates a projected event within a conditional future, looking back on it from the future moment. Rather than framing the archive as retrospective, this temporality emphasizes that the archive is always in a state of becoming: it is forward-looking and open to what is to come, without the expectation that it will ever coalesce into a stable, finalized state. The archive's inherent "incomplétude" maintains this condition, Derrida writes in *Mal d'archive*.[15]

While Derrida does not elaborate on the archival *futur antérieur* in *Mal d'archive*, his interest in this multiple temporality, which embeds an imagined past into a future, is reminiscent of the spectral temporality he describes in *Spectres of Marx*. The "future-to-come" is not only beyond the present moment, it also calls into question the very opposition between past, present, and future.[16] To be sure, the future perfect is not the same as the future-to-come. The future perfect contains the past within the future. But both are linked in Derrida's work by a disjointedness that dissociates the present moment from stability or identity, creating a spectral effect. In both cases, the "here-now" is always haunted: "A spectral asymmetry . . . de-synchronizes, it recalls us to anachrony," writes Derrida in *Spectres of Marx*.[17] This understanding of temporality and ontology—or hauntology, surpassing conventional forms of presence and being—allows for a projected, ongoing existence, or what Derrida calls *survie*. The archival state is similarly characterized by disjointedness, a haunting, a spectrality in which this multiple, shifting temporality unseats the present moment. The spectral effect prompts an interrogation of a presumed linear trajectory from draft to finished, published text. In the archive, the before and after are blurred by the mere survival—the living-on, in the Derridean sense of spectral haunting—of artifacts, remnants and revenants of the creative process.

Like Derrida's *futur antérieur* and the spectral effect of his "future-to-come," Carolyn Dinshaw's concept of "asynchrony" provides a way to understand archival temporality beyond teleological, linear progression. Specifically related to the experience of consulting texts and manuscripts, asynchrony describes the "dissonance" that occurs when we perceive "different time frames or different temporal systems colliding in a single moment of *now*" and gives the sense of a "complex and vascular" present moment.[18] Dinshaw's view of archival temporality is textured, suggesting a material awareness of time that I borrow in this chapter. The contingency of artifacts is rooted in a dynamic materiality that is experienced in the asynchrony of archival consultation.

This chapter builds on the advantageous instability of archival materials. My readings of volatile materials highlight the dynamic potential of archives. As we have seen, materials have a symbolic resonance in those of Cixous's books that feature the scene of writing, such as *Manhattan* (2002) and *Tours promises* (2004). Easily reused and rearranged, Post-it notes and loose-leaf papers reinforce the potentiality of the work in process in Cixous's archives. Ephemera found in Derrida's library at Princeton University are similarly unstable: scraps, notes, and letters interleaved in books were rerouted to the IMEC, and Cixous's correspondence there was amended to include some of these artifacts. Thinking about material contingency offers a perspective on the concept of *destinerrance* in Derrida's *La Carte postale*, a formally experimental text that evokes the materiality of textual objects, which I explore in relation to the archived dossier of *La Carte postale* and other significant artifacts at UC Irvine. As they shift between collections, these materials run the risk of losing their place or being lost. It is in this risk that I locate their particular force.

Cixous's Material Contingency

Cixous's published texts retain the dynamic fermentation of the work in process, whether by representing the physical act of writing and the material conditions that surround and enable it; by giving voice to the writer's hesitations as narrative tension; or by formal interventions into chapter structures that give the impression of a text coming into being. As we have already seen, the books written around the time her archives were set up at the Bibliothèque nationale de France represent Cixous's process in extensive material detail, such as the writer's interest in the endurance of certain materials such as pencil and paper in "Une chemise JAUNE" ("A yellow FOLDER") in *Manhattan* (2002), and in *Double Oubli de l'Orang-Outang* (2010). Other books develop an interest in material contingency through textual objects that are easily displaced and thus allow for repeated readings made constantly new. In *OR: Les Lettres de mon père* (1997), the narrator contemplates whether to open and read an archive-like box of letters written by her father to her mother, remarking on the "gisements de cartons encore animés" ("deposits of still animated boxes," my translation) as a prelude to the active materials contained inside.[19] *L'Amour même dans la boîte aux lettres* (2005) tracks the growth of an eclectic archive of emotionally charged letters and ephemera from a love affair. These books feature letters explicitly in order to foreground concerns about the letter's material and temporal contingency. Other textual objects represented in these books—ephemera, loose-leaf pages, notebooks, and Post-it notes—come under the same influence of chance and change. The manuscript dossiers of these texts reinforce an understanding of the principle of contingency so crucial to Cixous's writing process. Both texts and archived artifacts share in a project to keep writing and reading in a state of constant renewal, the writing process channeling what is animate, unfinished and unfixed.

The narrator of *L'Amour même* is collecting memories of a past relationship, using the term "feuilles" to refer to the sheets of loose-leaf paper on which she notes these memories. The "feuilles" distinguish themselves from the writer's notebooks in the chapter "Vie des cahiers":

> Quelle différence entre l'aspect des pages sauvages et celui des pages de cahier! Sur les grandes feuilles tout est disjonction, altercation, tout est grand de traits, les phrases sont brisées, inachevées, battues, les membres tranchés n'importe comment, beaucoup de ratures, parfois deux mots puis un mot sur une ligne . . . Les cahiers : tout le contraire. L'écriture est dense, petite, serrée, l'espace est occupé entièrement, c'est qu'on cherche à remplir la valise ou la boîte au maximum, si on l'emportait sous le coup d'une attaque ou d'un incendie, on entasse le temps, ce sont des coffres, des réserves.

> What a difference between the appearance of the wild pages and that of the notebook pages! On the large sheets everything is disjunction, altercation, everything has large features, there are large blanks between slender paragraphs, the sentences are broken, unfinished, beaten, the limbs are cut off any which way, many crossings-out, sometimes two words then one word on a line . . . The notebooks: completely the opposite. The writing is dense, small, crowded, the space is entirely occupied, it's because one is trying to fill up the suitcase or the box to the maximum, one might have to carry it out if there's an attack or a fire, time is piled up, they are trunks, stores.[20]

In the notebooks the writing is denser, more readable, with less room for correction. Writing has been packed into the notebook pages to fill them to capacity. It would seem in this comparison that the notebooks are more analogous to the archive, being described as "des coffres, des réserves" ("trunks, stores"). Yet these miniature archives have not been transferred to the BNF: to date, the *fonds* Cixous does not include her notebooks. Occasionally, a photocopied notebook page appears in a dossier of very preliminary preparatory notes. While the act of writing in a notebook is for the narrator an archival gesture—packing up, preserving as much as possible in a storage space, a *réserve*—this kind of writing is less representative of a work in its provisional state. Writing on loose-leaf paper, on the other hand, allows for more space, more intervals between phrases and lines—which is to say, the possibility for correction, change, and for the vicissitudes of the writing process. The continuity of writing in the notebooks contrasts with the fragmentation of writing on the sheets of loose-leaf, where it spreads out, unbounded and wild, because it is cut: "les cahiers c'est le fil, les feuilles sauvages: la coupure" ("the notebooks form the thread, the wild leaves: the cut").[21] The sentences themselves are truncated, broken, and beaten. Loose-leaf pages illustrate separation both in their distribution of writing and in their singularity, each detached from the other, creating an interval of space and time at the moment of writing. When read later on, the interval on the page remains, retaining the potentiality of writing. In her descriptions of notebooks and loose-leaf paper in *L'Amour même*, Cixous highlights the use of loose-leaf to increase the fluidity of the text in progress. Because of their material form, these *feuilles* can shuffle around and rearrange themselves, slipping out of order. It is not notebooks but loose-leaf pages (and their close cousins, the letters and ephemera that accumulate around them) that figure the archival state of writing-in-process, its unstable potential.

The sheets of loose-leaf paper, organized into sheaves in Cixous's manuscripts at the BNF, bear varying amounts of writing: sometimes no more than several lines, sometimes a few paragraphs dispersed over the page.[22]

The scarcity of corrections on these pages is striking: very few traces of erasure, very few strike-throughs. Of course, such pages could have been thrown away—another advantage of loose-leaf. The overall impression is that Cixous's writing takes place with little revision, so that the handwritten manuscript closely corresponds to the published text. But an attentiveness to the numbering of these pages reveals that it is in the sequencing that Cixous's books come together. Handwritten page numbers accumulate in the corners and the margins, crossed out and rewritten—multiple times, in some cases. On one page of the manuscript of *OR* (f° 55, sous-chemise 3), the following numbers read from left to right (the numbers in parentheses are circled on the manuscript page, and the grayscale represents differences in emphasis and writing implements):

(67) 61bisA (57bisA) 54bisA~~53bisA~~
= (55)

I reproduce the layered pagination here to show how many times this page shifted sequencing during the writing process: at least five times. "Bis" and "bis A"—which Cixous uses frequently, along with "bis B" and others—indicate that this page was inserted into a sequence. The intervals on the loose-leaf page and between pages allow for expansion during the writing process. In the archive, too, they remain unbound, maintaining this impression of dynamism and contingency, as if content could still be added, removed, or rearranged. Cixous maximizes the flexibility of her text in progress through simple technologies. Loose-leaf pages and other mobile writing supports, such as Post-it notes, subtly attest to the writing that remains in process up until the moment they are transcribed into a nearly final-state typescript—or longer. The passages of her texts are carefully ordered, but the archived manuscripts retain the volatility of the writing process.

Phenomenology of Post-its

Cixous's Post-it notes illustrate the contingencies of archived works in progress, capturing ideas at a preliminary stage of reflection. The notes alight on many of Cixous's manuscripts, often to evoke moments of inspiration or to flag work to be done on a certain passage. Just as for other contemporary writers who compose by longhand, the Post-it note is an ordinary material, but its presence in the archive is symbolically evocative, and requires specific archival preservation techniques. For these reasons, the notes are of interest to a study of a writer's materials in the archive. The physical presence of these small textual objects in Cixous's manuscripts evinces a writing process fueled by telegraphic inspiration, relying on materials that can be shifted and reordered as the text takes shape. The notes' small size, their striking colors, and their mobility stand out on handwritten pages of Cixous's preliminary notes and drafts. The sticky strip leaves the note's two bottom corners free—but how much can be seen underneath the note? How many times can the note be lifted and reapplied before the sticky strip wears out? Perhaps even more than loose-leaf pages, the Post-it note implicates the researcher and the archivist in the present potentiality of the work in progress. These notes' specific volatility is clear: as their adhesive wears off or dries up, the notes risk becoming detached, losing their specific location in the manuscript; and as a note's glue permeates the paper to which it is affixed, its chemicals might corrode it. Yet to fasten them permanently also obviates their specific use. Post-its pose a challenge to archival conservation, since it is still unclear how they will age over time. They represent an unknown quantity, conjuring up the ephemeral, fragile nature of the archive and the risks of conservation. Their physical makeup shows what is at stake in preserving the vitality of a writing process: the challenge of ensuring not only the physical conservation of the material but also the provisional, experimental spirit of a text's preliminary stages. In the text of *OR*, Cixous emphasizes the role of the interval and of separation in maintaining the continuing dynamism of writing; this archival principle is also at play in the artifacts that compose the writer's manuscript pages.

A manuscript page of *OR* demonstrates the dynamism of Post-it notes and loose-leaf paper and serves as an example of Cixous's use of Post-it notes more generally in her writing process. This folio (f°1 in Chemise 3, "Notes," from the manuscript of *OR: Les Lettres de mon père*), the first page of preparatory notes in an A5-sized notepad (sold as a "bloc de correspondence"), contains several groupings of text, several blank areas, and many abbreviations and dash marks showing the speed of a preliminary notation. Two pale yellow Post-it notes, bearing penciled handwriting, have been affixed to the page. The larger of the two Post-its almost completely covers the writing on the middle of the page, which remains partially legible through the limited transparency of the Post-it note. The note serves multiple purposes in this preliminary draft: with its sticky end affixed to the blank between the first two groupings of lines on the A5 page, it has the quality of an insertion; as it is placed over a block of writing, it also has the status of a correction. The notes' dual nature is best understood through their visual representation, which adds a graphic dimension to the page. Varying in size and placement with respect to the page's other material and handwritten components, and variously managing the page's blank space, the notes organize relationships between elements on the page, and with the reader.

The corresponding content on the Post-it notes and the A5 page (and, eventually, the published text) gives the impression of a dynamic process of writing in which words and phrases are repeatedly used in resonant experimentation, which is apparent above all in the artifact's makeup. In order to read the writing covered over by the larger Post-it, the viewer must plunge into the yellow rectangle to distinguish between layers of pen and pencil marks. Through this phenomenological act of reading, the manuscript page becomes a three-dimensional space. My eyes dart from one element of the page to the other, switching between directions and levels of reading to make connections between the semantic meaning and the disposition of the page. This kind of reading is just as tactile as it is visual. The sticky edges of the Post-it notes parallel the top and left margins of the page so that the free edges align with the direction of writing and reading, drawing the eye over and under from top to bottom and left to right. Simultaneously, the notes' corners that lift up from the page seem to invite further movement. The text beneath the large Post-it, barely legible through the yellow paper, increases the impression of continuous writing and reading, curtailed only by the red BNF stamp straddling the bottom edge of the note and the page beneath it, which seems to anticipate the temptation to lift the flap and peek underneath. In addition to identifying the page as part of a manuscript belonging to this institution, the red BNF stamp reinforces the Post-it's specific position on this page: here it was placed and will remain. On the margins of this Post-it note, the limits of preservation and the desire to maintain a sense of experimentation come into tension.

In its layout and its distinct materiality, this manuscript page orchestrates a temporality of writing, editing, and reading. The layout of the page redirects the gaze through the materiality of the page itself, and by the graphic markings on it, including writing and symbols such as stars, points, arrows, and numbers. What came first? What was the order of writing? What was the causal relationship between two parts, or two pages? The components of this archival arrangement provoke such questions about temporality and order, highlighting the role of contingency within processes of writing and researching. The interplay of the textual and material interfaces speaks to the dialogic nature of interaction between archivist, archived artifacts, researcher, archival institution, and writer, and to the divergent temporalities they inhabit. Consulting this document encourages a recognition of the ongoing potentiality on the manuscript page across varying times and places, provoking a sense of "dissonance" and "asynchrony"—feelings Carolyn Dinshaw attributes to communities of readers who converge across the ages around medieval manuscripts when they perceive "different time frames or different temporal systems colliding in a single moment of now," giving the sense of a "complex and vascular" present moment.[23] The resulting alternate temporality brings into focus what is contingent, touching together (from the Latin *con- tangere*), highlighting the many kinds of relationships that exist around, on, and with these objects.

On the manuscript page of *OR* under discussion (the first page of the notepad in Chemise 3, "Notes"), a project for dealing with the family photo archive tentatively unfolds. The first block of handwritten lines can be discerned under the larger Post-it note that covers them:

En fait ce qu'il faudrait faire: 1 tri des photos
20–30 photos
Il y en a beaucoup il surgit 30 à 40 photos qu'il
serait bon de séparer des autres
Certains st vraimt d'1 très gde beauté
Il faudra à côté de ces photocopies voir l'histoire de cette
photographie—

In fact: sorting the photos would be necessary
20–30 photos
There are a lot of them 30 to 40 stand out which
would be good to separate from the others
Certain photos rlly hv great beauty
Next to these photocopies you'd need to see the story of this
photograph—

Then, uncovered, after a break in the writing, three lines follow:

Ça me fait envie.— de sortir le + beau de ces albums
Pr ça faut pas tant de tps que ça—
Faut aussi—être capable de découper—[24]

It's tempting.— to take the most beautiful out of these albums
Don't need that much time to do that
Also need—to be able to cut out or up—

The photo albums are presented as material whose aesthetic and historical aura triggers nostalgic emotions as well as a new creative project that would require a significant reworking and reordering. If these materials were to be put to use, the first task would be to sort them ("un tri"): to separate out, to cut through the collection, and thereby to create an interval between the individual photos themselves, and between their current state and another existence. In the descriptions of notebooks and loose-leaf papers in *L'Amour même*, the interval makes space for change; here, on the manuscript page of notes, the interval marks a change in the status of the materials in question (the photos) as well as the materials that combine to create this archived artifact. The interval of processing, sorting, and separating discussed on the folio characterizes the archival mode.

On this manuscript page, and in the narrative of *OR: Les Lettres de mon père*, the spatial and temporal orchestration of reading and writing creates intervals which promote contingency and dynamism favorable to the writing project. The narrator of *OR* hesitates to consult her archive of family photos and letters, and this deferral gives the book a narrative tension. But it is not only a question of whether or not to read, and when. The book is also preoccupied with the issue of how best to store materials worthy of attention and care long after the original author and recipient—the narrator's father and mother—are gone. The narrator grapples with questions of inheritance, legacy, and appropriation as she weighs what to make of this newly discovered trove, and whether these artifacts will serve as material for a new written work. Separation is key: the narrator in *OR* is preoccupied with the creation and maintenance of intervals created by cutting and separating. "Il me garde séparée . . . À cheval sur l'intervalle," says the narrator of *OR*, of her father, his legacy, and the psychic acrobatics it requires ("He keeps me separate . . . Straddling the interval").[25] The interval that the narrator straddles facilitates the keeping of the family archive. This is reflected in the use of materials and the layout of the manuscript pages of *OR*, where separation is a creative, archival principle at work on the artifact. Similarly, the Post-it note enacts the separation described on the manuscript page. But on the artifact, the material subject to sorting and separating is the stuff of writing, not a trove of photos. The creative act of the writing process links the two, underscoring the aesthetic drive at work—"sortir le + beau," as the text claims. Of course, the archival impulse works both ways. Separation is a kind of destruction, inescapable in the archive.[26] One has to be capable of cutting, of carving out, in order to enact the creative transformation this project calls for.

The writing on the Post-it note itself, whose subject matter appears to veer away from the archival photo project, discusses the need to carry on in the face of tragedy, drawing inspiration from the force of character the narrator's mother musters in the wake of her husband's untimely death:

> *Maman était là elle lui a pris le pouls*
> *∝ [et] elle a senti que le pouls s'était arrêté*
> *Maman investit cent fois moins que moi*
> *C'est ce que tjs dis—*
> *Maman est 1 réaliste*
> *Ça n'a pas été 1 cataclysme—Elle a été peu*
> *sentimentale ac ns*
> *Ms elle n'est pas tombée ds le tombeau*
>
> *Mama was there she took his pulse*
> *& she felt that the pulse had stopped*
> *Mama is a hundred times less involved than I*
> *That what alwys say—*
> *Mama is a realist*
> *It was not a cataclysm—She was not very*
> *sentimental w us*
> *bt she didn't fall in the tomb*

Through the tentative project of sorting through photos, reworked by a Post-it note describing a postmortem emotional state, on a manuscript page of a work in progress, Cixous proposes that the violence of separation is a restorative, creative necessity. "Il faudrait faire: un tri"; "il / serait bon de séparer"; "Faut aussi—être capable de découper": the interval is at work in the handwriting that composes these very lines, with its halting staccato.

The manuscript emphasizes the archival principles that are significant to the project described in *OR*: dynamism and change through separation and the creation of intervals. The Post-it note intervenes in the archival project, covering or adding onto the aesthetic project with a "realistic" attitude towards death, which the narrator also inherits from her mother. These two passages—the one written on paper and the other on the added Post-it note—are intimately related through their arrangement on the manuscript page and the writing process, which involves separating, sorting, and editing, illustrated here in theory and in practice. The artifact joins archiving and writing, material care and lack of sentimentality, and the creative act of mourning. The creative process at work on the manuscript page plays out in dynamic materials that come together on this artifact.

Ephemera and Other Letters

If separation is the ordering principle at work in *OR*'s photo project, other archives are built by accumulation. In both cases, the material dictates the direction the archive takes. In *L'Amour même*, the narrator's attempt to save all letters from a love affair launches an obsessive metonymic economy by which everything related to her lover is worthy of preservation. In the chapter "Quand je deviens une gardeuse frénétique," envelopes of all sizes, as well as used Kleenex and gauze, become sacred objects: "Il m'a paru impossible de jeter cette trace" ("It seemed to me impossible to throw out this trace").[27] But it is their particular physical makeup—small, loose—that makes these objects difficult to manage. "Le rangement de traces est une autre affaire. . . . Le mélange de papier sacré et de papier non sacré en tous genres se fait naturellement" ("The storage of traces is something else. . . . The mixture of sacred and non-sacred paper of all kinds happens naturally").[28] The accumulation of material "traces" of various forms creates an eclectic archive formed without organizational principles. Yet this amalgam is not a homogeneous mass: as with the consultation of Le Carton and its contents in *Double Oubli* (discussed in chapter 1), described as "un ensemble nombreux—des centaines peut-être—de feuillets, de différentes consistances et épaisseurs" ("a large collection—hundreds, maybe—of sheets of paper, of varying consistencies and thicknesses"), each artifact retains its individuality.[29]

The contingent nature of this archive—its randomness and disorder—is further assured by the instability of these separated, singular objects:

"J'imagine qu'elles vivent par ensembles séparés. Certaines sont d'ailleurs glissées dans des cahiers, il y avait peut-être un dialogue entre ces feuillets, je n'ai jamais exercé d'autorité sur les mouvements de ces âmes" ("I imagine that they are living in separate groupings. Some of them moreover were slipped into notebooks, there was perhaps a dialogue between these little sheets, I never exercised authority over the movements of these souls").[30] As mobile materials that act independently from a human "authority" yet are in dialogue with each other, the sheets of paper form an eclectic ensemble, living separately together, an assemblage of communicating, contingent ephemera whose volatility confers vibrancy—or, put differently, an agentic force, or a "soul." These letters, envelopes, and scraps tend to get away from the narrator, to hide, to slip into notebooks, allowing them to be encountered and rediscovered again and again.

Because letters are written with an awareness of the contretemps between sending and receiving and highlight geographic and temporal distance, they parallel an emotional contretemps, a disjointedness, that plays out in *L'Amour même*. Each time the narrator rereads letters from her former lover—a total of three times in the chapter "Fidèlement pour toujours" ("Faithfully Forever")—she registers a sense of distance both from the letters' writing and from her previous readings. Not only has more time elapsed since the moment of writing, but other intervals of time can also be measured out from one reading to the next. As these intervals of temporal distance accumulate, the narrator's relationship to the letters and to this past relationship changes. In particular, the word "fidèlement" with which her lover has signed each letter triggers the pain of realizing that a letter is never completely faithful: it is possible to read the word divided into two words, as *fidèle* and *ment*, creating an interval out of which additional meaning arises ("faithfully" becomes "faithful" and "lie"). Yet the letter's betrayal, its inconstancy, is also the condition of its repeated return.[31] For Cixous, the separation that letters carve out in time and space seems limitless, but it affords continuous possibility for renewed writing and reading, for the letter to arrive repeatedly. The intervals of separation materially and temporally orchestrate this halting existence. As we will see in chapter 5 with the rediscovery of a Post-it note in *Hyperrêve* and a manuscript in *Insister*—similar to the "revenance" of the first drafts of *Le Prénom de Dieu*—the surprise encounter with these artifacts is so powerful that it can transport the reader into an alternate reality in which it is possible to communicate with the dead.

But how is this force at work in the archive? And how can it be preserved?

An Eclectic Archive

In her published texts, as in her archive at the BNF, Cixous favors materials that are easily moved around, stored between and in books and other textual objects. Derrida used his own personal library in a similar way, stashing files, papers, letters, photos, and ephemera in and between books on the shelves. This organized index indicates "an alternate use of the Library as an ad-hoc topical filing system," according to Princeton's finding aid, which suggests that Derrida used his library as a highly personalized archive—"ad hoc" would indicate the particular use Derrida made of his shelves. His method conjures up a network of correspondences and meanings that were specific to Derrida's working process. This network was, furthermore, contingent on the specific spatial organization of Derrida's "sublime"—his attic—and the overflow into other spaces of his home in Ris Orangis. Derrida's library highlights the contingency at stake in archives that deal with ephemera. While the presence of ephemera is not uncommon in literary archives, Cixous's and Derrida's treatment of such materials draws attention to their use as correspondence between writers and within collections, and to the archival methods of conserving them. Materially eclectic artifacts illustrate the dynamism of archival arrangements and inspire new methods of consulting them in view of literary criticism.

When Derrida's library was acquired by Princeton, archivists sought to preserve it as an archive, giving attention to the original order of the materials and their groupings. Most books retain their original contents, including papers, bookmarks, and Post-it notes. The thousand-page finding aid lists books in Derrida's original shelving order, creating a catalog of physical space vastly changed since the books departed the house, yet it enables the researcher to engage in "the virtual reconstruction of the contextual placement of works on his Studio shelves." But certain archival principles necessarily destabilized this order, superseding the original order as a priority. Archivists recognized the need to separate materials that contained handwritten annotations and ephemera for safer storage. As Derrida's books were being processed for transfer to Princeton University's Special Collections in 2014, some papers, letters, and ephemera were removed from between the pages. When possible, materials written by others—especially handwritten ones—were sent to other collections.[32] The changes these materials underwent during archival processing destabilized the special meaning conferred by Derrida's bookmarking. The significance of this indexing system is accounted for through cataloging and encoding in the finding aid, but the archival configurations of the books and their contents create new possibilities for material conversation based on the artifacts' contingency—literally, the physical proximity of materials touching each other. The documents thereby acquire new meaning. Derrida's collections highlight the potential for renewed vitality of the archives through the volatile materials that circulate within and between them.

The decisions made in processing Derrida's library have created links across institutions, including Princeton, the IMEC, and the BNF. In particular, several "versements" or deposits to the Derrida collection at the IMEC occurred during the processing of the library. Artifacts began to appear at the IMEC in 2013 and 2014, including new items in the folder of correspondence from Hélène Cixous to Jacques Derrida.[33] At least four textual objects had been extracted from the pages of Cixous's books and sent back to France. Their treatment in archival processing and their presence among other more traditional "correspondence" gives them an aura of rarity and mystique, despite being composed with conventional materials: two notes written on very small pieces of paper which have been crumpled, smoothed, and folded several times; a note written on a pink Post-it stuck to a photo of Cixous; and a note faxed to Derrida, dated (1991-07-17). Each artifact is stored individually in a folded sheet of paper on which an archivist has written the title of the book in which Derrida had stashed it (*Entre l'écriture*, in two cases). Each has been unfolded, their creases askew across the small width and length of paper.

The IMEC's treatment of Cixous's notes to Derrida creates an eclectic collection of materials that are unconventional for "correspondence": though addressed, in a certain fashion, to Derrida, they have neither envelope nor stamp. If these materials are not quite letters, neither are they manuscripts—they resist any cohesive, all-encompassing description, and it is difficult to know how to name them. Notes? Scraps? The Princeton finding aid calls them "courts messages amicaux" ("short friendly messages"); an archivist at the IMEC referred to them as "billets" ("notes" or "missives"). Beyond the fact that they were written, sent, or given to Derrida by Cixous, they share a material diversity and instability that facilitates movement within archives and between institutions. "Ephemera" could be an appropriate term, though an ironic designation, given the promises of fidelity and endurance these traveling artifacts carry.

Notes that Derrida had not stored in books have a different trajectory: they have remained in Derrida's library at Princeton under cover of other materials. One of three folders labeled "Documents: Hélène Cixous" contains a thick, uneven pile of newspaper clippings, invitations, theater playbills and tickets, and a cassette tape recording of a radio appearance. Opening up the folded program for a lecture and reading Cixous gave at the University of Alicante in 1999, I find a small note, no larger than two square inches. Its sturdy off-white paper has been folded in half; two corners stuck together form a tiny pocket. The exterior of this makeshift envelope is covered in Cixous's handwriting conveying a concentrated burst of *vœux*—well-wishes—"bénédictions et joies," in the note's own language.

Bénédictions et joies
encore toujours
jeune fort
∝
jusqu'au
centième an

Bon pour J

____ *[fold]*

heureux

HJ *[Cixous's signature]*

Benedictions and joys / still always / young strong / until the / hundredth year / happy

[vertical text] Voucher good for J

"Bénédictions" are not only what the note conveys; it is also the word that best describes what this object is: a good saying, a good word, a good note (insofar as "mot" can mean both word and note—"un court message," according to *Le Petit Robert*'s definition of "mot," reaffirming the Princeton finding aid's term). The note is also, by its own estimation, a "bon," a voucher, a promise for future goods to be redeemed. Demonstrating the art of the *bon mot*, Cixous deploys the force of writing that confers the benefits of the words literalized by "injonction télégraphique," a kind of wish come true in the performative presence of this artifact's creation and continual activation, which Derrida analyzes in Cixous's writing.[34] Transmitting more than simply the *vœux* of good thoughts, words, or wishes (on a birthday or anniversary?), this tiny packet of "bénédictions et joies" maintains the integrity of its message: the placement of words and symbols on the page suggests a multidirectional reading. If its recipient is wished to be "young," "strong," and "happy" "until the hundredth year," the *bon* itself also promises to retain its own youthful, joyous vigor well into the future. Then, too, as an archival find the note is a "joy" to discover unexpectedly in the library, skirting the intended recipient to display its integrity to the researcher.

The note of "bénédictions et joies" left behind in the folder of Cixous documents in the Derrida Library at Princeton is folded to create an improvised pocket. Carefully slipping my fingers between the two sides, I extract two pressed leaves, joined together at the stem. This pocket and its contents could be read as representations of the archival modality of enclosing, protecting, covering. Indeed, the folding and enfolding of Cixous's notes in Derrida's archival collections—within books, leaflets, paper, *chemises*, archival folders, and boxes—illuminates processes of conserving these and other kinds of artifacts. But in the case of Cixous's notes to Derrida, it is not so easy to separate the container from what it contains when faced with the artifacts themselves. The leaves can be read not only as fragile, precious content stored within this folded note, but for their own exploration of material endurance and contingency. The elongated central lobe, flanked by two smaller lobes, suggests that the leaves' provenance is an ivy plant (*une lierre*), a vine (*une liane*). Reading the leaves in this provisional interpretation, we could then draw from the plant's cultural symbolism, and from the etymological and homophonic resonance of its name. A symbol of fidelity and eternal life, the ivy vine keeps its color year round—these two dried leaves are surprisingly green. The leaves' vibrant preservation extends metonymically to the materials that surround it, by the literal contingency of one leaf rubbing up against another. "Jeune, fort, heureux . . . jusqu'au centième an," the note says, as if its well-wishes could extend further to other materials that surround it in the folder of "Documents: Hélène Cixous"—the newspaper clippings, the program for the Alicante event, the cassette tape. The leaves touch each other and the papers that surround them, a closeness that illuminates the fact that paper and ink have historically been made from plants, which replaced rags in the nineteenth century.[35] Yet if the leaves convey vitality, it is not because of their origin as plant matter but because of their attachment to other textual objects. The note's promise is the continuous renewal of its "bon pour," its voucher never cashed in. Beyond its intended recipient, the note can keep its word if it links to a wider network. Tapping into *hedera*, ivy's botanical name from the Latin *haerere*, "to be attached,"[36] these two leaves could be understood as a means of communication, an attachment, a telepathic telephone between archives (a concept discussed further in chapter 5), formed through both textual content and material form. The note's well-wishes and promises of vitality resonate in the material contingency of this archival assemblage.

This attachment extends virtually across institutions. The "bénédiction" note at Princeton links up with two counterparts in the dossier of Cixous's correspondence at the IMEC's *fonds* Derrida, described as "short friendly messages." One note echoes the language of the "bon magique" and "bénédiction toute puissante." On the second note, Cixous has written thirteen lines of praise for Derrida in tight script. The economy of writing correlates with the force invested in each word, symbol, or letter, or what Derrida called, quoting from Cixous's book *OR*, telegraphic: "Le télégraphique, c'est ce qui va le plus vite possible, dans le transport de mots brefs, réduits à l'infime de la longueur et du poids, le vol ailé de vocables courts, furtifs, agiles et légers" ("The telegraphic is what goes as fast as possible, in the transport of short words, reduced to the minutest length and weight, the winged flight of short, furtive, agile, and light terms").[37] The telegraphic appears here as a mode of connection and exchange in which links are made instantaneously, distilled in the shortest of words. In his analysis of Cixous's published texts, Derrida focuses on the linguistic, but the telegraphic can extend to the materiality of writing more broadly: these archived notes are "short, furtive, agile, and light" and take "winged flight" as they connect the two archival institutions. Beyond the "vocables" written on them, the notes could be understood as telegrams (fitting in the category of correspondence), if the *gramme* can also account for nonlinguistic material traces. This goes to the heart of the question about material vitality: who or what can make traces, can write, can *be*?

The attention to the significance of material and form intensifies when these notes are in close proximity to other non-textual matter: flowers, feathers, and leaves that push at the limits of literary artifacts. At the IMEC, three small, thistle-like flowers are enclosed in an envelope labeled "Cueillies dans le jardin de Heidegger" in Cixous's distinctive handwriting, and two stark white feathers are perfectly preserved, with no textual accompaniment, in a transparent plastic sheath.[38] In conversation with these items, the ivy leaves and the note that contains them are activated, as their material form stands out from the conventionally sized paper and envelopes that dominate the collection. They give an expansive meaning to the notion of a literary artifact, lending their extratextual yet evocative forms to the materiality of writing. The challenges they pose to interpretation invite a reading that straddles the supposed distinction between the physical surface and the handwritten marks made on it, allowing for a broader understanding of what is on or in an artifact.

Although these artifacts are made of familiar, everyday materials, they do not appear ordinary in the archive: their distinctiveness and the charge of their evident use even make them seem, for a glimmer of a second, capable of transforming into something else. Paper becomes fabric; leaves and flowers, dried and flattened, come to resemble the *feuilles* that contain them, which in turn are highlighted as plant matter. Folded in half again and again, the small size of paper condenses down into a coin-sized packet. The creases are easy and deep, and the paper is slightly crumpled and resmoothed, as if it had been used, touched, opened and closed. Repeated handling has softened the paper to the touch, like a delicate fabric, again recalling the material history of papers once made from rags. These materials might become "fichus," doomed to disintegrate into ragged scraps worn down by repeated folds and the touch of many hands, highlighting the material contingency of ephemera.[39]

The artifacts' volatility is based in their material, emblematized in cases where it resists being fixed into a simplistic, identifiable package of information or aesthetic content. Changeable and fragile, the manuscript object is always becoming something else, reworking and reconfiguring its material composition. Along with other kinds of artifacts, not readily identifiable, it conveys unexpected glimpses, not only of what could have been, but also of what could still be: its potentiality registers here as animated because changeable. Wherever they are found, these artifacts give the impression of seeming out of place: neither quite at home with Cixous's correspondence in the IMEC, nor readily understood in between playbills and cassette tapes. Jolted out of Derrida's filing system, these notes, scraps, feathers, and leaves are caught up anew in their movement, wandering in *destinerrance*.

Derrida's *Destinerrance*

Change, which is crucial to the survival of literary artifacts, impacts the preservation of their creative potential. Derrida's term *destinerrance* describes the movement of materials that would allow for change. Introduced in *La Carte postale* along with the term *adestination*, and further developed in Malabou and Derrida's cowritten *La Contre-Allée*, Derrida's treatment of *destinerrance* is rooted in materialism and its inherent contingency, and is closely related to Lucretius's materialist conception of the *clinamen* of atoms colliding in their fall through space.[40] The analysis of archival materials in this chapter aims to enrich the idea of *destinerrance*, bringing a focus to the role of contingency, both material and temporal, in the dynamism of literary artifacts. Deferring a concern for the reception or arrival of the "letter"—and archived artifacts more broadly understood—to the second half of this book, I focus in this chapter on materials still in transit, at risk of becoming lost, damaged, or destroyed. The letter is most keenly subject to *destinerrance* when it is *en souffrance*, at risk of not arriving in the interval between sending and receiving. The interval points up the material contingency inherent to letters, as well as many other kinds of literary artifacts, especially free-floating ephemera. The texts that make up Derrida's *La Carte postale* illustrate this, through the formal experimentation of accumulated fictional letters in "Envois," followed by a theoretical dialogue surrounding Edgar Allan Poe's story "The Purloined Letter."[41] In these texts, and in the archived dossier for this book at UC Irvine, we can see the importance of chance and contingency in Derrida's conception of the archive.[42]

In "Le Facteur de la vérité," the penultimate text in *La Carte postale*, Derrida calls attention to the contingency of the letter's arrival by challenging Lacan's reading of "The Purloined Letter." In contrast to Lacan, Derrida is interested not in the arrival of the letter but in what happens before this event. According to Derrida, in the time between sending and receiving, the letter can be further fragmented and therefore cannot be assured to arrive intact at its destination: "[une lettre] peut se morceler sans retour et c'est ce de quoi le système du symbolique, de la castration, du signifiant, de la vérité, du contrat, etc., tente toujours de la garder . . . Et sans cette menace . . . le circuit de la lettre n'aurait même pas commencé. Mais avec cette menace, il peut toujours ne pas finir" ("[a letter] can always be fragmented without return, and the system of the symbolic, of castration, of the signifier, of the truth, of the contract, etc., always attempts to protect the letter from this fragmentation . . . And without this threat . . . the circuit of the letter would not even have begun. But with this threat, the circuit can always not finish").[43] To account for the risk that the letter endures in the interval between sending and reception, Derrida amends Lacan's statement: "Non que la lettre n'arrive jamais à destination, mais il appartient à sa structure de pouvoir, toujours, ne pas y arriver" ("Not that the letter never arrives at its destination, but it always belongs to the structure of the letter to be capable, always, of not arriving").[44] The uncertainty of the letter's arrival gives rise to the insistent, excessive deployment of this motif—"une lettre peut toujours ne pas arriver à destination" ("a letter can always not arrive at its destination")—in the accretion of texts that make up the volume *La Carte postale*: three essays, a long text composed of a fragmented epistolary correspondence, and a preface. It is as if Derrida's letter to Lacan, itself an unsolicited response, never received delivery confirmation. Stuck in the interval, *en souffrance*, the possibility of never arriving at any destination translates into an interminable textual output that never ceases to illustrate, display, explain, and attempt to prove its point, elaborating the original argument without ever uncomplicating it. About the letter Derrida always has something more to say.[45] *Destinerrance* is in this way an integral aspect of the archive, as Derrida conceives of it: deferring the possibility of arrival creates an interval of space and time where materials, letters, and texts can accumulate. Because it is fundamentally unstable, the archive is perpetually at risk, but its dynamism is also its advantage.

An Archive of Letters

Throughout *La Carte postale* (1980), Derrida calls into question the reliability of the letter: both its relationship to truth and delusion and its ability to withstand physical damage in transit. This interrogation is illustrated in "Envois," the first and longest section of *La Carte postale* and one of Derrida's most extensive experiments with form. The narrative thread of "Envois" spools out of a discovery of a postcard bearing an image of Socrates and Plato, taken from a medieval manuscript in the Bodleian Library. Seemingly incongruously, this discovery stimulates a series of dense, repetitive, enigmatic love letters and a melodrama of excess and *souffrance*, in both senses of suffering and waiting. Echoing the framework of an epistolary novel, "Envois" represents an archive of correspondence that accumulates as more letters are written.[46] The growth of this "archive terrifiante" ("terrifying archive") is exponential, outpacing the letters themselves:[47]

> Dès lors que, à la seconde, le premier trait d'une lettre se divise et doit bien supposer la partition pour s'identifier, il n'y a plus que des cartes postales, des morceaux anonymes et sans domicile fixe, sans destinataire attitré, lettres ouvertes, mais comme des cryptes. Toute notre bibliothèque, toute notre encyclopédie, nos mots, nos images, nos figures, nos secrets, un immense château de cartes postales.
>
> As soon as, in a second, the first stroke of a letter divides itself, and must indeed support partition in order to identify itself, there are nothing but post cards, anonymous morsels without fixed domicile, without legitimate addressee, letters open, but like crypts. Our entire library, our entire encyclopedia, our words, our pictures, our figures, our secrets, all an immense house of post cards.[48]

This passage highlights the importance of division and separation in the archive, the creation of an interval that is both material and temporal (which we have also seen in Cixous's letter-heavy texts and manuscripts). Paradoxically, as the letters divide into postcards and fragments, they create progressively larger ensembles of books (libraries), knowledge (encyclopedia, secrets), and language (words, figures, images). The correspondence contaminates "toute notre mémoire, nos noms, les lettres, les photos, les petits objets, les clés, les fétiches, etc." ("our entire memory, our names, the letters, photos, small objects, keys, fetishes, etc.").[49]

From the beginning, the question of whether to keep the letters or destroy them is raised, with a particular interest in the form a potential destruction should take. Ultimately, the best solution, the narrator suggests, would be "un grand incendie holocaustique, un brûle-tout" ("a great holocaustic fire, a burn-everything").[50] Such a totalizing erasure would in fact be an ideal archival gesture: "Le néant sublime, tu sais qu'il garde tout," the letter-writer bemoans—or sighs with relief (185; "Sublime nothingness, you know that it preserves everything," 171).[51] A partial archive is finally agreed upon, as this would better preserve the secrets by virtue of its incompleteness: "La 'correspondance' sera mieux détruite si on fait semblant d'en sauver quelques fragments dérisoires, quelque clichés bons à mettre entre toutes les mains" ("The 'correspondence' will be destroyed better if we pretend to save several laughable fragments of it, several snapshots good enough to put into everyone's hands").[52] Yet the project of publishing these letters reveals more than a basic dualism between material, immanent presence and immaterial, transcendent absence. The preface tells us that these letters passed through fire, and "Envois" is made up of the legible remains of this "holocaust." But the text also preserves the illegibility marked by incineration, in a typographical neutralization that replaces each burn mark, each unique gap or defect, no matter how large or small, with the same sign, "un blanc de 52 signes":

> Quelle que soit leur longueur d'origine, les passages disparus sont signalés, au lieu même de leur incinération, par un blanc de 52 signes   et cette étendue de la surface détruite, *un contrat* veut qu'elle reste à jamais indéterminable. . . . Quant aux 52 signes, aux 52 espaces muets, il s'agit là d'un chiffre que j'avais voulu symbolique et secret—bref un cryptogramme savant, entendez très naïf, qui m'avait coûté de longs calculs.

> Whatever their original length, the passages that have disappeared are indicated, at the very place of their incineration, by a blank of 52 signs   and a contract insists that this stretch of destroyed surface remain forever indeterminable. . . . As for the 52 signs, the 52 mute spaces, in question is a cipher that I had wanted to be symbolic and secret—in a word a clever cryptogram, that is, a very naive one, that had cost me long calculations.[53]

The fifty-two spaces mark out an interval that materially recalls the vulnerability of the letters *en souffrance*, before publication: an unvarying blank space that offers a secret in place of what is destroyed, regardless of the length of the original content. Both destruction and secret are unknowable, linking the past (destruction) to the future (the secret) in a commemorative gesture. Though it neutralizes, the secret also memorializes the singularity of each mark of destruction, and the 52 signs do in fact encrypt the "passages disparus" through the overdetermined calculus, both "savant" and "naïf," by erasing both their content and their material specificity.

As an archival gesture, the blanks enact both preservation and destruction—one by means of the other. Fueling a tension between the desire to save and to destroy, *La Carte postale* prefigures the psychoanalytic "pulsion d'archive" (echoing and countering the Freudian death drive) which Derrida later describes in *Mal d'archive*. The materiality of the "letter"—highlighted by the trauma it has undergone, the fragility of its form—would draw attention away from the secret truth of the liaison, which cannot be represented. This is of course paradoxical, since one of the functions of the letters or postcards of "Envois" is to mimic the scandalous correspondence of a secret love affair whose tantalizing details offer the hope of figuring out the truth—perhaps even autobiographical—of the story, recalling the detective work that drives Poe's "The Purloined Letter." This is the trap into which the reader must not fall. So while the letter-writer claims that the materiality of the letter (and the holes that riddle the correspondence) are deployed in order to hide the secrets of intimacy, the project of "Envois" is in fact designed as an exploration of that material contingency under cover of an epistolary love affair.

The "bad" reading of *La Carte postale* would thus be the one that seeks out the autobiographical experience—a love affair—which might have inspired Derrida to write or publish these fragmented letters. Derrida's biographer Benoît Peeters admits to being lured into this trap in *Trois ans avec Derrida*, the logbook accompanying his biography of Derrida and detailing his experience of conducting archival research and extensive interviews. After following up on several suggestive comments made by an interviewee that the secret correspondence in "Envois" might allude to Derrida's relationship with Sylviane Agacinski, Peeters realizes he has reached a dead end: "Qui pouvait avoir écrit ces lettres? Après deux ans de recherches, je n'en ai pas la moindre idée" ("Who might have written these letters? After two years of research, I haven't the slightest idea").[54] In the ten days Peeters spent with the Derrida papers at UC Irvine, his time with the dossier of *La Carte postale* was limited to solving the mystery of the secret love affair, and he finds the biographical research he conducted at Irvine disappointing ("décevante") on the whole.[55] Certainly, the dossier of *La Carte postale* held at UC Irvine contains no correspondence laced with burn-marks. Peeters's experience of the archive illustrates the kind of reading and detective work that "Envois" discourages, with its emphasis on chance and contingency.

In fact, the autobiographical element that appears in the archives is not the red-herring love story—*une aventure*, a liaison or love affair—but instead Derrida's interest in the materiality of manuscripts: specifically, a medieval manuscript in the Bodleian Library. The adventure of a contingent, chance encounter with a manuscript, tracked down through correspondence, is highlighted in the archival processing of Derrida's own manuscript at UC Irvine. Some of the documents in *La Carte postale*'s dossier are typical for Derrida's writing practice, such as a late-stage typescript of "Envois," amended to include supplemental letters and instructions for the *mise-en-page* of the book, including the formatting of the blanks interspersed in the text (Box 27, Folder 5). The extensive preparatory materials included in the dossier are more uncommon: correspondence, articles, notes, images, and mock-ups of the book's cover, as well as the Socrates-Plato postcard featured in the text ("Notes," box 27, folder 3). Eighty-four notes, diverse in size and color, mostly handwritten, have been gathered into archival envelopes (f° 21–47) or written in a 2 × 3" notepad, the cover graced with a kitschy illustration of a child with galoshes and umbrella amid splashy raindrops (f° 52–81). The notes consist mostly of fragmented phrases, few of which relate explicitly to "Envois." The exceptions can be found in a series of preliminary notes (f° 15–20 in Box 27, Folder 3) that include the phrase "Tout aura commencé par la reproduction," which appears several times, as well as the repeated phrases "la catastrophe," "tout à coup, je suis tombé en arrêt," "une hallucination," "une transformation," "Spectacle renversant," "en un seul coup par le spectral d'une catastrophe," and "immédiateté." These phrases, explored in Derrida's preparatory notes, can be located in the published text of *La Carte postale*.[56] Yet this method of tracing the development of the text from its final state back to an *avant-texte* yields little by way of critical interpretation of Derrida's writing process and his interest in chance and material contingency. Ironically, this is one of the most extensive dossiers of preliminary notes in any of the Derrida collections. Yet although it seems to have been preserved *as* the manuscript of "Envois," and despite the handful of incipient phrases, quoted above, that carry through to the final version, these preparatory notes do not represent a preliminary version of the text: instead, they demonstrate the principles of contingency that the "Envois" letters illustrate most adamantly. Unbound ephemeral materials, gathered together in folders and envelopes, without consistent contextual connections to the final text: these artifacts give the impression of the provisional state of a work in progress.

Within this dossier of preparatory materials, a folder of "Correspondence" (Box 27, Folder 1) offers another indication that these documents have been processed to illustrate and echo the archival significance of the text. The "Correspondence" includes research Derrida conducted from afar and by proxy to investigate the manuscript containing the image of Socrates and Plato that arrests the narrator and launches the whole project of letter-writing in *La Carte postale*. Several letters confirm the existence of this illustration in the Ashmole Manuscript 304 at the Bodleian and describe it in detail. It appears from this correspondence that Derrida was also interested in adjacent illustrations in the same manuscript, including most significantly a fortune-telling table titled "In prenostica Socratis basilei . . . scribuntur."[57] A photocopy and a hand-made tracing of this table, made directly from the manuscript, appear in a separate folder (Box 27, Folder 4): Derrida clearly studied the illustration, though it is not explicitly mentioned in the published text of *La Carte postale*. The coincidental, even fortuitous conjunction of the Socrates/Plato image and the fortune-telling game is a crucial representation of the principles of chance and contingency at work in *La Carte postale*. Indeed, manuscripts from the medieval period, of which Ashmole 304 is a specimen, are characterized by the circumstantial combinations of texts brought together by the commissioning patron or the head of the manuscript workshop, resulting in different configurations from one manuscript to the next: the proximity of the fortune-telling wheel to the image of Socrates and Plato is unique to Ashmole 304. The chance encounter of these two images is a feature not only of the narrator's or Derrida's discovery of them, but also of the material composition of that specific manuscript and its contingent preservation throughout the centuries.

Chance, *le hasard*, and contingency underwrite "Envois" from the beginning of Derrida's work on this text. But if the contents of the *Carte postale* dossier show that, from the beginning of the project, Derrida was interested in the materiality and contingency of manuscripts, it is not through a direct correlation between *avant-texte* and published text. The preliminary notes and eclectic correspondence, which seem to have been gathered together to create an illustrative genetic dossier of *La Carte postale*, have the illusory quality of a staged demonstration. They recall the ruse of evidence hidden in plain sight, borrowed from Poe's "Purloined Letter" discussed by Lacan, then Derrida, in these texts, as well as Derrida's comment in "Envois": "La 'correspondance' sera mieux détruite si on fait semblant d'en sauver quelques fragments dérisoires, quelque clichés bons à mettre entre toutes les mains" ("The 'correspondence' will be destroyed better if we pretend to save several laughable fragments of it, several snapshots good enough to put into everyone's hands").[58] *La Carte postale*, and "Envois" in particular, encourages the reader to look beyond the most obvious textual content to something else—not to the depths of the text, where one might expect a secret to be revealed, but to the material form of the text, which would provoke the experience of chance, discovery, and dizzying *destinerrance*: the adventure of *La Carte postale*. In parallel, "Envois" encourages the researcher in the archive to abandon any expectations of finding an identifiable manuscript for the text, and to query instead the other materials that surround a text's creation. These do not constitute a substitute manuscript, a stand-in for what is not there, but can be read as independently significant materials, illuminated artifacts that shed light on the workings of *La Carte postale*.

Chance and Randomness in Derrida's Notecards

Despite the prevalence of late-stage typescripts in his collection, which give a sense of fixity and stability that pencil, paper, and Post-its do not, material contingency and chance are an important part of Derrida's writing process. This comes to the fore in a dossier called "Notecards," whose moveable nature demonstrates the importance of change and dynamism within a literary archive. The notecards' material contingency is highlighted in Derrida's use of them, as well as in their archival processing. Early on in the UC Irvine finding aid, Thomas Dutoit and Eddie Yeghiayan discuss Derrida's general use of notecards as additions to the main text of manuscripts, based on a system of graphic insertion. The finding aid thus guides the researcher: "Note that several of the manuscripts have cards inserted with quotations or other text to be added to the manuscript. Derrida marked several of these cards with a symbol, and he also marked the manuscript with the same symbol to indicate where the text on the card belongs in the manuscript."[59] The marks must be visually similar enough to link the two documents together, indicating how they can be pieced together. Yet the card itself remains free-floating, loose, capable of slipping out, or shifting around in the folder. The symbols gesture towards order, but the actual distance between card and manuscript page must be acknowledged, and then breached, by the act of reading, which may temporarily bring the notecard's text to its destination. The unfixed insertions of the notecards are akin to Cixous's Post-it notes and show that Derrida's writing process also allows for change both at the time of writing and later, in the archive.

This use of index cards may seem prosaic, but their treatment in the archival collection encourages further reflection on their use in the writing process and their function in archival practices of processing and consultation. In addition to the note about notecards in the UC Irvine Derrida collection's finding aid, "Notecards" constitutes a separate entry in the category of "Publication and conference activities," as if it were the title of a published text, appearing alphabetically between the entries "Nombre de oui" and "Notes on Marx." This grouping gathers together over 700 palm-sized index cards or *cartes Bristol* into their own separate category. Although the authors of the finding aid write that it is "impossible to tell which cards go with which material" and they "cannot be identified as belonging to any particular manuscript," many of the cards bear notes explicitly related to texts such as "Fors," "Survivre," "Cartouches," "La Loi du genre," and "Signéponge," when the handwriting is legible.[60] The collection was processed by scholars of Derrida's work who preferred, we can assume, to keep the notecards together despite the fact that they were well placed to collate the notecards with corresponding texts.[61] Even though the notecards *could be identified*, the archivists decided to keep them all together in one stack.

The scholars dealing with these materials in the first round of processing took the idea of original order to its fullest expression—not only by placing all of the notecards together, but in their treatment of individual cards. Each card bears a bracketed number in an archivist's pencil in the bottom right-hand corner, added during processing. While archivists now favor a "series-level processing" that allows them to work more efficiently and quickly through an ever-increasing amount of material, in order to make it more readily accessible to the public, we see in the case of Derrida's notecards an "item-level processing" whose attention to detail invites a certain amount of fetishization of the material on the part of the researcher.[62] This commitment to original order—even preserving the original orientation of wayward upside-down or overturned notecards in the stack—indicates a hypersensitivity to Derrida's particular writing process, highlighting the materiality of these cards. This processing seems to maintain the impression of the chaos of preliminary, provisional writing, yet paradoxically the detailed numbering of each card removes a certain amount of mobility as it fixes the notecards' order. A researcher consulting the notecards can register this chaos and informality, but cannot experience it materially, since the numbering system compels the researcher to respect the order and orientation of the cards.

And yet the notecards do communicate some amount of contingency in their archived state. Taken out of their intended context, without symbols to indicate where they belong, the content of certain cards resonates with their placement in the archive. One fortuitous notecard commands, "bien marquer que ceci est un fragment" (folder 3, card 93; "note well that this is a *fragment*"). The accidental self-referentiality of this notecard comes to the fore when read in the archive, recalling the importance of contingency in context and location. This fragment renews itself in each particular context of reading, in the rhythm of reading that each reader brings to the scene. Each notecard, on which perhaps five words are scrawled, appears as a cliché, a fragment, separated from what precedes and follows it. Flipping through these notecards, a rhythm of reading emerges, particular to the researcher. The slight variations in the cards—the size and legibility of handwriting, the different inks and pencil leads, the color, weight, and texture of the paper, the edges worn or sharply new—produce a sensorial variety that enlivens the experience of consulting. It is a daunting task to flip through 700 notecards. I notice their material makeup as much as, if not more than, their handwritten content, which is at times indecipherable. The pause between cards may be short or long, but every interval constitutes a hiatus that separates out each card, making the experience similar to a slideshow or a moving picture.[63] Like the reader of *La Carte postale*, the researcher will find that "tous les accidents peuvent arriver dans l'intervalle qui sépare le sujet (qui dit je) et son attribut" ("all possible accidents can happen in the interval that separates the subject [who says I] and their attribute")—which is also to say, in the interval between writing and reading, or between the sending and receiving of a letter.[64] With increasing rapidity and shortened intervals, the pictures may coalesce into an intelligible whole, but the inherent structural fragmentation enables a syncopated temporality to develop, one that allows for contingency, disorder, or freedom of movement. In cases like this, efforts to create order in the archive, or to maintain the original order of manuscripts, actually enhance the experience of a temporality *en décalage*, the disjointed hiccup of time. Interactions with literary artifacts such as these notecards bring an awareness of contingency to the fore, emphasizing their capacity for transformation.

✦

Although the file "Lettres d'Hélène Cixous à Jacques Derrida" at the IMEC contains many letters from Cixous to Derrida, mostly concentrated in the late 1960s and 1970s, at the beginning of their friendship, the bulk of the correspondence between the two authors is stored at Cixous's apartment in Paris: Derrida returned her letters to her before his death so that the two sides of the correspondence would be joined. In the future, this correspondence will enter the *fonds* Cixous at the BNF, though it will not be immediately accessible.[65] Most of the letters Cixous and Derrida wrote to each other are therefore stored together, separate from the authors' official archival collections.

The absence of correspondence between Cixous and Derrida in their archives is an opportunity to rethink what is expected from letters in archival research, and to shift the framework of correspondence to focus on the material contingency of archived artifacts more broadly. Faced with their correspondence's intriguing absence, one possibility is to turn to materials that resemble letters, either materially or metaphorically, and explore the impact of certain ephemeral materials and their volatility on research methodologies and archival preservation. We have seen that other stray textual objects—ephemeral notes and short messages from Cixous to Derrida—are treated like letters at the IMEC, filed with Cixous's archived correspondence. These materials create a geographical and temporal rift that runs counter to the proximity their tone of intimate communication evokes. This tone may in fact be a ruse employed to keep the reader at a distance, or it may indicate an impossible desire for understanding, and yet the interval opened up between sending and receiving gives the chance for an event to occur. Yet with the possibility of experiencing a surprising event comes the possibility of risk, damage, or loss. This is what letters and other correspondence suggest about the materiality of ephemeral artifacts more broadly: their contingency allows for both the unexpected encounter and unfortunate destruction to take place. As we see in texts that foreground letters—Cixous's *OR: Les Lettres de mon père* and *L'Amour même dans la boîte aux lettres*, and Derrida's *La Carte postale*—the focus shifts *away* from letters themselves to other archivable materials and to questions of material and temporal contingency. Reading these texts together prompts a reconsideration of what belongs in the conventional category of correspondence in literary archives.

Consulting these archived materials does not magically transport the researcher back to the scene of writing, nor does it close the gap between institutions, archives, or two friends. But an awareness of the artifacts' role in creating and maintaining an interval of correspondence does draw out the creative potentiality that has been a part of the work from the beginning of (and perhaps even before) the process of writing and preserving, through a focus on the artifacts' capacity for movement and change. The archival contingency of materials also highlights the researcher's presence in the archive as part of a network of once and future readers. The interval of time between sending and receiving constitutes a reserve in which the "letter's" status is unknown: it is lost, missing, or absent from the archive, yet it can be accessed by others. The moment when it is received or read, whether for the first time or in subsequent readings, provokes surprise. This affective response momentarily closes the interval of waiting, postponed anticipation, or even wholesale forgetting. The withholding and unfolding of "letters" creates a temporality of punctured intervals, highlighting the risk and surprise of archival preservation and discovery. Research in the archive does not entail a moment of the work reaching its destination, but instead highlights the *destinerrance* that the work is still subject to. The relationship between reader and textual object shifts in this correspondence: the artifact is unstable, but its instability gives it dynamism and verve.

In this view of temporality, punctuating intervals allow for the arrival of a new event, for a chance encounter. While for Derrida the interval between sending and receiving is interminable, Cixous multiplies the intervals, and therefore the experiences of discovery and revelation. The long intervals between sending and receiving, between one reading and the next, are just as necessary as the feeling of surprise that interrupts them. As we will see in chapter 5, these surprise encounters offer the possibility of reestablishing lines of communication that have been suspended by death. Yet they are transformed in the interval: rather than acting as stand-ins for the absent friend, surprise encounters with literary artifacts serve as reminders of the limits of archival institutions. To counter this sense of limitation, Cixous and Derrida invent alternative forms of archiving that test the limits and potential of the accumulation of copies, doubling, and virtuality.

Chapter 3

✦

Create a Copy

Accumulations of Derrida's Facsimile Drafts and Cixous's "Book I Do Not Write"

Jacques Derrida's and Hélène Cixous's affective and actual archives return again and again to the matter of doubles: both to the material form that a copy or "double" of writing could take, and to the question of the simulacrum as a virtual artifact. In conversation with her friend in a waking dream, the narrator of Cixous's *Hyperrêve* notes that "il me rappelait d'en faire un double simultané à porter dans notre cœur" ("he was reminding me to make a simultaneous double to carry in our hearts").[1] This "double" takes the form of a scrawled note that channels the friends' surreal dialogue and is invested with the affective force of that encounter. In "Circonfession," Derrida emphasizes the doubling in the material workings of the floppy disks he uses, noting "la structure anamnésique, réitérable et vulnérable, des double-sided/double density, double poste, micro floppy-disks MF2-DD" ("the amnesiac, reiterable and vulnerable structure of the double-sided/double-density, double track, micro floppy disks MF2-DD").[2] In both cases, the material form acquires vulnerability and value through a process of doubling that seeks to reinforce the longevity of a miraculous encounter (for Cixous) and of the writing process (for Derrida).

Cixous's "double simultané" and Derrida's double/doubling floppy disks preoccupy them as they offer possibilities for archival innovation. They are two instances of what Derrida describes in *H. C. pour la vie* as the goal of writing: "dépasser ainsi l'espace et le temps, doubler l'espace et le temps" ("to overtake space and time, to pass or 'double' space and time").[3] In Derrida's view, Cixous accomplishes this goal through her facility for doubling, the French verb *doubler* indicating both to multiply and to overtake, as a vehicle passes another, as well as the cinematic technique of dubbing. Derrida explains Cixous's doubling writing in terms of a spectral substitution: "cela gagne en doublant, selon a loi du double, de la substitution de l'unique à l'unique qui vise en son spectre et en soi-même, se remplaçant lui-même à sa place, presque sans bouger" ("what gains *in* speed and *on* speed, time and space, gains in passing or 'doubling,' according to the law of the double, of the substitution of the unique for the unique, which aims for its own specter and for itself, replacing itself at its place, almost without moving").[4] By collapsing any distinction between original and copy across time and space with a "vitesse" that would "dépasser ainsi l'espace et le temps," writing can effectively create a copy that would eliminate the need for a copy. In this view, doubling would facilitate the preservation of materials and enable sharing across archives. But does the simultaneous double make for two different, twinned entities, or for a reinforced singularity? Can a copy be an exact duplicate of an original, overriding the interval of space and time that separates one from the other? Cixous's and Derrida's reflections on these questions provoke challenges for archival preservation, whether in the form of floppy disks or a memory stored in one's heart. Especially as their papers are transferred to and between archival institutions, the accumulation of copies, doubled and multiplied, creates a proliferation of virtual archives that work in tandem with their material counterparts to ensure the continuation of writing.

In this chapter, I trace the figure of the double or the copy through several texts and artifacts that demonstrate Cixous's and Derrida's interest in harnessing the potential of virtuality in archival contexts. The presence of literal photocopies in the Derrida collections at UC Irvine and the IMEC points to the limits of archival technologies, if we understand the photocopies as a stand-in for Derrida's hard drive, or to indicate its absence. Yet the relationship between photocopy and hard drive is not one of copy to original or actual to virtual; indeed, considering the two together destabilizes these binary oppositions. Furthermore, Derrida's photocopies and hard drive offer unexpected experiences in archival consultation when considered in their own right and not as faithful reproductions. After exploring the conjunction of virtual and material in these two kinds of artifacts in the Derrida archives, I will turn to two instances of doubling in Cixous where the relationship between material and virtual becomes even more imbricated, moving away from objects that can readily be called "artifacts." In the scene in *Hyperrêve* introduced above, Cixous explores the relationship between a waking dream and a note written on a scrap of paper as one of doubling that creates an affective portal between reality and another state of being, serving as a virtual archive of a precious moment. Similarly, a figure Cixous calls "Le Livre que je n'écris pas" ("The Book I Do Not Write"), developed around the time of her archive's creation, precludes the archive and outpaces it through its intimate connections to the material world of writing and everyday life. Even so, the shadow archive or virtual archive challenges what the archive can and should contain.

In Derrida's and Cixous's archival experiments, the double emerges as an evocative term, an alternative to the theoretically weighted terms "copy" and "simulacrum." These archival artifacts—photocopies, hard drives, dream notations, and virtual book—do not replicate or mimic an original artifact, concept, or event, and neither Cixous nor Derrida understands them as such. Instead, they are relational objects that carry their own power of signification and being. In this sense, they could be considered simulacra, as understood by Deleuze, in their productive relation to difference.[5] The simulacrum "interrupts the relation between original and copy," as well as between material and virtual.[6] In none of these artifacts can the material be separated from the virtual aspect. They indicate at once the fullness of the archive—sometimes overwhelming for the archival institution or for the researcher—as well as its absences or oversights. In doing so they suggest new venues for preservation and creation within the archive. As Derrida says in "Circonfession," his computer enables his writing to become "plus nue . . . grâce au simulacre" ("more naked . . . thanks to the simulacrum").[7] But how are we to understand his use of the term "simulacre" here? Tracing Derrida's "simulacre" in relation to virtuality and technology through his work in the 1990s, I show how his theoretical development of these terms is intimately related to his own experience with archival institutions.

Both Derrida and Cixous experiment with creating copies, with double or shadow archives, that attest to a desire to intensify, accumulate, stockpile, and create a reserve, but they do so in ways that challenge what material form that reserve might take. This has implications for overriding a material-virtual binary reinforced by institutional limitations of time, space, and archival convention. Thinking differently about the relationship between material and virtual might point to solutions to the institutional separation of archives that characterizes the Derrida and Cixous collections. The virtual artifact may have a different relationship to being and presence, yet it still can participate in the archive. It does so by pushing the limits of what conventionally falls outside the purview of archiving, and is particularly significant for overlapping collections such as those of Cixous and Derrida, which depend so much on virtual conversations, as we will see with dream-texts and seminar recordings in subsequent chapters.

Derrida's Photocopies

During a round table about the archives of the Collège international de philosophie at the IMEC in 1999, Derrida announced that plans for his own archive to be shared between the IMEC and UC Irvine were underway, nearly a decade after his first donation to Irvine's Special Collections.[8] At this public discussion, Derrida envisioned that his archives would be shared between the two institutions, and be accessible via new archival technologies for what he called "virtualization." These technologies would ideally transform the Collège—as well as his own archives—into an international, virtual, archival space: "Les recherches et les enseignements qui se produiront dans cet espace virtuel seront immédiatement des lieux d'archivation," Derrida explains

("The research and teaching that will be produced in this virtual space will immediately be places of archiving").[9] In linking his own archives to those of the Collège both through the archival institution that would house them and through the technologies that would permit their preservation and access, Derrida imagines the consequences of virtualization for his own papers. His writing would be opened up to institutional sharing, simultaneous access by international scholars, and the immediate archiving of his writing:

> Olivier Corpet [le directeur de l'IMEC] m'a proposé de partager les choses entre l'IMEC et Irvine, d'inventer un meilleur dispositif pour que justement l'archive soit à la fois ici et là, de faire en sorte que les mêmes documents puissent être simultanément et immédiatement accessibles ici et là, en Californie et à Paris. . . . le partage de l'archive devient possible, et celle-ci n'a plus un lieu unique.
>
> Olivier Corpet [the director of the IMEC] proposed that I share things between the IMEC and Irvine, to invent a better system so that in fact the archive is both here and there, to make it so that the same documents are simultaneously and immediately accessible here and there, in California and in Paris. . . . sharing the archive becomes possible, and it no longer has a single place.[10]

The "dispositif" (system) that Derrida evokes here would circumvent political borders and geographic distances to allow for a truly international community of thinkers and readers. It would multiply the "lieu unique" by at least two—here and there (repeated twice); California and Paris; IMEC and Irvine—and condense disparate temporal moments into the simultaneous and immediate. Limitless in its philosophical project and its international scope, the archive would become virtual in more than a technological sense: it would include the possibility of further developing itself, overriding the constraints of time and space that a traditional archival institution faces.

For his part, Olivier Corpet appears to have been enthusiastic and even optimistic about the project of developing a shared archival collection with UC Irvine. In a letter written to Derrida in 2000, a year after his remarks at the conference on the archives of the Collège international de philosophie, Corpet suggests that "on devrait sans trop de difficulté trouver une solution concrete, pratique," but his letter does in fact hint at difficulties: "Pour la question de vos archives et de l'intervention de l'IMEC . . . il est indispensable que nous nous revoyions très vite pour préciser un certain nombre de points pratiques, notamment en ce qui concerne les frontières et les modalities précises du partage avec Irvine" ("it should be possible to find a concrete, practical solution without too much difficulty"; "Regarding the question of your archives and the IMEC's intervention . . . it is essential that we see each other again very soon to clarify a few practical aspects, namely concerning the borders and specific modalities of sharing with Irvine").[11] On the copy of the letter he received, Derrida echoes Corpet's urgency, flagging this paragraph with blue ink and circling the IMEC's telephone numbers on the letterhead. Indeed, Corpet tells Derrida in the letter that the archival inventory was already underway, and several of Derrida's "boîtes d'archives" (archival boxes) were being processed by the archivist Christine Martin. Along with unspecified potential institutional loggerheads that would require the IMEC's "intervention," the problem Corpet and Derrida are trying to resolve is the geographic dislocation of two institutions, separated by legal and political borders (*frontières*): the *partage* (sharing) speaks both to this doubled location—split and shared—and to the possibility of a common, virtual space in which the archive could coexist.

In retrospect, the hope of realizing a shared archive "sans trop de difficulté" seems ill-fated. A virtual reading room in place at UC Irvine is a step toward realizing Derrida's call to "inventer un meilleur dispositif" ("invent a better system"), but we are far from "le partage de l'archive" (archive-sharing) between Irvine and the IMEC, and from what he imagined as a virtual, doubled archive. The legal struggles involving the two institutions following Derrida's death have left their marks on the two collections' finding aids:[12] although Derrida remained prolific until his death in 2004, Irvine dates the end of its collection to 2000, giving no account for the remaining years or the cutoff; and the IMEC's guide refers to a "supplemental collection," which it must do in order to explain the fact that most of its holdings are photocopies of the material housed at Irvine.[13] Notably, there is no equivalent collection of photocopied documents in the Derrida archives at Irvine; the university had tried to negotiate this toward the end of their three-year lawsuit against Derrida's estate to obtain additional materials, but this was abandoned when the lawsuit was dropped.

Photocopies are perhaps the "solution concrète, pratique" that Corpet alludes to in his letter to Derrida, though this does not seem to be what Derrida had in mind by a shared archive rooted in "virtualization," which would likely tap into digitalization and new media. Instead, the photocopies that constitute the bulk of the collection at the IMEC are an astonishing accumulation of perhaps the simplest technology of paper-based reproduction currently in use: xerography. The Derrida collection is full of photocopies of early, handwritten versions of certain texts and, more often, photocopies of annotated typescripts, and even photocopies of photocopies of these typescripts—sometimes in multiple sets with minor changes from one version to the next. It is nearly impossible to discern the difference between two versions, and especially between an original typescript printout and the photocopy of it. In these cases, the presence of the photocopy seems redundant, nearly absurd. What can these photocopies tell us, if anything, about the archive in general, and about Derrida's archives in particular? Is it possible to learn to read these typescripts "along the archival grain," in Ann

Laura Stoler's formulation, to consult them with attentiveness to the particular "pulse of the archive," with a sensitivity to "the archive's granular rather than seamless texture, to the rough surface that mottles its hue and shapes its form"?[14] Is there any grain on these smooth copies along which to read?

The history of xerography provides something to grasp onto, contributing to an understanding of these photocopies as an archival grain that textures reading, and suggesting that the facsimile is more than a simple stand-in. The "dry writing" of xerography (from the Greek *xeros* and *graphia*) distinguishes itself from processes like cyanotype that use liquid chemicals, and it works efficiently, without smell or liquid mess, to reproduce an image using a photoreceptor onto which the optical image of the document to be copied is scanned. This image is then transferred in the form of "cascading charged dry ink or toner consisting of polymer particles containing carbon black pigment" to plain paper, where the toner image is fixed with a solvent or with heat.[15] Like other technologies of reproduction, xerography's goal is to create a near-perfect copy, as suggested by the name of its predecessors, including the mimeograph and the spirit duplicator, produced by the Ditto Company—both invented in the later 1880s.[16] Unlike duplicating devices such as the printing press, lithograph, or even carbon paper, all of which use an intermediate step, copy machines make it possible to create a facsimile directly from a document at hand.[17] Photocopies do indeed act as facsimiles in their attempt—as the Latin *fac-simile* suggests—to make the same, or similar. The facsimile appears as a catachresis, a "secondary" original, a (more or less) failed replica—a simulacrum.[18]

In the Derrida collection at the IMEC, the presence of photocopies further highlights what is not there: the writer's hard drive, from which the typescripts were printed. Consulting the hard drive would make the photocopies unnecessary and would in fact reveal much more about the writing process, more efficiently. Furthermore, it would illuminate the existence of another archival collection (at UC Irvine) that has necessitated this "partage de l'archive" (archival division). But the photocopies' simulacrum also highlights what *is* there, making hyper-visible what would have otherwise gone unnoticed or been difficult to see: faint erasures, ragged edges or folds, traces of writing on the recto or the following page. The photocopy's unexpected granularity, along with an attention to the history of this medium, gives an enriched perspective on the presence of photocopies in the Derrida collection, and their relationship to notions of facsimile, simulacrum, and virtualization.

Understanding the photocopies as a hypothetical realization of the "solution concrète, pratique" that Corpet proposes would seemingly oppose them to the idealistic "partage de l'archive" that Derrida calls for—fueling the accusation that has at times been leveled against Derrida for being too abstract and too theoretical to fully grasp what archives are in actuality.[19] Yet Derrida's desire to "inventer un meilleur dispositif" ("invent a better system") does in fact involve the technological, the material: the "dispositif" he alludes to in his 1999 discussion at the IMEC recalls an apparatus, a device or a machine, and evokes the specter of the absent hard drive, the files that yielded the printouts that were then photocopied.[20] But when we consider both Derrida's comments on his own writing machine—hard drive, Macintosh, or *subjectile*, as he called it—and the possibilities of consulting new media afforded by innovations in digital humanities, including the "Derrida hexadécimal" project, it becomes necessary to rethink the relationship between Derrida's hard drive and his photocopied drafts.[21] Beyond the opposition of original and copy, of absence and presence, Derrida's use of technology, especially in relation to virtuality, prompts a renewed consideration of the relationship between what is material and immaterial.

An Archive "*sans limites*"

Derrida's remarks about a shared archive across two institutions evidence a link between virtuality and technology as he imagined the modalities of "le partage de l'archive" between UC Irvine and the IMEC. Beyond the specific remarks made during the "Questions d'archives" roundtable, Derrida's work on virtuality throughout the 1990s consistently invokes technology. *Spectres de Marx* (1993), *Mal d'archive: Une impression freudienne* (1995), and *L'Université sans condition* (given as a lecture in 1998, then published in 2001) explore techniques of doubling, multiplying, and accumulating in order to reflect on the relationship between the virtual and the material. The impact of this line of thought can be traced through certain artifacts in question—and perhaps in limbo—between the Derrida collections.

The subtitle of *Mal d'archive* should be taken quite literally: "impressions freudiennes" (Freudian impressions) refers not only to Derrida's reflection on, and demonstration of, the *pulsion d'archive* gleaned from Freud's work, but also to the physical impressions and marks left on Freud's body, doubled onto the corpus of the writer and its legacy. According to Derrida, Freud's circumcision, a form of corporeal inscription that binds the body to a community through ritual practice, finds a corollary in the paternal dedication inscribed into Freud's copy of the Talmud; both of these are linked to and inform Freud's figure of psychical inscription in the *Wunderblock*. *Mal d'archive* articulates the stakes of thinking between the material and virtual when it comes to technologies of archiving, and archiving technology, by bringing the body to the fore, and by conjugating the body with technologies of writing and archiving. The body itself is a technological apparatus.

Freud describes the operations of the psyche through his description of the *Wunderblock* in "A Note Upon the 'Mystic Writing-Pad.'" Using the metaphor of a technical device whose workings demonstrate the "mental apparatus," Freud suggests that there is an archival quality to the psychic process, in which "impressions" are imprinted on the mind, understood as an "ever-ready receptive surface." As Christopher Johnson has suggested, Derrida's reading of the *Wunderblock* in "Freud et la scène de l'écriture" reworks the binary between human and machine implicit in Freud's conception of the mind, and Johnson argues that a knowledge of cybernetics would have permitted Derrida to question the limits between "living and mechanical systems" and understand the trace itself as "working, productive" and imbued with "dynamism and autonomy."[22] Yet Catherine Malabou has demonstrated that cybernetics, with its reliance on concepts of system and program, is insufficient for a contemporary understanding of the way the brain works. Malabou argues that, following discoveries in neuroscience regarding synapses and the brain's plasticity—its capacity to "*form* and *reform* information"—the graphic metaphor is no longer relevant to our conception of mental activity, or of other biological components such as DNA.[23] Malabou's integration of the implications of neuroscientific research for the philosophical understanding of the mind, revising the model of impression and trace in thought, can be read alongside Derrida's reading of Freud when we consider that, in Derrida's reading, Freud's understanding of the "mental apparatus" involves more than a relationship between a surface and the accumulating traces that shape it. In particular, Derrida's reading of Freud has consequences for an integrated understanding of the relationship between mind and body, and between material and virtual, especially with respect to archiving. If *Mal d'archive* deserves to be considered a determining text for archive theory and archive studies, it is not because of its theory of archival abstraction, but because it demonstrates how the material and the virtual are deeply interconnected. This informs an understanding of the doubled archive we have seen in the Derrida collections at the IMEC and UC Irvine.

Derrida mobilizes questions of transmission and technology in *Mal d'archive* in order to elaborate a new understanding of virtuality. The virtual is first mentioned in *Mal d'archive* in relation to the imagined conversation that the historian Yosef Hayim Yerushalmi stages between Freud and himself—a conversation Derrida characterizes as "l'échange *virtuel*" ("the *virtual* exchange").[24] Derrida emphasizes the word "virtual" here to foreground what follows: an interrogation of whether such an exchange, or indeed any act, could be said to take place, if not *in actuality*. At this point, Derrida seems to consider *virtuel* in opposition to something that would actually exist; the archives that exist virtually exist *autrement*, or "otherwise" (this word is repeated three times over one page). But Freudian psychoanalysis is significant, for Derrida, in that it allows for the study of "une absence d'archive" ("an absence of archive"): it allows us to "tenir compte d'archives *inconscientes*, et plus généralement *virtuelles*" ("take into account *unconscious*, and more generally *virtual* archives").[25] Derrida makes this archival connection by affirming that "le propos de Freud, c'est d'analyser, à travers l'apparente absence de mémoire et d'archive, toutes sortes de symptômes, signes, figures, métaphores et métonymies qui attestent, au moins virtuellement, une documentation archivale" ("Freud's intention is to analyze, across the apparent absence of memory and of archive, all kinds of symptoms, signs, figures, metaphors, and metonymies that attest, at least virtually, an archival documentation").[26] But the qualifying phrase "au moins virtuellement," which seems to relegate the virtual to a stand-in or a consolation for an "actual" archive, gives way to a more comprehensive understanding: "L'inconscient ignore ici la différence entre le virtuel et l'actuel, l'intention et l'action . . . ou du moins ne se règle-t-il pas sur la manière dont la conscience . . . distribue les rapports du virtuel, de l'intentionnel et de l'actuel" ("The unconscious does not know the difference here between the virtual and the actual, the intention and the action . . . or at least does not model itself on the manner in which the consciousness . . . distributes the relations of the virtual, of the intentional, and of the actual").[27] Freud's psychoanalysis provides a model for an archive that could exist *autrement*, and which could go beyond psychoanalysis to explore, "dans sa plus grande généralité, le champ problématique d'une *archive du virtuel*" ("the problematic field of an *archive of the virtual*, in its greatest generality"):[28]

> Qu'en sera-t-il quand il faudra bien soustraire le concept de virtualité au couple qui l'oppose à l'actualité, à l'effectivité ou à la réalité ? Devra-t-on continuer à penser qu'il n'y a pas d'archive pensable pour le virtuel ? Pour ce qui arrive dans l'espace et le temps virtuels ? C'est peu probable, cette mutation est en cours, mais il faudra, pour tenir un compte rigoureux de cette autre virtualité, abandonner ou restructurer de fond en comble notre concept hérité de l'archive. Le moment sera venu d'accepter un grand remuement dans notre archive conceptuelle, et d'y croiser une "logique de l'inconscient" avec une pensée du virtuel qui ne soit plus limitée par l'opposition philosophique traditionnelle de l'acte et de la puissance.
>
> What will become of this when we will indeed have to remove the concept of virtuality from the couple that opposes it to actuality, to effectivity, or to reality? Will we be obliged to continue thinking that there is no thinkable archive for the virtual? For what happens in virtual space and time? It is hardly probable, this mutation is in progress, but it will be necessary, to keep a rigorous account of this other virtuality, to abandon or restructure from top to bottom our inherited concept of the archive, and in it to cross a "logic of the unconscious" with a way of thinking of the virtual which is no longer limited by the traditional philosophical opposition between act and power.[29]

Calling for an overhaul in the concepts of the archive and of the virtual as they are traditionally understood, Derrida alludes to the fact that this change (a "mutation") is already taking place. Derrida's statements in *Mal d'archive* are not merely a call for archival science to recuperate virtuality from an oppositional relationship with reality. They also suggest that the conceptual archive must heretofore account for the technical, technological, and scientific developments whose effects were already being felt (in the mid-1990s) within the realms of archiving and neuroscience.

Technological "mutations" contribute their own safeguards to archival preservation. The archival drive in *Mal d'archive* appears as an automatic, nearly mechanistic function of the mind—the psychic archive—and of all other archives: a "pulsion d'archive" that is both a desire to archive and to destroy or remake the archive. As a machine, the "pulsion d'archive" has the spectral quality and faculties of a ghost: "une réponse spectrale (donc instruite par une *tékhnē* et inscrite dans une archive) est toujours possible" ("a spectral response [thus informed by a *technē* and inscribed in an archive] is always possible").[30] This continuously possible response projects the archive into a state of future potential. As a feature of the *mal d'archive* as a drive or a "pulsion," the continually possible response is only guaranteed through a machine, or other technology, that would record and replay.

The conjunction of the machine and the ghost takes place in a curious simile. Updating Freud's *Wunderblock* as a modern-day answering machine, Derrida writes: "Cela parle, un fantôme . . . un peu comme ce répondeur automatique (*answering machine*) dont la voix survit à son moment d'enregistrement" ("A phantom speaks . . . a bit like the answering machine whose voice outlives its moment of recording").[31] In the attenuated simile ("un peu comme") employed here, Derrida seems to be cautioning against an understanding of the archival ghost-machine as mere metaphor, a supernatural impossibility. The spectral aspect of the archive is not to be understood as separate from its technical or technological aspect; the former is only possible through the latter. The technology itself is phantomatic, producing the "réponse spectrale" that is "toujours possible." The answering machine hearkens to other archival technologies that can themselves make ghosts speak. Using the answering machine as a metaphor for the archive, Derrida draws attention to the archive's form, since the claims of an unflagging futurity allude to, and indeed may rely upon, the physical state of the archive's content. In this way, those who are alive are affected by the "technique d'archive [qui] déborde la singularité de l'événement" ("an archival technique [which] overflows the singularity of an event") and can return to respond again and again.[32]

Derrida's call to think about the virtual beyond an opposition to action, power, effectivity, and actuality is a theoretical preoccupation during the 1990s. He links virtuality to the spectrality of technology in *Spectres de Marx*. In this text, Derrida counters the usage of "virtual" as synonymous with "ineffective" and "non-presence, non-effectivity, inactuality," while linking it to the notion of simulacrum.[33] Simultaneously, he relates virtuality to technology in order to develop the potentiality (i.e., the force) of the to-come (*à venir*). In *Spectres de Marx*, the *à venir* is figured as a ghost or specter, not opposed to the actual or real, as the traditional scholar (in the figure of *Hamlet*'s Horatio) would have it, but as a "hallucination ou simulacre, et virtuellement plus efficace que ce qu'on appelle tranquillement une présence vivante" ("a hallucination or simulacrum that is virtually more actual than what is so blithely called a living presence").[34] The simulacrum, through virtuality, allows us to rethink categories of life and death, suggesting other modes of living. The simulacrum of virtuality is also characterized by the capacity to preserve all alternate contingencies of time, that which could have been otherwise. But as technology, it is related to the media and to the "pouvoir techno-médiatique" ("techno-mediatic power") that makes use of "tant d'effets *spectraux*, de la nouvelle vitesse *d'apparition* . . . du simulacre, de l'image synthétique ou prosthétique, de l'événement virtuel, du *cyberspace* et de l'arraisonnement" ("so many *spectral* effects, the new speed of *apparition* . . . of the simulacrum, the synthetic or prosthetic image, and the virtual event, cyberspace and surveillance"), whether in the service of democracy or authoritarianism.[35] The "differential deployment of *tekhnē*" has foregrounded the question of virtualization, whose pervasiveness makes it impossible to oppose "presence to its representation, 'real time' to 'deferred time,' effectivity to its simulacrum, the living to the non-living."[36] Precisely as it is understood as a technological mode, virtuality no longer holds up in opposition to actuality or the real, but is in fact what breaks down the oppositions Derrida lists, and points to new ways of envisioning reality, presence, and the state of living or *survie*.

The actualizing, and in fact contemporary, power of virtuality can be seen most significantly in the extensive technological transformations that were changing the nature of work, community, and place in the 1990s, prompting a reconsideration of institutions such as the university. For Derrida, the role of technology in institutions—their establishment, their longevity—underwrites the inner workings of a virtual community that is unbound by constraints of time and space. Derrida's focus on the university as one such institution in *L'Université sans condition* echoes his reflections on the limits and potential of archival institutions. In *L'Université sans condition*, Derrida writes: "une mutation technoscientifique . . . affecte le télétravail, la virtualisation du travail et, en même temps que la communication du savoir . . . , que toute mise en commun et que toute 'communauté,' l'expérience du lieu, de l'avoir lieu, de l'événement et de l'œuvre" ("a techno-scientific mutation . . . affects tele-work, the virtualization of work, and at the same time the communication of knowledge, at the same time as any putting-into-common and any 'community,' the experience of place, of taking place, of the event, and of the *oeuvre*").[37] For Derrida, these technological developments were to be embraced as a means of realizing a university "sans limite" ("without limit") that could escape institutional strictures and ideological constraints on the freedom of thought—"la liberté académique, une liberté *inconditionnelle* de questionnement et de proposition" ("academic freedom, an unconditional freedom to question and to assert").[38] His hope is that virtualization would be possible through technologies of archiving, which would ensure unconditional and unlimited freedom for the university. It is the utopian aspect of his view—literally, an archive without a singular place—that informs Derrida's reflections on technology in relation to the archive: the boundlessness of the community it could create; the seemingly infinite capacity for storage. His vision of the possibilities of archival technologies presents virtuality as both place and space, both material and immaterial—enabling the transformation of "l'expérience du lieu, de l'avoir lieu" ("the experience of place, of taking place") that Derrida notes in relation to the university. The insistence on place echoes his remarks in *Mal d'archive*—first given as a talk in the Freud Museum, which houses the possessions and personal archive of the Freud family, in their former home—as Derrida highlights in his insistence on the *arkhè* as a place of "consignation" and "domiciliation," the archonte's "demeure" ("dwelling").[39] Derrida shows that the archive is not bound to a physical "domiciliation": instead of being fixed in a geographical location, it can also be characterized by its virtual existence.

Derrida's dream of a limitless university took form as the Collège international de philosophie, which was created in 1983.[40] As Derrida conceived it, the Collège would draw on the hybridity of "a kind of marginal or inter-institutional territory, a space that . . . is neither purely philosophical, nor purely scientific, nor purely aesthetic."[41] The Collège would be virtual in the sense that it would not be tied to a particular place. When the archives of the Collège international de philosophie entered the IMEC in 1999, Derrida once again brought up the importance of virtuality for that institution, returning, four years after *Mal d'archive*, to the notion of the archive in order to reflect on the foundation, history, and posterity of institutions, and the role of virtuality and technology in realizing an institution's goals. As we have seen, in "Le Futur antérieur de l'archive," Derrida refers to "[les] possibilités technologiques [du] développement accéléré des techniques d'archivation et de virtualisation. . . . Les recherches et les enseignements qui se produiront dans cet espace virtuel seront immédiatement des lieux d'archivation" ("the technological possibilities of the rapid development of archiving and virtualizing techniques. . . . The research and teaching that will be produced in this virtual space will immediately be places of archiving").[42] By emphasizing virtualization as immediate and simultaneous, Derrida underscores its affinity with actualization, rejecting a confluence with the absent or unrealized. The fact that the "virtual space" is not solely theoretical but is realized through technology would enable the Collège to fulfill its international vocation, in addition to providing and preserving a record of its intellectual work. As Derrida then says, expanding his comments on the Collège to his own archives, "le partage de l'archive devient possible, et celle-ci n'a plus un lieu unique" ("sharing the archive becomes possible, an archive that no longer has one single location").[43] It is as a multiplied, virtual space that the archive can be shared—not split—over two or more locations, but fully preserved and accessible across institutions. Furthermore, it can create apparent overlaps between other collections within those institutions. The connection between Derrida's own archives and those of the Collège, to be preserved under the aegis of the IMEC yet also reaching across an ocean and a continent to UC Irvine, is an example of the range of the virtual.

As we can see, Derrida's concept of virtuality emerges alongside a sustained reflection on technology, especially in relation to questions of legacy, transmission, and archiving. From *Mal d'archive* on, virtuality appears in conjunction with materiality, not in opposition to it. The consideration of technology, also riding the line between material and immaterial, leverages Derrida's ongoing theorization of the virtual. In practice, too, virtualization becomes crucial for Derrida's involvement in his own archives, as he mines the possibilities and challenges of integrating new media—including most notably his computer hard drive—at Irvine and the IMEC.

"*Mon subjectile*"

The relationship between the material, the virtual, and technology underlies Derrida's descriptions of his own writing process. His writing harnesses the cutting-edge synchronicity of the computer and the nostalgia and material beauty of older technologies of paper and mark-making implements, privileging neither, delighting in the quirks and contingencies of each. The computer in particular offered Derrida something of a laboratory for exploring the conjunction of materiality and virtuality. His "bloc Macintosh" was an essential part of his writing process, as we see in "Circonfession," where he explains that his computer complements his attic, which serves as library and personal archive: "[mon ordinateur] je l'ai surnommé *subjectile* comme j'avais baptisé mon grenier, là où je stocke les skizzes de ma circoncision, *mon sublime*" ("I've nicknamed [my computer] *subjectile*, like I'd baptized my attic, where I stock the skizzes of my circumcision, *my sublime*").[44] Although the doubling of the *subjectile* and the *sublime*, computer and attic, would seem to follow a binary logic opposing material and immaterial, we will see that this is far from being the case. Written on the eve of the creation of Derrida's collection as the cornerstone of the Critical Theory Archive at UC Irvine, "Circonfession" raises questions about materiality and virtuality with respect to writing and archival storage, prefiguring concerns raised later by Derrida and Olivier Corpet at the IMEC.

Mon subjectile would seem to be an ironic nickname for a computer, since *subjectile* is commonly used as an art historical term referring to the material support on which a painting or drawing is made. In *Artaud le Moma* and "Forcener le subjectile," Derrida discusses this term in relation to Antonin

Artaud, for whom the "subjectile" was a medium that could be physically damaged and could in turn transmit the force of that attack to the reader or viewer. The surface that receives the *jet* incorporates it and becomes a projectile itself. The notion of medium as both physical substance and means of transmission is significant for Derrida's conception of the computer as *subjectile*. The computer offers an intangible page for writing, a visual skeuomorph backed by a complex technical system of data preservation, yet it remains, at its core, physical, material hardware. Writing is inscribed on, or within, this *subjectile* by magnetizing areas of a glass or aluminum platter covered in metal—the hard drive—according to binary code: Derrida's computer writing therefore does constitute a physical, spatial relationship with a *subjectile*, though the inscription is not made by the writer directly. The term *subjectile* thus overrides an easy distinction between old and new technologies, between material and virtual ascriptions of writing.

Paired together, the *subjectile* and the *sublime*, computer and attic, form the storeroom of writing, "là où je stocke les skizzes." The computer's "space" of writing and storing, however, is not ordered according to familiar spatial referents: the oppositional doubles of up/down, above/beneath, and left/right do not map clearly onto the structure of the *subjectile-sublime*:

> Le mien [l'ordinateur] je l'ai surnommé *subjectile* comme j'avais baptisé mon grenier, là où je stocke les skizzes de ma circoncision, *mon sublime*, mes dessus dessous, car je n'ai ni haut ni bas, comme l'écureuil qui monte et descend à l'horizontale, la forme de mon monde, une littérature d'apparence, comme l'allure même de mon écriture, cosmonautique, flottante en apesanteur, marine et *high-tech*, plus nue, quoi qu'ils disent, grâce au simulacre.

> I've nicknamed mine [my computer] *subjectile*, like I'd baptized my attic, where I stock the skizzes of my circumcision, *my sublime*, my upside downs, for I have neither up nor down, like the squirrel climbing up and down horizontally, the form of my world, a literature that appears to be, like the very look of my writing, cosmonautical, floating in weightlessness, marine and *high-tech*, more naked, whatever they say, thanks to the simulacrum.[45]

As Derrida continues his description of this writing duo in Period 26 of "Circonfession," his use of doubling complicates geographies of writing and spatial orientation. In this passage, the archive is not hierarchically structured: one alternative is not privileged over the other, as we also see in Derrida's elaborate syntax. Instead, "la forme de mon monde" is dictated by the structure of the computer: "ma confession inaugure au lieu de se stratifier dans le bloc Macintosh, avec la structure anamnésique, réitérable et vulnérable, des double-sided/double density, double poste, micro floppy-disks MF2-DD, par exemple, de marque Sony" ("the amnesiac, reiterable and vulnerable structure of the double-sided/double-density, double track, micro floppy disks MF2-DD."[46] Resisting the "stratification" associated with the accumulation of paper archives, the computer and related technologies (here, the floppy disk) are structured differently. Even though this type of floppy disk is "ten times stronger for greater durability" with a "unique binder system [that] enables disks to withstand *twice* the number of passes,"[47] the disk is ultimately fragile and flighty, its name—floppy—a droll evocation of a limp, flaccid prosthetic, appropriate for "Circonfession," a text whose project is to "décrire mon sexe" ("describe my sex") in order to counter conventions of philosophical writing.[48] Far from offering a reliable system of preservation, this technological structure is instead "anamnésique, réitérable et vulnérable." The usefulness of this technology clearly does not lie in its stability, its capacity to serve as a faithful archival system.

The repetition of "double" in the passage cited above does more than evoke the increased storage capacity of a particular (and now obsolete)[49] form of technology, the floppy disk. The "double" raises trouble for widely accepted views about the personal computer—hardly ubiquitous at the time of Derrida's writing in the late 1980s—countering the opinion of traditionalists who believe that "l'ordinateur nuit à l'écriture" ("computers are harmful to writing") but also those who believe that the computer can "règle[r] enfin le problem des doubles ou de l'archive" ("sort out the problem of doubles or the archive").[50] The attitude Derrida is writing against is ambivalent: on the one hand, it scorns the computer for spoiling a tradition of handwriting, but on the other hand, it applauds the computer's improved ability to store and preserve—notions Derrida corrects in this period of "Circonfession." In fact, these new technologies—the computer and the floppy disk—are both more fragile and more at risk of obsolescence than paper and pen(cil), and as Derrida shows in "Circonfession" and elsewhere, writing on the computer is also writing by hand.[51] In addition, if the computer "ne règle pas le problème des doubles," for Derrida, this is because it is itself a double, coupled with the attic writing room—*subjectile* and *sublime*, respectively. With its doubling and doubled structure, the computer causes rifts in an archiving system that thinks it understands what must be saved, and in what order, with what technologies, and for how long. The integration of a new technology of writing into archival techniques might understandably provoke changes in the conventions of an institutional practice, but Derrida's insistence on the "problem of doubles" draws attention to the fact that this new technology might in fact raise challenges precisely where it appears to resolve them. Understanding the simulacrum of the machine both for its challenges and its particular potential is a way to harness this technology, which Derrida does in view both of writing and of archiving.

As we have seen, Derrida tells us that his writing has changed as he has adopted the use of the typewriter and then the computer. He details the history of his switch to "machines" in the essay "La Machine à traitement de texte": "J'ai écrit de plus en plus 'à la machine,' comme on dit, à la machine à écrire mécanique, puis à la machine électrique, en 1979, puis enfin à l'ordinateur, vers 1986–1987. Je ne peux plus m'en passer maintenant, de ce petit Mac, surtout quand je travaille chez moi" ("I wrote more and more 'straight onto' the machine: first the mechanical typewriter; then the electric typewriter, in 1979; then finally the computer, around 1986 or 1987. I can't do without it anymore now, this little Mac, especially when I'm working at home").[52] These new technologies have given his writing, as he describes it in the passage from "Circonfession" quoted above, "une littérature d'apparence, comme l'allure même de mon écriture" ("a literature that appears to be, like the very look of my writing").[53] But what does "mon écriture" refer to here—to the quality or style of writing, to his handwriting by pen? Or is Derrida referring to the handwriting that takes place *through* the computer, from the keyboard to the word-processing page? Not only would this writing increase in speed, but its character would radically transform in the realm of the born-digital. Writing in or on the computer, for Derrida, is a new kind of moving and being. Derrida insists on the physical movement, unconstrained by this technology, "cosmonautique, flottante en apesanteur, marine et *high-tech*, plus nue, quoi qu'ils disent, grâce au simulacre" ("cosmonautical, floating in weightlessness, marine and *high-tech*, more naked, whatever they say, thanks to the simulacrum").[54]

The "simulacrum" of this passage could be read as a reference to the skeuomorph of word-processing software—that is to say, the writing in binary code that is magnetized onto the metallic surface of the disk or drive *appears* on the screen as the image of the typeface and alphabet of our choice on what resembles a piece of paper.[55] In all likelihood, Derrida did not distinguish between word-processing software and the hardware that was his "bloc Macintosh." He admits, in "La Machine à traitement de texte," that "je ne sais pas *comment* ça marche. Je ne sais donc pas, je sais moins que jamais 'qui c'est,' qui va là . . . même si on sait jusqu'à un certain point s'en servir, on sait rarement, d'un savoir intuitif et immédiat . . . *comment* opère le démon intérieur de l'appareil" ("I don't know *how* it works. So I don't know, I know less than ever 'who it is,' who goes there . . . even if people know how to use them up to a point, they rarely know, intuitively and without thinking . . . *how* the internal demon of the apparatus operates").[56] For Derrida, the technical details that distinguish the computer from the typewriter do not seem to be of great importance, though the idea of the simulacrum or of "une littérature d'apparence" arises in particular with the enigmatic skeuomorph created by word-processing software. This software does more than approximate the visual (not tactile) experience of writing: the simulacrum it creates allows for writing to appear to be "plus nue." Evoking nakedness, Derrida suggests that computer-writing is itself a physical body, thus recalling his description of the floppy disks as rewriteable and therefore "vulnerable." This double is not the abstraction of something concrete. In unsettling the relationship of original to copy, the simulacrum also disturbs a clear distinction between material and virtual.

Archiving the Hard Drive

If the *subjectile* is a means of preservation on which and through which writing can be realized, it is also a material artifact that demands preservation of its own. The hard drive and the floppy disks that populate Derrida's scene of writing are clearly essential components of his oeuvre. Yet the double-sided floppy disks are by now quaint relics, along with the "bloc Macintosh," whose portrait appears in "Circonfession." The hard drive of this computer and others that Derrida may have used are subject not only to technological obsolescence, but to an additional danger: bit rot causes their data to decay over time, gradually making it inaccessible. The status of Derrida's *subjectile* in the archives highlights the technological and theoretical challenges of virtualization. Since 2008, three of Derrida's computers and some external hard drives have been housed at the IMEC. The main priority has been to increase the speed and scope of digitization in order to counter the technological obsolescence that risks rendering the digital content inaccessible.[57] In addition, approximately 500 floppy disks offer an additional, even more complex material for digital archivists. The "Derrida hexadécimal" team, based within the ITEM (Institut des textes et mémoires modernes), points to the likelihood that other more recent computers are still not present in the IMEC's collection, given Derrida's allusions to specific models and to his own writing practice.[58] Faced with this materially challenging and often uncommunicative material, a vast but somewhat inaccessible reserve, the "Derrida hexadécimal" project has devised a method of reading the files and digital content, made available by the IMEC, to establish a preliminary understanding of what a digital genetic dossier would look like: how to identify deletions and additions, for example, directly in the hexadecimal source code of the files. The team anticipates that the project could represent a shift in genetic criticism as its "fundamental laws and methodology" confront this unfamiliar material.[59]

Over the past two decades, the solutions invented by librarians, archivists, and digital humanities scholars working on born-digital materials, especially those faced with urgent issues of technological obsolescence, give a sense of the potential for conserving and consulting Derrida's hard drives in the future. At the IMEC and other institutions, including those that house Derrida's papers, the search for technologies suited to ensure the preservation, transmission, and accessibility of these materials, and for the measures that can be taken to ward off technological decline, as well as bit rot and obsolescence, becomes increasingly urgent as the amount of born-digital material accumulates. At UC Irvine's Critical Theory Archive, archivists have devised a virtual reading room for scholars to consult documents, both digitized and born-digital, and are expanding this to include audio and video materials, including recordings of Derrida's seminars.[60] The project "Derrida's Margins," based at Princeton University, provides scholars with an online database of digitized images of annotations and insertions in the books referenced in *De la grammatologie*, to demonstrate the activity of reading as part of Derrida's writing process. Virtualization promotes access to new media, giving a fuller picture of Derrida's working process even beyond its textual components.

In imagining the potential of a virtual space, Derrida draws on the meaning of "virtual" as denoting both digital (related to technology) and potential (yet-unrealized). With his enthusiastic, even optimistic use of virtual technologies, Derrida diverges from critics who, over the decades, have expressed anxieties about technological developments relating to archives.[61] But two decades after Derrida's remarks, it is impossible to ignore the major technological shifts in information access and forms of writing, and their theoretical and practical implications for archival studies. While some scholars of contemporary archives have taken a reactionary view, using the terms "virtual" and "digital" interchangeably and disapprovingly, others see the digital field as a venue for innovation and experimentation, and argue for the possibilities of archival innovation through digital humanities.[62] Within archival science, post-structuralism has inspired, for some, a new approach to archival materials, technologies, and the concerns of those who consult archival collections.[63] Derrida's views on virtualization parallel developments in archival science and the digital humanities, which have likewise found in Derrida a sympathetic source. In combining practical and theoretical aspects of archiving, these studies pave the way for a more careful analysis of what "virtual" means in relation to archives—for example, in Timothy Colburn's conception of software as a "concrete abstraction" and as a "machine made of text."[64] Dovetailing with work done in archival science, new media studies, and digital humanities, the technological innovations underway in archives and author collections make clear the conjunction of material and virtual, as well as of theory and practice.[65]

Faced with the urgent need to address the fragility of born-digital materials, archivists and digital scholars are working with realities of copying and doubling that reflect the pervasive materiality of the digital. Several products have been engineered to facilitate the migration of data between media formats, thereby preventing the loss of archival material due to hardware or software obsolescence and bit-level rot. Matthew McKinley, a digital project specialist with the UC Irvine Libraries, devised a system called LAMMP (Legacy Archival Media Migration Platform) "to rescue potentially valuable digital content from rapidly aging digital media formats."[66] Like other products of its kind, LAMMP works by transferring data to a digital repository from digital media storage devices such as floppy and ZIP disks, CDs, DVDs, and USB drives. The data is preserved in this migration from one form to another, but the process itself underscores a striking aspect of the digital:

the "paradoxical distance and disconnect" felt on the one hand is countered by "the ultimately unavoidable truth that nothing in this world is ever truly immaterial," as the digital media scholar Matthew Kirschenbaum puts it in his essay "The .txtual Condition."[67] Because "each access engenders a new logical entity that is forensically individuated at the level of its physical representation," this vital technique of preservation prompts the realization that what is saved is not in fact exactly the same as the original content.[68]

Not the same, but very close: here we take the measure of the power of the simulacrum that Derrida drew out synonymously with the virtual in *Spectres de Marx*, "Circonfession," and other texts. The effect provoked by technologies of archival preservation and consultation is closely linked to contemporary working conditions characterized by a conjunction of the material and virtual—as especially prominent in the archives of writers who worked primarily on computers. As more archival institutions try to make writers' hard drives and even their computers accessible, the goal, according to Matthew McKinley, is to "reliably captur[e] the work environments of digital content creators,"[69] creating, in one case, "a complete virtual emulation" of manuscripts, a filing system, games, the desktop organization, and thousands of e-mails, as Kirschenbaum describes the Salman Rushdie collection.[70] This experience changes the way researchers access material and understand the creative process through their own proximity to it. The intimacy experienced in consulting the hard drive can be even more intense than the handling of handwritten papers: the feelings of "queasiness," "creepiness and voyeurism" that arise when consulting computer-based documents, described by Benjamin Moser, suggest that the experience is a visceral one.[71] Despite the familiarity we may have with the digital sphere, archival materials that are "born digital" still have the power to be volatile and affecting. Derrida's statement that his writing becomes "plus nue . . . grâce au simulacre" ("more naked . . . thanks to the simulacrum") can be read in this light: the simulacrum of virtualizing technologies brings us into intimate contact with writing, which appears not as a mask or covering but as the bare skin of writing, exposed and vulnerable.

The quality of the simulacrum surrounds these documents and produces, in our proximity to them and in their proximity to something like an original, a "bewildering and vertiginous" effect: Daniel Smith uses this affective language in his analysis of the simulacrum according to Deleuze.[72] Unlike a copy, which is posited as a deferential counterpart to an original, the simulacrum, for Deleuze, is "*the Same*, the perfect double, the exact semblance, the *Doppelgânger*"—and thus much more powerfully subversive.[73] With its ability to approximate the material conditions of a writer at work, the virtual counterpart of Derrida's hard drive would offer a seductive version of his ideal archive. As a (near-)perfect copy, the simulacrum exposes the act of consulting a writer's "papers" as an unsettling experience of intimacy, whose proximity to the scene of writing, and to the body of the writer, is only heightened in this extrapolation. This effect attests to the success of the simulacrum's mimicry, its genius for creating a copy that dissimulates itself as the original, effacing the work of doubling even as it casts doubt on the very distinction between original and copy.

The hard drive and the potential mechanisms of its consultation draw attention to the importance of the perfect copy—the virtual simulacrum—in Derrida's understanding of an ideal archive both in theory and in practice. From earlier explorations of virtuality and technology, we have seen how Derrida was drawn to technological innovations in writing and archiving not for their ability to provide an exact replica, but for the creative potential they have as simulacra: linking a virtual community of researchers in simultaneous consultation, for example. As Kirschenbaum suggests with respect to consulting born-digital materials, "access is thus duplication, duplication is preservation, and preservation is creation and re-creation."[74] The simulacrum's infinite multiplication and the imperceptible changes it causes within the material mean that consulting the writer's hard drive can achieve the effect of the Same by posing as the perfect double. We have the impression of simultaneity, of intimate access, of exposure: this is how writing becomes "plus nue . . . grâce au simulacre." A technological inevitability—the challenge of integrating computer-based writing into an oeuvre, or into an archival institution—appears as a fruitful technique for invigorating Derrida's writing, stripping it down, launching it into (cyber)space and time, and giving it a renewed chance at survival.

Cixous Dreaming Double

Derrida aims to ensure that the archives are full by tapping into the power of media and technology to provoke a doubling or multiplication of the archive. The conjunction of the *sublime* and *subjectile* is one example of technologies that override mortality and invoke other ways of being. Virtual technologies offer solutions for conserving particularly fragile, vulnerable materials. Cixous shares the doubling impulse, developing it as an archival technique. In her work since her 1999 donation to the Bibliothèque nationale de France, she demonstrates an interest in and concern for what the archive cannot contain, especially in the face of death. What can the archive do to preserve memory from oblivion, and to preserve writing from decay or loss? Cixous's writing addresses this question by exploring techniques of doubling and copying that could preserve both materially and virtually; that is to say, whose virtual preservation passes through and depends on the artifact's materiality. It is not merely that the act of creating a copy reveals the failures of that copy to provide a perfect stand-in for the original; in putting to writing this archival impulse toward perfect preservation, Cixous suggests a way of moving beyond circular, mimetic impossibility. Two texts illustrate this process:

Hyperrêve (2006), which describes the fugue state of mourning in the wake of Derrida's death and of preemptive grief for the end of her mother's life, and *Tours promises* (2004), which describes the transfer of Cixous's papers to the BNF. Both texts convey an urgency of writing and innovative strategies to make use of virtuality in order to archive more fully. What's more, in Cixous's use of the double, virtuality itself becomes something worth preserving.

Hyperrêve is a book powered by the intensity of mourning, a *hyper-* intensity that is above, beyond, in excess. Written in the year following Derrida's death, the book contains numerous references to "mon ami J.D." alternating with scenes of a mother's decline through old age into extreme frailty of mind and body. Between two deaths, the narrator's search for solace takes shape in various forms of documentation and recording, which override temporal distinctions as well as the limits between dream, writing, and reality. In this sense, the word *hyper-* indicates a possible elsewhere that is by turns nightmarish and idyllic. The narrator's desire to reunite with her dead friend finds a counterpart in a desire to repair the imminent rift of her mother's demise. As time passes, the narrator anxiously grasps at the small details of a life that is slipping away. Despite the frustrations of their daily life together, everything is precious because it is ephemeral, on the brink of disappearance:

> Je veux retenir chaque instant, je veux garder l'exaspération insupportable je veux me souvenir tout de suite, à la minute et pour les temps des temps, de chaque intonation de ma mère, de chacune des centaines d'images par jour de ma mère, je veux enregistrer instantanément mentalement chaque picotement intolérable de mon être-avec-maman, je veux avoir un double simultané indélébile de tout ce qui compose la vie et l'œuvre de ma mère . . . je ne veux pas perdre une miette de ce tout ce qu'ai besoin de fuir et de balayer
>
> I want to hold on to every instant, I want to keep the unbearable exasperation, I want to remember right now, this very minute and for the time of times, each modulation of my mother's voice, each of the hundreds of daily images of my mother, I want to record instantaneously mentally each intolerable prick of my being-with-mummy, I want to have a simultaneous indelible double of everything that composes the life and work of my mother . . . I don't want to lose a crumb of everything I need to flee and to sweep away.[75]

In her wish to preserve the totality of her mother's life and work in all its minute details, the narrator becomes the archive of her mother's life: the intonations, images, and the composition of this oeuvre would be held and recorded for all eternity ("pour les temps des temps," "indélébile"). Moreover, this particular archiving machine works in temporal lockstep with reality: the double is simultaneous and instantaneous, archiving "tout de suite." Only in this way can the narrator be assured that nothing will be lost. This archival technique collapses the interval between the work and the archive, creating a perfect double that can bear no separation from the event itself.

The narrator's repeated invocations correspond to the infinite speed and power that Derrida ascribes to Cixous's writing. The insistent "je veux" ("I want") repeated in the passage cited above operates according to what Derrida describes as "l'accélération même et l'impatience absolue de mon désir qui voudrait le faire arriver aussitôt, sans attendre, vivement" ("acceleration itself and the absolute impatience of my desire, which would like to make it arrive straightaway, without delay, briskly").[76] The "vitesse" and "puissance" ("speed" and "might") of this writing, according to Derrida, outpace space and time to achieve an "accélération quasiment infinie" ("quasi-infinite acceleration").[77] He refers to this mode as Cixous's "injonction télégraphique" ("telegraphic injunction"), quoting from her own *OR*, distinguishing the "puissance" ("might") of her writing from the conventional subjunctive wish or promise, and insisting instead on its performative capability and, further, its ability to override the traditional opposition of virtuality and actuality, *dynamis* and *energeia*.[78] The force of Cixous's writing is such that it "doubles": *doubler* in French indicating at once the multiplication by two, the action of overtaking or passing, and the act of standing in for someone, as on a movie set or in a dubbed film. Indeed, Derrida cites this homonymic play as one example of Cixous's virtuosic style, a linguistic doubling. But this is at work throughout Cixous's writing: "ce qui gagne *de* vitesse et *sur la* vitesse, le temps et l'espace, cela gagne en doublant, selon la loi du double, de la substitution de l'unique à l'unique qui vise en son spectre et en soi-même, se remplaçant lui-même à sa place, presque sans bouger" ("what gains *in* speed and *on* speed, time and space, gains in passing or 'doubling,' according to the law of the double, of the substitution of the unique for the unique, which aims for its own specter and for itself, replacing itself at its place, almost without moving").[79] With the unique doubled, splitting and recombining into a ghostly self and other of itself, the simulacrum here is joined with simultaneity to unsettle not only the relation between original and copy, but the notion of selfhood as selfsame. By replacing, doubling actually multiplies, creates space, and expands time. In its doubling force, Cixous's call for a "double simultané indélébile" ("simultaneous indelible double") of her mother's life intensifies the present moment, opening it up to contain—and preserve—an expanse of memory and being. In this way the archival moment is both the same as and more than the original.

In *Hyperrêve*, the vast scope of Cixous's dream welcomes a wide range of materials, documents, and events: a record of what is inarchivable, the life, dreams, and encounters that are otherwise lost, a source of solace in memory and mourning. As we will see in chapter 5, the alternative archive is just as real as the institution's, preserving what the official archive cannot. This would be what both Cixous and Derrida imagine as the ideal solution for the future preservation of their writing—their dream archive, of sorts—as well as an actual, present reserve of vitality. But if this is a dream archive, it is not in the sense of an illusory impossibility or a motivating theory. Cixous's "injunctions" here constitute a kind of writing, a writing technique that is also an archival technique.

The narrator of *Hyperrêve* has other occasions to put this technique into practice, notably in a sequence involving a dream that doubles the material to be preserved through archival writing. We will see later on how Cixous's practice of dream transcription in particular contributes to the "telegraphic injunctions" of her writing, allowing her to communicate with her deceased friend. The technique of doubled, dictated writing is worth previewing here, in the context of a simultaneous archival simulacrum. *Within* her dream, the narrator transcribes a dream (a dream within a dream) of a telephone call she has received from her deceased friend:

> Je pensais, je notais, je revivais je recevais je riais je perdais je retrouvais, je saisissais la phrase, la voix, l'absolu, *en double*, tout en double; cet instant, et son double passé, le double de cet instant et son double futur; cette dictée et son double futur; ce rêve et le double qui en resterait; la réalité de ce rêve dans le rêve la réalité de ce rêve hors de ce rêve; . . . je faisais le rêve et son double, *dans* le rêve, suivant les indications de la voix de mon ami, je comprenais qu'il me rappelait d'en faire un double simultané à porter dans notre cœur.
>
> I was thinking, I was jotting, I was reliving I was receiving I was laughing I was losing I was finding again, I was grasping the phrase, the voice, the absolute, *in duplicate*, everything was double; this instant, and its past doubled up, a double of this instant and its future double; this dictation and its future double; this dream and its double, which would remain; the reality of this dream in the dream the reality of this dream out of the dream . . . I dreamed the dream and its double, *in* the dream, following the directions in the voice of my friend, I understood he was reminding me to make a copy, a duplicate to carry in our hearts.[80]

The dreaming narrator transcribes so quickly that she creates a perfect copy of the ephemeral, precious moment, multiplying one instant into further doubled moments in the past and future, indicating that doubling extends much further than two. Likewise, the act of transcription is not confined to a singular action or to a singular being: the transcriber thinks, notes, and relives, making or doing (*je faisais*) the dream within the dream, following a voice. In its active multiplicity, this writing technique is able to preserve fully.

Still dreaming, the narrator fears that the transcription will vanish on waking, though she is impatient to wake up "pour vérifier fiévreuse l'état de ces inscriptions" ("anxious to check on the state of the inscriptions").[81] Miraculously, as she awakens—"J'ai allumé si peu" ("I lit so little")—she perceives that the transcription has made it across from the dream to reality: "Tout—tout était couché—en grosses lettres gauches laides valables lisibles—par syllabes détachées chues—tout était disséminé dépiécé mais lisible comme un double intimidé" ("Everything—everything was lying there—in big gauche ugly round readable letters—dropped syllable by syllable—all was scattered chopped up but readable like a shy duplicate").[82] Is this in fact a dream within a dream? Or has the limit between the dream and waking states blurred in the desire to conserve the words of the beloved dead? The narrative of *Hyperrêve* overrides any distinction between realms of being to focus instead on the product of the experience: the transcription is a faithful copy of the dreamt telephone call. Rather than marking a distinction between a supposedly virtual state (the dream) and reality, the written account binds together the dreamt call, the dream itself, and the memory of it. Yet the transcription of the encounter ("ces inscriptions") does not return in *Hyperrêve*. It is replaced by another artifact, a concise handwritten note, which allows the narrator to revisit the dream encounter.

Echoing the dream's call to "faire un double simultané à porter dans notre cœur" ("make a copy, a duplicate to carry in our hearts"), the narrator writes herself a note containing a brief reminder of the dream, for solace later on. The two artifacts are yet another instance of doubling. Unlike the dreamt transcription, which would seem immense given the intensity of the temporal multiplication, this note condenses that intensity into a terse yet evocative dictum: "Il y a des permissions" ("there are leaves").[83] In chapter 5, I show how this note, lost and then rediscovered, demonstrates the affective power of the physical object. As the double of the transcription within the dream, the note challenges us to think about what an artifact preserves, and how it might itself act as an archive—albeit in miniature. In Cixous's estimation, it does so not as a singular object, but as a double. Far from remaining in the immaterial, unrealized realm, the desire ("je veux") and the dream in *Hyperrêve* enact an archival technique that actualizes what they preserve. The doubling Cixous proposes does not accrue in or on a stagnant copy, but multiplies moments infinitely. Like the conjunction of the *sublime* and the *subjectile* in Derrida's "Circonfession," Cixous's comments on the double archive or shadow archive enrich the view of material endurance and contingency associated with her mourning work. The richness of materiality refutes the idea that multiple copies devalue a work by stripping it of rarity.

The Perfect Copy of "Le Livre que je n'écris pas"

Yet the potential of a shadow archive to bypass mortality is hard-won, and the morbidity of archives gives the writer pause, especially in the early stages of the transfer of Cixous's papers to the Bibliothèque nationale de France, as we have seen in chapter 1. In *Tours promises*, written as the *fonds* Cixous was being set up, the practicalities of archiving weigh on the narrator. Faced with the disorder of boxes being prepared for the BNF, the writer spirals into a deep, nearly tragicomic fixation on the tomb-like nature of her papers in their pre-archival state. As she assesses the "morbidité d'une résurrection des morts morts par l'artifice des fouilles" ("morbidness of a resurrection of the dead dead from the artifice of excavation"), the boxes undergo a ghoulish transformation: "Ce ne sont pas des cartons dans lesquels je plonge les mains pour en extraire des liasses d'enveloppes, . . . des grouillances de sentiments flétris pourris, mes pauvres mains envoyées dans la purée cadavérique . . . ce sont des boîtes à hontes et démons" ("These are not boxes into which I plunge my hands to extract bundles of envelopes, . . . swarmings of wilted rotten feelings, my poor hands sent into the cadaveresque goo . . . these are boxes of shames and demons").[84] The nightmarish trance is broken by the writer's mother, who appears at the door with a glass of orange juice in hand, ordering her to drink "Main-te-nant" ("Now"), bringing her back to the here-and-now.[85] *Tours promises* is filled with these seemingly inconsequential flashes of the quotidian. Tiny bursts of the personal erupt onto the scene of writing that runs through *Tours promises*, alluding to the physical world that surrounds writing and enables it. The *jus d'orange* is one of many "sacred details" of everyday life that the writer cherishes: "Tous les détails sont sacrés. Je fais mes comptes: le jus d'orange, les cannelés . . . la douche de Selma . . . les mouches" ("All the details are sacred. I do my accounting: the orange juice, the cannelés, Selma's shower . . . , the flies").[86] Demarcating the literary space of the book, the sacred details shake the writer from a state of paralysis and despair by alluding to another world, that of unnoticed, mundane life, which is not represented textually. What is unwritten is parceled off under the enigmatic name of a book: "J'aurais pu noter le nom du restaurant. Mais cette scène se passait dans le Livre que je n'écris pas" ("I could have noted the name of the restaurant. But this scene took place in the Book I Do Not Write").[87]

Arriving on the scene with the sacred details that banish the writer's archival anxiety, the Livre que je n'écris pas (abbreviated here as LQJNP) is directly associated with the Bibliothèque nationale de France. Over the course of *Tours promises*, it becomes the counterpart to the official archive, shadowing it and outpacing it. In the interval between the unwritten work and the lived moment, the anonymous details that escape being written form an inverse, parallel archive under the guise of this infinite, impossible book, which itself is beyond the scope of the BNF:

> [Le Livre que je n'écris pas] s'étend sans maître et sans ordre dans des dizaines de tiroirs dormants, en un vrac secret partout sur mes étagères, . . . la maison tout entière est peinte de ces phrases sublimes . . . dans

> chaque objet que vous croyez voir est gardé l'événement d'une scène dans tous ses détails, je me fais du souci. Puis-je transférer le Livre intégralement en apparence illisible à la BN?[88]
>
> [The Book I Do Not Write] spreads out unmastered and disordered in dozens of dormant drawers, in a secret miscellany all over my shelves . . . the whole entire house is painted with these sublime phrases . . . in each object that you believe you see is stored the event of a scene in all its details, I worry. Can I transfer the Book integral and whole apparently illegible to the BN?

Cixous's rhetorical question exposes the limits of the institutional archive in the face of the LQJNP's overwhelming totality. Beyond the punctuating interruptions of its sacred details, the LQJNP here introduces a different modality, permeating material objects, insinuating itself into every part of the physical house, transforming it into a kind of counter-archive, a term coined by Paula Amad to explain the challenge that early film presented to archival positivity, with its "sacred myths of order, exhaustiveness, and objective neutrality."[89] Like film, Cixous's LQJNP can be understood as a "counter-archival record of reality," with "its attraction to the everyday fragment as the history of the present."[90] The LQNJP's counter-archival mode is generative. From this early scene in *Tours promises* to a sustained reflection on its nature in "Le Livre que Tu n'écriras pas," a 2005 interview between Cixous and the poet Frédéric-Yves Jeannet, the Livre que je n'écris pas comes to be understood as a source of creative potential: "au-dessus au loin à l'infini, celui qui me manque, le LQJNP, mais dont je pressens que le manque est retourné en combustible" ("above afar infinitely, the one that escapes me, the BIDNW, but whose lack I sense becomes fuel").[91] The LQJNP acts as a safeguard for Cixous's writing by continuing to exist in its dynamic potentiality—not only as a shifting archive, but as renewable material. But what kind of book is it, if it is illegible? What kind of archive is it, if it escapes preservation at the BNF? The ontological enigma of the LQJNP is crucial to its ability to act as a shadow archive.

The LQJNP distinguishes itself by name from the figure of the Book that is recurrent throughout Cixous's work: in lieu of a proper name (*Le Livre*), it goes by an unfinished "syntagm," a shifting appellation that reflects the morphing, moving thing in question.[92] Cixous alternatively refers to this figure as *LQJNP*, *livrequejen'écrispas*, *le Livre-que-je-n'écris-pas*, *le L. que . . .* , and *l.q.j.n.p* elsewhere in *Tours promises* and in *Rencontre terrestre* (2005), a book of extended correspondence with Jeannet. More than a simple riddle of naming, these aliases have the paradoxical effect of conferring the quality of a character, an alien entity, on this book. Moreover, Cixous affirms that the LQJNP differs from the trope of the ideal, impossible Book of Mallarmé and Blanchot.[93] She writes in "Le Livre que Tu n'écriras pas," the correspondence out of which *Rencontre terrestre* emerged: "Tu vois que je parle, non pas du livre à venir, mais du livre immense dont je n'attends même pas la venue, parce que d'une certaine manière il est là tout autour à côté de moi, mais je ne l'écris pas, il ne se pose pas" ("You see that I am speaking not of the book to come but of the immense book whose coming I do not even await, because in some manner it is all around next to me, but I am not writing it, for that's not where the book alights").[94] The temporality of the LQJNP is not teleological; it is not an echo of the Blanchotian "book to come"; it does not attempt to become actualized in written, textual form; it does not defer this actualization in the constantly receding notion of a Derridean *à venir*.[95] Its presence is virtual, not as an unactualized potential, but because it exists otherwise.

In naming as well as in being, the LQJNP asserts its difference and its multiplicity to become a powerful double or shadow companion to Cixous's written, archivable work. It is not one thing, stable and fixed; it is protean. The LQJNP is figured and named as a being that at times appears a mystical beast "qui détale devant moi [et] fait courir tous les impurs chevaliers" ("that darts out before me and makes all the impure knights give chase"); at other times, it is a voice whispering "je, suis, là, même, quand, je, suis, pas, là" ("I, am, there, even, when, I, am, not, there").[96] Its movement, dynamism, and vitality are not bound to a distinction between animate and inanimate, but instead suggest a different mode of existence, fragmented and dispersed: "Il n'est pas exclu qu'il se sécrète, dans mes cahiers, dans mes notes et rêves, mais tout ça reste dispersé, désassemblé" ("It is not impossible that it secretes itself, in my notebooks, in my notes and dreams, but it all remains dispersed, disassembled").[97] The LQJNP models a different kind of writing, as Derrida himself suggested to Cixous: "De ce livre Jacques Derrida me disait: celui que tu n'écris pas s'écrit autrement" ("Of this book Jacques Derrida said to me: the one you don't write is written otherwise").[98] Written otherwise, it exists otherwise, recalling the other-life of manuscripts and textual artifacts that hold Cixous's interest as the "avant d'un livre."[99] The archival afterlife made possible by the LQJNP depends on its otherness.

This shadow archive is tied from the beginning to the Bibliothèque nationale de France. The LQJNP first appeared in Cixous's work at the 2003 conference "Genèses Généalogies Genres," held in honor of the writer's recently acquired archives, in Cixous's keynote address titled "Le livre que je n'écris pas." Impossible not for its unwrittenness, but because it is written everywhere, differently, the LQJNP constitutes a body of writing *en creux*, a corresponding counterpart, by alluding to a virtual, living world, flashing out in small details like the glass of orange juice. Its absence from the BNF, first seen as a cause for concern, is its ultimate virtue: that which the BNF is unprepared to accommodate will fall under the protection of the LQJNP, Cixous suggests. Extracting the writer from the fear that archiving is death, tomb, or sepulcher, the LQJNP allows the writer to see the archive's potential for living on virtually.

Like the slivers of everyday life that punctuate *Tours promises*, the LQJNP punctuates *Tours promises* textually. The essay titled "Le Livre que je n'écris pas" is spliced into *Tours promises* in large chunks, sometimes directly contextualized as a speech given at the BNF conference, at other times imperceptibly cited. The LQJNP is therefore tied to the archive materially as well, as an "avant d'un livre," weaving itself into the manuscript of *Tours promises* that is stored at the BNF. The written text of "Le Livre que je n'écris pas" enters the *fonds* Cixous not as a unique text with a separate dossier, but inserted into the manuscript of *Tours promises*. The text binds the LQJNP to the archive as a conceptual space for preserving and prolonging writing and as a physical collection at the BNF: the interjections of the LQJNP within this book and its manuscript sketch out the shadows of the physical archive's virtual counterpart. The manuscript of *Tours promises* enacts what Cixous proposes in the text, alluding to a virtual archive (represented by the LQJNP) that further preserves Cixous's writing by doubling it. It does so by insinuating itself into physical walls, shelves, and objects—including, but not limited to, the literary artifacts that make their way to the BNF.

With figurative archives in the form of the LQJNP, Cixous creates channels of communication between the BNF, her own personal archives, and live, mutating texts. Through these conduits, the work generates a rich, resilient double of itself. Multiplied and projected in its limitless potentiality, a virtual archive grows out of and yet outpaces—doubles—its material counterpart. By considering the archive as an alternate space of poetic creation, Cixous takes the preservation and the extension of her work into her own hands. The understanding of the archive as doubled, shadowed, or copied affects not only the way Cixous writes, but also the ways readers and researchers approach her work, whether in the form of published text or archived artifacts at the BNF. Cixous's experiments with techniques of intensifying preservation in her writing encourage the reader and researcher to wonder what is left out of the work, and whether this absence is all the better preserved "autrement" (otherwise). In this way the writer involves the researcher and reader in the process of archiving. Understanding the physical textual object as a double that evokes or even preserves vastly more than itself, the researcher is invited to conjure up spaces and moments beyond the present, participating in writing's virtuality and therefore its sustained vitality.

✦

Cixous seeks to create a virtual archive that could outpace the BNF and account for that institution's inevitable shortcomings. Derrida's call for an archive shared across institutional divides is motivated by a digital optimism, an interest in technologies of virtualization. In both cases, virtuality is a desirable feature of an archival setup, yet for neither author is the virtual opposed to the material. The conjunction of virtual and material is instead made clear in the structures and techniques of doubling, copying, and reproduction that feature in Cixous's and Derrida's archival texts.

If Cixous can "faire un double simultané à porter dans notre cœur"; and if Derrida's "double-sided/double density, double poste, micro floppy-disks MF2-DD" can overcome their vulnerability, it is because of a view of the double that does not reduce it to a limp, lifeless copy—a work without aura in the age of mechanical reproduction.[100] Rather than bemoan the reproduction of the work, Derrida and Cixous look to copies, and especially doubles—technological and psychic—for their archival potential. As Derrida recognized through his analysis of Cixous's writing, the kind of doubling that can "dépasser ainsi l'espace et le temps" ("overtake space and time") is that which works through "la substitution de l'unique à l'unique qui vise en son spectre et en soi-même, se remplaçant lui-même à sa place, presque sans bouger" ("the substitution of the unique for the unique, which aims for its own specter and for itself, replacing itself at its place, almost without moving").[101] What is ghostly about the double is its uncanny familiarity, the convincing allure of the perfect copy. But if the simulacrum can step in when the material is most at risk, it can only offer itself as an "enduring ephemeral" because it is itself material. Derrida's attachment to his *subjectile* dramatizes this, as does a different kind of apparatus present in Cixous's Livre que je n'écris pas.

The virtuality explored through doubled archives allows for alternative forms of communication and community. Artifacts participate in creating networks of circulation and transmission between friends, future readers, and institutions. If the materiality of writing contributes to the survival of literary artifacts in an archival state, it also impacts the modes of transmission the artifacts are subject to, as does anyone or anything coming into contact with them. The first three chapters of this book have explored the capacity for endurance, transformation, and creation in certain configurations of archival materials. Derrida and Cixous's attention to the materiality of artifacts has the effect of opening up distance, and intervals, between the writer and writing, which enables written artifacts to circulate more freely. Stripped of its status as authorial property, matter comes into focus as contingent and dynamic, not opposed to virtuality but in lively conversation with it. In the second half of this book, we will see how these aspects—materiality, contingency, and dynamism—contribute to creating connections between readers that will continue to animate the work long after the writers named Hélène Cixous and Jacques Derrida are alive.

Part II

✦

Live Transmission

Chapter 4

✦

Share with Others

Handling Manuscripts between Friends

meilleure
(trop fatiguée au début)
et la dernière page
n'est pas encore écrite =
mais j'ai songé que
cela t'amuserait
peut-être de me
prendre en flagrant
delit—[1]

better
(too tired at the beginning)
and the last page
hasn't been written yet =
but I thought that
you'd find it amusing
perhaps to catch
me in the
act—

This handwritten note, cramped into the narrow top-left margin of the manuscript of Hélène Cixous's *Le Prénom de Dieu*, invests the unfinished text with playfulness and desire as it is shared with a reader. A closer look at this penciled fragment reveals that the annotation's beginning and end have been half-erased. The full text invokes an individual reader and, despite the erasure (in italics here), is mostly legible:

> *Cher George = ceci est le travail de la δƷ'∠∩ = un jeu—j'y ai un peu pensé à toi—La 2*[e] *partie est tellement* meilleure (trop fatiguée au début) . . . cela t'amuserait peut-être de me prendre en flagrant delit—*Puisque inévitablement, il s'agit aussi de toi là-dedans*
>
> *Dear George = this is the work of δƷ'∠∩ = a game—it made me think of you a little—The 2nd part is so much* better (too tired at the beginning) . . . you'd find it amusing perhaps to catch me in the act—*Because inevitably in there it's also about you*

Erasing the personal elements of this address makes room for the anonymous reader, the unforeseen recipient of this note, though it also makes some words difficult to decipher (represented in alternative characters above). Indeed, we might be surprised not to read "Cher Jacques" on this draft, given the legend of Jacques Derrida as the first reader of *Le Prénom de Dieu*. But whether it is "George" who reads this text for the first time, or any subsequent reader—including whoever encounters it in the Bibliothèque nationale de France—the reader will remark the call to catch the writer red-handed, "en flagrant delit [*sic*]." A *délit* is a crime or misdemeanor. But the underlined *delit*, missing an accent, could also indicate a form of unreading (*dé-lire*) or a delirious state, evoking the verb *délirer*, to babble incoherently or deliriously. To write and to read the manuscript in progress would be to find yourself in an exalted state—to go out of your mind, to hallucinate, or to be overjoyed. *Délit* calls up the Latin *delectare*—to charm—and its link to delight: "cela t'amuserait" and "j'ai songé" belong to the same delightful register.

The annotation functions as a poetic *envoi*, a call to the reader, inviting a response through the handling of the draft. This is a temporal trick, but also a physical one, the challenge being raised to witness the live act of writing. The writer calls for the reader to apprehend her (*me prendre*), evoking the hands that grasp the pages in question. *Me prendre* could also be read as *méprendre*, if we follow the casual attitude towards accents here: what is taken could always be mis-taken—and that possibility seems to be at play in this marginalia. Perhaps the *me* has in fact been mistaken: if it is a direct object pronoun, to whom or to what does it refer? Can *me* be confidently linked to the first person of *j'ai songé*? Who or what is being taken, surprised, caught in the act?

This question leads to others: what exactly is being shared here, offered up by a marginal annotation, and what kind of sharing does this invitation offer? If the manuscript's material makeup indicates its dynamism and its liveliness, as we have seen in the first half of this book, how do these qualities affect the way an artifact is transmitted and received? In the three chapters that comprise this book's second half, I explore forms of archival sharing and transmission between Hélène Cixous, Jacques Derrida, and their readers. This chapter looks in particular at manuscripts and literary artifacts that circulate between them. Particularly as the two writers invite each other to serve as readers—and sometimes repositories—of their writing in progress, it becomes difficult to confidently identify manuscripts as discrete objects belonging to an individual writer or collection. Sharing manuscripts and other literary artifacts has consequences for conventionally categorized single-author collections, as we will see over the next three chapters: the practice challenges generic designations of autobiographical writing based on individual authorship and subjectivity. Both writers touch the other's texts in a contingent close reading, leaving physical, reparative traces that lace their texts together across a corpus of artifacts. Furthermore, Cixous's and Derrida's practice of sharing and handling manuscripts is a way of ensuring an afterlife for writing, especially when the manuscripts are physically transformed in the hands of the reader.

Shared Manuscripts

Throughout their decades-long friendship, Derrida and Cixous shared manuscripts and were often each other's first readers, going back to Cixous's first forays into writing: in 1965 she sent the manuscript of what would eventually become *Le Prénom de Dieu* to Derrida, whose work she had read but whom she had only recently met, asking him to gauge its potential. Since that initial reading, drafts and proofs of yet unpublished work form the basis of many of the texts they have written about each other. In considering their "bibliographical crossings," in the words of Laurent Milesi, it appears that two manuscripts in particular set off several series of texts circulating between Cixous and Derrida: the manuscript of Derrida's "Circonfession" and the jointly written manuscript of *Voiles*.[2]

The first grouping of texts exchanged publicly between the two writers centers on Derrida's "Circonfession." Derrida had given the manuscript of this text to Cixous, who writes about it in "Contes de la Différence Sexuelle," an essay delivered at the conference "Lectures de la différence sexuelle" (1990).[3] At the same conference, and immediately following Cixous's presentation, Derrida delivered "Fourmis," an essay whose title evokes a dream Cixous recounted to Derrida over the telephone. "Fourmis" is thus not based on a manuscript or draft of Cixous's work; Derrida instead refers to his talk as a way of giving "un corps d'écriture publique" ("a body of public writing") to the dream, of attempting to "lui tailler un corps" ("carve out a body of writing") for the dream, giving it material form.[4] In this way, "Fourmis" appears to be an outlier: no physical artifact inspired the writing of "Fourmis," and it is unclear whether Derrida's preliminary notes for the essay ever reached Cixous's purview.[5] It therefore complicates notion of exchange, derailing what would otherwise be a back-and-forth around "Circonfession." Ten years after the 1990 conference, Cixous volleys back to Derrida with another body of writing in *Portrait de Jacques Derrida en Jeune Saint Juif*. In this book-length essay, first presented at the 2000 conference titled "Judéités: Questions pour Jacques Derrida," Cixous returns to "Circonfession," giving it a physical treatment inspired by the text itself. But in the interval between Cixous's two readings of "Circonfession," another manuscript sets off textual echoes between the two writers: the manuscript of *Voiles*.

Several years after the "Lectures de la différence sexuelle" conference, Cixous gave the manuscript of her short text "Savoir" to Derrida, who in response wrote his essay "Un ver à soie" while traveling between Buenos Aires, Santiago de Chile, and São Paulo. "Savoir" and "Un ver à soie" were published together twice: first with other texts in an issue of the journal *Contretemps* (1997), and then separately in *Voiles* (1998). Derrida then gave Cixous the entire manuscript of *Voiles*, combining both essays. The manuscript's unexpected rediscovery is the subject of Cixous's *Insister à Jacques Derrida* (2006). A half-year after Derrida's death, Cixous writes, "le manuscrit de *Voiles* a fait revenance depuis un de mes tiroirs où il dormait totalement oublié de moi" ("the manuscript of *Veils* made its ghostly return from out of one of my drawers where it had been sleeping utterly forgotten by me").[6] Even though the manuscript is in fact two manuscripts, two texts, written separately across an ocean, calling it "le manuscrit de *Voiles*" is one way of keeping it together, of highlighting Cixous's care not to see it split in two. Written nearly in parallel with *Insister*, Cixous's *Hyperrêve* echoes her concern with another manuscript: the volatility of Derrida's manuscript of *Fichus* causes it to disappear and reappear in Cixous's writing room. Along with *Fourmis*, we will see in chapter 5 that *Fichus* suggests alternative forms of communication, beyond physical handling. For now, we note that the "flying manuscripts," as Cixous calls *Voiles*, are beginning to multiply and pile up.[7]

In *Insister*, we learn that Derrida also entrusted Cixous with the manuscript of *Genèses, généalogies, genres . . . et le génie: Les Secrets de l'archive* (2004). One of Derrida's last published texts, *Genèses* . . . proposes to address the challenges of Cixous's archival collection at the BNF through readings of Cixous's *Rêve je te dis* and *Manhattan*, unpublished at the time. *Genèses* was given as a keynote speech at a conference inaugurating Cixous's archives, and on this same occasion Cixous presented the text titled "Le Livre que je n'écris pas," which was then interwoven into her book *Tours promises* (2004). Continuing the practice of weaving together Cixous's and Derrida's publicly read texts, *Tours promises* can be seen as an indirect response to Derrida's *Genèses*. However, although a late-stage typescript of *Tours promises* is conserved in the Derrida Library at Princeton, the location of the manuscripts of *Rêve je te dis* and *Manhattan*, which Derrida would have consulted to prepare *Genèses*, is undetermined.

Derrida entrusted the manuscript of *Genèses* to Cixous in a "geste d'urgence" ("urgent gesture") as an important object to be cared for and preserved.[8] According to Cixous, Derrida handed off the manuscript with a command to save and not to open it: "Cette fois c'est déposé entre mes mains que tu 'envoies,' . . . ceci écrit d'un très loin intérieur, dans une enveloppe fermée. À ne pas ouvrir. Sauf et sinon" ("This time it is deposited into my hands that you 'send,' from a wholly other great distance, this text written from a very distant interior, in a closed envelope. Not to be opened. Except and unless").[9] Cixous tells Derrida that this gesture parallels the previous one of receiving *Voiles*: "Tu remets à mes soins 1995 la garde d'un pli secret, en me recommandant de ne pas l'ouvrir" ("In 1995 you put into my care the keeping of a secret envelope, a secret fold, while recommending that I not open it"). In Cixous's description, Derrida's gift of his *Genèses* manuscript takes on an archival impulse, as she receives the manuscript, "déposé" ("deposited"), like an archival institution or an archivist.[10] The archival impulse here is furtive, secret, and urgent: best given to a friend, one who can act as an archive, a vault, both for the secrets contained within and as a caretaker for a delicate artifact.

From this series of manuscripts given and received, we could say that Derrida and Cixous considered the friend as a kind of archive particularly suited to ensuring the survival of a manuscript. Drafts of Cixous's manuscripts, often in their final stages, are preserved in the Derrida Library at Princeton.[11] Cixous was not the only recipient of Derrida's works in progress: he habitually entrusted his writing to a friend while traveling, fearful for a manuscript's loss or destruction. Speaking about the manuscript of *Le Toucher*, Derrida describes this habit: "Je laisse, par habitude, prudence et superstition, mon texte inachevé sur disquette à une amie dont je venais de faire la connaissance. Je pense toujours dans ces moments-là, entre autres choses, à l'accident d'avion" ("I leave, by habit, prudence, and superstition, my unfinished text on a disk with a friend whom I had just met. In these moments I always think about plane crashes, among other things").[12] Remarkable here is the floppy disk left in the care of someone Derrida barely knows but whom he trusts with this unfinished work, as if receiving the disk itself establishes friendship. Sharing a manuscript with others changes the status of the relationship, and can have effects on the status of the manuscript as well. Elisabeth Presa, the artist who received *Le Toucher*'s floppy disk, made use of this draft for her own purposes: she printed out a copy, and then folded, cut, and joined the paper into new forms, rendering the text itself unreadable, as Derrida himself noted.[13] From the floppy disk to the paper printout, the unfinished text continues to be reworked across media, and as a result the work continues on in a radically new form. The result of Derrida's safeguarding strategy, then, and its advantage, is not that it preserves the work in its original state, but that the transfer to another person invests the work with fluidity, shifting the physical form of a text as well as its content and intention.

This anecdote regarding *Le Toucher* suggests that Derrida's manuscripts may have been disseminated to many readers and friends. Focusing on manuscripts circulating between Derrida and Cixous in particular reveals a practice of giving, manipulating, and preserving that enhances the textual friendship between the two writers beyond their lifetimes. This comes through especially when, as we will see, the artifacts respond to and enfold each other in a way that physically transforms them. Cixous's and Derrida's awareness of this process and its effects on their archives comes through in discussions of their approaches to sharing manuscripts.

The concatenation of Cixous and Derrida's textual dialogue forms a dense archive that attempts to incorporate the two writers' friendship. This results in a material overlap that complicates notions of property when it comes to archives—especially as the manuscripts become enfolded, as they regularly are, into new work. *Voiles* becomes part of *Insister*, just as "Circonfession" is integral to *Portrait de Jacques Derrida en Jeune Saint Juif*, and *Le Prénom de Dieu* is imbricated in *H. C. pour la vie* as well as in *Double Oubli de l'Orang-Outang*. In whose archives does the manuscript of each of these texts belong? In which collection? In which dossier? The manuscripts of *Rêve je te dis* and *Manhattan*, two major texts by Cixous, are missing from the archives: they are neither in Derrida's collections nor in Cixous's. Similarly, the original manuscripts of several of Derrida's major later works, "Circonfession," "Un ver à soie," and *Fichus*, are absent from Derrida's collections, where these rare and valuable handwritten artifacts would stand out against the printouts of final drafts and proofs with minor handwritten annotations that populate the Derrida collections at the IMEC and UC Irvine. They would seem instead to belong in the BNF's *fonds* Cixous, especially as they become integrated into her writing: *Portrait de Jacques Derrida*, *Insister*, and *Hyperrêve* include readings of "Circonfession," "Un ver à soie," and *Fichus* respectively, making specific reference to the manuscripts of these texts. Questions of belonging, property, and appropriation become especially important in Cixous's treatment of the manuscripts, which serves to continually reinvigorate the writing of and between the two writers, and to extend their friendship in posthumous archival collaboration. The archival conventions of provenance, authorship, and chronology (original order) are complicated when sharing a manuscript suggests a form of reading that reactivates an affective connection through handling and touch.

Reading a manuscript does not necessarily entail preservation, but instead actively transforms the artifact at hand. Although this could be understood on some level as destructive reading, as it submits the manuscript to the risks of damage and disintegration by heavy hands, I see it instead as reparative reading, in both an affective and a physical sense. In her essay "Paranoid Reading, Reparative Reading," Eve Kosofsky Sedgwick develops the reparative mode, borrowed from psychoanalysis, as a method of reading that accounts for emotion and affect, which have too often been disparaged by hermeneutics, in her view. According to Sedgwick, the "hermeneutics of suspicion" is characterized by a paranoid attitude whose goal is to expose and exhibit the content of a text in order to avoid being (unpleasantly) surprised.[14] For the reparative reader, on the other hand, surprise is not always unpleasant and can be a pleasurable, necessary attitude toward reading. Archive and manuscript studies have benefited from Sedgwick's discussion of reparative and paranoid reading. Recent methodologies devote attention to the surface level of the text, which is reinvested with meaning after having long been associated with superficiality and artifice, as opposed to a more authentic depth in which truth hides.[15] Citing Sedgwick's earlier work on the secret in *Epistemology of the Closet*, Anjali Arondekar writes against the archival methodology of exposure and extraction in relation to sexuality in colonial archives, and emphasizes the need to develop alternative methodologies of reading and archival practice.[16] In this chapter, I identify strategies of reading between Derrida and Cixous that constitute psychological and physical reparative reading. Building on the affective charge of the reparative mode, I show how the sensual, tactile engagement with a friend's text is crucial to maintaining a dialogue interrupted by death. This form of close reading has as its goal not the discovery of new meaning or textual analysis, but the maintenance of relationships. Communication, connection, and care take place at the surface level of the literary artifact.

As Cixous becomes a reparative reader in her attempts to continue her conversation with Derrida after his death and to reinvest mourning with creative potential, the archive becomes a source of solace and of material for new writing. This material often consists of actual physical literary artifacts that act as affective nodal points connecting the two writers, repairing the rift death has wrought between them. But the "exchange" between Cixous and Derrida is not easily traced through discrete documents: manuscripts shared between the two writers may turn up in unexpected places, or not exist at all. Instead of identifying and studying a set of significant individual manuscripts, then, I propose to focus attention at a more granular level, tracing points of contact on the artifacts' surfaces as records of the rhythms of correspondence between Cixous and Derrida. Literary artifacts consist of accretions of writings and readings that take shape through annotations, which attest to the vibrancy of a document that has passed through many hands. Taking these accretions into account, I suggest an expansive view of annotations: to annotate is to make a mark, whether in the form of marginalia, hand- or fingerprints and other traces of touch, highlighting, coloring, underlining, cuts, staples, folds, creating points of contact that can be understood as additions, supplements, renewals, comments, dialogue, marking a territory, a sign of life or of presence. These points of contact or points of attachment stitch together successive readings and writings, across readers and archives.

The split manuscript becomes emblematic of the separation between Cixous and Derrida, as well as of the potential for reconnecting through reparative reading. As we have seen in chapter 1, the material presence of the manuscript as other—though not as a stand-in for the beloved dead—destabilizes the idea of identity and property associated with single-author manuscripts. It does so by overriding the metonymic connection between manuscript and author, by being physically handled by someone else. The friend must literally "porter l'autre" ("carry the other"), as Derrida has said in *Béliers*, must become responsible for the other's afterlife in manuscript form. Through this connection of friend to archive, putting a manuscript back together—as we see in the case of *Voiles* and "Circonfession"—becomes a way of re-membering, re-living friendship, making it live on.

Sharing and Repairing "Circonfession"

"Circonfession" is shot through with a desire for a re-membering reading. The text is concerned with the changes in Derrida's writing process over time through different technologies of writing, and the implications for the limits of the body and writing technologies, of the body *as* writing technology. As we have seen, "Circonfession" explores how writing's materiality can ensure its survival as an "unpredictable thing" working between technologies of writing, between Derrida's *sublime*, his attic space filled with books and manuscripts, and his word-processing computer, nicknamed *subjectile*—and how a focus on materiality in "Circonfession" ensures that writing is more than an extension of the author. At stake in this text is a concern for the legacy of writing: how it will be received, read, and preserved.

As we have seen in chapter 3, "Circonfession" begins with what appears to be a conventional metaphor of writing, that of words flowing like blood onto the page. The writing is likened to the writer's life force:

> Je rêve d'une plume qui soit une seringue . . . une fois trouvée la juste veine, plus aucun labeur, aucune responsabilité, aucun risque de mauvais goût ni de violence, le sang se livre seul . . . le volume de sang, incroyable pour l'enfant que je reste ce soir, expose au-dehors, donc à sa mort, ce qu'il y aura eu de plus vivant en moi.
>
> I dream of a pen that would be a syringe . . . once the right vein has been found, no more toil, no more responsibility, no risk of bad taste nor violence, the blood delivers itself all alone . . . the volume of blood, incredible amount for the child I remain this evening, should expose outward, and thus to its death, what will have been most alive in me.[17]

In the ideal writing scenario Derrida describes here, the writing instrument—"une plume," a quill or a fountain pen nib—allows for interiority and life (*vivant*) to be drawn out onto the page, without any effort on the part of the writer. The "risk" that the writer runs is not in the disclosure of content that spills out onto the page, but that the act of exposure confronts "le vivant" with its death. Yet this exposure is not grounds for anxiety: it provokes instead a "glorieux apaisement" ("glorious appeasement"), a sense of relief or peace.[18] The syringe pen evokes transfusion, calling up possibilities of contamination but also of a life-saving process of fluid transfer. This kind of mark-making is more than a facile metaphor linking ink and blood that would seamlessly connect the identity of writing to the biological identity of the writer in a supposedly perfect autobiographical pact[19]—it also reinforces the provisional state of writing, favoring the act of writing in its unstable state over the result or product.

The marks evoked in "Circonfession"—the *skizzes*, as Derrida calls them, "stocked" in the attic as "le corpus infini, ma skizzolâtrie en carnets" ("the infinite corpus, my skizzolatry in notebooks")—do not consist of discrete points, but rather of dynamic liquids, including bodily fluids.[20] The fluidity of the *skizzes* illustrates the writer's desire for sharing with others, for reaching across the borders of the artifact and spilling over, exceeding and excessive. Indeed, the word *skizzes*, German for "sketch," is close to the Italian *schizzo*, a squirt, splash, stain, or spot: a mark made by misbehaving liquid. With his focus on *skizzes*, Derrida draws attention to liquidity, evoking ink on the manuscript page along with the bodily fluids that accompany "les skizzes de ma circoncision," including blood, as well as saliva, sweat, and sperm: "*le mélange sur cette cène incroyable du vin et du sang, le donner à voir comme je le vois sur mon sexe chaque fois que du sang se mêle au sperme ou à la salive de la fellation*" ("*the mixture on this incredible supper of the wine and blood, let people see it how I see it on my sex each time blood is mixed with sperm or the saliva of fellatio*").[21]

The liquid *skizzes* of writing are embodied and physical to the point of intimate seduction. In Period 30, it seems that the bodily fluids Derrida seeks to mobilize in writing are not, in fact, mere metaphor. He aims to "*décrire mon sexe . . . jusqu'à crever le papier, faire baver, mouiller les lèvres, en haut et en bas, de tous les lecteurs . . .*" ("*describe my sex . . . until the paper breaks, make all the readers drool, wet lips, high and low . . .*").[22] Derrida quotes from his handwritten *skizzes* notebooks (italicized above and in the text), drawing a parallel between, on the one hand, the project in which he sets out to "décrire mon sexe" in order to seduce his readers, and, on the other hand, the legibility of his handwriting, suggesting that it is not merely a matter of content that will provoke the intended corporeal effect of getting his readers' juices flowing. Over the years his handwriting has "perdu sa verticalité interrompue, presque à chaque lettre, pour se lier de mieux en mieux mais se lire de plus en plus mal depuis près de vingt ans" ("lost its uninterrupted verticality, almost with every letter, to be bound better and better but be read less and less well over almost twenty years").[23] If his handwriting has become less legible over the years, it has become more connected, giving the effect of an increased fluidity. This is the inverse of what is said to be a transformation of Derrida's writing style from the dense, difficult philosophical texts of the 1960s and '70s to the more "reader-friendly" autobiographical and political texts of the 1980s onward—a second "period" that "Circonfession" inaugurates. So if Derrida becomes more readable over the years, it is because he adopts the typewriter and the computer as writing implements; his handwriting, on the other hand, is increasingly unreadable yet more fluid. The fluidity of writing is crucial to the transfer from writing to reading body that Derrida calls for in "Circonfession."

The effect Derrida seeks to achieve through his *subjectile* and its *skizzes* draws out the reader's desire in the form of sensual secretions. This diverges markedly from Derrida's first assessment of the *subjectile* in Antonin Artaud's drawings. Artaud's *subjectile* is riddled with "une opération de la main, voire d'une arme à feu, d'une sorte de foudre qui attaque le support même du *Sort*, mimant ou préparant des coups portés au destinataire" ("an operation of the hand, or even of a firearm, a sort of lightning that attacks the very support of the *Sort*, miming or preparing blows striking the addressee").[24] Both for Derrida and Artaud, the *subjectile* is the crucial medium of interaction, though it is unclear if for Derrida the *subjectile* he alludes to in Period 36 is a paper support ("faire crever le papier") or the computer *subjectile* that appears later in "Circonfession." But while Artaud's *subjectile* carries the physical force of the *jet*, the force behind the thrown pro*ject*ile, the *jet* in Derrida's *subjectile* is more fluid: a spurt, squirt, or spray.[25] Evoking the transformation of his own handwriting over the years, Derrida prompts another question about the future of his writing and its legibility: what happens to the marks when the accumulation of *skizzes* causes the paper to burst?

Despite their idiosyncrasy, their intimacy, their secrecy—or perhaps precisely because of these—the *skizzes* can and must be shared. The *skizzes* are one of the "unpredictable things" that allow for an afterlife of writing, "des choses improbables qui déstabilisent, déconcertent, surprennent à leur tour le programme de G . . . *unpredictable things* pour lui survivre" ("improbable things which destabilize, disconcert, surprise in their turn G's program . . . *unpredictable things* to survive him").[26] If "Circonfession" can escape a totalizing "programme" of indexing and interpretation, it will do so through a desirous, shared writing: "il faut . . . retrouver la jouissance indéfiniment réactivable, ce qui donne envie d'écrire comme de jouir au moment de démanger l'effet de circoncision pour le donner en partage" ("we must . . . rediscover the indefinitely reactivable enjoyment, what makes one want to write and to come at the moment of itching the effect of circumcision to share it with others").[27] If effective, the text will provoke a writing akin to *jouissance* that is continuous in part because it is shared with someone else. Derrida ups the ante by suggesting that reading will not be enough; the reader will be prompted in turn to write, and thus to "reactivate" the pleasure of the text.

As a reader of "Circonfession"—perhaps the text's first reader—Cixous is attuned to the sharing the text desires and demands. Her reading, fully developed in *Portrait de Jacques Derrida en Jeune Saint Juif*, involves physically manipulating the text: Cixous cuts, staples, photocopies, and annotates Derrida's "périodes." Despite the violence of some of these acts, the various annotations that comprise Cixous's physical treatment of "Circonfession" in fact reframe it as a reparative reading process. Cixous's reading method in *Portrait* is represented in colored handwritten annotations made onto passages of "Circonfession," interspersed throughout the published text. The annotations emphasize letters, words, and phrases, recopying them in the margins where they are reordered to constitute a new key to reading Derrida's text. From Period 17, for example, Cixous pulls *l'histoire*, *li*, *ile*, *lie*, *secret*, *lis*, *il*, *littérature*, *philosophie*, *religion*, *politique*, *sca*, *escarre*, *sk*, *l'i*, and *sec*, in which she finds anagrammatically encrypted the phrase "Les lits secrets d'Elie, ou l'hypothèse." Her syllabic interpretation is at once heard phonetically and made visual, resulting in a multisensorial apprehension for Cixous as well as for the reader. This close reading is the assiduous work of textual explication, a methodical reading process with a religious genealogy: Talmudic hermeneutics, followed by the exegesis of Christian Church Fathers, opened up to the interpretation of secular and poetic texts with the rise of the discipline of philology in the nineteenth century.[28] The method Cixous uses in *Portrait de Jacques Derrida en Jeune Saint Juif* is the hermeneutic and philological work of passionate attachment to language, to the letter of the text. But when Cixous takes Derrida literally, she also means physically. Her reading is a demonstration of linguistic and poetic virtuosity applied to Derrida's text "Circonfession," as Cixous explains: "J'ai compris qu'il fallait le prendre au mot, à la lettre, à la cime, littéralement, à la virgule aussi . . . minutieusement en poussant l'attention jusqu'au tatillonnement" ("I realized I had to take him at his word, to the letter, to the summit, literally, to the comma as well . . . meticulously, being attentive to the point of finickiness").[29] This is a literal close reading that seizes upon words and letters, taking hold of them in a new color, and in this way it distinguishes itself from the "hermeneutics of suspicion" Sedgwick characterizes as paranoid reading. In Derrida's phonetic and thematic constellation, illuminated through Cixous's reading, each letter can be felt to resonate—we hear *tâtonnement* (fumbling) within *tatillonnement*—so that reading "Circonfession" becomes just as tactile as the writing of the text.

Frédéric Regard calls Cixous's method "highlighting," an operation that corresponds, as he notes, to the annotations made in the manuscript of *Portrait de Jacques Derrida* at the BNF.[30] Cixous used yellow, pink, and orange highlighting markers on the passages of "Circonfession" to signal the letters and phonemes relevant to her reading.[31] Caressing the surface of the paper, the highlighter is translated typographically by printing letters in blue or orange ink to correspond to Cixous's handwritten annotations that decorate the margins. In her manuscript, the pages Cixous highlights are not re-transcriptions of passages from "Circonfession," nor are they simple photocopies of the volume *Derrida*, where Derrida's *périodes*, each spanning four pages, are printed on thirteen or fewer lines on the bottom third of the page under Geoffrey Bennington's text "Derridabase." Cixous assembles her own copy of the passages. Having photocopied the four pages of a *période* from the published book, Cixous cuts Derrida's text off the bottom of each page and staples the parts to a blank sheet of paper. The *période*, once a horizontal margin in the published volume, is now a vertical column on a single page, allowing for a nearly continuous reading of the entire passage. This reconfiguration is then photocopied to facilitate Cixous's highlighting work. The marks of the staples render visually, though not palpably, on the photocopy that Cixous highlights, and the manuscript is marked by a slight gap every thirteen lines, like scars or stretch marks that accompany the staples' sutures. Cixous's reading method engages this symbolic visual aspect of marks on a textual body: "Je lis aussi d'un œil attentif à ce qui arrive à la peau et la chair du texte, incision, greffe d'un fragment prélevé sur une autre partie du temps . . . sur papier mais gravé au couteau sur l'âme" ("Here too I read attentively watching for what happens to the skin and flesh of the text, incision, graft of a fragment lifted from another segment of time one stitches it up again . . . on paper but scored with a knife in the soul").[32] Just as Cixous determines that "il fallait le prendre au mot, à la lettre," ("I had to take him at his word, to the letter"), the manuscript of *Portrait de Jacques Derrida* also show traces of "what happens" to writing, which is especially significant in a text thinking through the implications of cutting the body.[33]

During a public discussion in 2007, Cixous affirmed that the *mise-en-page* of the annotated, color-coded passages interspersed throughout *Portrait de Jacques Derrida* was intended as "un retour au manuscrit de 'Circonfession,' à la page telle qu'elle s'était *déroulée*, précisément, dans le mouvement de la première coulée, . . . au plus près de la source de l'écriture, de la manuscripture de Derrida" ("a return to the manuscript of 'Circonfession," to the page as it had unfolded, precisely, in the movement of the first flow, . . . as close as possible to the source of writing, to Derrida's handwriting").[34] Returning to the manuscript, which Derrida had given her in 1990, Cixous's reading of "Circonfession" is based on the physical form of the artifact. As we can see from the page of the manuscript that is reproduced in the book *Portrait de Jacques Derrida*, each long passage of "Circonfession" was confined to a single page. Cixous works from this formatting in her analysis of Derrida's text. Indeed, Derrida continued this *mise-en-page* from the manuscript of "Circonfession" to the typescripts, which are conserved at UC Irvine: each period takes up one full printed page, a layout that is maintained in successive versions. These various forms of "Circonfession"—in Cixous's papers, in a university's special collections, and in Cixous's preliminary annotations at the BNF and published in *Portrait*—reiterate a textual format that diverges from the layout published in the volume *Derrida*. Although Cixous claims that her work hews closely to Derrida's "manuscripture" found on the manuscript of "Circonfession" in her possession, the "mouvement de la première coulée" ("movement of the first flow") in fact extends beyond those handwritten pages to the layout on the computer, from the first drafts of the text.[35] Taken together, the archival presence of this text and Cixous's readings in *Portrait* create an alternative status for Derrida's text beyond its publication trajectory.

Furthermore, Cixous's work in *Portrait de Jacques Derrida* is not a simple reconstitution of Derrida's texts. Cixous also describes the pages she prepared for *Portrait* as "[des] greffe[s] d'un fragment prélevé sur une autre partie du temps" ("graft of a fragment lifted from another segment of time").[36] Alluding to Derrida's work on the graft and its implications for notions of body, writing, self, and other, the "greffe d'un fragment" in Cixous's *Portrait* also echoes the structure of "Circonfession," in which Derrida grafts selected passages from Saint Augustine's *Confessions* as well as from his own handwritten notebooks of autobiographical and scholarly notes on circumcision.[37] None of these notebooks are preserved in any of Derrida's collections, but the "Circonfession" dossier at UC Irvine does contain photocopies that extract from the notebooks the passages Derrida intended to integrate into his typewritten periods: a form of "prélèvement," in Cixous's words, a sample collected or lifted from a body for a medical procdure.[38] Cixous's treatment of "Circonfession," with its *greffes* and *agrafes*, grafts and staples, and the *mise-en-page* of *Portrait de Jacques Derrida*, echo the techniques Derrida employed in his essay.

Neither highlighting nor stapling is mentioned directly in *Portrait*, but Cixous's reading method, which is in evidence on the annotated pages of "Circonfession" in the archived dossier of *Portrait*, make use of these techniques to significant symbolic effect. The *agrafe* in particular, with its phonetic proximity to the *greffe*, proves to be a richly reparative gesture that links up the two texts. This operation does not reverse time or conjure up an *avant-texte* in order to restage a nostalgic moment. Cixous remakes the manuscript of "Circonfession" for her annotations even though she has Derrida's handwritten manuscript with her as she writes *Portrait*. The resulting text is not simply a restitution of the text's original, manuscript form, making Derrida's "periods" all fit on one page instead of running along the bottom margin of the book object. This metaphor would cast Cixous as a surgeon of Derrida's body-text, mangled in the operation of circumcision or of publication, and restored in the archive. Instead, her reparative reading lingers again and again over what is present—the *greffe*—toggling between the manuscript artifact she has received and the published text with its unique layout. What she repairs is not the manuscript's original state, but the experience of activated, physical reading that animates Derrida's essay from the beginning.[39] She is thus able to "retrouver la jouissance indéfiniment réactivable," as Derrida suggested in "Circonfession" ("rediscover the indefinitely reactivable enjoyment"), grappling with a physical presence in order to ensure that writing survives and continues on in a new form created through her reading, as she leaves traces of her engagement with the beloved artifact.[40]

Cixous's treatment of Derrida's manuscript is a literal rendering of the autobiographical experience that Derrida's text seeks to portray and problematize: the physical and psychic scars left by the incisions of circumcision, and the tenuous link between the circumcised body and a religious tradition. Derrida questions the validity of this link in several ways in "Circonfession": by interweaving the Christian Saint Augustine with his own research on circumcision as a Jewish rite; by exploring the consequences of his mother's illness, which prevents her from recognizing her son; and by evoking his decision not to circumcise his sons, breaking with his family's religious tradition and lineage.[41] As an ambiguous autobiographical text, then, "Circonfession" casts doubt on the writer's ability to characterize himself as Jewish. Cixous's reading emphasizes Derrida's exploration of circumcision's effects and its implications for autobiographical writing.

The dialogue between "Circonfession" and *Portrait de Jacques Derrida* stages an interrogation of the limits of life writing as an individual practice by foregrounding autobiographical elements the two writers have in common. In *Portrait*, Cixous reminds the reader that, like Derrida, she was brought up Jewish in Algeria. She writes, "nous avons en miroir un nombre de stigmates précis et datés: Algérie 1940" ("we have in common a number of precise and dated stigmata: Algeria 1940"), referencing the expulsions and exclusions of the pro-Nazi Vichy regime in Algeria.[42] Cixous recasts the "stigmates" as "noblessures" in a joint interview with Derrida in which the two writers discuss their connection to Algeria.[43] Born into Jewish families in El Biar (Derrida) and Oran (Cixous), stripped of French nationality by the Vichy regime, both Cixous and Derrida experience exclusion and, ultimately, voluntary exile (both writers left Algeria for Paris).

But what occurs in *Portrait de Jacques Derrida* is not simply the recognition of a similar shared experience. The graft as theme and technique has implications for whether this book can be designated an autobiographical text. Mara Negrón describes Cixous's autobiographical pseudo-portraiture as a "greffe de genre" and as a literal operation of grafting through the colored "greffes electives" of the highlighted letters in the published text.[44] Genre grafting is at work at the surface level of the manuscripts of Cixous's and Derrida's two texts. With her treatment of the manuscript as a body, Cixous's grafting operation complicates the idea that life writing is performed by an individual, human subject. Her method of reading accounts for the inscription of text on a physical surface that is both the support of writing and becomes a textual body itself.[45] Just as human bodies are marked by various techniques of engraving, and can thus be taken as interpretable surfaces, the literary artifact can be understood as an inscribed body of a different kind. Cixous's reading suggests that we take this correlation literally, as she offers a novel approach to textual analysis that reads the entire artifact as a body, distinct from human life, including from the individual who created it. The question is not *whose* body the manuscript represents, but *what kind* of body we are holding in our hands when we read this text, and what kinds of life writing, or live writing, are at work on these artifacts. Cixous's reading foregrounds the artifact, emphasizing the archival afterlife of "Circonfession."

Touching, Stitching, and Folding *Voiles*

If "Circonfession" and *Portrait de Jacques Derrida* destabilize the unique, singular autobiographical subject by requiring and enacting a physical, sensual sharing of the text, *Voiles* makes further inroads into life writing by questioning the text as property belonging to the author, friend, or reader. Published in 1998, *Voiles* combines two texts in dialogue: Derrida's essay "Un ver à soie" ("A Silkworm of One's Own") is a reading of Cixous's "Savoir" (the title is maintained in the English translation) that provokes a meditation on gender and the Jewish faith (like "Circonfession"), in this case through the religious laws governing the appropriate use of the tallith, the prayer shawl, meant to be worn exclusively by men. As it spirals out from Cixous's text, "Un ver à soie" becomes one of Derrida's most poetic pieces of writing. This can be seen most clearly in its final pages: a dense italicized coda about a "souvenir d'enfance" ("childhood memory") of raising and observing silkworms. Set in an Algerian summer, the scene of wonderment provoked in the narrator, on the brink of puberty, by these creatures (*des vers*) is, Derrida says, the in*ver*se of a dream (*un rêve*), and an awakening to an awareness of subjecthood, truth (*vérité*), and poetry (*le vers*). In presenting this childhood memory of raising silkworms as a moment of metamorphosis, Derrida highlights the instability of identity: of the silkworms', and of his own.

Observing the silkworms, the narrator of this childhood memory first highlights their radical otherness and indecidability. Although it was possible to "trouver un sens à la chose" ("find some sense in the thing") by sorting out which end was the head and which was the tail, Derrida recalls that "il était impossible de discerner un sexe" ("it was impossible to discern a sex").[46] It is also difficult to see where the silkworm begins and ends, to distinguish between the silkworm and the silk it secretes: "Il sécrétait une chose qui ne lui serait jamais un objet . . . Il ne se séparait pas de son œuvre . . . une chose qui lui appartenait et lui revenait en propre" ("It secreted a thing that would never be an object to it, an object for it . . . It did not separate itself from its work . . . a thing that belonged to it, to whom it was properly due"). If the product of the silkworm's labor, its biological process, belongs to it and is "proper" to it, this preliminary state will give way, Derrida suggests, to a secondary stage, wherein the larvae will transform into moths and thereby be separated from their "œuvre."

In this way, the silkworms' irrevocable shift from larva to moth, which appears to the human observer to be a total transformation, is paralleled in the coda of "Un ver à soie" as a *crise d'adolescence*, a coming-of-age: Derrida's memory takes place "avant mes treize ans" ("before I was thirteen"). After weaving themselves into a silk cocoon, the silkworms begin to darken. They are marked by the appearance of "[une] tache humide . . . un sang inconnu, rouge presque noir" that announces a rupturing of the silkworm's skin "pour ouvrir le passage aux ailes du papillon" ("the damp patch would finally appear . . . an unknown blood, a red almost black"; "that open the way for the moth's wings").[47] The visual marker of maturation is rendered by the term *véraison*, in bold in Derrida's text to figure the change in color the term signifies, a change reinforced by the mulberry leaves the boy feeds the silkworms (in French, *mûrier* contains *mûr*, "ripe"). The darkening of *véraison* evokes ink, linking the coming-of-age to a coming-to-writing.[48]

Though it concludes the essay, the silkworm seems an apt figure for an initiatory scene, figuring the time before an author begins to write: this is the autobiographical status of the silkworm in this text. This scene could also prefigure a scene of writing in which the silkworm is likened to the *avant-texte*, a term that describes an indeterminate, as-yet unidentified state of textual production, before it is transformed into a published text, which would represent its mature, adult, ripened state. Indeed, the word *avant* is repeated throughout "Un ver à soie," serving as a "point," a stitch, that sutures the text from beginning to end: from the opening "Avant le verdict, le mien" ("Before the verdict, my verdict," a phrase that is bolded, in a typographic link to the worms' darkening at the end), to the beginning of the italicized worm-text, "Avant mes treize ans" ("Before I was thirteen").[49] The text is preoccupied with the prepositional preliminary state, with a temporality that accounts for the indeterminate and undecided, a moment before transformation, before "revelation" (a word Derrida also uses), where wonder can exist: a moment of naive pleasure in looking, touching, and reading. Read in this way, memory and remembering would not lead to wholeness, to recovering a lost moment in one's life, but could instead reactivate the indeterminateness of the past, preliminary state in the present. If the silkworm and its secretion metaphorically correlate to the adolescent writer-to-be and the *avant-texte*, the manuscript of this text would also be linked to the writer ("il ne se séparait pas de son œuvre"; "it did not separate itself from its work"). But the relationship between the writer and the manuscript of "Un ver à soie" is complicated by being in dialogue with another text: Cixous's "Savoir."

Immediately before the dense account of raising silkworms, Derrida explains how he came to recall this childhood memory: "Je venais de lire *Savoir*. Et avant de fermer les yeux pour céder au sommeil, je me laissai envahir, comme on dit . . . par un souvenir d'enfance" ("I had just read *Savoir*. And before closing my eyes to give in to sleep, I let myself be invaded, as they say . . . by a childhood memory").[50] After having read Cixous's text, Derrida allows himself to be invaded, taken over, overwhelmed or engulfed, by the memory that follows. The narrator is transformed by otherness and projected into a new state of being that is poetic writing. The silkworms are not a fiction, a tale he has spun, but are instead "un vrai souvenir d'enfance, l'envers d'un rêve, et là je ne brode plus" ("a true childhood memory, the opposite of a dream, and here I embroider no longer").[51] Yet the relationship between fiction and reality, truth and poetry, dreaming and waking, is complicated by a question of authorship. The "souvenir d'enfance" seems to arise of its own accord: "je me laissai envahir . . . par un souvenir d'enfance." But invoking "Savoir" shifts the driving force behind the memory and the final section of "Un ver à soie" to an unidentified other, suggesting that it is not Derrida who spins out this tale, but that "Savoir" is its maker: "Pour ce qui arrive (l'opération que je n'opère pas, celle qui m'opère) il faut *Savoir*, un autre *Savoir*, le voici, celui de l'autre" ("For what happens [the operation I don't operate, the one that operates me], you must *Savoir*, another *Savoir*, here it is, the other's"), Derrida writes to introduce the final section of "Un ver à soie."[52] But who is "l'autre" here? Whose "*Savoir*" is being invoked here? Derrida describes Hélène Cixous's writing as "l'opération d'écriture poétique" ("the operation of poetic writing") earlier in "Un ver à soie," and the link of the "opération" suggests that her writing—here, "Savoir"—is what triggers "ce qui arrive" ("what happens") at the end of Derrida's text.[53] If, as Derrida suggests, we read the closing passage as "un autre *Savoir*, le voici, celui de l'autre" ("another *Savoir*, here it is, the other's"), and if it is impossible to distinguish between the maker and the product, then the writing of this coda is itself akin to the silkworm's operation. Derrida writes: "Ce que je m'appropriais sans le retourner vers moi . . . c'était l'opération, l'opération à travers laquelle le ver lui-même sécrétait sa sécrétion. . . . Il sécrétait une chose qui ne lui serait jamais un objet, . . . il ne se séparait pas de son œuvre" ("What I appropriated for myself . . . was the operation, the operation through which the worm itself secreted its secretion. . . . It secreted a thing that would never be an object to it, . . . it did not separate itself from its work").[54] But it is unclear in this parallel whose operation, whose oeuvre, this is. Who is the silkworm here? Derrida, Cixous? "Savoir"?

To get out of this metaphoric tangle, I propose to consider "l'opération d'écriture poétique" that projects Derrida into this "autre *Savoir*" as a *metonymic* relationship established through touch. Although Derrida does not explicitly mention holding "Savoir" as he drifts off, the sensual reading experience is physically enfolded into the reader's consciousness: this is suggested by the published text as well as the manuscript. His reading involves a kind of touching that, by increasing proximity (*vers*), creates something new.[55] This metonymic relation allows for the possibility of mutual transformations between manuscripts and readers in contact: a passage through difference represented by a tactile gesture that is crucial to Derrida's elaboration of

Voiles's final pages. Touch links "Savoir" to "Un ver à soie" as well as to Derrida's tallith, which is discussed in the main section of his essay. The tallith is "une châle de prière que j'aime à toucher plus qu'à voir . . . alors même qu'il demeure enveloppé dans un sac de papier où je plonge la main dans la nuit les yeux fermés" ("a prayer shawl I like to touch more than to see, . . . even when it remains wrapped in a paper bag into which I stick my hand at night, eyes closed"), a gesture echoed when Derrida finishes reading Cixous's text "avant de fermer les yeux pour céder au sommeil" ("before closing my eyes to give in to sleep").[56] Touch links up four elements: tallith, silkworm, "Savoir," and "Un ver à soie." All four are textual-textural objects determined by their tactile relationship to self and other as *vivant*, living. As textiles, the tallith and the worm's silk are inseparable from the living beings that produced them: the silkworm "ne se séparait pas de son œuvre" ("did not separate itself from its work"), and the tallith's material must necessarily be "pris sur du vivant" and, of equal importance, "porté par du vivant."[57] Derrida elaborates on the meaning of "vivant" here: "Vivant, c'est à dire qui aura eu quelque rapport à soi. Le vivant, c'est la possibilité de l'auto-affection, du temps et du retard: ce qui, dans l'affection de soi, aura pu se toucher" ("The tallith must be something living taken from something living worn by something living. . . . Living, that is something that will have had some relation to itself [*à soi*]. The living is the possibility of auto-affection, of time and delay: what, in self-affection, will have been able to touch itself").[58] The tallith is inseparable from the animal it is made from, and its auto-affection is enhanced by the woven textile folding over onto itself. But this is not unique to the textile objects involved in *Voiles*; touching affects the texts as well. Just as "le tallith *se touche*" ("the tallith *touches itself*"), Derrida establishes that "le toucher de *Savoir* est un se-toucher des lèvres" ("the touch of *Savoir* is a self-touching of the lips"), drawing a parallel between Cixous's essay and the tallith.[59]

The dense text of "Savoir," Derrida suggests, is rendered phonetically richer by the play of labial consonants, as if written by lips instead of by hand: a designation that emphasizes speech as tactile and embodied.[60] Derrida's reading of Cixous's text is animated by a sensitivity to the "vocables en V."[61] The Vs "fabrique[nt]" ("fabricate") what Derrida calls "l'unique poème" that is Cixous's text.[62] Derrida draws out the "se toucher des lèvres" ("self-touching of the lips") in his emphasis on certain consonants in the chain of key words, including *véraison*, *ver*, *rêve*, and *vrai*. The phonetic thread contained in *véraison* links the worms (*vers à soie*), a near anagram of "Savoir," *l'envers* (reverse, flipside, inside), and a dream (*un rêve*), as well as poetry (*le vers*), truth (*vérité*), and even sight (in an evocation of the Spanish verb *ver*, "to see," resonating in geographic proximity as Derrida composes the essay on a trip to South America). The phoneme that traverses "tous les morceaux grouillants de mots en *ver*" ("all the crawling bits of words with *ver*-"), from *ver* to *véraison*, becomes a thread connecting "Un ver à soie" to "Savoir," the foundation of Derrida's reading and analysis.[63]

The insistent V appears as a tactile aspect of the physical text. In "Un ver à soie," Derrida proposes to imagine his essay as "un parchemin [dont] les autres mots, les mots sans V auraient été brûlés" ("Imagine too a parchment on which all the other words, the words without V have been burned"),[64] emphasizing the provisional, archival quality of his text and its physical state, susceptible to burn marks, which would touch the non-V words and thereby eliminate them. The marks he makes on his typescript copy of "Savoir" have the inverse effect: the Vs are all underlined in thick blue and black marker.[65] Derrida's textual annotation is an "operation" that echoes Cixous's "opération d'écriture poétique," as it underscores the labial play, the "se toucher," of Cixous's text. Each underlined V becomes a key to the Vs referenced in "Un ver à soie," and each V echoing between the two texts thus constitutes a V "piqué sur l'autre voile" ("stitched on the other veil"), referencing the subtitle of Derrida's essay. The ambiguity of this formulation further reinforces the two texts' connection: the Vs could be stolen from or stitched onto ("piqués"); and "l'autre voile" could refer to "Savoir," "Un ver à soie," or the annotated typescript. This indeterminacy continues beyond Derrida's essay to further readings by Cixous and others. Derrida's annotations on Cixous's typescript reinforce his reading, and examining the manuscript reveals that not only the Vs but other marks also act as reparative stitches to ensure the connection between the two essays.

Derrida's annotated Vs stitch the manuscript to the published text, and stitch the two essays together. Other marks on the manuscript of "Un ver à soie" encourage the reader to consider the preliminary drafts of Cixous's and Derrida's essays together as one manuscript. Discovering Derrida's handwritten manuscript half a year after his death, Cixous realizes that "Points de vue piqués sur l'autre voile" was the essay's original title—later changed to the subtitle of "Un ver à soie." *Points* becomes the watchword for Cixous's reading of the manuscript in *Insister*. The title's "points" take shape on Derrida's manuscript in the form of large black dots, much larger than standard punctuation marks, darkened by hand. Marking out intervals in the text, these dots serve both to separate the text and to stitch it together: this is the double meaning of "des points piqués," both stolen and applied, that the title indicates. As they structure the manuscript page, they also serve as *points de repères*, signposts or bearings for the reader. Feeling lost as she confronts the manuscript, wondering how to read it, Cixous herself asks, "quel genre de lecture peut-on effectuer lorsque l'on se trouve quelque peu invité, invitée, logé(e), dans le texte à lire?" ("what kind of reading can one perform when one finds oneself to some degree invited, lodged, within the text to be read?").[66] The black marks rise up as invitations "logées" within the manuscript, and then quickly transform into a kind of mirror for the reader, who identifies with the dot: "Je me trouve soudain quelque ressemblance avec ce • point noir qui flotte entre tes strophes *dans le manuscrit* . . . Ce • ce serait tout à fait moi: Un point de vue. Je veux dire un point sans vue, une pupille sans lumière" ("I find suddenly that I resemble somewhat that •, the black dot that floats between your stanzas in the manuscript . . . This • would be altogether me: A point of (non-)view. I mean a point without sight, a pupil without light").[67] The inability to see that plagues the narrator of "Savoir"—a severe myopia, but not quite blindness—is rendered in Derrida's manuscript as a black dot. But in the published text of "Un ver à soie," Cixous notes, the points are replaced by arrows, causing her again to feel unmoored. The identification that Cixous first felt is quickly swept away, and she asks repeatedly in *Insister*, "Où me mettre? Où me mettre pour pouvoir jouir en paix donc sans 'moi,' franchement, de la beauté de ce texte?" ("Where to place myself now? . . . Where to go to be able to delight in peace therefore without 'me,' frankly, in the beauty of this text?").[68] Paradoxically, the ability to "identify" with the dot, to locate oneself in the text, is what allows the reader to lose her sense of self and experience the pleasure of the text. As the dot is replaced, the reader is drawn outside of herself.

The transformation from points to arrows, from the manuscript to the published text of "Un ver à soie," can be traced on a set of annotated proofs conserved in the IMEC's *fonds* Derrida. In this set of proofs, arrows had been inserted to mark the beginning of each section in the text. Whether this was a decision on the part of the editor or copyeditor unable to find a typographic mark resembling Derrida's large dots is unclear. In the first section of the proofs, Derrida calls for changing the arrows back to points: the arrows are crossed out, and a note in the margin reads : "Remplacer ces fleches par un point noir: assez gros (O) À moins que ce ne soit trop difficile: dans ce cas laisser la flèche aigue: ce n'est pas un mauvais trait finalement" ("Replace these arrows with a black dot: fairly large (O) Unless it's too difficult: in which case leave the arrow: it's ultimately not a bad mark").[69] This second possibility wins out in the end: the note is crossed out and a second annotation reads "OK garder la flèche" ("OK keep the arrow"). By the second section of the essay, Derrida has stopped correcting the arrows. It seems that he quickly embraced the potential of this alternative mark. The arrow symbolizes the text written in transit, taking off from—and with—Cixous's essay in an airplane, and then ultimately sent off in publication as an *envoi* toward other lands and other readers. As a symbol of address, the arrow indicates the interval between call and response, Cixous's text and Derrida's, the movement of the preposition *vers* (towards) which evokes both the approach and the distance left to travel.

Moreover, the transformation of the black dot into an arrow can be read as an illustration of the silkworm scene that closes "Un ver à soie." The dot Derrida observes on the silkworm corresponds to the large black dots on the manuscript, literalizing the "ripening" that would characterize the manuscript as *avant-texte*. The wet stain or smudge ("la tache humide") that marks and announces the imminent transformation of the worm into a moth makes way for the wings to pass through, "pour attendrir et percer la peau, puis ouvrir le passage aux ailes du papillon" ("to soften and pierce the skin, then open the way for the moth's wings"), indicating a movement from the "point" to the insect's flight, from the point to the arrow on the manuscript.[70]

The dream of becoming something new, of leaving behind an old body, which characterizes this transition and this account of a childhood memory, extends to the manuscript. Enclosed in an envelope, left to metamorphose in a desk drawer, the manuscript of *Voiles* becomes a "flying manuscript" when Cixous rediscovers it and opens it up—"Le Manuscrit Volant" is the title of the chapter in *Insister* that features this rediscovery and restages Cixous's reading of *Voiles*. The manuscript also occupies an important place within *Insister*: eight pages of it are reproduced in the center of Cixous's book. *Voiles* thus forms the core of *Insister*, enclosed in Cixous's text. Just as Derrida's reading of Cixous's manuscript ("Savoir") envelops her writing, creating a new veil for it, Cixous puts his manuscripts under wraps, veiling the text in a gesture of protection, but not of concealment. Like the silkworms' cocoon in Derrida's "Un ver à soie," the protective enfolding allows for *éclosion* (hatching) and metamorphosis—for a new body to emerge through this reparative reading that stitches the two texts together.

But although the manuscript pages are reproduced in the center of *Insister*, Cixous's book further counters the notion that the manuscript is the exact reverse (*l'envers*) of the text, like the inside (*l'envers*) of a glove. *Insister* ends with a "Note descriptive sur le manuscrit original de *Voiles*" ("Description of the Original Manuscript of *Veils*"), which appears after the endnotes in the back matter of the book. This one-page "note" parallels the coda to "Un ver à soie," Derrida's italicized memory of silkworms. The "descriptive note" that ends *Insister* inventories "the first drafts of the text" ("les premiers états du texte") of *Voiles* one by one, meticulously detailing ink colors, paper dimensions, and distinct documents. The note begins without any indication of authorship, the writer implied in passive construction, and later refers to an unnamed "author's hand" ("main de l'auteur"). Later on, the note refers to "two documents by Hélène Cixous" ("deux documents d'Hélène Cixous") which it says are "joined" to the previous documents, without further specification. The final section of the note describes in detail the "cardboard file folder" ("une chemise cartonnée," "un dossier cartonné") that encloses the foregoing documents, referred to as "Le tout" ("All this"). This "dossier cartonné" itself bears "numerous handwritten notes" ("de nombreuses notes manuscrites") (written by whom? the note demurs), and is the outermost handwritten artifact gathering together all the rest. Joined together and enfolded into two protective coverings, the manuscript of *Voiles* encompasses the variety of artifacts described in this authorially vague yet materially detailed note.

The published text of *Insister* reinforces the link between Cixous's and Derrida's two essays and draws from the manuscript to do so. The descriptive note that closes *Insister* is a gloss of the actual artifact—the manuscript of *Voiles*—and acts as an echo to the pages reproduced in the center of the book. The visual representation of the manuscript is supplemented by the descriptive note, which serves to emphasize the archival quality of *Voiles* and, through this quality, the connection between "Savoir" and "Un ver à soie." The interplay between the artifact and the published text strengthens this bond and creates opportunities for it to continue on for further readings.

The Risks of Repair

Cixous's reading of *Voiles*—which was published in *Insister* the year following Derrida's death—is a way of keeping their two texts together, inextricably. Instead of being further separated by Derrida's death and the creation of both Cixous's and Derrida's separate archives, "Savoir" and "Un ver à soie" remain linked in publication and in manuscript form. Cixous's discovery of "le manuscrit de *Voiles*" in her desk drawer seems to solidify the manuscript as one combined text. Her reading draws out the "points" visible on the original manuscript as literal illustrations of the title: "Points de vue piquées sur l'autre voile" ("Points of view stitched on the other veil"). *Piquées* references the physical operation of stitching, sewing, putting something back together—but "piquées sur" has the double meaning of stitched onto and stolen from. *Voiles* indicates a type of writing and sharing that challenges notions of property, belonging, and appropriation. This reparative mode of reading, bringing two texts and two writers together and solidifying their bond, impacts an understanding of authorship in autobiographical writing and the use of traditional archival strategies of manuscript preservation. The literary artifact shared between Cixous and Derrida does not fall into clear alignment with designations of single-author collections and provenance, since it does not clearly bear the mark or signature of one author.

The reparative readings that Cixous and Derrida perform in and around *Voiles* have implications for other wounds and trauma in the two writers' overlapping biographies. The "noblessures" and "stigmates" that Cixous revisits with Derrida do not amount to nostalgic reflections on a past that, when shared, serves to connect two people in a similar experience. Rather, Cixous returns to the wound and even, in the case of "Circonfession," re-creates some of these wounds: the marks of reading in *Portrait de Jacques Derrida* representing "the closed lips of the wound" ("les lèvres de la plaie rapprochées"), the stitches of reading that would "stitch up" ("recoudre") the wound.[71] To what end does Cixous "repasser au plus près de la blessure" ("go back as close as possible to the wound"), in the words of Frédéric Regard?[72] Revisiting and re-presenting the wound constitutes a mode of connection, of dialogue that is a form of reparative care for the manuscript. But does this repair seek to heal the wounds and the rifts that death has perpetrated, or to maintain them? What are the risks of passing over, over and over, the record of violence shared between Cixous and Derrida? Is reparative reading a way of nursing one's wounds—an "entretien de la blessure," to echo Cixous's work on Genet? Anticipating the task of the surviving friend to "porter l'autre" ("carry the other"), autobiographical writing *à deux* enables Cixous and Derrida to share in the "noblessures" and "stigmates" of separation and death. Cixous does not repair in order to heal or to erase, but to ensure that two manuscripts, and two friends, remain inseparable.

Many of the marks, points of contact, and annotations discussed in this chapter are potentially, if not actively, detrimental to the literary artifact they engage with: heavy hands, paper bursting under the weight of *skizzes*, corrosive staples and ink. Each of these forms of touch could degrade the manuscript, physically transforming it or destroying it beyond recognition. The reparative strategies employed by Cixous are particularly destructive and seem to flout the care she has committed to giving the manuscripts Derrida has entrusted to her. The scene of Cixous's promise is described in *Insister* in relation to the manuscript of Derrida's *Genèses . . .* :

> Cette fois c'est déposé entre mes mains que tu "envoies," d'un très loin tout autre, ceci écrit d'un très loin intérieur, dans une enveloppe fermée. À ne pas ouvrir. Sauf et sinon. J'ai promis. À plus d'une reprise tu m'appelles et tu dis: "Tu ne l'as pas ouverte au moins." Cette scène nous peint. "Je te jure que je n'y touche pas. —Ah si je pouvais te croire!"
>
> This time it is deposited into my hands that you "send," from a wholly other great distance, this text written from a very distant interior, in a closed envelope. Not to be opened. Except and unless. I promised. More than once you call me and you say: you didn't open it at least. This scene depicts us. I swear to you I haven't touched it. —Oh if only I could believe you![73]

Although she swears that she has not opened the envelope which contains the manuscript—more precisely, that she does not *touch* the envelope—the scene ends with the mention of a "couteau" brought in for the purpose of cutting up ("pour découper") *Voiles*, the book: a knife to slice open the folds of the book's leaves in order to read it.[74] It is as though it is impossible not to touch *Voiles* in some way.

The threat of the broken promise, wielded here like the knife that cuts the book to allow it to be read, parallels the laws of the letter that can always fail to arrive at its destination, discussed by Derrida in *La Carte postale* and illustrated in the "Envois" that form the bulk of that text. The "menace" is necessary to the continuation of the letter's sending, being in play, being alive, in suspension. Yet even as it threatens the letter with destruction, the risk of fragmentation ("se morceler") enables the letter's circulation.[75] Accordingly, the risk of sharing and sending, illustrated by the manuscript of *Genèses* stored in an envelope, is necessary for the survival of the manuscript. The points of contact on a manuscript shared between Cixous and Derrida have potential for renewal as well as for loss and destruction. Although the fragile or contingent state of a manuscript can contribute to anxiety about the archive's ability to preserve the work for future readers, strategies to alleviate these concerns often make use of the manuscript's materiality, especially as it implicates close contact with a reader or a friend. Even the most delicate, careful forms of touch and contact highlight the fragility of the literary artifact and the separation in space and time between two friends.

It would be tempting to discuss the trajectories of these manuscripts in terms of appropriation, gift, or exchange: by giving Cixous these manuscripts, and others, Derrida has taken rare, and therefore valuable, textual objects out of the scope of his own archives; they seem instead to "belong" in the BNF's Cixous collection, especially as they become integrated into her writing. But these economic models limit the manuscripts' field of play, understanding them as discrete objects exchanged between distinct individual agents. Instead, looking at Cixous and Derrida's shared manuscripts as a form of reparative reading opens up onto a consideration of the possibilities of transsubjectivity that occur in the manuscripts' circulation.

Stripped of its status as property, the manuscript becomes a place where the uneven texture of its material traces morphs to make new forms of being and, in turn, change the reader who touches it. This speaks at once to the instability of the trace, even within Derrida's own conception of it: a volatility stemming from its unstable ontological status that eschews any selfsame identity. By virtue of their material makeup, the literary artifacts in question here transform all that surrounds them and all who encounter them, whether human or nonhuman. Derrida's "Un ver à soie" interrogates the ability to "se séparer de son œuvre" ("separate oneself from one's work") especially when the "œuvre" in question is a friend's manuscript. Cixous loses herself in front of the manuscript of *Voiles*, and even as she attempts to keep this manuscript and that of "Circonfession" together, she can only do so by radically altering it at the material level. Sharing manuscripts is a physical act that transforms both the material artifact and the reader. This transformation provides the possibility of living on. Instead of giving clues to a writer's life through identity, belonging, and experience, the manuscript becomes the vehicle for sharing, difference, and metamorphosis, allowing for an unstable, ever-shifting, ever-continuous operation of reading. Ventriloquizing Derrida in *Portrait de Jacques Derrida*, Cixous describes what she sees as his unflinching respect for difference: "Non, je ne suis pas toi, murmure-t-il, je ne suis pas moi non plus, cependant il arrive parfois que je te sois ou que tu me traverses" ("No, I am not you, he murmurs, I am not me either, however it sometimes happens that I be you or you traverse me").[76] This citation also speaks to the physical encounter with the shared manuscript, volatile and changing.

Reading the manuscript enacts a reconfiguration of subjectivity, as we have seen in Derrida's memory of being infused with a childhood memory after reading "Savoir." Similarly, in the rediscovery of *Voiles*, Cixous writes in *Insister*: "Je contemplai la main. Je cessai la mort. Cette essence de présence était en moi. Elle était moi" ("I contemplated the hand. I halted death. This essence of presence was in me. It was me").[77] In this passage, Cixous likens her encounter with the manuscript to resurrection or *revenance* that operates in an abrupt shift, from "cette essence de présence était en moi" to "elle était moi." In this way, the textual object acts as an agent of metamorphosis that transforms the reader who comes into contact with it. It is not a matter of reproducing or resurrecting in flesh and in spirit the exact likeness or being of the other; Jacques Derrida will not appear as in life before Hélène Cixous. Rather, what will appear within her, through her, is the "présence vivante" ("living presence") of the "figure de la main de Jacques Derrida" ("face and shape of the hand of Jacques Derrida"). In this way Cixous manages to "porter l'autre," but "l'autre" here is not her dead friend—it is the marks on the manuscript. Similarly, in *Portrait de Jacques Derrida*, Cixous shoulders the finitude of life not to oppose it or reject it, but to split and share it, to strip it of its individuality, proposing an alternative to the understanding of death as a proper end, an idiosyncratic experience that closes and completes one's own life. She writes, channeling Derrida: "La mort est en moi, ce n'est pas la personne morte qui est morte, c'est moi qui suis porteur ou porteuse de sa mort. On partage la mort comme on partage la vie. En outre cette mort ou cette vie sont aussi partagées, la vie par la mort et la mort par la vie" ("Death is within me, it is not the dead person who is dead, it is I who am the bearer of her death. One shares the death as one shares the life. Furthermore, this death or this life are also divided, the life by the death, or the death by the life").[78] In this view of mortality, life and death are not one's own, but are transferrable; they are not whole, but are separated by the other. Expanding the double meaning of *partager*, Cixous confounds separation and sharing. The resulting operation is one of multiplication, not division: rather than parceling out lives and deaths, sharing allows for an extension of existence.

Through their practice of sharing manuscripts, Cixous and Derrida challenge distinctions between drafts and published texts, between intellectual property and authorship, and even between individual texts: "Circonfession," *Voiles*, *Portrait de Jacques Derrida*, and *Insister* create a dense textual registry of resonances and responses. Their authors' reparative reading of each other's manuscripts implicates fidelity, appropriation, and mourning to overcome the divide between self and other, and between life, death, and afterlife. In the next chapter, I explore forms of ventriloquizing in the two writers' dialogue in more detail. What Cixous calls "secrécitation," and what Frédéric Regard calls "citational grafting," indicate a telepathic mode that Cixous and Derrida explore in their writing. As we will see, these come into play in the afterlife, as Cixous mourns Derrida, and as both writers imagine what "survie" might entail for techniques and technologies of writing and communication that resist archival preservation: telephone calls and dreams.

Chapter 5

✦

Dream On

Other Conversations

Throughout "Fourmis" ("Ants"), his first text on Hélène Cixous, Jacques Derrida insists that the essay's eponymous insects are not his own—or at least were not at first. Instead, they were given to him over the telephone: "Il y aura donc eu le coup de téléphone d'Hélène, il y a quelques jours, le 'allô, fourmi, allô, il y a un fourmi dans mon rêve de cette nuit' " ("There will have been the telephone call from Hélène a few days ago, the 'hello, *fourmi*, hello, there was *un fourmi* in my dream last night' ").[1] Cixous had called to tell him she had dreamt about an ant. Derrida gives his account of this telephone call, highlighting that the ant in the dream was not exactly an insect, but instead the word "fourmi," with a masculine article (*un fourmi*) instead of the grammatically correct feminine *une fourmi*. With this call, Derrida says, Cixous has in essence transferred the *fourmi* to him. But he hesitates: did she give him the *fourmi*, or did her dream give it to him? "Hélène m'a fourni sans le savoir, me le donnant ainsi, le mot *fourmi*. Son rêve me l'a donné sans savoir ce qu'il faisait" ("Hélène provided me with the word *fourmi without knowing it*, giving it to me in this way. Her dream gave it to me without knowing what it was doing").[2] If Derrida received this *fourmi*, it was a gift made without the donor's explicit knowledge—"sans le savoir": the only truly generous way to give without expecting anything in return, according to Derrida.

How can a dream be given? What form does the dream take? How could it be preserved and archived? The dreams shared between Cixous and Derrida, most often over the telephone, test the limits of the archive. In Cixous's doubled archive, Derrida's virtual archive, and their shared manuscripts, we have seen that the material limits of what the archive can contain, and how well it can conserve its contents, provoke Cixous and Derrida to envision alternative modes of archival preservation. But what of the forms of communication of which there are no records? What traces remain of the phone call, or of the dream account? What possibilities for conversation and connection exist when two friends are separated by distance or by death? Sharing dreams, on the telephone or even telepathically, is one of several modes of communication and transmission that weave throughout the Derrida-Cixous dialogue, pointing up questions of appropriation and influence. This chapter explores the effects of these modes of communication on the concept of the archive, as well as the archive's effects on this conversation. Depending on how their physical traces are preserved and archived, certain artifacts can offer the chance of an afterlife of writing as they prompt the reader and the archivist to negotiate the possibility of preserving physical traces alongside the impossibility of accounting for what is untraceable.

This chapter considers the implications of Cixous's and Derrida's claims about untraceable writing for literary criticism and for archival preservation, and investigates the possibility that the writers can sustain their conversation beyond death by communicating through telephone calls, dreams, and telepathy. If two voices in dialogue are inextricably linked, but the dialogue is untraceable, then both the telephone and the dream seem to offer modes of cognition and communication that sidestep conventional modes of archiving. In *Genèses, généalogies, genres . . . et le génie: Les Secrets de l'archive* (2004), Derrida sets up Cixous's dream texts as the eponymous secrets of the essay's subtitle. The dream texts deploy their own preserving mechanism within the archive, keeping the secrets of her writing under wraps and thereby ensuring that the oeuvre is continually renewed and enriched for future readers. Sharing dreams on the telephone is a recurrent topos through which the two writers reflect on how thinking and writing are shared between two minds.[3] Much of Cixous and Derrida's friendship played out in telephone calls, and by alluding to this in their published texts they challenge the boundaries between public and private conversation, unrecorded and unverifiable. The telephone further highlights the enfolded, undetectable overlap at work in other venues of shared writing. In *Insister* and *Hyperrêve*, both published in 2006, Cixous offers "secrécitation" as a name for how two bodies of writing come together. This strengthens the connection between the two friends in a tightly knit intertextual web, one that is further intensified when Cixous uses the concept of telepathy as a bridge between Derrida's essay "Télépathie" (1981) and her own *Philippines* (2009).

The forms of writing and of dialogue I investigate in this chapter—dreams, telephone calls, and telepathic communication—form an eclectic archive that is intentionally difficult to identify and access. They provide a counterpoint to other, more conventional archival artifacts explored in the majority of this book. Their presence in this chapter acts as an interrogation of what is considered archivable, and in particular what materials can be ascribed to a single author's collection. The creation and preservation of this archive of alternative materials, and the continued interaction with it, highlight the potential of transmission that so interested Derrida and Cixous in their textual conversation. As Derrida suggests in "Fourmis," the shared dream illustrates the challenges and the innovations of archiving *à deux*. Returning to the subject again and again, Cixous's and Derrida's writings about dreaming together pile into a tangle of repetitive, inextricable texts, creating a form of co-writing that is not quite collaborative, even though it is the result of close conversation. By dreaming and archiving together, the friends allude to an afterlife in and of embodied writing.

"*Un corps d'écriture publique*" ("A Body of Public Writing")

Derrida takes up the question of the untraceability of the dream in "Fourmis" by focusing on the body of the ant, the dream, and the place of sexual difference within it. Cixous and Derrida opened the 1990 conference "Lectures de la différence sexuelle" with mutually referential texts: Cixous's "Contes de la différence sexuelle," a reading of the manuscript of Derrida's "Circonfession," and Derrida's "Fourmis." By sharing the *fourmi* of Cixous's dream with the audience, Derrida publicly affirms his friendship with Cixous and opens the intimacy of their friendship to a wider public. The ant dream passes from Cixous to Derrida to the reader, engaging all of them in the same oneiric sphere. It is this chain of shared dreaming that motivates Derrida to "sceller ce qui se passe aujourd'hui dans la cire d'une contingence exemplaire, de ce qui arrive en me touchant . . . et qui provient, cet événement, d'Hélène" ("to seal what is happening today in the wax of an exemplary contingency, of what happens in touching me . . . and coming, this event, from Hélène").[4] Derrida's "desire" ("désir") here is to provide a record of provenance for this dream, ascribing it to "Hélène" and setting it down as an exemplary event. The material he would use for this is "la cire d'une contingence exemplaire," a substance that alludes to the amber in which insects are fixed, but which is more malleable, better suited to the contingencies of dreaming. This recalls the wax of Freud's *Wunderblock* and Derrida's insistence on the material support of writing as an integral aspect of the trace's transforming operation. By the end of "Fourmis," Derrida's project takes on this contingent quality. He writes: "Tout ce que je voulais faire, c'est peut-être donner un corps d'écriture publique au fourmi qu'Hélène m'avait seulement soufflé au téléphone" ("All I wanted to do was perhaps to give a body of public writing to *le fourmi* that Hélène had only whispered to me on the telephone").[5] Adverbally qualified and provisional, the "désir . . . de sceller" ("desire to seal") that Derrida first avows is ultimately described in a series of overlapping actions: "Je lui ai soufflé le mot qu'elle m'a soufflé, je le lui ai volé, non, je le lui ai emprunté, j'ai fait semblant de le lui prendre le temps de lui tailler un corps d'écriture. En rêvant à mon tour de le lui rendre. Et tendre" ("I whispered to her the word she whispered to me, I stole it from her, no, I borrowed it from her, I have pretended to take it from her for time enough to carve out a body of writing for it. While dreaming in turn of returning it, and holding it out to her").[6] The verbal swirl (*donner*, *soufflé*, *volé*, *emprunté*, *prendre*, *rendre*, *tendre*) serves to problematize both the act of "giving" a dream, and, further, of "giving" what Derrida calls "un corps d'écriture" to the dream.

Especially since it is presented publicly at a conference, we could assume that the essay "Fourmis" itself is the "corps d'écriture publique" which Derrida has fashioned for the dream. Yet in repeating this expression, Derrida distinguishes between the dream itself, which Cixous recounted to him over the telephone; the word "fourmi" in that dream; and the essay "Fourmis." If a dream cannot be materialized in its entirety, at least a word can: the only part of the dream that makes its way into the essay, taking on a "corps d'écriture publique," is the word itself—*fourmi*. The content of the dream, Derrida explains, will remain secret: "un rêve d'Hélène qu'à ma connaissance je suis seul à connaître, dont je ne dirai vraisemblablement rien, rien de direct" ("a dream of Hélène's that as far as I know I am the only one to know, about which I will apparently say nothing, nothing direct").[7] Derrida preserves the content of the dream for himself as the presumed sole recipient even as he exposes the *fourmi* for all to see—that is, to read: the ant is "voué au noir de l'aveuglement mais promis par là même à la lecture" ("doomed to the obscurity of blindness but promised in this way to reading").[8] Because the ant's sex cannot be identified by looking at the body of the insect ("d'une fourmi il est bien difficile de voir, sinon de savoir, la différence sexuelle," 71; "it is very difficult to see, if not to know, the sexual difference of *une fourmi*," 18–19), the article, masculine or feminine, does the work of conferring a gender within the binary grammatical system.[9] This dream's *fourmi—un*, not *une*—illustrates the workings of sexual difference, which takes place in a shift from seeing to reading: "passant de *voir* à *lire*," Derrida writes (96; "passing from *seeing* to *reading*," 36). The body is not inherently sexed, but rather it has traces and markings that can be read and interpreted as a particular sex: "Il peut y avoir de la trace sans différence sexuelle, par exemple pour du vivant asexué, mais il ne peut y avoir de la différence sexuelle sans trace" (74; "There can be traces without sexual difference, for example for unsexed living things, but there can be no sexual difference without traces," 21). The word *fourmi* in the dream is the body that Derrida reads, and therefore it is already textual. But if it already has a written body, is the "corps d'écriture" that Derrida proposes to give it redundant? Derrida's hesitation about what exactly he is doing with, for, or to the *fourmi* (giving, stealing, whispering, etc.) indicates the uncertain status of this body. The word *fourmi* is the trace that remains of Cixous's dream as Derrida publicizes it, but this trace demonstrates the impossibility of fully reading or knowing the ant dream in its entirety. The essay publicly memorializes the uncertain *fourmi* in writing, linking the question of the material form of writing and its limits to sexual difference.

If the "fourmi" does not have a visibly discernible sex, neither does it have a clear author: the "gift" of the dream is precisely that it sidesteps authorship. Derrida calls the *fourmi*'s provenance into question, shifting from

Cixous herself to "un rêve d'Hélène," stemming from Cixous's unconscious. Derrida flags dreaming as the ideal mode of giving—that is to say, without ulterior motive or even awareness of the act. Only in a dream is it possible to give without knowing: "On ne peut donner que sans savoir—et si la conscience aussi bien qu'un certain inconscient sont des figures du savoir, alors permettez-moi de voir dans le rêve la figure au moins de ce don qui se porte entre les deux et au-delà des deux" (73; "One can only give without knowing—and if consciousness as well as a certain unconscious are figures of knowledge, then allow me to see in the dream at least the figure of this gift that is borne between the two and beyond the two," 20). The true act of giving would bypass the restrictive, binary economic system that structures exchange as well as sexual difference. In "Fourmis," the dream, the word *fourmi*, and the phone call seem to take place via the impersonal *il y a*: "Il y aura donc eu le coup de téléphone d'Hélène, il y a quelques jours, le 'allô, fourmi, allô, il y a un fourmi dans mon rêve de cette nuit' " (89; "There will have been the telephone call from Hélène a few days ago, the 'hello, *fourmi*, hello, there was *un fourmi* in my dream last night,' " 31). Derrida is careful to insist that it is the "rêve d'Hélène" ("Hélène's dream") that has affected him: "Son rêve me l'a donné sans savoir ce qu'il faisait" (80; "Her dream gave it to me without knowing what it was doing," 24); "Tout cela s'est passé, tout cela s'est donné en rêve, depuis le rêve d'Hélène" (80; "All of this took place, all of this was given in a dream, from Hélène's dream," 25).

Derrida's attempts to receive and to give the *fourmi* a "corps d'écriture publique" (a "body of public writing") raise questions about ownership and preservation: to whom does a dream belong? What is the responsibility of the dreamer toward the dream, and when that dream is shared, what kind of responsibilities does the recipient have to its provenance? If Cixous is not the author of the dream, as Derrida suggests, will she be credited in any way for this linguistic innovation? How can the legacy of certain texts and concepts be traced through unconventional citation or appropriation? These questions are particularly charged within a framework of sexual difference when the work of marginalized voices is often passed over or appropriated by the dominant discourse. Furthermore, "Fourmis" is significant for the issue of how dreams can be archived. What is the status of a written dream with respect to the dream itself? When "Fourmis" is archived, where and how will it be preserved? Indeed, the case of Derrida's essay proves emblematic here: the manuscript of the essay "Fourmis" is never mentioned in Derrida's and Cixous's published writings, unlike other important manuscripts passed between Cixous and Derrida, such as *Voiles* and "Circonfession." But the question of archiving dreams persists in their dialogues: Derrida returns to the subject fourteen years later, laying out the stakes for the emerging relationship between a body of work and a national institution.

Derrida's book *Genèses, généalogies, genres . . . et le génie: Les Secrets de l'archive* was written for the inauguration of the Cixous collection at the

BNF in 2003. It would be his last text about Cixous before his death. In *Genèses*, as in his other studies of her writing, he worked with manuscripts of her most recent texts, focusing in particular on Cixous's *Manhattan*, a book about libraries and archival research, and *Rêve je te dis*, a collection of unedited dream-texts. Positioning himself as a continuous reader of her work and offering guidance to her future readership, Derrida participates in launching the legacy of Cixous's oeuvre within the French patrimony. Yet he does so mainly through a series of warnings about the impossibility of interpreting and conserving Cixous's work—her dream-texts in particular.

Derrida's warnings echo Cixous's "Avertissements," her preface to *Rêve je te dis*. As in "Fourmis," Derrida reiterates Cixous's words, giving them a doubled presence that is shared between their bodies of writing. In her preface, Cixous explains the process of selecting and publishing the dreams that follow while discouraging the work of interpretation the dreams might seem to invite:

> Je n'ai aucunement "corrigé," censuré, touché en rien aux récits enregistrés par la main entre chat et loup. Ils sont reproduits intégralement, bruts, innocents, tels qu'ils s'ébattaient dans l'aube préanalytique. Je pourrais, pour mon propre profit, les analyser. Moi seule pourrais le faire, puisque j'ai seule les clés. Je ne le fais pas ici. . . . Je me suis tenue éloignée de l'analyse et de la littérature. Ces choses sont des récits primitifs. Des larves. J'aurais pu, les couvant, les porter à papillons. Alors ils n'eussent plus été des rêves.
>
> I have in no way "corrected," censored, touched up the tales set down by my hand in the twilight hours. They are reproduced in their entirety, unpolished, innocent, such as they disported themselves in the preanalytic dawn. I could, for my own benefit, analyze them. Only I could do this, since only I have the keys. I do not do this here. . . . Analysis and literature I have kept at arm's length. These things are primitive tales. Larvae. I could, by brooding on them, have transformed them into butterflies. They would no longer have been dreams.[10]

Assembled and published in the wake of the archive's creation, *Rêve je te dis* mirrors archival gestures of collecting, sorting, and ordering that Cixous's dream-texts undergo at the BNF. By proscribing interpretation, Cixous warns against reading the dreams as part of a complete *dossier génétique* of a published text; instead, they constitute a unique type of material, even a genre, in their own right. Mairéad Hanrahan advocates for this view of Cixous's dreams, positing that "le rêve ne fournit pas qu'une matière première, un matériau brut que la *technē* de l'écriture transformerait par la suite" ("the dream does not merely supply a raw material, a crude matter that the *technē* of writing would go on to transform").[11] For Cixous, dreams are a material, but the metaphor of raw material to be transformed and indeed refined into a finished product is insufficient in understanding Cixous's writing process. They are texts that invite a different approach to reading and analysis. Derrida further suggests that Cixous's dreams resist interpretation altogether, posing problems for those who would presume to read, understand, and thereby fully integrate them into her oeuvre: "lecteurs, interprètes, philologues, décrypteurs de toute espèce" ("readers, interpreters, philologists, cryptologists of all ilk").[12] Decoding is impossible. "La porte est condamnée, mais entrez donc," Derrida enigmatically states in *Genèses*, perhaps ventriloquizing the archived texts themselves, or the archive ("The door is barred but please come in").[13] How is a reader to understand this invitation, couched in a warning?

As in Derrida's treatment of the *fourmi*, another kind of encounter is required here, beyond conventional understandings of knowing, reading, and giving or receiving. Cixous's writing provides an occasion for Derrida to address the question of donations and gifts, linking Cixous's archiving to his own work (especially *Donner la mort* and *Donner le temps*) and, further, to his own archives which were, at the time of writing *Genèses*, mired in a complicated institutional triangle between the IMEC, UC Irvine, and Derrida's estate. Beginning with "La Pharmacie de Platon," Derrida emphasizes that the gift is double-sided: it is also a poison, just as hospitality is tinged with hostility.[14] As the recipient of Cixous's archives, the BNF is the main target of Derrida's warnings in *Genèses*. This institution is necessarily affected (or infected) by the donation it has just received. Although Derrida's essay discusses the implications of the entirety of Cixous's oeuvre for the BNF, he focuses on dreams in particular, as they represent a significant portion of her output and a vital aspect of her writing process. The dream-texts included within this gift, according to Derrida, cause the most trouble for the archival enterprise and the research it presumes to facilitate. First, the sheer volume of this collection—"des dizaines de milliers de notations de rêves" (53; "tens of thousands of dreams noted down," 43)—would constitute a massive undertaking for archival processing: their inclusion in the *fonds* Cixous "imposera à la BNF de redoutables et, je le crains ou l'espère, je ne sais pas, d'insolubles problèmes . . . La BNF en fera les frais," Derrida warns (34; "will cause the BNF daunting and, I fear or hope, I'm not sure which, insoluble problems . . . The BNF will pay the piper," 24). These problems operate from within the archive, and their subversion is "bien pire que l'opposition, le conflit, la hiérarchie oppressive ou le refoulement" (34; "worse than oppositions, conflict, oppressive hierarchy or repression," 24) because they implicate the BNF in the dream's encrypted secrets, "la puissance cryptopoétique qui met tout sous scellés" (56–57; "the cryptopoetic power that seals up everything," 46). The BNF must preserve the secrets in order to complete its job in good faith. By including dream-texts in her donation, Derrida suggests, Cixous has effectively demanded of the BNF that it admit its own powerlessness with regard to its primary function to know, preserve, and present on behalf of future readers: "La BNF . . . doit donc avouer ne pas comprendre ce qu'elle comprend. Elle doit avouer . . . ne pas regarder ce qu'elle garde, ce qu'elle garde sauf—mais sauf son inconscient. Sauf par-devers son inconscient" (43; "The BNF . . . must avow it does not comprehend that which it comprehends. It must avow . . . that it does not regard that which it guards, that which it keeps safe—saving its unconscious. Save in its unconscious," 32–33). The paradox of archival secrecy may be a general condition of all archiving, and perhaps literary archiving especially, but this aspect is highlighted in Derrida's analysis of Cixous's archives by the dream-texts being in dialogue with the institution. The magnetizing presence of pre-analytic dream material directly targets the archive's unconscious: "On n'a jamais si bien parlé à l'inconscient d'une bibliothèque," he writes (43; "Never has anyone so well addressed a library's unconscious," 33). Derrida alludes to a form of communicating with and through the archive that might yield an afterlife of writing and transmission. This talent (this gift?) is part of Cixous's *génie*.

Cixous's dreams are a microcosm of her work as a whole. According to Derrida, the genius of Cixous's writing is that it speaks to the library's unconscious, not in a simplistic antagonistic challenge, but by involving itself in the conversation. Derrida ascribes the structure of a psychic apparatus to the Bibliothèque nationale de France by evoking the unconscious and *refoulement*. He suggests that it is only through the unconscious that the BNF, or any future reader, can approach Cixous's writing, invested as it is with "la puissance cryptopoétique" (56; the "cryptopoetic power") that is "le secret de la littérature" (46; "literature's secret"). This formulation recalls the psychoanalytic concept of the crypt, developed by Nicholas Abraham and Maria Torok, as the psychic location of an introjected "dead object" that characterizes melancholia, an emotional state bent on maintaining a "secret tomb" instead of digesting the dead object in the process of mourning.[15] Yet Derrida's use of the word "cryptopoétique," and the repetition of "crypte" throughout *Genèses*, suggests that the secret and secrecy are in fact crucial to maintaining the power of literature accessible to future readers. Only if the crypt is broken and the code is cracked, decrypting the secret, would the "puissance" of Cixous's enigmatic dreams die. The psychoanalytic paradigm of mourning is thus not the ideal position for understanding how to read literature in general, or how to read dream-texts in particular. In that view, the BNF's inability to incorporate Cixous's dreams would indicate a failed or faulty mourning, as if the only way it could process this reactive material would be to consider it as dead and entombed.[16] Derrida's and Cixous's dialogue with the archive suggests another mode of interpretation that would preserve its dynamism and creative potential. Paradoxically, the BNF's "faulty burial" (to use Frédéric Regard's phrase) of Cixous's dreams enhances archival survival.

Beyond the specific archival institution that is the BNF, Derrida's warning can also be understood as an address to psychoanalysis as an authoritative interpretative method. Certainly, the issue of interpretation (and more broadly of interpretability) is at stake here: both Derrida and Cixous reject interpretation as a possibility or a goal in their use of their own and others' dreams. It would thus seem that, despite their ongoing engagement with psychoanalysis, both writers do not consider the method to be sufficient for studying dreams, archived materials, and literary texts.[17] For both writers, dreaming poses a challenge to interpretation and reading. Cixous and Derrida contest a Freudian understanding of the dream as a psychic manifestation correlating directly to mental processes that can be understood through a scientific methodology; instead, they are interested in dreaming as a rich reserve of literary innovation, as an experience of difference, and as a model for archiving.

Of course, Freud also recognized the limits of dream interpretation. His descriptions of the dream structure in *The Interpretation of Dreams* involve the figure of the *ombilic*, which constitutes a node of intensity in the dense knot of unconscious dream thoughts. The *ombilic* is a point of resistance that "cannot be unraveled" through conscious psychoanalytic interpretation: it is "unplumbable" and "has to be left obscure."[18] This tangle is located in the "unknown," as Freud says, and is discernible from the perspective of the awakened dreamer and analyst through the *ombilic*, the "tangle of dream-thoughts" that is the dream's "navel" and constitutes a point of contact with the unconscious.[19] For Freud, this is the point where interpretation must stop: the unconscious cannot be accessed at this point, where the entangled dream-thoughts indicate an unmanageable psychic intensity. Rising up from the tangle of dream-thoughts, "like a mushroom out of its mycelium," as Freud writes, the *ombilic* is a node of resistance that unsettles the act of interpretation.[20] Freud describes the "intricate network" and "meshwork" of the mind as a rhizome.[21] For Cixous, and for Derrida in his reading of Cixous, the *ombilic* is the point of access to the "other side," although this access is not obtained through interpretation.

We have seen that, particularly for Cixous, the dream constitutes a double or supplemental life, opening up onto another state of being, another mode of thinking, another temporality. In *Hyperrêve*, the "vie à hyperrêve" is a "vie autre," or "cette autrevie" which the narrator seeks to preserve by dreaming double ("hyperdream life," "other-life," "otherlife").[22] If writing down dreams is a way of preserving "[des] coulées venues de l'autre monde" ("flowing from the other world"), or of mixing "extreme familiarity with extreme strangeness," accessing this otherness can only happen a flash: suddenly the dreamer is "transported to another world; no, you are not transported, you *are* already in the other world."[23] As portals onto this alternate reality, the dream-texts are the means by which the reader or researcher can find themselves on the other side of the archive, in its unknown or unconscious.

This is one way of understanding Derrida's pseudo-invitation, "la porte est condamnée mais entrez donc" ("the door is barred but come in"): Cixous's dream-texts are *ombilics*, points of resistance that connect to another side, portals through which one must pass in one quick leap, foregoing the slower work of interpretation.[24]

Events and remnants of "l'autre côté" arrive unexpectedly, like a surprising dream or a phone call. Tapping into this network, especially after Derrida's death, Cixous's switchboard becomes the "intricate network" of dreams that would put her into contact with her friend on "the other side." Dreams and dream-texts appear from the other side, materializing in the "écriture publique" of a conference or an archival institution. They call up other textual objects which are also charged with this telepathic or teleporting power, acting as portals to the "other side." This unusual archive poses challenges for interpretation and for conservation, even as it suggests cryptic modes of communication. Cixous's and Derrida's attention to the embodiment of dreams in textual objects offers the chance to consider alternatives to hermeneutic interpretation in the form of intimate encounters with hypercharged artifacts. Considering these artifacts in light of the importance of dreaming for Cixous's and Derrida's archival practice and friendship reveals their potential for living on.

Surprise Encounters

In the year following Derrida's death, Cixous writes about two surprise encounters with manuscripts. In *Insister à Jacques Derrida*, Cixous and Derrida's co-written manuscript of *Voiles* "fait revenance," reappearing in her desk drawer.[25] In *Hyperrêve*, the narrator tucks a talismanic Post-it note into Derrida's manuscript of *Fichus*, which disappears and is found again amid the stacks of books and papers in Cixous's study. We have seen from previous chapters that *Hyperrêve*'s Post-it note illustrates the volatility of materials (in chapter 2) and that the *Voiles* manuscript skirts confining notions of property (in chapter 4). In both cases, artifacts offer the possibility of existing otherwise, of creating new afterlives. Yet if these are joyful experiences for Cixous, mourning Derrida, she also acknowleages that the manuscripts which return are not proxies for her absent friend. These affectively charged manuscripts offer the relief of communication in moments of surprise encounters.

The Post-it note in *Hyperrêve* is one of the "vestiges . . . du fameux rêve intitulé *Une Permission*. Rêve qui était lui-même une permission valable pour une journée des deux côtés" ("vestiges . . . of the famous dream entitled *A Leave*. A dream which was in itself a leave good for one day on both sides").[26] This dream itself is remarkable: the narrator has often dreamed *about* her friend since his death, but this one is "une *permission exceptionnelle*, c'est *autre chose qu'un rêve*" ("a *special* leave: *something other than a dream,*" 142)[27]—it is a "hyperdream" that surpasses a distinction between reality and dream, between one side and the other side of life or death:

> Ainsi je venais d'apprendre qu'après l'événement tranchant, le grand séparant, après l'écho des derniers mots de l'Essai de l'Amitié éteint, il pouvait y avoir un royaume autre non totalement clos-et-néant, un royaume de rétention non pas absolument retranché dans un jamais, mais avec des suspens des rémissions des hésitations des permissions, des brèves levées d'écrou.
>
> Hence I had only just learned that after the knife falls, the great separator, after the last words of the Essay of Friendship ceased to resound there, could be an other realm not totally closed-and-nothingness, a realm of retention not utterly cut off in a neverness, but with suspensions, remissions hesitations leaves, brief liftings of the latch.[28]

Cixous describes a state of being that eschews the absolute division of mortality that would separate or "cut" two friends. This state is fleeting and porous, the "permissions" indicating a kind of conditional mode that unseats death's absolute finality. Within this "royaume autre" ("other realm"), it is possible to "rétablir la communication dont se nourrit l'amitié" ("reestablish the lines of communication that nourish friendship"), to conduct "quelque réparation de réseau" ("a sort of repairing of the line"), but this is only truly possible between two people who have had "le temps de penser ensemble et de nous parler si longtemps et si souvent au téléphone et même peut-être jamais" ("time to think together and to talk to each other at such length and so often on the telephone and maybe even never").[29] Not all lines of communication can be repaired.

Moreover, the "permission" that allows the two friends to continue their dialogue leaves a "deposit" that is at once affective and material: "Ce que la permission m'a laissé en dépôt après l'écoulement du répit: une exaltation folle et triste, aussi triste qu'enthousiasmée" (195; "What the leave left me on deposit after the grace period expired: a crazy sad elation, as sad as it was exciting," 147).[30] In order to preserve the memory of and the belief in this experience, the narrator of *Hyperrêve* puts these affective traces into written form as they accumulate. She writes, for example, "'*il y a des permissions*' sur un post-it rectangulaire" ("'there are leaves' on a rectangular post-it") that she sticks to the window and later slips into "la copie manuscrite de *Fichus* que mon ami m'a confiée en août 2001" ("into a manuscript copy of *Fichus* my friend entrusted me with in August 2001").[31] But when she decides to "revenir à ma réserve" ("come back to my reserve") in order to fortify herself against grief, she finds neither the Post-it note nor the manuscript.[32] The loss of these two textual objects signifies the loss of access to the other world and to the possibility of communication with her friend: "La douleur d'avoir perdu le rêve de Permission, donc la Permission, est si violente que c'est presque une réplique de la douleur d'avoir perdu mon ami" ("The pain of having lost the dream of the Leave, therefore the Leave, is so wrenching that it almost amounts to reliving the pain of losing my friend").[33] Although she does not go so far as to equate the loss of the Post-it with the loss of her friend, the concatenation of loss does lead her to mourn the Permission and to celebrate its return in the last pages of *Hyperrêve*: "Il est *revenu*. Je ne l'ai pas *retrouvé*. . . . Les êtres perdus reviennent d'eux-mêmes, parfois" ("It has *come back*. I didn't *find* it . . . Sometimes the lost find their own way back").[34] What returns is not her friend, but the artifact—the pronoun *il* carries a shadow of ambiguity—and along with it the possibility of communication with him. This possibility is embodied by a different kind of "être perdu": an object that channels the experience of a link to the "other side."

Cixous's treatment of these artifacts is significant not only because of her detailed description of their physical makeup and her handling of them, but also because she ascribes an archival quality to these scenes. The Post-it note in *Hyperrêve*, penned to serve as a reminder of an oneiric conversation with Derrida, is described as a "réserve" that was "laissé en dépôt" ("left on deposit")—two terms with archival connotations, which suggest that the note itself has the capacity to contain and preserve this valuable experience.[35] Similarly, in *Insister*, Cixous recalls that Derrida had entrusted her with the manuscript of *Voiles* for safekeeping: "Tu remets à mes soins 1995 [*sic*] la garde d'un pli secret" ("In 1995 you put into my care the keeping of a secret envelope, a secret fold").[36] This gesture, "remettre sous la garde, ici la mienne" ("turn it over to another's keeping, here mine"), is linked in her memory to the manuscript of *Genèses . . .*, "déposé entre mes mains" in 2003 ("deposited into my hands").[37] Here, Cixous places herself as the guardian of the manuscript, its archonte or archivist, as if the archival scene is most apt to produce the intense encounters Cixous seeks. But unlike in *Double Oubli*, where the narrator's discovery of the manuscript of *Le Prénom de Dieu* immediately leads to the idea of giving the manuscript to her archivist at the Bibliothèque nationale de France, in these two scenes featuring manuscripts by Derrida—*Voiles* and *Fichus*, in which the Post-it note is stashed—neither of his archival collections are mentioned, nor does a reference to the BNF enter into play. In these moments, the intensity and intimacy of the encounter with the artifact eclipses any institutional consideration.

The narrator's encounter with the manuscript of *Voiles* is imbued with affective intensity: "J'ai d'abord pris joie à l'apparition du visage de ton écriture manuscrite. Joie, joie. . . . Joie augmentée d'une autre joie née du sentiment de rareté. . . . Joie entristée à la vue comme du Voile de Véronique. Joie voilée" ("I was first of all seized by joy at the apparition of the face of your handwriting. Joy, joy. . . . Joy amplified by another joy born of the feeling of rarity. . . . Joy ensorrowed as if at the sight of the Veil of Veronica. Veiled joy").[38] The multiplied "joies" differentiate themselves, accumulating in affective intensity around the "voiles," linked to the assonant "joie." Just as she is "frappée de joie" ("overwhelmed with joy") at the discovery of Derrida's handwritten annotations on the typescript of *Le Prénom de Dieu*,[39] Cixous describes in detail how she is struck by the heightened emotion of the encounter with *Voiles*, which appears to take place suddenly, without warning: "Triste bonheur mais bonheur en vérité à retrouver, à l'improviste, un manuscrit dont chaque trait me saute aux yeux, et tous les graphes, apocalypse à la maison mais éblouissante, je vois d'un coup tout et je ne vois rien" ("Sad good fortune but good fortune in truth to come upon again, unexpectedly, a manuscript whose every feature leaps into view, and all the graphisms, apocalypse in the house but dazzling, I see at once everything and I see nothing").[40] The apocalyptic moment of the "coup" is a condensation of time whose intensity blinds the reader to any content. Instead, the marks of writing, the "traits" and "graphes" that jump out at her, provoke the emotional shock.

The immediacy and intensity of the experience are described in terms of an encounter with another being. But Cixous repeatedly distinguishes the "visage de ton écriture manuscrite" ("the face of your handwriting") and "un visage figuré sur papier" ("a face depicted on paper") from that of the person who wrote it—the face of handwriting, the face of Derrida's hand ("la figure de la main de Jacques Derrida"), and the face of the manuscript ("le visage du manuscrit") appear on this object, not the face of Derrida himself.[41] The manuscript is not simply a representation. It cannot be read, but can be contemplated, in an act that stops death in a moment of coexistence: "Il ne me vint pas à l'idée de *lire* ce trésor. Je contemplais la main. Je cessai la mort. Cette essence de présence était en moi. Elle était moi" ("It never occurred to me to *read* this treasure. I contemplated the hand. I halted death. This essence of presence was in me. It was me").[42] The intimate proximity between Cixous and this manuscript contrasts with the distance at which Derrida wrote and sent it: Derrida's text starts off with the project to "s'éloigner au bout du monde . . . aussi loin que possible, s'enfermer avec soi en soi" ("go off to the ends of the earth . . . as far as possible, lock oneself away with oneself in oneself").[43] By the time the manuscript reaches Cixous, this project has spiraled from a statement of solitude and individuality to another kind of enclosure, where the "essence de présence" of the manuscript enters into the reader—much like Derrida's reading of Cixous's text causes him to be "envahi" ("invaded") in *Voiles* (as discussed in chapter 4). Throughout Cixous's encounter with the manuscript, this "présence vivante" ("living presence") works within her to become her, making one body the vehicle for another.[44]

Cixous demonstrates that manuscripts have a way of returning, of showing up unexpectedly. The scenes of (re)discovery in *Hyperrêve* and *Insister* speak to Cixous's and Derrida's trust in the materiality of textual objects, the anxiety of the limits of archiving, the contingency of uncontrollable events, and the surprise of loss and rediscovery. The "visage" and the "présence" of the manuscript, repeated throughout these scenes, suggest the possibility of survival through physical written artifacts. But who, or what, is haunting in these scenes? Who, or what, survives? In her encounters with these artifacts, Cixous proposes a mode of living on that enhances Derrida's work on haunting and *survie*, emphasizing the shock and surprise of discovery and the dreamlike state in which they take place.

Insister and *Hyperrêve* present encounters with another being, with otherness—both in the "presence" and "figure" of the artifacts, and with an "other world" or an "other side." Stored within the pages of another object charged with meaning (*Fichus*), the Post-it note in *Hyperrêve* acts as a transportive device that the narrator hopes to use to access an alternate reality: the state of *hyperrêve* where she can communicate with her friend. As links to the "other side," concentrations of written artifacts become nodes of resistance or *ombilics* that flag the points where connections become most intense. The "other side" of dreams can be accessed not by unraveling the *ombilic* through interpretation, but by passing directly through it, "d'un coup."[45] The instantaneity and speed of the "coup"—cut, blow, or telephone call (*le coup de téléphone*)—runs counter to the slower work of interpretation and overrides the limits that seem to irrevocably separate day and night, life and death, waking life and dream-state. The "coup" joins the telephone and the dream as modes of communication and modes of being, both heightened as *survie* in an afterlife state. These "coups" leave traces, both material and affective, that bind the two friends together in a communication unbound by the death of one or both writers.

"*Secrécitations*"

In *Hyperrêve*, a bed acts as a mediating object that allows the narrator to experience the state of *hyperrêve*, access "the other side," and enter into communication with her deceased friend. The narrator's mother tells her that she had once purchased "un sommier," a box spring, from a fellow refugee in Paris, "un M. Benjamin [qui était] en train de déménager" ("a certain Mr. Benjamin, he's in the midst of moving").[46] The narrator makes a cognitive leap, believing the former owner Benjamin to in fact be the writer Walter Benjamin, and regrets having learned about the improbable provenance of Benjamin's bedding too late: Derrida, the author of *Fichus*, would have been especially interested to hear about this bed. *Fichus* borrows its title from a dream Walter Benjamin had while in an internment camp in 1939. In his account of the dream, written in French in a letter to Gretl and Theodor Adorno, Benjamin writes of poetry becoming *fichu*: "À un moment donné je disais textuellement ceci: 'Il s'agissait de changer en fichu une poésie'" ("At one point I was saying this, *verbatim*: 'It was about changing a poem into a *fichu*' ").[47] Derrida comments on the double meaning of *fichu*, both a scrap of fabric or a scarf, and an adjective meaning doomed or done for. Similarly, in *Hyperrêve*, the "sommier" and the Post-it "Permission" doubly indicate a physical object and evoke a psychic state. These objects act as intertextual connections between the three writers.

Cixous channels Benjamin's correspondence with the Adornos, writing to Derrida about her experience with the "sommier." The book *Hyperrêve* itself is a potential form of communication with her friend after his death. The narrator wonders, "suis-je peut-être en train d'écrire un livre pour poser à mon ami toutes ces questions que je n'ai pas eu le temps de poser au téléphone?" ("am I perhaps writing a book in order to ask my friend all these questions that I hadn't time to ask on the telephone?").[48] We might expect the question to end differently—no time to ask him before his death—but the question instead identifies the telephone as a venue for their conversation. This rhetorical question alludes to the power Cixous and Derrida ascribe to the telephone and other related means of communication to establish unexpected, otherworldly connections. The "sommier" acts as a telephonic object in *Hyperrêve*, opening up possibilities for intertextual connection that go beyond a simple reference to another text.

When the narrator decides to "essayer le sommier" ("try the bed"), she is transported almost immediately into a state of hyperdream where she takes dictation from her friend at his insistence: "Je comprenais qu'il me rappelait d'en faire un double simultané à porter dans notre cœur" ("I understood he was reminding me to make a copy, a duplicate to carry in our hearts").[49] As the narrator transcribes this dream sequence, one phrase in particular strikes her with its resonances of friendship. Cixous introduces the term *secrécitation* to describe this particular form of intertextuality:

> Et là à ces mots . . . j'ai reconnu avec une extase d'émotion que mon ami me faisait en toute hâte un de ces signes qu'il m'a toujours fait de la manière joueuse et enfantine qui était une des conventions de notre amitié que nous appelions *faire citation* ou parfois *secrécitation*. Nous n'avons jamais cessé, en l'amitié de quoi je demeure seule à parler, d'assaisonner le discours de l'un de quelques mots de l'autre, d'un air si naturel et si apparemment spontané qu'aucun tiers ne retrouverait plus la trace de la soudure dans l'alliage de nos phrases signées dessus et par-dessus le marché soussignées. Lui surtout le plus grand des Citateurs ayant coutume de m'envoyer des messages, dits "Échos" entre nous, en retournant vers moi des lignes ou des syntagmes que j'avais naguère frappés et qu'il avait été le plus prompt au monde à recevoir tout comme s'il allait justement les écrire ou venait à l'instant d'écrire les mêmes lui-même, si bien qu'entre nous antériorité et simultanéité se mêlait l'une en l'autre, et dès qu'il prononça "toutes-puissances-autres" j'eus un coup au cœur comme si

> debout sur un quai de la gare le visage tendu vers le train qui estompe le voyageur j'avais aperçu à l'extrémité de l'image l'agitation d'un mouchoir.
>
> And at these words . . . I was thrilled to see my friend rapidly signaling to me in one of those gestures he was forever making, playful and childlike in the manner that was a convention of our friendship, which we called *making a citation* or sometimes *secretcitation*. We've never ceased, in the friendship I alone remain to speak of, seasoning the discourse of the one with words of the other, so naturally, so apparently spontaneously that no third person would ever detect a trace of soldering in the alloy of our phrases we the above signed and above all we undersigned. He especially greatest of Citers was in the habit of sending me messages we between us called "Echoes," him batting back in my direction a few lines or syntagms that I'd once hit, that he'd been fastest in the whole world to receive as if he himself were just about to jot them down or had just that instant written the same himself, so that between us priority and simultaneity were mixed up, and as soon as he pronounced "omnipotence others" my heart shook as if standing on a train platform, eyes straining in the direction of the train that blurs the traveler I caught the flicker of a handkerchief way off at the other end of the image.[50]

This passage characterizes the dialogue between the two writers. The affective charge of recognition that the citation provokes in the narrator ("un coup au cœur" and "une extase d'émotion"), as well as the playful, childlike, natural and spontaneous manner in which this conversation takes place, underscore the fact that *secrécitation* is above all an act of friendship, and not an exclusively writerly or intellectual act. Furthermore, the terms Cixous uses to describe this practice suggest alternative forms of communication that do not rely on writing, including "convention," "message," and "signe" (echoed in the "faire signe" of the frantic handkerchief—another sign that recalls Derrida's *Fichus*). Calling them "Échos" and even "assaisonnements" further underscores this distinction. The fact that the "secrécitations" take place beyond writing emphasizes their authorial and material indeterminacy.

Indeed, the speed and simultaneity of "secrécitation" make it difficult to know to what extent the crossovers are intentional, overriding concerns of appropriation or intellectual property. It is impossible to tell who said or wrote what first, to ascribe ownership to specific concepts or phrasings. Frédéric Regard calls this practice "citational grafting," identifying it as the modality par excellence of *écriture féminine*, since it "flouts the law of differentiation [as well as] the difference between male writing and female writing, understood as manifestations of ontological or biological identities."[51] *Écriture féminine* does so in its characteristic gesture, *voler*, to fly and to steal:

displacing property and language between categories of identity, *écriture féminine* cannot be ascribed to one kind of writing or one gender.[52] Within the wider context of Cixous's oeuvre, especially regarding a writing freed of individual subjecthood, Cixous's "secrécitation" homes in on the particularity of friendship. Just as Derrida had claimed a "corps d'écriture publique" for the shared *fourmi*, Cixous invokes a corpus teeming with unidentifiable references.

Perhaps the most striking aspect of the passage shown above is the "trace de la soudure de l'alliage" of their friendship. Akin to the "porte condamnée" of Derrida's invitation-warning in *Genèses*, this trace indicates a bond, yet is indiscernible: "aucun tiers" ("no third person") would be able to locate it. It bars access to the secret language of this friendship. The bond is thus both manifest and secret, linking the two writers in a kinship that cannot be unraveled. In *Insister*, Cixous calls their dialogue a "conversation inintérrompue" ("uninterrupted conversation"), reading Derrida's assessment of their friendship in *H. C. pour la vie* as a "révélation . . . d'une parenté vierge d'héritage entre deux écritures tout autres qui n'auront jamais cessé de se retrouver" (a "revelation without guilt, in a parenthesis, of a kinship untouched by legacy between two altogether other writings that will never have ceased finding themselves/each other").[53] This is more than an intertextuality that can be puzzled out, identified, and named—through Benjamin's *sommier* and his *fichu*, for example.[54] Instead, Cixous claims an irrevocable bond for her friendship with Derrida within, through, and beyond writing, a bond that has no precedent or inheritance. The dovetailing and overlap of their texts is the means by which their friendship can solidify, take shape, and be sustained, even beyond death.

Nor can we point to the fortuitous conjunction of Derrida's *Mémoires d'aveugles: L'Autoportrait et autres ruines* and Cixous's "Autoportraits d'une aveugle" (a chapter in *Jours de l'an*) as an example of *secrécitation*. This pairing is often cited to indicate the closeness of the two writers' friendship and their thought, particularly given their works' obviously similar titles. The texts were written around the same time, yet the overlap was unconscious, Derrida affirms, "sans que nous nous soyons jamais donné le mot" ("without our ever having spoken of it").[55] It may be possible to envision a project tracing parallel echoes through the two texts. Such an assiduous comparative study would seek to prove a textual dialogue between the two writers through explicit evidence, and might aim to further reinforce the connection between the writers. I willfully set aside such a project here, choosing instead to follow the implications of Cixous's resistance to this kind of approach for literary criticism and manuscript study within the context of the *secrécitation*. Significantly, the dovetailing of *Mémoires* and "Autoportraits" in these two texts occurs blindly, between two "aveugles," and constitutes a ground on which to elaborate a different kind of life writing, a challenge to the limits of life and the consequences of these limitations for two bodies of writing in conversation. Instead of constituting a traceable interconnection between Cixous and Derrida, the salient marks of intertextuality gesture toward a vast, intricate network of connection between the two writers that resists being brought to light in any methodical way. By investigating the inner workings of these connections in *Hyperrêve*, Cixous demonstrates the potential for telepathic writing, beyond intertextuality: the dream and the telephone become venues where these connections can be realized "autrement" ("otherwise").

Incorporating Dreams

In *Insister*, Cixous describes the importance of dreaming and sharing dreams for both her own and Derrida's writing, as well as their friendship:

> Le désir du rêve *nous* a toujours occupés. . . . Toute la vie *nous* en parlons, du Rêve-et-du-texte, de rêver, d'écrire, de ne pas rêver, des sorts différents qui *nous* sont faits, qui *nous* sommes, que *nous* sommes . . . Que *nous nous* soyons depuis toujours si souvent entretenus de rêves, de rêver . . . Toute la vie *nous nous* racontons nos rêves jusqu'à la fin. *Nous nous* donnons à "lire" ces chapitres par lui non écrits pour la plupart, quoiqu'il en ait noté certains, tous écrits pour ma part. Je veux dire : *nous nous* les disons, lisons, citons, à haute voix. *Nous nous* montrons nos trouvailles. (Emphasis added)

> The desire of the dream has always preoccupied us. . . . All our lives we talk about it, about the Dream-and-the-text, about dreaming, not dreaming, the different lots that have fallen to us, who we are, that we slumber, he the intermittent dreamer, me impenitence itself . . . That we have so often and for so long spoken of dreams, of dreaming . . . Throughout life we tell each other our dreams right up to the end. We give each other these chapters "to read," for him unwritten for the most part, even though he has noted some of them, as for me they are all written. I mean: we say them, read them, cite them to each other, out loud. We show each other our lucky finds.[56]

Through homophonic play, polysemy, double genitive ("le désir du rêve," read as the dream's desire and the desire for the dream), and detached referents (especially the expansive, ambiguous *nous*), Cixous builds up an equivocality of dreamers and dreaming that resonates like an infinite echo chamber. The "sommes" in particular vacillates between the conjugated verb "to be" and its other meanings: a sum total, a burden, an order, or a nap, recalling the "sommier" that features in *Hyperrêve*, published in the same year. The hypnotic repetition of *nous nous* highlights the reflexive and reciprocal verbal structure: the *nous* mirror each other as they are refracted across the page. In conversation about and through dreaming, Cixous and Derrida are no longer two individual writers but a doubled unit sharing in harmonic play.

Throughout *Insister*, Cixous's use of *nous* makes it difficult to separate their shared plurality of dreaming from individual concerns. Telephonic technology brings the impression of aural intimacy and interconnectedness further into relief. "La plupart du temps," Cixous explains, "nous nous sommes 'donnés' les rêves comme en rêve, par téléphone. À l'oreille on voit mieux, c'est-à-dire on rêve mieux, . . . on se surveille moins, à distance, on fait peu de style" ("Most often we 'gave' each other dreams as if in a dream, over the telephone. With the ear one sees better, that is, one dreams better, . . . One doesn't watch oneself as much, at a distance, one cares little about style").[57] The dream is ideally told to "une personne qui n'interrompt pas, ne pulvérise pas la frêle valeur, qui goûte sans bruit, à presque personne. À soi-même, près de soi-même. À un supplément de soi" ("to a person who does not interrupt, does not crush the frail vapor, who tastes noiselessly, to almost no one. To oneself, near to oneself. To a self supplement").[58] The telephone makes it possible to confuse oneself with one's interlocutor, in the absence of the other person, and through the intermediary of a nonhuman apparatus.

Especially as it is shared over the telephone through Cixous's description of this technology's effects on selfhood and sensation, the dream could be one of the untraceable "secrécitations" that echo throughout Cixous's and Derrida's writing, linking them up in an oneiric web. Cixous includes several of Derrida's dreams in *Insister*, forming a corollary to Derrida's desire to give "Fourmis" "un corps d'écriture publique" ("a body of public writing"). *Insister* begins with an italicized epigraph titled "Rêve d'avril 2005" ("Dream, April 2005"), yet no author or dreamer is ascribed to the text, which features another "sommes": "toi et moi nous sommes deux souris vêtues sport" ("you and I are two mice in sports clothes"). At the other end of the book, six short texts comprise a section titled "J. D. rêvant" ("J.D. dreaming"). Narrative signposts such as "Il me raconte: trois rêves. Trois bouts de rêve dit-il" ("He recounts to me: three dreams. Three bits of dreams he says") give some context without calling the dreamer directly by name.[59] The dreams seem to have been directly transcribed, using a "je" that ventriloquizes "J. D." These dreams stand alone, without interpretation or analysis, and serve as a final reminder of *Insister*'s overarching assertion that life and friendship can be preserved through shared dreams, though the limits of individual lives and voices are blurred in this communication.

But the records of their shared dreams are not found solely in published texts: the conjunction is at work at the level of language and multiplied voices. In Cixous's description of their telephonic dialogue, with the repetition of "nous nous" introducing a mesmerizing harmonics, it is nearly impossible to distinguish one from the other. The notion of selfhood dissolves in the process. The repetition of "nous" enacts a simultaneous joining and separation, challenging the notion of symmetrical exchange and reciprocity. We have seen that Derrida and Cixous explore the porous boundary between self and other, notably in *Voiles* where Derrida allows himself to be "envahi" by "un vrai souvenir d'enfance, l'envers d'un rêve" ("a true childhood memory, the opposite of a dream") after reading Cixous's essay "Savoir."[60] In *Insister*, Cixous's encounter with the *Voiles* manuscript also lets the other in: "Cette essence de présence était en moi. Elle était moi" ("This essence of presence was in me. It was me").[61] At the conjunction of the surprise encounter with a manuscript and a quasi-dream state, the melding of modes of being—between sleeping and waking, between human and nonhuman interlocutors, whether objects or dreamed *revenants*—underscores the possibility of living on, close to the text.

The overlapping of voices, bodies, and written traces characterizes this mode of conjoined writing as physical and embodied. Derrida experimented with doubled and intertwined voices formally and theoretically, exploring the hymen and the tympan as surfaces of inscription and figures for sexual difference.[62] In "Chorégraphies," a 1982 interview with Christie MacDonald on the subject of sexual difference in his work, Derrida rejects the idea that terms such as "hymen" have an anatomical specificity that would make them the sole property of women. He describes his vision for opening up embodied language via "la multiplicité de voix sexuellement marquées . . . ce nombre indéterminable de voix enchevêtrées" ("the multiplicity of sexually marked voices . . . this indeterminable number of blended voices"). Imagining the future of non-binary, non-heteronormative sexual difference, Derrida insists on multiplicity, calling for "des chorégraphies incalculables" ("incalculable choreographies") and "une sexualité innombrable" that would "[venir] nous protéger, comme un rêve, contre un implacable destin qui scelle tout à perpétuité du chiffre 2" ("a sexuality without number [that] can still protect us, like a dream, from an implacable destiny which immures everything for life in the figure 2").[63] Derrida's use of the word "dream" is not a figure for an unattainable utopian future or a personal desire. Instead, the dream becomes the vehicle for the "enchevêtrement des voix" ("blended voices") that Derrida proposes: "rêver l'innombrable. Oui, peut-être, pourquoi pas ? Mais d'où viendrait alors le 'rêve' de l'innombrable, si c'est un rêve ? À lui seul ne prouve-t-il pas ce dont il rêve et qui doit bien être là pour faire rêver ?" ("dreaming the innumerable. Yes, perhaps; why not? But where would the 'dream' of the innumerable come from, if it is indeed a dream?").[64] Repeated over and over, the word *rêve* acquires a hypnotic quality, as if the speaker is testing its semantic and idiomatic limits through the multiplicity it would permit. The "voix enchevêtrées" that come together in this dream have a performative function, materializing the possibility of the dream. Derrida returns to the idea of sexual difference figured as intertwining voices in the 1999 film *D'ailleurs, Derrida* by Safaa Fathy, giving voice to the paradigm of "différences sexuelles" as a "tresse de voix" ("braid of voices") even within individuals, acknowledging a "plurivocité qui travaille chaque voix" ("a plurivocity working within each voice"):

> Dès que "je" parle, ce je est constitué par cet enchevêtrement des voix, une voix habitant l'autre, hantant l'autre. . . . Alors la multiplicité des voix est aussi l'espace ouvert aux fantômes, aux revenants, ce qui est exclu, forclos. J'essaierai de penser ensemble la multiplicité des voix, la hantise, la spectralité, et aussi tout ce dont nous parlons depuis un moment du côté du meurtre et des répressions des différences sexuelles, de la femme, etc.
>
> As soon as "I" speak, this I is made up of this tangle of voices, one voice inhabiting the other, haunting the other. . . . The multiplicity of voices is then too the space open to ghosts, phantoms, that which is excluded, foreclosed. I will endeavor to think together the multiplicity of voices, haunting, spectrality, as well as all that we speak of in terms of the murder and repression of sexual differences, of woman, etc.

This understanding of sexual difference rejects the notion of a singular identity based on or linked to a singular sex, gender, or sexuality. An individual can be "traversée" by phantomatic otherness, opening up to difference within oneself, and to the shifting of these differences over time. Derrida uses the same term, *enchevêtrement*, in *Genèses . . .* with regard to Cixous's dreams, referring to "le tissu enchevêtré qui relie [les rêves de Cixous] à l'œuvre publiée" ("the tangle of threads that ties [Cixous's dreams] to the published work").[65] The figure of entanglement, with crossed lines, gives a physical form to dreaming and to writing, echoing the figure of "secrécitation" between Cixous and Derrida.

A Telegraphic Force Field

With the *ombilic* that invites the reader to enter the archive though the door is barred, and with the incorporated *cryptopoétique* of Cixous's dreams, we have seen that both Cixous and Derrida mine psychoanalysis for models of transmission and communication. The embodied dreams in *Insister* and "Fourmis" distinguish Cixous's and Derrida's take on shared writing and reading from a Freudian understanding of telepathy. Whereas Freud kept his distance from the concept of telepathy, Derrida and Cixous's interest in telepathic forms takes shape in embodied dreams, animated objects, telephony, and telegraphy, all of which allow for communication at a scene of co-writing.

Freud approached the subject of telepathy over the course of his career in several written lectures that were never delivered publicly, including "Psychanalyse et télépathie" (1921), "Rêve et télépathie" (1922), and "Rêve et occultisme" (1932). Throughout these essays, Freud relates telepathy to dreaming, and especially to dreams of premonition, where the content of the dream appears to materialize in the following days or weeks. Derrida addressed Freud's skeptical attitude toward the subject in his essay "Télépathie," where he characterizes Freud's dismissal of telepathic dreams as a fear of otherness, and explores the relationship between telepathy and dreams as a privileged mode of communication. Cixous weaves direct and indirect references to Derrida's "Télépathie" into her own book *Philippines* (2009). Some of the most direct of these include individual words that are not explicitly cited, such as "le premier pas," "le lac," and the figure of twins. Like *Hyperrêve*, which is haunted by echoes of Derrida's *Fichus*, *Philippines* seems to serve as a response to Derrida's writing, a way of staying in communication with him after his death. But Cixous's reading of "Télépathie" and of *Fichus* is not solely a means of continuing their textual dialogue; by engaging with these texts, she explores their shared interest in the metaphysical access made possible through dreams and telepathy, emphasizing the strangeness, otherness, and unknowability of certain forms of communication. Neither writer affirms an abstracted belief in telepathy; both Cixous and Derrida experiment with its potential concrete form, in the figure of the telephone, in the anatomical reverberations of voice and sound, and in dynamic textual objects, as we see in Cixous's encounters with surprising, "flying" manuscripts, and with Derrida's experience with the manuscript of *Le Prénom de Dieu* as an unidentifiable flying literary object.

In *H. C. pour la vie*, Derrida characterizes Cixous's writing as "telegraphic" (a word he borrows from her own writing, in *OR*) through his theorization of virtuality in her work. The intensity of the telegraphic relation counters the distance (*tele-*) it implies with a *cele-* of acceleration and infinite speed, creating the impression of a jump or a "coup," a break, into otherness. Just as her encounters with lost manuscripts transport her into another state, Cixous's writing unsettles the integrity of "being" or "essence," according to Derrida, allowing the dreamer and reader, like the letter, "to go from one point to another in space or time, on the page, for example, or between pages, or between dreaming and awakening, phantasm and reality," and "even faster than all these speeds" in a "quasi-infinite acceleration" ("se déplac[er] pour se rendre d'un point à un autre de l'espace ou du temps, sur la page, par exemple, ou entre les pages, ou entre le rêve et le réveil, le phantasme et la réalité"; "encore plus vite que toutes ces vitesses"; "accélération quasiment infinie").[66] The displacement that occurs here is not bounded by a particular form of reality or spatial fixedness, but can occur in or around a literary object ("entre les pages"). Both as speed and as movement through space, Cixous's writing, according to Derrida, orchestrates an instantaneous *coup*.

Derrida calls this technique "injonctions télégraphiques" ("telegraphic injunctions"), borrowing the term from Cixous's book *OR*.[67] Derrida once again grafts Cixous's writing, declining to invent a new term or interpretation of her work. Instead, he expands this particular phrase to describe Cixous's writing on the whole. For Derrida, Cixous's oeuvre is characterized by a desire and demand to be transported into otherness, into an elsewhere, at top speed. Her "injonctions télégraphiques" operate according to "l'accélération même et l'impatience absolue de mon désir qui voudrait la faire arriver aussitôt, sans attendre, vivement" ("acceleration itself and the absolute impatience of my desire, which would like to make it arrive straightaway, without delay, briskly"), as Derrida puts it.[68] This "changement de vitesse" and "accélération infinie" constitute the force (*puissance*) of Cixous's writing.[69] The speed of her writing gives the effect of instantaneity: "Comme si dans le temps, dans l'intervalle du temps, tout allait si vite qu'il n'y avait plus le temps. . . . c'est l'accélération infinie de la vitesse. D'un coup d'œil, à l'instant, d'un clin d'œil même (*Augenblick*): vite la vision" ("As if in time, in the interval of time, everything went so fast that there would be no time anymore. In the interval that spaces out the times and tenses, there is no more time, and this is the infinite acceleration of speed. At a glance, right now, in the twinkling of an eye even [*Augenblick*]: vision, quick").[70] The "coup" that Derrida extolls here transports the dreamer as well as the reader.

Just as the *coup* takes place instantaneously, at top speed, and is nearly imperceptible, it is also difficult to pin down spatially: "You are not transported, you *are* already in the other world," Cixous writes in *Three Steps on the Ladder of Writing*.[71] Derrida describes the dislocation and displacement of Cixous's writing in terms of a foundational, underlying "puissance d'impuissance" ("potency in impotence")[72] that takes places "par-dessous, de façon sous-marine, entre le dessous du subjonctif et le dessous de la substitution" ("underneath, in a submarine fashion, between the underside of the *sub*junctive and the underside of *sub*stitution").[73] This is a writing that reworks spatial hierarchies of above and below, and reworks assumed hierarchical binaries between activity and passivity; a writing "dont la venue, l'événement, l'arrivance consisterait justement en cette efficace, en ce coup qui abolit la différence entre *faire venir* et *laisser venir*" ("whose coming, event, and *arrivance* would lie precisely in this effectiveness, in this *coup*, which abolishes the difference between *making come* and *letting come*").[74] Writing, reading, dreaming, and giving oneself over to otherness—even by being cited by another writer—involve a voluntary disappropriation.

For Derrida, Cixous's writing is a force field: "tout l'œuvre . . . se trouve aimanté, tenu en vibration, à haute tension dans la puissance à la fois actuelle et virtuelle d'un sous-sol magnétique, d'un fond qui recharge chaque unité verbale de la mémoire et de la projection de toutes les autres" ("the whole work . . . is magnetized, held in high-tension vibration, by the power of a magnetic subsoil at once actual and virtual, a bedrock [*un fond*] that recharges each verbal unit with the memory and projection of all the others").[75] This description is not solely figurative, but alludes to a real spatial and physical arrangement of Cixous's work. Derrida opens up the possibility of dreaming as its own *fonds*, or reserve, of power and meaning, permeating all of Cixous's writing and thus also her archive. What Derrida calls the *fond* of Cixous's work—homophonically and etymologically related to the archival *fonds*—sets up an undercurrent that connects the body of work through each of its individual parts. Each small unit is infinitely capable of containing and regenerating the entirety of the work; by tapping into one of these currents, the reader can access a portal into the work.

In *Genèses*, Derrida brings this force into direct connection with the dream-writing so crucial to Cixous's practice. The speed and immediacy of this "saut" ("leap") is the "interruption dans l'interruption" ("interruption in the interruption"), the breakdown of the "césure" ("rupture") between two temporalities or two states of being.[76] There is no divide, no *partage*, between dreaming and waking; her "opération littéraire" ("literary act proper") carries over from "un tout autre réveil" ("a completely other waking") which is the dream state.[77] Derrida writes that "ce réveil dans le réveil est donc l'extrême vigilance de la conscience littéraire" that seeks to "*faire fond* sur le secret de la littérature . . . c'est-à-dire sous le signe ou le verdict de cette condamnation qui non seulement n'a jamais empêché personne de lire, mais ouvre au contraire *un champ infini* à la lecture et à ses jouissances" ("this waking within the waking is therefore the extreme vigilance of a most refined and practiced literary conscience," "founding itself on literature's secret . . . that is marked with the sign or verdict of this boarding up which not only has never kept anyone from reading, but opens on the contrary an infinite field to reading and its pleasures").[78] Derrida paradoxically links "le secret de la littérature" to "le verdict de cette condamnation" that bars the reader from complete interpretation. And yet this condemnation ensures that the pleasure of the text remains infinitely available. *La porte est condamnée mais entrez donc*. Precisely because it is forbidden, precisely because of the secret, you may enter. The vigilant literary consciousness creates a virtual space (*un champ*), preserving the pleasures of the text in an archival gesture that seeks to *faire fond(s)*.

Thus Cixous's "injonction télégraphique" both describes the interconnected network of her writing and, at the same time, offers a means of tapping into this network. For the telegraphic or telepathic reader to enter into communication with the *fonds* or the *champs* of a magnetized and magnetizing literary force field, perhaps all that is needed is to tune the antennae in the right direction. At the end of "Fourmis," Derrida wonders whether the telephonic relation is "un supplément secondaire ou une antenne essentielle à travers toutes les séparations, la télépathie la plus fidèle" ("a secondary supplement or an essential antenna across all separations, the most faithful telepathy").[79] This form of communication with the other—on the telephone, sharing dreams—involves the *fourmi* and all its counterparts that circulate between the two friends. But is dream-writing or telephonic, telepathic writing enough to preserve the network fully and faithfully? Is the "corps d'écriture publique" ("body of public writing") that Derrida proposes for Cixous's dream archivable? Is the BNF, the IMEC, or any other institution prepared to deal with the issues these *fonds* raise, particularly regarding single authorship and materiality? Or are these challenges better left unresolved, to resonate with archival possibility? Can co-writing constitute a legacy that is accessible to a wider network of future friends and readers?

✦

Cixous and Derrida's interwoven dialogue creates an echo chamber resonating throughout their work. The "secrécitations" that connect the two writers are imperceptible, but they are by no means fragile: they create a bond within a pervasive *fonds*. Like an institutional archival *fonds*, this *fonds* can be accessed, though the door is not wide open. The authors challenge the researcher to reflect on the demands they make on literary archives and archival institutions, particularly their expectations regarding access and transparency. If we cannot trace the connections between texts, cannot unravel or even accurately detect the "soudure de l'alliage" ("soldering in the alloy") of texts, how can we understand their relationship to each other? Derrida and Cixous's conversations offer alternative models of reading and interacting with texts, beyond interpretation and analysis. Transmission and conversation between Cixous and Derrida appear not as exchange, in which one text responds to a previous one, creating a pattern of chiasm and crossing, but as a record of dissymmetry and overlap. The calls and responses they make bind the two in friendship: sometimes immediately, crossing geographic or metaphysical distances in an instant, and other times with delayed effects. Both extremes have their own frequencies, but waiting for the belated arrival of a response can be just as intense as the synced-up and hyped-up speed of simultaneous dialogue. Different rhythms of correspondence create a texture in the archival record, an "archival grain" (to use Ann Laura Stoler's formulation) that is not only tactile and textual but can also be aural or even supersensory. Tuning into this frequency requires that the reader enter, perhaps uninvited, into this intimate exchange.

Through dreams, telephone conversations, and telepathic reading, Derrida and Cixous's experimental dialogues test the limits of material traceability and archival presence. As such, they offer the potential to exist otherwise, in a state of afterlife or *survie* that builds on, yet also diverges from, more conventional technologies and techniques of writing. Especially to the grieving friend, they offer the surprise of connection and the immediacy of communication, bridging the interval of separation in the blink of an eye. This kind of synchronicity verges on an impossible proximity, a speed nearly too fast to measure. The risk is that discrete materials and conversations cannot be tracked or traced by archival standards, and that they might not arrive in the writers' institutional collections at all. But their challenges to archival techniques are also a call for reimagined methods and configurations of archival networks. In the next and final chapter, I look at seminar recordings as another instance of the struggle to archive materials when multiple voices are in play, and when the "material" at hand is indeterminate or unpredictable. If the goal is to preserve the work such that it can be reactivated by future readers, what surprise encounters can serve as invitations to participate in this conversation?

Chapter 6

Return to the Scene

The Seminar as Virtual Archive

The short film "La Phrase début" is composed of beginnings of Hélène Cixous's seminar sessions. Over the years, we see Cixous set up her books and notes, adjust her hat, and comment on ambient light or sound. The room changes, as do the style of her clothes and the character of the recording media. Each clip cuts off as soon as she has pronounced the first sentence of the seminar session. This document is the work of Manuel Irniger, who has recorded many years of Cixous's seminars and stores these recordings at his home.[1] By giving attention to the prelude to each session, Irniger reveals the particularities of Cixous's teaching and offers an intimate view of her seminars. In its use of recordings, this film preserves extra-textual aspects of the seminar, providing a counterpoint to conventional archiving and publishing techniques that would privilege textual or linguistic content. The recording captures the particular environment that converges around the event: the pedagogical style created in community, its fullness and liveliness, beyond professorial discourse.

Seminar recordings are emblematic of the communities that sustain the work of thinkers such as Hélène Cixous and Jacques Derrida. But the question of documenting the seminar, whether through recordings or notes, looms large: can a seminar be lived or relived by interacting with its material support, as a paper, digital, or analog recording? How does the material's vulnerability impact the experience of consulting the archived seminar and the possibility of experiencing it as an event, even for the first time? The archived material affects the legacy of writing, thinking, and teaching, especially as new technologies and forms of archival preservation allow for a network of voices to emerge.

The seminar record outpaces a writer's official institutional archive: not solely the instructor but all participants leave traces of this collectively experienced event, whether in the form of notes, recordings, whether authorized or secret, or in memory. Taking an expansive understanding of "media" and its capacities for transmission and preservation contributes to the decentralizing, anti-hierarchical work of the seminar: along with recording devices, as well as students, the pedagogue can serve as the media or medium who facilitates transmission, allowing students to take control of the seminar work. The archived seminar, *partagé* in the sense of split or divided, highlights the separation between what is said (*l'énoncé*) and the moment of saying it (*l'énonciation*). Technology further highlights this divide. The media of seminars, refracted in the archive, counter a view of a flattened, comprehensive media space, and capture and transmit the work of a community across a variety of formats instead of representing or replicating a single, fixed pedagogical discourse.[2] By multiplying voices and media, the seminar emerges as a dynamic, interconnected, virtual network that destabilizes a linear temporality of vertical transmission from master to student, challenges pedagogical conventions of authority and mastery, and creates opportunities for continued conversations. "Comment esquiver la maîtrise?" ("How to elude mastery?") Roland Barthes asked in his essay "Au séminaire" ("To the Seminar").[3] Derrida's and Cixous's answers to this question are tethered to the power of the seminar community and to mediating recording devices.

In the first half of this book, we have seen that the materiality of the archive opens up possibilities for afterlives of writing. We then saw that these possibilities include new forums for contact and communication made possible as the archive's materiality destabilizes notions of authorship, provenance, and property. Cixous and Derrida seek to create a virtual shared archive by harnessing technologies, telepathy, and dreams. This final chapter explores the reach of this virtual archive to unknown, future participants. The seminar is a venue founded in community. Recording a seminar poses particular material challenges that impact its preservation and future access, expanding the seminar community over time. The community that both writers hope to create through their shared archival networks expands beyond a dyadic notion of friendship to allow new kinships, affinities, and genealogies to form. By harnessing the performative power of the seminar and recording technologies, Derrida and Cixous reflect on the seminar's potential both within the moment of teaching and in filmed appearances that speak to recordings and pedagogy more broadly.

Publishing a Seminar

The seminar has come to be recognized for its contributions to the legacy of contemporary French thought, and to the mythologies and genealogies of its major figures, as seen in increased—and ongoing—publication efforts over the past two decades, including Derrida's lectures and seminars at the École normale supérieure, the École des hautes études en sciences sociales, and international visiting appointments; Roland Barthes's and Michel Foucault's seminars at the Collège de France; and Cixous's seminars at the Université

Paris 8 and the Collège international de philosophie. Most often, the "grands séminaires" of a thinker constitute an extensive, even colossal output, often untapped in archives. The projects of editing and publishing critical theory seminars confront the issue of how best to use archival material to make the seminars accessible while preserving the individual pedagogical tenor that distinguishes one thinker's seminars, and also distinguishing the seminar from other kinds of intellectual work, such as monographs, conference proceedings, and creative endeavors.

Derrida's seminar publications arise from the typescripts he wrote out in advance and read, nearly verbatim, in each session. Yet the published volumes highlight the complexity of transforming a live event into a published text, configuring material from media and recording devices to give the impression of the preliminary, contingent "parole enseignante" (speech of instruction) and its difference from Derrida's published oeuvre. The ongoing project to publish Derrida's seminars draws from nearly 14,000 typed pages, working alongside recordings of his seminar to integrate the improvised remarks added *en cours*.[4] Since Derrida did not himself rework the texts for publication, the editors of his seminars seek to preserve the preliminary status of the written texts, explaining their goals in the "Note des éditeurs" that accompanies each volume. They seek to "présenter le *texte* du séminaire, tel qu'il fut *écrit* par Jacques Derrida, *en vue* de la parole, de la lecture à voix haute, donc avec certaines marques d'oralité anticipée et quelques tournures familières" ("to present the *text* of the seminar, as it was *written* by Jacques Derrida, *in view* of being spoken, of being read aloud, and thus with some marks of anticipated orality and some familiar turns of phrase").[5] In this way the published seminars offer "la chance d'un contact . . . avec la parole enseignante du philosophe"[6] ("the opportunity to encounter the philosopher's teachings"). But in the attempt to provide direct written access to the spoken word, this editorial work is made invisible: in the difficult choice between what Derrida had written and any improvised deviations or substitutions captured by audio or video recordings, for example, the editors must necessarily forego a certain amount of the seminar's dynamic potential as live event. In the second volume of the seminar *La Bête et le souverain*, for example, the editors detail the process of triangulating between typescripts, photocopied passages from texts in multiple languages, layers of annotations on these photocopies and in the books tracked down in his personal library, and translations, sometimes improvised or modified multiple times, that Derrida made of his own seminar script when he gave sessions in English. What is at stake here is how to represent and preserve the contingent nature of the event and its divergence from texts written solely for publication, while also providing an accurate, readable record of the seminar's content.

At the opposite end of the spectrum, documentation of Cixous's long-running seminar exists primarily in the form of audio and video recordings—some of which date back to the seminar's first setting at the

Université expérimentale de Vincennes in 1969. Cixous has developed an idiosyncratic, exploratory teaching style covering a range of corpora, themes, and registers over decades of seminars given in experimental venues, some of her own design: as director of the literature division of the Université expérimentale de Vincennes, as founder of the doctorate and Centre d'études féminines, and in collaboration with the Collège international de philosophie. Cixous's seminar diverges from the legacy of *grands séminaires* in postwar France in that it is entirely improvised, unfurling from open books and Post-it notes over the course of several hours on Saturday mornings into the early afternoon. These sessions have been recorded in various formats by different attendees. Transcriptions of reused cassette tapes, professional and amateur video camera footage—these materials are what remain of Cixous's seminars.[7] They have recently been acquired by the Bibliothèque nationale de France, yet the institutional website of the *fonds* Cixous does not include any information about these recordings' material form, presence, or availability.[8]

The task of expanding the preservation and access of these materials is especially urgent as Cixous's seminars are prepared for publication: this is a project that must grapple with the status of the recordings and the possibilities for translating their dynamism and experimental quality into a written form.[9] Recordings have informed the ongoing publication of Cixous's seminars under the editorship of Marta Segarra, as well as two earlier, separate volumes from Cixous's seminar. Verena A. Conley's edition of *Readings: The Poetics of Blanchot, Joyce, Kafka, Kleist, Lispector, and Tsvetaeva* (1991) contains materials authored solely by Cixous, whereas in *Writing Differences: Readings from the Seminar of Hélène Cixous* (1998), editor Susan Sellers presents Cixous's words alongside texts by a number of participants who contributed to the seminar. Both volumes work from recordings and transcriptions, as well as from pre-written texts, smoothing them over for publication. In her introduction, Conley refers to Cixous's seminars as a "laboratory" and as "material" that "is elsewhere transformed poetically in her fictional writings. In these pages she explains what her fiction performs."[10] But the material published in *Readings* is not raw; it has been transformed editorially: oral effects, including verbal tics and repetitive phrasings, have deliberately been erased.[11] Because of this and "because of the pedagogical tenor of the seminars," Conley suggests, the *Readings* are "eminently readable."[12] Marta Segarra's edition of Cixous's seminars acknowledges the orality of the seminar, while deferring to the textual nature of the publication, explaining for example the editorial decision not to include circumstantial anecdotes "puisqu'ils n'étaient pas faits pour être lus mais pour être entendus" ("because they were not told to be read but to be heard") and because their tonal complexities would be lost in transcription.[13]

How in fact is a reading transformed into a transcribed, published text? Where does the preliminary material go? How can it be preserved in an archival setting? What are the material effects of publishing a *reading*? If improvisation and community (of attendees and texts) contribute to the creative force and particular style of Cixous's seminars, which I maintain is the case, then the end goal of publication must strive to highlight this. As Lucy O'Meara describes the publication of Roland Barthes's seminars, the goal would be to preserve, however paradoxically, "the contingent nature of the material" in a "quasi-archival mode."[14] But as Conley's use of the word suggests, it is unclear in what sense the seminar consists of "material." On the one hand, each year of Cixous's seminar could be understood as a genetic dossier, as preparation for the book Cixous writes during the following summer: this has long been the rhythm of Cixous's creative process. But the seminar "material" could also be understood as a specific form of improvisational writing in its own right. If the latter understanding of the seminar is prioritized, then the seminar material would warrant a specific strategy of archival preservation, processing, and cataloging, with the goal of allowing expansive access to researchers and students of all kinds.

The publication of Roland Barthes's lectures at the Collège de France provides a counter-example of an editorial attempt to evoke an intermedial portrait of teaching, giving an archival quality to the published artifact. Prepared in collaboration with the IMEC, home to the Barthes collection before it was transferred to the BNF, the volumes balance Barthes's own preparatory notes with recordings and students' notes, and are supplemented by audio recordings of these lectures available on CDs and online. The publication harnesses an archival component through a variety of media to convey the contingent and improvisational qualities of the seminar event. Barthes's notes, written out before his lectures and read with "minimal improvisation," amount to what editor Éric Marty calls an "infratexte."[15] The decision to preserve the archival quality of the seminar in publication—"the contingent nature of the material" in a "quasi-archival mode"—contributes to the liveliness of the document, giving the reader the impression of witnessing the event unfolding.

Unlike other forms of teaching, such as the lecture, the seminar provides a form in which the idea of mastery and absolute knowledge can be challenged. Barthes draws out the collaborative, anti-authoritarian nature of the seminar in "Au séminare," an essay written as an homage to and explanation of this particular form. In the seminar, he writes, "aucun savoir n'est transmis (mais un savoir peut être créé), aucun discours n'est tenu (mais un texte se cherche)" ("In the seminar, . . . no knowledge is transmitted [but a knowledge can be created], no discourse is sustained [but a text is sought]").[16] According to Barthes, the seminar is characterized by the collective work of production and composition, fueled by desire: "Ou bien quelqu'un travaille, cherche, produit, assemble, écrit devant les autres ; ou bien tous s'incitent, s'appellent, mettent en circulation l'objet à produire, la démarche à composer, qui passent ainsi de main en main, suspendus au fil du désir" ("Either someone works, seeks, produces, gathers, writes in the others' presence; or else all incite each other, call to each other, put into circulation the object to be produced, the procedure to compose, which thus passes from hand to hand, suspended from the thread of desire").[17] The improvised, contingent nature of the seminar is rooted in its collective aspect, which can extend beyond the context of the seminar event to the seminar's afterlife. If it is to continue its collective, creative work, the seminar must foster the "suspension" of desire, extending it across time and space to future participants who would continue to access and circulate the object of desire. Cixous describes her seminar in similar terms, using an archival metaphor to evoke the seminar as a place where the participants are "guardians" of the text: "I use the word 'guardian' . . . not just in the passive sense, but as someone who breathes on the fire, runs to fetch fuel for it: fosterer of the vital flame," she explains.[18] Cixous highlights the importance of collaborative work in sustaining the seminar as a living archive in which pedagogical style, practiced in community, amounts to an active archiving technique.

Performing the Pedagogue

None of Derrida's archival collections contain recordings of his seminars. The most extensive holdings of his seminar recordings are part of filmmaker Safaa Fathy's archives at UC Irvine, in the form of unused footage Fathy shot for her 1999 documentary *D'ailleurs, Derrida*. The location of these recordings speaks to the importance of the student, and of the performative and creative qualities of pedagogy. Filmed recordings of Derrida performing a pedagogical role give a sense of the potential for "suspending" the seminar moment and opening it up to a virtual archive that can be accessed by future participants. Three feature-length films include footage of Derrida teaching. In addition to Fathy's film and *Derrida*, the Kirby Dick and Amy Ziering Kofman documentary (2002), Derrida participated in Ken McMullen's experimental film *Ghost Dance* (1983). In all three films, Derrida draws attention to the recording devices present, revealing the structures that underwrite a performance of authority and knowledge that he interrogates on camera. His performances suggest that he found the seminar to be a space particularly hospitable to haunting and virtuality, especially in the presence of recording devices. These scenes of teaching are crucial to Derrida's work on the performative event in the context of the university. Pedagogy, spectrality, and media come together to allow for the surprising, performative event to occur, countering a model of constative, absolute knowledge that Derrida rejects.

Derrida's interest in legacy and transmission is linked to haunting. A pedagogical aspect underlies his explorations of spectrality, particularly in *Spectres de Marx*, where Derrida introduces the term *hauntologie*. The text of that book opens with a pedagogical scene: the spectral condition is essential to the project of learning to live, Derrida writes. It is necessary to "apprendre à vivre *avec* les fantômes, dans l'entretien, la compagnie ou le compagnonnage, dans le commerce sans commerce des fantômes" ("to learn to live *with* ghosts, in the upkeep, the conversation, the company, or the companionship, in the commerce without commerce of ghosts").[19] Earlier, in his appearance in the film *Ghost Dance*, Derrida participates in a pedagogical conversation about ghosts. His affirmation that technology can "décuple[r] le pouvoir des fantômes" ("heighten the power of ghosts") establishes a link between technology and haunting, but the pedagogical scene is also reversed, as the roles of student and teacher shift during filming and in a viewing, years later. Taken together, Derrida's work on spectrality in *Spectres de Marx* and on the value of communication and dialogue with ghosts in *Ghost Dance* reveals an essential instability in the roles of student, teacher, and ghost.

Mastery is unsettled by the presence of technology, including the devices that record a seminar or other pedagogical scenes. In *Ghost Dance*, Derrida plays a philosophy professor instructing and advising a young, rebellious student interested in philosophy, played by Pascale Ogier. They have arranged to meet in the professor's office. Leaning back in his chair behind a desk covered in papers and books, Derrida expounds on the topic of ghosts and technology in philosophy. His lecture is interrupted by a phone call, which gives the professor the opportunity to draw attention to the ubiquity of technologies and recording devices and their ability to increase the presence and power of ghosts: he asserts that "les développements de la technologie et de la télécommunication décuplent le pouvoir des fantômes, le retour des fantômes" ("developments in technology and telecommunication heighten the power of ghosts, the ghosts' return"). Derrida improvised his speech in each take of the scene, but was instructed by McMullen to conclude each take by asking Ogier's character whether she herself believed in ghosts. The camera registers the professor's surprise at her unhesitating affirmative response, then cuts to Ogier's face, in close-up. Her repeated "Oui, maintenant oui" resonates over and over again as the scene fades out.

Derrida's performance of a professor knowledgeable on the subject of ghosts in philosophy and in control of his meeting with the curious student in *Ghost Dance* contrasts with his experience viewing the film later on, described in *Échographies de la télévision*. Ogier had died unexpectedly of a heart attack after the film was released, and Derrida is shaken by the experience of watching her on-screen presence repeatedly affirm that yes, she does, "now," believe in ghosts. The question he had posed to Ogier over and over again, a rhetorical question that was meant to conclude the scene and his improvised discourse, resonates with the certainty of the student's temporally open-ended answer, as the "maintenant" of filming extends to the "now" of Derrida's viewing. When he watches the film years later, his initial position of expertise as professor is unsettled and the roles are reversed, as he finds himself prompted by Ogier's spectral image to reflect on death, ghosts, and the capacity of technology to facilitate their return. In his retrospective meditation on his experience of working with Ogier, Derrida emphasizes his position as a student, as he recalls learning about acting techniques from her: "Pascale Ogier . . . m'avait enseigné pendant les intervalles" the importance of "eyelines" before filming the scene: "le fait de se regarder les yeux dans les yeux" ("During the breaks Pascale Ogier had taught me . . . looking each other in the eye").[20] In his experience of filming *Ghost Dance*, Derrida was the student of Ogier's expertise, just as in viewing the film, Derrida places himself in the position of learning from a ghostly apparition.

Through the eyelines orchestrated between actors and viewers, and through the repetition of Ogier's ghostly affirmation, framed by references to phantomatic recording devices, Derrida creates a feedback loop that implicates his own appearance in the film and the viewers who will encounter his image and voice after his own death. Derrida's performance creates an experience of haunting that does not reproduce the event, but instead dislocates time and space, creating the spectral sense of being that Derrida later calls *hauntologie*. In Derrida's performance in *Ghost Dance*, recording technologies emphasize the desire to maintain conversation and exchange, albeit curtailed and frustrated, beyond the event and beyond the grave.

In the two documentaries featuring Derrida, the subject is transformed into material via an awareness of recording devices, which Derrida himself encourages. The attention to material recorded, edited, and shaped into a film frames the documentaries with an archival quality, as if the specter of the archive were lingering just beyond the final cut. The transformation of professor into material is at work from the moment recording begins. Amy Ziering Kofman and Kirby Dick's documentary, *Derrida* (2002), includes footage from the inauguration of Derrida's archives at UC Irvine, and from one of his lectures in a large amphitheater. Derrida opens the session with a disclaimer that draws attention to the camera, requesting the audience's permission to be filmed, and commenting on the ever-present recording devices. He then draws a parallel between the amphitheater's previous use as a dissection and operating theater, and the "operation" of the lecture itself, noting the potential ethical risks of technique and technology—whether animal dissection, close reading, or invasive recording. By drawing attention to recording devices, highlighting their potential for the virtual and the spectral, and by challenging the students to be aware of their responsibilities faced with the "material" at hand—in some cases, the material being the teacher himself—Derrida draws out an archival awareness of the seminar. Recordings underscore the seminar as a virtual space subject to the risks of transmission.

Safaa Fathy's documentary *D'ailleurs, Derrida* (1999) offers a portrait of Derrida's work and its intricate relationship with his life, including his career as a university professor—a biographical experiment that necessarily relies on the intimacy and dedication of the filmmaker, who regularly attended

Derrida's seminars. Fathy spent years amassing an archive of filmed material from Derrida's seminars, from which she drew for the film. This material is stored in Fathy's archival collection at UC Irvine, along with additional recordings.[21] In one of the opening scenes of *D'ailleurs, Derrida*, filmed at his home in Laguna Beach, near UC Irvine, Derrida likens the filmmaker's work to that of a writer, telling Fathy: "Vous êtes en train, vous, d'écrire, c'est-à-dire d'inscrire des images que vous allez à votre tour monter, éditer, sélectionner, couper, coller, . . . et moi je suis là, une espèce de matériau pour votre écriture" ("Right now you are writing, which is to say you are inscribing images that you will in turn assemble, edit, select, cut, paste . . . and there I am, a kind of material for your writing"). Derrida's self-identification as "material" resonates throughout the documentary, especially in the scenes that stage him among his personal archives—in his library attic "sublime" and his garden storage shed, for example. The student (Fathy) is positioned as the inheritor not just of the professor's thought, his legacy, but also as the inheritor of a "material" that will be molded and shaped by the student. Derrida is the material, but the film's material also consists of the physical items stored at UC Irvine: the creator of these documents is not Derrida, but Fathy. By acknowledging that Fathy's work has transformed him into "une espèce de matériau," Derrida relinquishes a certain amount of control over his legacy and transmission. His seminar material does not coalesce into one collection under his own name, but is part of the network that makes up the Critical Theory Archive as a whole at UC Irvine—significantly, in the unused material of his student's film. The seminar is generative for future work—both intellectual and creative—beyond the moment of pedagogical instruction.

In his reflections on the university, Derrida links the mastery imbuing the figure of the pedagogue to the power of profession as a performative act. He writes in *L'Université sans condition* that the goal of the professor is to "[produire] des événements, par exemple en écrivant, et en donnant lieu . . . à des *œuvres* singulières" ("produc[e] events [for example, by writing] and by giving rise to singular *œuvres*").[22] Without elaborating on the nature of these "œuvres," Derrida makes it clear that he is not referring to an epistemological project. Knowledge, for him, remains constative, reinforcing the status quo by presuming to speak from a preestablished position of authority.[23] A true event within the university would have to be performative, according to Derrida: through this kind of speech act, the teacher or professor can create new works, new events, and new ideas. The seminar offers this possibility, but only insofar as it is an event in which many participate. Derrida sees the seminar as a collective act of interpretation, writing in "Mochlos ou le conflit des facultés" that the performative act and responsibility of the university is to continually reinscribe and reinvent the contract of community through the act of interpretation.[24] In this view, teaching is a communal, performative event capable of creating and maintaining a community.

Cixous's Seminar as an "*Opération Poétique*"

In *H. C. pour la vie*, Derrida presents Cixous as a practitioner of the ideal "opération poétique" that constitutes a truly performative act. He does so by challenging the notion of expertise, and positing a temporal relationship between Cixous's texts and his own reading that would contribute to preserving her work for future readers. Instead of presenting himself as the foremost expert on her texts because of his position as her first reader, he rejects textual mastery in order to characterize her work as truly performative, surprising, and new.

Derrida positions himself as an unknowing, incapable reader from the beginning, when he first encountered Cixous's writing in the early 1960s. In his description of this scene of reading, Cixous's drafts arrive unexpectedly, like "un objet littéraire non identifiable" ("an unidentifiable letter and literary object"), provoking a series of questions: "Qu'est-ce que c'est que ça? me suis-je à peu près demandé. Qu'est-ce qui arrive là? Qu'est-ce qui m'arrive? Quel genre? Qui pourra jamais lire ça? Moi?" he writes in his first description of this scene of reading ("What *is* this? I asked myself more or less. What is happening here? What is happening to me? What genre? Who could ever read this? Me?").[25] Towards the end of *H. C. pour la vie*, he restages his incredulous reaction with another nearly identical volley of questions: "Mais qu'est-ce qui arrive là? Qu'est-ce qui se met au monde et dans la littérature, etc.? Ou 'qu'est-ce qui m'arrive là'; 'Qu'est-ce que je vais faire, moi, avec ça?'; 'Qu'est-ce que ce type? ce nouveau type d'autobiographie délirante et sublime?'; 'Qui est-ce?'; 'Qu'est-ce qu'elle veut, celle-là?'" ("What on earth is happening here? What is brought into the world and into literature, etc.? Or 'What is happening to me here?'; 'What am I going to do with this?'; 'What on earth is this type, this new type of raving and sublime autobiography?'; 'Who is this?'; 'What is it that she wants?'").[26] The doubled scene stages a preliminary and ever-repeating position of interrogation and surprise vis-à-vis Cixous's writing, framed as a philosophical attitude of questioning.[27] Derrida taps into the Socratic method to enact a reversal of a hierarchical pedagogical and epistemological model, a reversal favoring doubt and uncertainty. Distancing philosophical inquiry from scientific inquiry, Derrida suggests that the former is equipped to encounter and respect the unknown, whereas the latter is concerned with extracting measurable knowledge from discernible objects of study. But Derrida not only shrugs off the possibility that *he* will ever be able to master Cixous's text—he models this as an ideal position of reading: abandoning the need to know and understand, abandoning oneself to the text.

This initial scene of reading and questioning sets the stage for a disorientation to which Derrida applies several modes of textual analysis in order to demonstrate the insufficiency of each one. The explorer, surgeon, and radiologist offer three metaphors for hermeneutic methodology. In each case,

Derrida chips away at the scientist's reliance on absolute knowledge (*savoir absolu*) and instead insists on the unconscious, the invisible, and on imagination as favored modes of reading experience. The three discredited scenes of reading give way to a final approach in which Derrida casts himself as Cixous's prophet, a figure that further disrupts conventions of textual mastery and its reliance on linear models of transmission: he is a follower, but he precedes what he announces.[28] The combination of the prophetic figure with a theorization of the event's arrival is consistent with Derrida's writing at this time: the *à venir* (to-come) has been read as an onto-theological concept, a constantly deferred arrival that takes on a messianic structure of expectation and hope—which Derrida has qualified as a "messianicité sans messianisme" (in *Spectres de Marx*). But Derrida's reading of Cixous's writing operates within a different temporality, since Cixous's writing has already arrived, however unidentifiable and constantly surprising it may be.

Derrida's prophetic pronouncements are ripe with undertones of irony as well as with the importance of fiction, as repeated in Derrida's constant exhortation to imagine, dream, pretend, and *faire comme si* (to pretend, or to make believe).[29] At the beginning of *H. C. pour la vie,* he writes: "quelqu'un en moi, l'un de moi rêve encore d'être le premier à parler d'elle, c'est à dire à l'annoncer, à prédire, à dire, à ceux qui ne l'ont pas encore vue, qu'elle va venir, qu'elle est déjà venue et qu'on ne l'a pas encore reconnue. Comme si j'étais voué à être son prophète" ("someone in me, one of me, is still dreaming about being the first to speak of her, that is to say, to announce her, to predict, to say to those who have not yet seen her that she is coming, that she has already come, and that she has not been recognized yet. As if I were destined to be her prophet").[30] With this allusion to the gospel of John (1:10–11), Derrida adopts an overtly religious tone that echoes throughout the text in his ascription of "toute-puissance" (omnipotence) to Cixous's writing (an *Écriture* read as scripture?). When Derrida returns to the idea of prophecy at the end of *H. C. pour la vie*, he draws the audience into his performance: "permettez-moi de jouer encore un peu au prophète pour mon avant-dernier commencement. . . . Je prévois, donc et je prédis, j'annonce ce que se passera un jour, quand on la lira enfin" ("allow me to play the prophet a little longer for my next to last beginning. . . . I foresee, therefore, and I foretell, I announce what will take place one day, when one reads her at last").[31] Here, Derrida's play-acting echoes the "rêve" and the "comme si" of the earlier passage. The performative aspect, almost heavy-handed in his demonstration, is emphasized by the bookending structure that opens and closes *H. C. pour la vie*: Derrida tells the tale of his first encounter with Cixous's writing twice; he twice restages his incredulous attitude with a litany of questions; and twice he adopts a tone of quasi-ironic prophecy. All of this establishes a narrative framework for his reading. Fiction contributes to the power of performativity, according to Derrida, because it overrides a distinction between the constative and the performative within speech act theory.[32] Derrida harnesses fiction and irony to create a surprising new event, announcing the arrival of Cixous's writing, which he characterizes as a "poétique de l'événement" ("poetics of the event") and an "opération poétique" ("poetical operation").[33]

Derrida's invitations to future readers in *H. C. pour la vie* and *Genèses, généalogies, genres . . . et le génie* make it clear that his prophetic positioning is a generous one, seeking a community composed not of "les élus" ("the happy few") and "les premiers alliés" ("the first allies") but of a group of readers diverse in "la situation, la compétence, la position sociale ou linguistique d'un bout à l'autre du monde, le savoir institutionnel ou la culture nationale" ("their situation, competence, social or linguistic position from one end of the world to the other, institutional knowledge or national culture").[34] In his reading of Cixous in *H. C. pour la vie*, Derrida continues to work against the possessive, even predatory attitude towards knowledge and reading, emblematized in the figures of the scientist that Derrida rejects. Presenting himself as an avid reader of Cixous, but not as an authority on her work, Derrida rejects the figure of the master in favor of the figure of the prophet, laying the groundwork for a community of future readers. Reversing a conventional understanding of Cixous as the student of Derrida, or as a follower of deconstruction, Derrida announces Cixous's future success like a spectral presence, already removed from the present time of his speech. As in the filmed recordings of Derrida teaching, here Derrida highlights spectrality and virtuality across time, proposing a kind of haunting that can move backwards and forwards, instead of a conventional linear transmission.

This opening-up of time is at work in the "opération poétique" ("poetical operation") of Cixous's seminars, which are improvised, unforeseen, and radically new: a true performative event. As such, her seminar cannot be understood as the preliminary sketches of an eventual written poetics, the *avant-texte* of her publications; it cannot be understood to "explain," preemptively, what her fiction then performs. Both as an oeuvre in itself, and within a broader genre of intellectual and literary creation, Cixous's seminar creates a literary community through improvisation and the development of a virtual space and temporality. Like the seminar which Barthes elegizes, Cixous's seminar rejects explanatory "enseignement," or teaching. "Dans le séminaire (c'en est la définition), . . . aucun savoir n'est transmis (mais un savoir peut être créé), aucun discours n'est tenu (mais un texte se cherche)," Barthes writes in "Au séminaire" ("In the seminar [and this is its definition] . . . no knowledge is transmitted [but a knowledge can be created], no discourse is sustained [but a text is sought]").[35] Certainly, in Cixous's seminar style, "un texte se cherche" ("a text is sought"), but it is not a search for a specific text, a search that will culminate in a predetermined publication. Indeed, the "texte" that is searched for here is not necessarily even Cixous's—her reading of other texts involves a searching, a researching, echoing one of the most frequently read texts in her seminar, Proust's *À la recherche du temps perdu*.

In Cixous's seminar, the methodology and theme of "la recherche," a textual meandering, correlates with the itinerant nature of the seminar, which has moved among various institutions and venues over the years. Within the expansive setting of Cixous's seminar the "opération poétique" can do its work, and the unexpected can occur. Cixous speaks of "un certain style" that she developed, afforded by the freedom of time and space that characterized the Université expérimentale de Vincennes:

> Quand on parle de mes séminaires on fait allusion à quelque chose qui se passe là dans cette scène-là, qui est une scène au fond sans limite.s. La limite c'est la limite de nos forces. Quand on est fatigué.e.s on arrête mais sinon c'est illimité dans tous les sens. . . . mes séminaires se poursuivent sans interruption, c'est-à-dire que c'est pas un séminaire par an, c'est perpétuel, voilà, c'est le séminaire perpétuel.[36]

> When people talk about my seminars, they allude to something that takes place there in that place, which is ultimately a place without limits. The limit is the limit of our strength. When we're tired we stop but otherwise it's unlimited in all ways. . . . My seminars follow along without interruption, which is to say that it's not one seminar per year, it's perpetual, yes, it's the perpetual seminar.

Although Cixous gives her seminar a unique title and description every academic year, and although it respects the academic calendar with a summer break, a thematic and bibliographic continuity from year to year connects the seminar into a whole: it is a perpetual seminar, as Cixous calls it. Furthermore, the seminar takes place over several hours, beginning at 9:30 a.m., ending when "on est fatigué.e.s" ("when we're tired"), and often continuing after a coffee break around noon. This is not a discussion-based seminar—Cixous speaks with only occasional interventions from those in attendance—but in her conception the work of the seminar cannot be done in isolation. Aside from the first-person possessive pronoun in the passage quoted above ("mes séminaires"), Cixous describes the seminar and its style either as a collective product ("nos forces," "quand on est fatigué.e.s") or as an independent agent that is taking place ("quelque chose qui se passe là") and continuing on ("se poursuivent"). The texts that circulate in Cixous's seminar are as much a part of the conversation—if not more—than the fifty-plus participants in the auditorium. Cixous refers to the texts studied in the seminar as "nos compagnons, ceux que nous ranimons et qui nous raniment" ("our companions, those who reanimate us and whom we reanimate").[37] In her associative improvisations, Cixous brings texts and authors into dialogue, acting as a medium to bring out unexpected commonalities and resonances.

If Cixous is able to "reanimate" the textual "companions" at hand in her seminar, she also reanimates the interventions of the human "companions" who are invited to participate. Derrida was one of these: as well as being one of the most consistently read authors over the years, he was regularly invited to participate in the last session of the year.[38] But their *séminaire à deux* was an extension of Cixous's pedagogical style, not an exception to it: it continued the practice of bringing together texts—including Derrida's—as "compagnons." Therefore, his death did not signal the end of the "séance rituelle": through animated texts channeled in the seminar, the conversation can go on. Cixous's performances of improvisational readings act as a medium that amplifies the texts she reads, transforming them into ghostly, and therefore powerful, presences in the seminar.

Referring to texts as "compagnons" creates an expansive, non-anthropocentric view of the seminar community. As nonhuman participants, the recording devices make explicit the seminar's archivability and transmission through their uncanny presence. Cixous's role as medium is transmitted through these media. Seen in this light, the seminar recordings that accompany Cixous in each of her seminar sessions are not just a supplement to or a simulacrum of an event. They instead play an integral part in the style of the seminar, participating in the work of reanimation; they are "guardians" who care for the "vital flame."[39] These archived seminar materials are not passive receptacles in the hands of active archivists or researchers, masters and manipulators of the knowledge stored within, but are invested with the potential to actively convey the seminar experience.

Returning to Vincennes

Material matters. If the seminar is intended to be an open-ended, virtual community that gathers together readers both present and absent across temporalities of reading, then technologies of preservation and access contribute to the possibility of revisiting or returning to the scene of the seminar. Ideally, a recording would channel the limitlessness and ephemerality of the seminar, the freedom from constraints of time and place that characterize Cixous's improvisational pedagogical style. By preserving the interruptions, the idiosyncrasies of the location, and the changes of light and temperature specific to a particular session, material traces can contribute to the texture of the seminar as an intellectual and affective event. But whether filmed to a digital file, magnetized to the tape of an audiocassette, or captured in pieces by handwritten notes, no medium can replicate the seminar as an individual lived experience. To conclude this chapter, I grapple with the inevitability of loss and incompleteness in my own attempts to imagine, or reimagine, Cixous's seminar. Notes taken during a session I attended, alongside archival photographs of Vincennes, are evocative material traces that channel memory, affect, and desire. They constitute an oblique archive that can host a "virtual exploration," in the words of one photographer who has documented the former site of the Université de Vincennes, where Cixous's first seminars were held.

Though there is nothing particularly remarkable about my own handwritten notes, taken during the last meeting of Cixous's 2014–15 seminar on June 13, I have been consulting them as a reminder of the atmosphere of her seminar and the theme of that session, which involved returning to a specific place in space and time, whether to Athens (for Freud and Derrida), or to the forest of Vincennes, for Cixous and some of her seminar attendees. As I type up my seminar notes in a word-processing file on my computer, they dispatch me, years later, to the scene of the seminar. Cixous is speaking and I am writing. My notes transcribe her voice "sur le vif" (from life), quickly and cutting to the quick: I recognize urgent emotion in my handwriting. For example, I have written:

> . . . *rien ne disparaît, tout est conservé et peut réapparaître* . . .
>
> . . . *nothing disappears, everything is conserved and can reappear* . . .

This fragment resonates for my virtual exploration of archival materials. But I am not a reliable medium, and my notes cannot serve as faithful citations. I am writing what sticks "à un rhythme imprévisible" ("at an unpredictable rhythm"), as Barthes wrote of notes taken during a seminar. These notes, he says, are "ce qui naît d'une écoute étourdie" ("what is born from an absent-minded listening"): and certainly when I wrote the fragment my mind may have wandered off, pursuing a tangent Cixous had gestured towards.[40] However, those words constitute a form of production in their own right, as Barthes asserts: "La note est détachée du savoir comme modèle (chose à copier); elle est écriture, non mémoire; elle est dans la production, non dans la représentation" ("Notes are detached from knowledge as a model [a thing to copy]; what is recorded is writing, not memory; the note is production, not representation."[41] Perhaps precisely because my words do not copy faithfully and accurately, because they are not an exact representation of the seminar event, but instead retain an urgent, scattershot quality taken *sur le vif*, they are invested with a transportive power. They are incomplete and unreliable—yet for me, "tout y est conservé": everything is preserved there. When I return to them, I return, in some way, to the seminar, and through it, improbably, to Vincennes.

By the time I started to attend Cixous's seminar in 2004, the Vincennes years were long gone. In my notes on the June 2015 session, Cixous describes her own recent visit to the forest of Vincennes with a film crew who were attempting to pinpoint the exact placement of the Université expérimentale de Vincennes. Cixous had been there from the beginning, in 1968, bringing together a group of writers and thinkers including Michel Deguy, Gilles Deleuze, and Michel Foucault in her role as *chargée de mission*, appointed by the French minister of education, Edgar Faure.[42] With the goal of translating the turbulence of May, in all its fragility, into something more enduring, a university was built on the former military grounds of the Bois de Vincennes.

I search for a photograph of the buildings, seeking more information about their purportedly provisional nature. I'm surprised to find that some of them were four stories high, nearly as tall as the surrounding pine trees. As part of the university's own archives, the photo conveys a material presence that attests to the endurance of the university's history. In 1980 the minister of universities, Alice Saunier-Seïté, ordered that Université Paris 8 be moved from Vincennes to Saint-Denis, and the "provisional" buildings at Vincennes would be destroyed. I return to my notes. I had written, channeling Cixous:

> *peut-être quelque chose en moi a toujours su*
> *que c'était un lieu mortel*
> *voué à la disparition*
>
> *maybe something in me always knew*
> *that it was a mortal place*
> *destined to disappear*

Because she had founded the university and taught there from the start, and thus had an intimate knowledge of the institution's early years, Cixous's presence on the 2015 documentary excursion serves not only to correctly identify the precise location—a task which proves impossible—but also, more keenly, to register the extent of the destruction of this university's first home. To return to Vincennes is ultimately to bear witness to absence and destruction.

> *au moment où on a rasé Vincennes, la destruction a voulu être totale—et elle est totale*
>
> *the moment they scraped Vincennes, the destruction was meant to be total—and it is total*

When Cixous returns to Vincennes, after having waited so long, the site is unrecognizable. The buildings have been destroyed, the material removed, and the vegetation has overgrown any physical markers of the site. I try to capture the scene of this revisiting in my notes.

> *est-ce qu'on va y arriver ?*
> *il n'y a pas de chemin, il y a des chemins qui mènent nulle part—*
> *à travers boisements et végétation*
> *l'équipe cinéma a posé un fauteuil*
> *et a dit—<u>c'est là.</u>*

are we going to make it?
there is no path, there are paths that lead nowhere—
through forestation and vegetation
the film crew set down an armchair
and said—there it is

Arriving at Vincennes becomes returning to Vincennes: the "là" set up, seemingly at random, by an armchair in the middle of the overgrowth, is a location in space and time that may not fully correlate to the actual place where the campus was located, but its approximation carries a certain force and enables the return: *c'est là*, I wrote, underlining decisively, as if to make my own place for Vincennes. I cannot return to the Vincennes campus because I've never been there, but the seminar and my notes are a form of access. In the seminar, in my notes, there we were. The moment that Cixous decides to go there, sharing this expedition with the seminar participants, Vincennes begins again.

The process of dismantling the Université de Vincennes was documented by the visual artist and professor emeritus Jean-Louis Boissier in 1980. His photographs give a sense of the university's physical presence, countering the school's administrative designation as "provisional." Boissier accounts for the living presence that was Vincennes and its buildings, transformed into vast piles of rubbish.[43] In one photo, an excavator pulls down a massive structure among shrubby trees that are on the verge of being overtaken by the building material. In another photo, a close-up of the detritus reveals bent structural rebar and crumbling drywall as well as light fixtures, furniture, and wall decorations, remnants of life at a human scale. The destruction recorded in these photographs is evidence of the violence of the university's displacement. Preserved in the university's archives, and featured in the documentation for its fortieth anniversary, Boissier's photographs capture a specific moment in time and space that gives life to the university's past.

A later series of photographs that Boissier made in 2008 shows the regrowth of the forest over "l'emplacement approximatif" of the university, leaving only a grouping of trees whose shadows are echoed by that of the photographer appearing in the bottom right corner. His photographs are part of a larger multimedia installation titled "L'Illumination de Vincennes," celebrating the fortieth anniversary of the university's founding, and placing it within a longer tradition of humanities work going back to Rousseau and his "illumination" in the same forest in 1749. Along with the archival images preserved by Université Paris 8, Boissier's photographs trace the erasure of the university's Vincennes site over several decades, and Boissier's written testimony gives a sense of the pace of the destruction. Only several months after the buildings were dismantled, Boissier writes:

> Il était déjà difficile de repérer où était l'entrée, les bordures en ciment de la route étaient refaites, des alignements de jeunes arbres traversaient de biais l'espace où était le "campus." En 2008, aujourd'hui, 27 ans après ce premier retour, seuls des plans en archives ou une mémoire des configurations de grands arbres permettraient de retrouver les lieux où nous étions.[44]
>
> It was already difficult to make out where the entrance had been, the cement borders of the road had been redone, rows of young trees cut across the space where the "campus" had been. In 2008, today, 27 years after this first return, only archived maps or a memory of the placement of tall trees would allow us to find the places where we had been.

The administration did not content itself with tearing down the buildings; reconstructing the road and planting new trees were another level of erasure of the site's previous use. But these "lieux" ("places") have not been entirely stripped of their memory: archival documents, as well as the memory of certain mature trees, permit some level of certainty as to where the university buildings once stood—where "we had been," in Boissier's words. The project combines "un travail sur les archives et la mémoire, des performances enregistrées sur le territoire de Paris 8 au bois de Vincennes, un environnement virtuel interactif et encore un film" ("archival and memory work, performances recorded on Paris 8's land in the Vincennes forest, an interactive virtual environment, as well as a film").[45] Through the "resonance" produced by the interaction of the documents from the past with archival research in the present, this "exploration virtuelle," as Boissier describes it, seeks to reconfigure the Université de Vincennes at its original site.

Similarly, Cixous's seminar serves as an "exploration virtuelle" that gives an expansive meaning to the idea of returning to Vincennes, conjuring it up in memory as well as through textual "companions" that evoke the idea of a virtual, psychic return. Her description of returning to Vincennes in the June 2015 seminar session appears as an interlude in her reading of two visits to Athens: Freud's in "A Disturbance of Memory on the Acropolis" and Derrida's in *Demeure, Athènes*. From these texts, Cixous spools out a meditation on the *ville éternelle* as a virtual space that allows for visitations and returns in memory, archaeology, and literature. Specifically, Cixous channels Freud to explain her own return to Vincennes. In my notes from the June 2015 seminar session, I track the shift from Freud's virtual travels to the seminar in a meandering meditation that describes the pleasure of Cixous's own improvisational pedagogical style:

Freud s'autorise un voyage d'une minutie incroyable—voyage virtuel—ça ne peut servir à rien pour ma démonstration
il ne peut pas s'empêcher de se laisser emporter par le fantasme

On écoute le maître, on se laisse aller, même quand il nous dit quelque chose
'parce que j'en ai besoin'—
irresponsabilité de pédagogue qui fait expérience de la jouissance.

Freud allows himself a voyage that is incredibly detailed—virtual voyage—it is in no way useful for my demonstration
he can't help but let himself be carried along by the fantasy
we listen to the master, we let ourselves go, even when he tells us something "because I need to"—
irresponsibility of the pedagogue experiencing pleasure

Cixous notes that while Freud's return to Athens is logically entirely beside the point of his "demonstration," his desire for returning, for being transported and taking his reader along with him, is irresistible. We cannot help but let ourselves be taken along, Cixous suggests. The pedagogue's virtual visit, as "irresponsible" as it may be, opens up "jouissance" (enjoyment) as a shared experience. My own notes are a rough portal to that world and the worlds in its orbit. Through Cixous's reading of Freud, the seminar also becomes a virtual space for haunting and for the spectralization of friends and textual companions, demonstrating the potential for an afterlife of friendship in the seminar.[46] Cixous highlights the importance of pleasure and fantasy in the seminar space, the importance of letting oneself be taken along by the "maître" or the "fantasme."[47] When the "maître" lets him or herself go, pursuing pleasure, those who listen in are also transported. It is because the "maître" (here, Freud, or any "irresponsible" pedagogue) cannot resist the pleasure of this journey, a deep personal need to revisit Athens in memory, that the "voyage virtuel" can take place. The study of texts becomes an intimate conversation across time, made possible in the virtual space which Cixous's seminar creates.

There is no monument at the site of the Université expérimentale de Vincennes—no plaque, no map, not even ruins, or a clearing—but this absence is fully significant. In its collective signification, its temporal range, and the contingencies of its history, Vincennes does not constitute a specific site or an originary moment to which one can return, but instead serves as a *lieu de mémoire* (place of memory).[48] The forest and the university converge in their geographic and symbolic significance: Vincennes constitutes a virtual archive that combines several layers of cultural history, including the contemporary theaters that have taken up residence in the Cartoucherie (another cultural institution in the Bois de Vincennes on which Cixous has left her mark).[49] Cixous's seminar, the Université expérimentale de Vincennes, and May '68 are part of this virtual archive, but so is the history of French colonization and cultivation that transformed the forest of the Roman-named Vilcena into a military ground and a public park.[50] The forest itself is a *lieu de mémoire* in the French cultural imaginary, and as such constitutes a virtual monument:

the forest channels ephemerality and outsideness, an anarchic endurance: the forest, from the Latin *foresta*, is literally "outside"; that which can take over, destroy, ruin, and overgrow.[51]

How is it possible to locate the site of the university when the destruction has been so thorough, and when the forest has taken over? Is returning to Vincennes in fact a recognition of its absence and loss, an acknowledgment of the power of the forest to complete the work of destruction and regrowth? Like the forest, the archives of Vincennes, of the university, and of Cixous's seminar weave between vulnerability and resilience. New media and new technologies offer the allure of extensive documentation, yet digital video and audio recordings are susceptible to bit rot and technological obsolescence. Cixous's seminar recordings are fragmented and dispersed. Handwritten notes on paper are not any more reliable as records, but like photographs, they offer a glimmer of past life as they capture a discrete moment. But this accumulation of media shares with the forest its burgeoning resilience, its ability to multiply in interconnected networks. This convergence of the digital, virtual, and material is particularly pertinent to archival projects such as the preservation, editing, and publishing of Cixous's seminars, especially as they extend beyond the individual pedagogue to channel a community of texts and friends.

The Voice Survives

As Cixous's and Derrida's archives and archive-minded writing illustrate, archives are more about an *alternate* existence in time, made possible virtually, than about stability and preservation. Their virtual state accounts for the impossibilities, silences, resistances, and risks that accompany the physicality of archival materials and encounters with them in real time. In Derrida's and Cixous's writing, archival haunting and spectrality is multidirectional: the past can come back to haunt the present, but the present can also revisit the future in a kind of projected haunting, anticipating a readership to come.

The material conditions of inheritance, and technologies of inscription and transmission in particular, are at the forefront of Derrida's reflection on archives: in *Mal d'archive*, he asserts that "[la] technique archivale ne détermine plus, et ne l'aura jamais fait, le seul moment de l'enregistrement conservateur, mais l'institution même de l'événement archivable" ("archival technology no longer determines, will never have determined, merely the moment of the conservational recording, but rather the very institution of the archivable event").[52] For Derrida, the spectralizing force of video recordings in *Ghost Dance* and, in *Mal d'archive*, of the answering machine's recording technology was such that "la voix survit à son moment d'enregistrement" ("the voice outlives its moment of recording").[53] Recordings allow for the survival of the voice and body, projected into an undetermined, anticipated future whose temporality Derrida identified as the *futur antérieur* or the "future-to-come," the spectral temporality of *Spectres de Marx*.[54] Consequently, the recorded moment is always deferred, incomplete in the present moment, and is defined by this incompleteness and "incoercible differ*a*nce.[55] Derrida rejects a retrospective point of view for the archive itself and the archived moment in favor of a temporality that is better suited to the unknown and unpredictable.

Yet it is worth considering another temporal relationship at play in the consultation of archived seminar recordings: the sense of belatedness, of arriving too late to the party. If the performative and spectral force of the recordings reaches forward into the future to haunt those who will have received the transmission and who will consult it, fulfilling the desire of the voice and body in the archived moment, what is the status of desire on the receiving end? Consulting the archived seminar can conjure up a wish to return to the scene of the seminar, to haunt the past from the present moment. Objectivity may be impossible in this case, but once it is set aside, an archival approach that accounts for and even harnesses affect can arise. The experience of consulting archived seminar materials requires this kind of affective methodology: legacy, transmission, and generational belonging are particularly charged with personal significance in the seminar community. The archival temporality of the seminar encourages an attention to the researcher's position vis-à-vis the material consulted. It is not only a matter of conjuring up the seminar scene to replay it—it is also a matter of inhabiting a virtual past. Or returning to it, again, for the first time.

Conclusion

✦

"Les Incorruptibles"

What does it mean to consider Jacques Derrida and Hélène Cixous as part of a larger "generation" of critical theorists whose work is now being archived, their collections mined for unpublished works, seminars, controversy, and unexplored connections? In the months before his death, Derrida linked himself to his peers via a nickname borrowed from Cixous: "les incorruptibles." To close this study on the potential for writing to live on through friendship, and for friendship to live on through archived artifacts, I return to Derrida's quote to explore its implications: on the one hand, what does this nickname mean for the legacy of critical theory? Moreover, what does this nickname entail for Cixous? Finally, can the terms "incorruptibles" and "insister," extended to artifacts in the Derrida and Cixous collections, reach beyond the two writers to reaffirm their longevity in an archival afterlife? As manuscripts, folded notes, Post-its, floppy disks, cassette tapes, and other documents inevitably break down and become fully ephemeral, their ironic incorruptibility remains contingent, touching and rubbing up against an ongoing material existence that projects them ever forward.

A Generation of *Incorruptibles*

In *Apprendre à vivre enfin*, the last published interview before his death, Derrida explains that he considers himself to be one of the last "survivors" of a generation of writers and thinkers associated with the 1960s.[1] Though admitting that the term "generation" could further be problematized, he nonetheless speaks of an obligation to remain faithful to the "exigences partagées" ("shared exigencies") among this group (in which he includes by name Lacan, Althusser, Lévinas, Foucault, Barthes, Deleuze, Blanchot, Lyotard, and Kofman) and to continue their "débat vivant" ("living debate").[2] Derrida suggests that "un *ethos* d'écriture et de pensée intransigeant, voire incorruptible" ("an *ethos* of writing and of thinking, an intransigent or indeed incorruptible *ethos*") defines this group, and he notes that "Hélène Cixous nous surnomme les 'incorruptibles'" ("Hélène Cixous calls us the 'incorruptibles'").[3] Since it precedes Derrida's confession of his own archival anxieties, the title Cixous confers—*les incorruptibles*—resonates powerfully and prophetically: the designation "incorruptible" suggests that this generation of writers will retain its integrity and its potency into the future, rather than being condemned to the dustbin of modern thought. But this generation also shares a concern about a radical shift in the "techno-culture" which has consequences for the modalities of inheritance and legacy via the archive, as Derrida explains:

> Les gens de ma "génération" . . . croyai[en]t savoir que telle œuvre pouvait ou non survivre, en fonction de ses qualités, pendant un, deux, voire, comme Platon, vint-cinq siècles. Disparaître, puis renaître. Mais aujourd'hui, l'accélération des modalités de l'archivation, mais aussi l'usure et la destruction, transforment la structure et la temporalité, la durée de l'héritage. Pour la pensée, la question de la survie prend désormais des formes absolument imprévisibles.
>
> The people of my "generation" . . . thought [they] knew that a particular work might or might not survive, based upon its own qualities, for one, two, or, perhaps, like Plato, twenty-five centuries. Disappear, then be reborn. But today, the acceleration in the forms of archivization, though also use and destruction, are transforming the structure, temporality, and duration of the legacy. When it comes to thought, the question of survival has taken on absolutely unforeseeable forms.[4]

The survival of these writers is not a matter of fitness or virtue based on the inherent value of their work. Instead, it is increasingly apparent that survival depends on technology. This may certainly have been true throughout the centuries, but Derrida suggests here that new technologies deployed at the turn of the twenty-first century ensure that anyone's work can be archived and therefore survive, in a sense. Survival becomes banal. Most of the "incorruptible" writers Derrida mentions are now deceased, their papers and computers archived: Althusser, Barthes, Cixous, de Man, Foucault, Guattari, and Kofman have substantial archival collections. The question of their living on in a significant sense remains to be seen. It is this risk—the danger of falling into disregard, or disrepair—that now constitutes the force of their ephemeral existence. In their wake, friends, loved ones, and scholars take up the burden of ensuring their posterity: the circulation of their work, the stewardship of their writing, the safekeeping of their material documents and written artifacts.

Considering Cixous and Derrida as part of a larger generation or trend in thinking (whether called post-structuralism, postmodernism, critical theory, French theory, *la génération de '68*, or *les incorruptibles*, in Cixous's formulation) also raises the issue of historicization and canonization.[5] Does the creation of critical theory archives in libraries and special collections legitimize or neutralize the work done by these writers? Does the move to archive suggest that critical theory is worn out, passé, and can no longer do the hard theoretical, political, or aesthetic work it once performed? That it is time to retire it to the archives? Or rather, is the archiving of this work characteristic of its subversive engagement with the institution? Given the trend of grouping together theorists' papers in library collections, it becomes urgent to ask what archives have to offer these writers, and what critical theory is doing in archives, especially when the work challenges notions of subjecthood and sovereignty.

The *grand séminaire* has become a privileged genre contributing to the mythologies and publication records of thinkers such as Lacan, Althusser, Foucault, Barthes, Derrida, and Rancière, all of whom variously occupied and interrogated the figure of the *maître* in philosophy and social science theories, consolidating mastery through their seminars. Genealogies and cycles of transmission ensure the transfer of authority from master to student, often solidifying a patriarchal lineage, in spite of some of these thinkers' attempts to interrogate this pattern of transmission.[6] Yet they did not work alone: institutional weight contributed both to the authority of the individual thinker and, less overtly, to reconfiguring networks of thought and intellectual communities, controlling access, and managing transmission. Prestigious institutions such as the Collège de France and the École normale supérieure welcomed many of them; others, including Derrida, found themselves less welcome.[7] Other venues came to prominence for innovative research and teaching, including the École des hautes études en sciences sociales (EHESS) and the Université Paris 8's Saint-Denis location, in the wake of the Vincennes campus destruction. Many thinkers decamped to the United States, forming institutional alliances in public and private institutions alike. New cross-disciplinary networks and patterns of transmission appeared in this transatlantic move. The concern for archiving the work of these thinkers, teachers, and writers arises from these networks of institutional teaching and scholarship. Particularly in the 1990s, archival collections grew out of institutions of higher education: first the Critical Theory Archive at UC Irvine, and then the Feminist Theory Archive at Brown University's Pembroke Center. In parallel, the Institut Mémoires de l'édition contemporaine (IMEC) was founded in Paris, and then moved to the Abbaye d'Ardenne in Normandy, where a state-of-the-art facility was designed in order to better conserve its growing collections. Barthes's and Foucault's papers were first held there, before being moved to the Bibliothèque nationale de France. The creation and transfer of Derrida's and Cixous's archival collections contribute to this institutional swirl and to the connections wrought and undone by transfers and new technologies of archiving.

These collections of critical theory archives developed and transformed alongside what has come to be known as the "archival turn" in the humanities and social sciences. Over the course of several decades, scholars have increasingly turned to archives and collections not solely as repositories of unexplored material to be uncovered and analyzed, but as a means to reflect on the methodologies, institutions, and power structures that underwrite the production and transmission of knowledge. Most recently, the field of critical archive studies proposes to interrogate the fundamental power structures at work at the intersections of archival science, humanities, and social science disciplines, whose marginalizing and silencing techniques must be rectified.[8] This new perspective of critical studies can be brought to bear on the designation "critical theory" and the understandings of archives that have come out of this "generation," including most often Derrida and Foucault. Moving from "critical theory" to "critical archive studies" draws out unforeseen connections and relationships between writers and thinkers and across collections and institutions. Taken together and read along a material grain, Cixous's and Derrida's archival practices and theories illuminate the advantages and pitfalls presented by archives shared between intellectual and artistic communities. They encourage an awareness of unconventional literary objects that raise the stakes of literary studies within the growing field of critical archiving, which participates in the important cross-disciplinary work being done to rethink hierarchies and undo mastery, nationalism, and institutional strictures.

As metaphor, institution, and as a supplement to published work, an archive of writers' papers (*fonds d'auteur*) consolidates a single author's work under their proper name, seeking to establish a totalizing and identifiable collection. Yet the element of connectivity in the archive undermines this totalizing impulse, resisting the separation into single-author *fonds*. Going beyond a notion of textual stability and fixed authorship, Rosalind Krauss's definition of the "paraliterary" re-situates writing within a "dramatic web of many voices, citations, asides, divagations," highlighting dialogue and exchange and allowing it to continue to resonate: paraliterary texts are "a space of debate, quotation, partisanship, betrayal, reconciliation; . . . not the space of unity, coherence, or resolution that we think of as constituting the work of literature."[9] Applied to the archive, Krauss's description of the paraliterary suggests that connectivity relies on difference and dialogue. As a paraliterary space, an archive creates a community and enables the circulation of ideas and documents within it. The "dramatic web" that characterizes intellectual archives evokes both materially and theoretically the "champ de tensions" (field of tensions) that Benoît Peeters described after his research at the IMEC: "Ce qu'on ressent en se plongeant dans les archives, c'est qu'on est au cœur même de la vie . . . La vie intellectuelle [est] . . . une série de relations, c'est une série de croisements, c'est une série permanente d'alliances et de conflits . . . La vie intellectuelle . . . c'est un champ de tensions" ("What you feel when you dive into archives is that you're at the heart of life itself . . . Intellectual life [is] . . . a series of relationships, a series of crossings, an ongoing series of alliances and conflicts . . . Intellectual life . . . is a field of tensions").[10]

Peeters points to "la vie" of archives and the materials they contain: relationships, crossings, alliances, and conflicts are all indicative of life in the archive.

As they put disparate collections into conversation, archives constitute communities. Derrida noted this at the inaugural ceremony of the Critical Theory Archive at UC Irvine, where his papers were to be housed, remarking with a wry smile, "the question is not only *where*, but *with whom* I am buried."[11] At Irvine, where Derrida lived and taught for part of the year from the mid-1980s to the early 2000s, his papers would be stored alongside those of J. Hillis Miller, Paul de Man, Safaa Fathy, and other friends and fellow writers. Pivoting from the question of *where* could be a way of acknowledging the apparently eccentric decision to create his primary archive outside of France (a decision Derrida would later counter with the creation of his collection at the IMEC), highlighting a concern with center and periphery: where is the writer from, and how do the national and international boundaries and trajectories that have shaped the course of his life determine where the archive belongs? Institution and patrimony embroil the archive in matters of geographic location. Derrida deflects from the question of *where* to *with whom*, as if to take comfort in the idea that his writing would be in good company, surrounded by other friendly works, by the magnetic pull of affinity. His remarks suggest how archival configurations can bypass the designation of "critical theory," allowing for writing to emerge and circulate within other, continuously shifting networks.

Incorruptibles and *Insisters*, Split and Shared

Borrowing Cixous's nickname, Derrida states that "Hélène Cixous nous surnomme les incorruptibles" ("Hélène Cixous calls us the incorruptibles"). Is Cixous a part of this *nous*? Does she include herself as an "incorruptible," or does she confer this title on a group from the outside? Does being an "incorruptible" entail participating in the survival of the work and thought produced in the web of debate and dialogue among this generation? Are the "incorruptibles" responsible for guaranteeing their own legacy, or are others needed to carry on this ethos into the future? At the beginning of the present study, I discussed the risks of considering Cixous as the inheritor of Derrida's thought. The gendered implications of this relationship are of particular concern for intellectual history. Cixous's decision to place her papers with the BNF instead of the IMEC, where Derrida and other critical theorists already had collections,[12] seems to reinforce her status *à part*, a writer and thinker in her own right, not primarily as the executor of deconstruction. But considering Cixous separately from Derrida and from the generation of *incorruptibles* she names has implications not only for gender dynamics within intellectual history, but also for the archival techniques that contribute to literary afterlives.

Cixous's choice of the BNF as an archival institution is a testament to a view of the archive as a virtual space that can maintain a literary friendship and continue to foster new networks and connections between writings. The materiality of writing, along with the institutional ethos both writers fostered through forums such as Vincennes and the Collège international de philosophie, ensure that connections and dialogue are maintained through virtualization and alternative conversations which develop not in spite of their disparate locations, but because of them. Whereas certain institutions may have attempted to solidify, legitimize, and claim an institutional status for critical theory by grouping together certain writers, the dissemination of this work across multiple institutions, and beyond institutions entirely, more effectively reinforces the critical, incorruptible spirit of this kind of thinking, living writing.

Furthermore, in choosing to create an archival collection at the BNF, Cixous inscribes herself within a literary genealogy that deviates from the IMEC's network. In the BNF's Département des Manuscrits, with her physical proximity to canonical literary predecessors such as Montaigne, Stendhal, and Proust, with whom she has formed a kinship through her work, she confronts the nationalistic project of establishing cultural patrimony with the idiomaticity of her own writing and archival materials, including dream-texts and seminar recordings. Derrida draws attention to this paradoxical status—both existing within a canon and applying a critical lever to it—in his essay *Genèses, généalogies, genres . . . et le génie: Les Secrets de l'archive*. He ironically subverts the title of the *fonds* Cixous's inaugural conference, "Genèses Généalogies Genres," with his addition of *génie* (genius). In this essay, as in *H. C. pour la vie*, Derrida adopts the role of Cixous's prophet, modifying his voice into a preemptive echo beyond the grave, into the supposedly eternal time of the archive. He thereby highlights the paradox of *génie*: though defined as exceptional, timeless, and independent from historical context or personality, genius is appropriable, since the accession of Cixous's manuscripts into the BNF is also an entry into French cultural patrimony, into the collection of exemplary writers that, through their assembled exceptionalism, are intended to represent the panoply of French linguistic and cultural value. As is the case for each "genius" present in the Département des Manuscrits, Cixous's idiomaticity asserts itself; the kinship she claims in her affective association with Montaigne, Pascal, Stendhal, and Proust disrupts her designation as a French feminist theorist within the critical theory canon.

Both writers' penchant for unsettling normative, gendered lineage and inheritance makes inroads into conventional archival configurations. In the documentary *Derrida*, Derrida infamously proclaims that a philosopher could not be his mother, and would have to be his daughter:

> I'll try to tell you why it's impossible for me to have any philosopher as a mother. . . . Because the figure of the philosopher is, for me, always a masculine figure. This is one of the reasons I undertook

> the deconstruction of philosophy. All the deconstruction of phallogocentrism is the deconstruction of what one calls philosophy, which since its inception has always been linked to a paternal figure. . . . So the philosopher that would be my mother would be a post-deconstructive philosopher, that is, myself or my son. My mother as a philosopher would be my granddaughter, for example. An inheritor. A woman philosopher who would reaffirm the deconstruction. And consequently [she] would be a woman who thinks, not a philosopher. I always distinguish thinking from philosophy. A thinking mother—it's what I both love and try to give birth to.

This statement has certainly raised concerns about the place of women in Derrida's thought and his claims for women in philosophy. But it can also be read as a reworking of temporality and kinship, and a dismantling of hierarchies in pedagogy, philosophy, and sexual difference. Through the figure of the daughter, Derrida claims deconstruction as an inherently feminist project, a takedown of the paternalistic foundations of philosophy. The mother figure is reworked as the daughter, creating an alternative relationship to genealogy and generation, especially since Derrida casts himself in the role of the one who gives birth, taking the place conventionally assigned to the mother. Claiming his legacy involves reworking his own role within the tradition he challenges. Similar to the role of the prophet which Derrida adopts vis-à-vis Cixous, this figure of the mother-daughter thinker scrambles patriarchal transmission, challenging what is expected from the inheritor or the survivor projected into the future.

Further destabilizing linear inheritance and kinship models with a counterpart to this deconstructive daughter, Cixous and Derrida experiment with the figure they coin as a shared nickname: the "insister." Like other words and texts volleyed between Cixous and Derrida, this word creates a powerful bond, as Cixous explains in *Insister*:

> —Tu es *my insister*, me dit-il. . . .
>
> Ce qui me plaît merveilleusement dans ce mot, dont tu me fais présent, ton trouvée, ta trouvaille de génie, ce ou cette intraduisible, c'est que je peux te le retourner également. Toi aussi tu es *my insister*. *Mon insister. Mon insisteur.*

> —You are *my insister*, he says to me. . . .
>
> What pleases me to no end in this word, which you give me as a present, your found object, your genius discovery, is that I can likewise turn it round on you. You too you are *my insister*. *My insisting*.[13]

Like the "incorruptible," characterizing a certain penchant for "un *ethos* d'écriture et de pensée intransigeant" ("an intransigent *ethos* of writing and of thinking"), the insister can continue the "débat vivant" and thus ensure the survival of writing and thought. The insister's bond is conceptual and playful, rooted in a shared language of hybrid citationality to override binaries of masculine-feminine, French-English. It does not easily replace the exclusionary political and philosophical imperative of fraternity, and sits uneasily as an object of appropriation or belonging.

But are these insistent conversations *à deux* enough to maintain the "life" of writing and thought, even within the protective space of the archive? If the scope of the insister and the incorruptible is expanded beyond fixed categories of age and gender, it could further include other friends, colleagues, and allies (though also enemies, competitors, antagonists), as well as readers, archivists, and researchers—along with the material vestiges of writing. The manuscript of *Fichus* insists, in dreams and dream-texts; seminar recordings demand constant upkeep to ward off technological obsolescence; folded notes resist interpretation even as they invite delicate handling. The physical makeup of these "incorruptibles" will of course break down and disintegrate. And yet their ephemerality invests the material with volatility, with the potential to change and elicit an affective response. An affection for artifacts opens up the kinship network beyond dualistic friendship, beyond a reliance on an anthropocentric notion of authorship, and beyond the finality of death. The bonds of the insister and the incorruptible *partagent*: they share, split, morph, transform, rework, reshape, assemble, animate, and enliven. Whether in the form of penciled annotations, dream-texts, digital recordings, ephemera, or virtual doubles, literary artifacts circulating in and around the archive insinuate themselves into the dialogue to become the *survie* of writing, between friends and beyond.

NOTES

Introduction

1. Manuscript of *OR: Les Lettres de mon père* (Box 636/929: Folder 10). Other manuscripts and typescripts by Cixous at Princeton's Firestone Library are found in "Documents: Hélène Cixous": *Rêve je te dis* and *Tours promises* in Box 635/928: Folder 3; and *La Ville parjure* in Box 635/928: Folder 4.

2. In this study, I use the term *fonds* to indicate "the entire body of records of an organization, family, or individual that have been created and accumulated as the result of an organic process reflecting the functions of the creator," according to the Society of American Archivists' glossary (https://www2.archivists.org/glossary/terms/f/fonds).

3. Benoît Peeters, *Derrida* (Paris: Flammarion, 2010), 370.

4. Personal interviews with Hélène Cixous (November 3, 2013) and Marie-Odile Germain (May 23, 2014).

5. Chemise 8 "Docs," Sous-chemise 2, Manuscript of *Double Oubli de l'Orang-Outang*. See also the Manuscript of *Le Prénom de Dieu*, Boîte I, Chemise B "verte avec mention PRENOM," "Texte dact. sur 'Le Prénom de Dieu,' 4e de couverture," Département des manuscrits, Bibliothèque nationale de France.

6. Derrida appears to have lifted this quote from the text of Cixous's *OR: Les Lettres de mon père* (Paris: Éditions des femmes, 1997), 191.

7. Cixous cites Derrida's account of her first encounter with him in *H. C. pour la vie*: "'Auparavant, m'a-t-elle dit depuis,' je cite, 'de longues années auparavant, quelque sept ans auparavant, elle m'avait, elle, vu et entendu—mais de dos.' . . . Je le cite me citant, citant, des dizaines d'années plus tard, une scène de procès à laquelle j'assistai par hasard, . . . moi face à son dos" (Hélène Cixous, *Portrait de Jacques Derrida en Jeune Saint Juif* [Paris: Galilée, 2001], 13). "'Before that, she has since told me,' I quote, 'many long years before that, some seven years before, she had seen and heard me—but from behind.' . . . I quote him, quoting me, quoting, dozens of years later, a trial scene at which I was present by chance, . . . me facing his back" (Cixous, *Portrait of Jacques Derrida as a Young Jewish Saint*, trans. Beverley Bie Brahic [New York: Columbia University Press, 2004], 5–6).

8. See Christa Stevens, "La Première fois plus d'une fois"; Laurent Dubreuil, "Leurs biographies d'auteurs," in *L'Événement comme écriture: Cixous et Derrida se lisant* (Paris: CampagnePremière, 2007), 220; Ashley Thompson, "Voir à lire," in *L'Événement comme écriture: Cixous et Derrida se lisant* (Paris: CampagnePremière, 2007), 328 ff.; and the first pages of Ginette Michaud's *Battements du secret littéraire*.

9. See the chapter "Ruptures" in Benoît Peeters's biography on Derrida. In *The French Joyce* (Ann Arbor: University of Michigan Press, 1990), Geert Lernout

links Cixous to the *Tel Quel* group via her writing on Joyce (14)—a tenuous link beyond the articles on English literature Cixous published in the journal (Verena Andermatt Conley. *Hélène Cixous*. Toronto: University of Toronto Press, 1992, 1–2).

10. A program which Derrida defended when it was revoked by the Barre government in 1980 (see "Lettre au ministre de l'Education nationale en appui du DEA d'études féminines," 219DRR/23/2, fonds Derrida, IMEC).

11. See the book *Pour Nelson Mandela* (1986), with texts by Derrida ("Admiration de Nelson Mandela, ou Les lois de la réflexion") and Cixous ("La Séparation du gâteau"). See also page 100 of Peeters's *Derrida* and the accompanying photo.

12. Derrida and Cixous discuss their childhoods in Algeria in the interview "Du mot à la vie." Derrida's year at Harvard (1956–57) was arranged "sous le prétexte d'y consulter les microfilms des inédits de Husserl; en réalité, ces documents n'arriveront que plus tard" (Peeters, *Derrida*, 107). Cixous traveled to the East Coast in 1963 to consult Joyce's manuscripts at Buffalo and Yale (Cixous and Calle-Gruber, *Photos de racines* [Paris: Éditions des femmes, 1994], 210).

13. I echo here the title of Mairéad Hanrahan's *Cixous's Semi-Fictions*. Studies focusing on connections between Derrida and Cixous began to appear in the early 2000s, around the time of Cixous's bequest to the BNF and the publication of Derrida's *H. C. pour la vie*. See especially the conference proceedings in *L'Événement comme écriture: Cixous et Derrida se lisant* (published 2007); the special issue of *Paragraph* called "Cixous, Derrida, Psychoanalysis" (2013); and Ginette Michaud's two-volume study *Lire Jacques Derrida et Hélène Cixous* (2010).

14. Hélène Cixous, "Contes de la différence sexuelle," in *Lectures de la différence sexuelle*, ed. Anne Berger and Mara Negrón (Paris: Éditions des femmes, 1994), 31. In "Appels" (in *L'Événement comme écriture*), Anne Berger points out that Cixous cuts off the dialogue at the crucial moment that would determine the identity of each speaker through the gendered agreement of the past participle "précédé·e" (87).

15. Jacques Derrida, "Fourmis," in *Lectures de la différence sexuelle* (Paris: Éditions des Femmes, 1994), 69; "Ants," trans. Eric Prenowitz, *Oxford Literary Review* 24 (2002): 17.

16. Described by Marcel Mauss as the *potlatch* in *Essai sur le don*, the structure and concept of the gift is analyzed in Derrida's *Donner le temps*.

17. Laurent Milesi, "Portraits of H. C. as J. D. and Back," *New Literary History* 37, no. 1 (2006): 67–69.

18. Ginette Michaud, *Battements du secret littéraire: Lire Jacques Derrida et Hélène Cixous*, vol. 1 (Paris: Hermann, 2010), 6, 13, 30, 31.

19. Michaud, *Battements du secret littéraire*, 33.

20. On the intellectual exchanges of these "couples," see *Beauvoir and Sartre: The Riddle of Influence* (Daigle and Golomb, eds., 2009); and Dana Villa's *Arendt and Heidegger: The Fate of the Political* (1995). Curiously, the Arendt-Heidegger relationship has also generated fictionalized accounts: *Martin et Hannah: Roman* by Catherine Clément (1999) and *Martin Heidegger à Hannah Arendt: Lettre jamais écrite* by Pio Colonnello (2014).

21. Laurent Dubreuil, "The Presences of Deconstruction," *New Literary History* 37, no. 1 (2006): 111–12. See also, for example, Verena Conley, *Hélène Cixous*; Susan Sellers and Ian Blyth, *Hélène Cixous: Live Theory*; and Laurent Dubreuil's "Leur biographies d'auteurs," which describes Cixous's writing on Derrida after his death as "des sépultures pour sauver la vie qui reste" (230; "sepultures to save the life that's left"). Mairéad Hanrahan explicitly resists this understanding of Cixous and Derrida in *Cixous's Semi-Fictions* (Edinburgh: Edinburgh University Press, 2014), 57–65. Claire Colebrook warns against framing Cixous in this way in "Cixous and Derrida: Friendship, Seduction, and Text," *Angelaki: Journal of Theoretical Humanities* 13, no. 2 (2008): 114.

22. These two works have remained largely unexplored in studies of Derrida's "late" works. Peggy Kamuf addressed the problem of this text's reception at the colloquium "Jacques Derrida and the Question of Life" in June 2005 (cited in Ginette Michaud, "Derrida & Cixous: Between and Beyond, or 'What to the Letter Has Happened,'" *New Literary History* 37, no. 1 [2006]: 91, 105).

23. Cixous, "Contes de la différence sexuelle," 96–97; "Tales of Sexual Difference," trans. Eric Prenowitz, in *The Portable Cixous*, ed. Marta Segarra (New York: Columbia University Press, 2010), 36.

24. Derrida, "Fourmis," 74–75; "Ants," 29. Marta Segarra's essay "L'Amitié, la trahison, la traduction" (in *L'Événement comme écriture*) recalls the Latin *amare* as the root of both "amour" and "amitié," and the Greek distinction between *eros* and *philia* in the context of Cixous and Derrida's friendship (181).

25. See Derrida, "Fourmis," 80–81; "Ants," 25; Hélène Cixous, *Insister à Jacques Derrida* (Paris: Galilée, 2006), 95; *Insister of Jacques Derrida*, trans. Peggy Kamuf (Edinburgh University Press: 2007), 128, 130; and Hélène Cixous and Jacques Derrida, "Du mot à la vie: Un dialogue entre Jacques Derrida et Hélène Cixous," with Aliette Armel, *Magazine Littéraire* 430 (2004): 2, 7.

26. Jacques Derrida, *H. C. pour la vie, c'est-à-dire* (Paris: Galilée, 2002), 54, 68–69, 136; *H. C. for Life, That Is to Say . . .* , trans. Laurent Milesi and Stefan Herbrechter (Stanford, CA: Stanford University Press, 2006), 56–57, 75–76, 158–59.

27. Cixous, *Insister à Jacques Derrida*, 42; *Insister of Jacques Derrida*, 52.

28. In *Qu'est-ce que la philosophie?* Deleuze and Guattari suggest that the friend is a "conceptual persona" foundational to philosophy (*What Is Philosophy?*, trans. Hugh Tomlinson and Graham Burchell [New York: Columbia University Press, 1994] 2–5).

29. "Disruptive Kinship" was the title of a roundtable discussion between Judith Butler, Hélène Cixous, and Avital Ronell that took place on October 24, 2011, at the New School in New York City, organized by the Villa Gillet's "Walls and Bridges" series. Intellectual history offers many examples of alternative kinship structures in issues of legacy. Famous executor sisters include Isabelle Rimbaud and Elizabeth Förster (Nietzsche's sister). Reversing the model of female inheritors, we can cite Leonard Woolf and Ted Hughes, whose role in Plath's archive is treated in *The Haunting of Sylvia Plath* by Jacqueline Rose and *The Unraveling Archive* (ed. Anita Helle). On these and other duos, see Michel Lafon and Benoît Peeters, *Nous est un autre: Enquête sur les duos d'écrivains* (2006).

30. Jacques Derrida, *Politiques de l'amitié* (Paris: Galilée, 1994), 310; *The Politics of Friendship*, trans. George Collins (New York: Verso, 2005), 278–79.

31. Derrida, *Politiques de l'amitié*, 114; *The Politics of Friendship*, 92.

32. Derrida, *Politiques de l'amitié*, 12; *The Politics of Friendship*, viii.

33. Several scholars have emphasized the importance of asymmetry in Cixous and Derrida's relationship: see, for example, the essays by Segarra (190), Negrón (261), and Thompson (335) in *L'Événement comme écriture*.

34. Tom Conley compares Cixous and Derrida's friendship to that of Montaigne and La Boétie in "Tours de force" (in *L'Événement comme écriture*, 155).

35. Derrida, *Politiques de l'amitié*, 42; *The Politics of Friendship*, 24. Marta Segarra also points out that Cixous and Derrida have both insisted on "la structure testamentaire" of friendship ("L'Amitié, la trahison, la traduction," 183).

36. The interconnectedness of death, writing, and community was a central concern for French postwar critical thought, particularly in the work of Maurice Blanchot, Emmanuel Levinas, Roland Barthes, and Jean-Luc Nancy, all of whom explore the idea of writing as afterlife or a state beyond or outside of life. On this theme, Simon Critchley's article "Il y a—A Dying Stronger Than Death (Blanchot with Levinas)" and the collected essays in *Dead Theory: Derrida, Death, and the Afterlife of Theory* (ed. Jeffrey R. Di Leo) are particularly illuminating.

37. Hélène Cixous, *Three Steps on the Ladder of Writing* (New York: Columbia University Press, 1993), 110, 12–13.

38. Jacques Derrida, *Donner la mort* (Paris: Galilée, 1999), 115; *The Gift of Death*, trans. David Wills (Chicago: University of Chicago Press, 2008), 82.

39. Derrida, *Donner la mort*, 75; *The Gift of Death*, 76.

40. Nearly half of the essays in *Cixous after/depuis 2000* focus on the presence of Cixous's mother in her writing.

41. Frédérique Chevillot, "Une contre-lecture de *Ciguë*, ou la mise à mort de la mère en mots," in *Cixous after/depuis 2000*, ed. Elizabeth Berglund Hall et al. (London: Brill, 2017), 106.

42. Mairéad Hanrahan, "Reversals and Revirements: The Mother *in extremis*," in *Cixous after/depuis 2000*, ed. Elizabeth Berglund Hall et al. (London: Brill, 2017), 123–40.

43. On the trace and *différance*, see Jacques Derrida, *De la grammatologie* (Paris: Minuit, 1967), 82–92; *La Dissémination* (Paris: Seuil, 1972), 9–11; and "La Différance" in *Marges de la philosophie* (Paris: Minuit, 1972), 1–29. See also Geoffrey Bennington, "Derridabase," in *Jacques Derrida*, by Geoffrey Bennington and Jacques Derrida (Paris: Seuil, 1991), 56; Juliet Fleming, *Cultural Graphology: Writing after Derrida* (Chicago: University of Chicago Press, 2016), 7; and Christopher Johnson, *System and Writing in the Philosophy of Jacques Derrida* (Cambridge: Cambridge University Press, 1993), 70–75.

44. Jacques Derrida and Jean Birnbaum, *Apprendre à vivre enfin* (Paris: Galilée, 2005), 33; *Learning to Live Finally*, trans. Pascale-Anne Brault (Hoboken, NJ: Melville House, 2007), 32.

45. Pascale-Anne Brault and Michael Naas, "Introduction," in *Chaque fois unique, la fin du monde*, by Jacques Derrida (Paris: Galilée, 2003), 18–19; "Introduction," in *The Work of Mourning*, ed. Pascale-Anne Brault and Michael Naas (Chicago: University of Chicago Press, 2001), 4.

46. Brault and Naas note that Derrida approved the project and "encouraged us throughout" (*The Work of Mourning*, viii).

47. Derrida, *Chaque fois unique*, 10.

48. Jacques Derrida, *Béliers: Le Dialogue ininterrompu: Entre deux infinis, le poème* (Paris: Galilée, 2003), 23; "Rams: Uninterrupted Dialogue—Between Two Infinities, the Poem," trans. Thomas Dutoit and Philippe Romanski, in *Sovereignties in Question: The Poetics of Paul Celan*, ed. Thomas Dutoit and Outi Pasanen (New York: Fordham University Press, 2005), 140.

49. Derrida, *Béliers*, 76; "Rams," 161.

50. Claire Colebrook, "Friendship, Seduction, and Text: Cixous and Derrida," *Angelaki: Journal of Theoretical Humanities* 13, no. 2 (2008): 123.

51. Frédéric Regard, "Faulty Burials," in "Cixous, Derrida, Psychoanalysis," special issue of *Paragraph* 36, no. 2 (2013): 255–69.

52. Derrida, *Apprendre à vivre enfin*, 34; *Learning to Live Finally*, 33–34.

53. Derrida, *Apprendre à vivre enfin*, 34–35; *Learning to Live Finally*, 33–34.

54. Derrida, *Apprendre à vivre enfin*, 27–28; *Learning to Live Finally*, 27.

55. Derrida, *Apprendre à vivre enfin*, 28; *Learning to Live Finally*, 27.

56. Derrida, *Apprendre à vivre enfin*, 28, 29; *Learning to Live Finally*, 27, 28.

57. Jacques Derrida, *Mal d'archive: Une impression freudienne* (Paris: Galilée, 1995), 13; *Archive Fever*, trans. Eric Prenowitz (Chicago: University of Chicago Press, 1998), 2.

58. Derrida coined this term in his 1995–1997 EHESS seminar "L'Hostilité et l'hospitalité." See his eponymous essay published in 1999.

59. Acknowledging Germain's work in *Genèses, généalogies, genres . . . et le génie: Les Secrets de l'archive* (Paris: Galilée, 2003), Derrida writes: "Cette gardienne de nobles héritages du passé se trouve être aussi . . . l'avant-gardienne audacieuse et prophétique . . . des chefs-d'œuvres auxquels . . . l'avenir est promis. Une telle avant-gardienne est vitale pour la Toute-puissance-autre de la littérature . . . [Ma gratitude] est due . . . à la personne de Marie-Odile Germain" (66). "This keeper of the past's noble heritage is also . . . the bold and prophetic avant-guardian, I dare say, of masterpieces to which . . . a future is promised. Such an avant-guardian is vital for the Omnipotence-other of literature . . . I express my gratitude . . . to Marie-Odile Germain" (*Geneses, Genealogies, Genres, and Genius: The Secrets of the Archive*, ed. Beverley Bie Brahic [New York: Columbia University Press, 2008], 55, translation slightly modified).

60. Hélène Cixous, *Tours promises* (Paris: Galilée, 2004), 98; Hélène Cixous, *Double Oubli de l'Orang-Outang* (Paris: Galilée, 2010), 62, 133.

61. The finding aid for the library of Jacques Derrida at Princeton, discussed above, is available to consult at http://arks.princeton.edu/ark:/88435/vq27zr16f.

62. The IMEC's web page for the Derrida collection lists the following associated collections: "Aubier-Montaigne, John Calder, Collège international de philosophie, Centre culturel international de Cerisy-la-Salle, Michel Deguy, Michel Foucault, Critique/Jean Piel, Sarah Kofman, Le Seuil, Jean Wahl." http://www.imec-archives.com/fonds/derrida-jacques/.

63. "Plan de classement" presented on the IMEC website (https://portail-collections.imec-archives.com/ark:/29414/a011433424761LQUFTQ).

64. In Jacques Derrida, "Le Futur antérieur de l'archive," in *Questions d'archives*, ed. Nathalie Léger (Paris: Institut Mémoires de l'édition contemporaine, 2002), 50.

65. For an account of the "affair," as Thomas Bartlett puts it, see his article "Archive Fever," as well as extensive documentation (including Derrida's letter to UCI's Chancellor Ralph J. Cicerone) available at http://www.jacques-derrida.org/UCI%20Affair.html, a website created by Geoffrey Bennington and Peggy Kamuf, the literary executors of Derrida's papers at UC Irvine.

66. Interview with Alexandra Bisio, processing archivist for UC Irvine's Critical Theory Archive, June 26, 2014.

67. *Hélène Cixous: The Writing Notebooks* includes many reproductions and transcriptions of Cixous's handwritten manuscripts and notebooks. Color images of her papers, including Post-it notes and folders, are included in *Brouillons d'écrivains*, based on the exhibition of the same name at the BNF.

68. According to Manuel Irniger and Geoffrey Bennington, Eric Prenowitz also made and still has additional recordings of Cixous's seminar. Interviews with Marie-Odile Germain, May 23, 2014; Geoffrey Bennington, January 23, 2015; and Manuel Irniger and Claudia Simma, June 28, 2015. The recordings have since been transferred to the BNF, according to Marta Segarra in her introduction to the edited volume of Cixous's seminars, *Lettres de fuite*, published in 2020.

69. E-mail communication with Christine Kim, public services and archives assistant, Special Collections and Archives, UCI Libraries, January 20, 2015.

70. On Sontag's hard drives, see Benjamin Moser; on Salman Rushdie's computer and other issues associated with born-digital materials, see Kirschenbaum's "The .txtual Condition."

71. Derrida, "Le Futur antérieur de l'archive," 43. See also Nathalie Piégay-Gros, *Le Futur antérieur de l'archive*, on the future perfect as the modality of the archive.

72. Jacques Derrida, *Spectres of Marx*, trans. Peggy Kamuf (New York: Routledge, 2006), xix, 6, 37, 45, 48.

73. Derrida, *Mal d'archive*, 56; *Archive Fever*, 33–34.

74. Derrida, *Apprendre à vivre enfin*, 33; *Learning to Live Finally*, 32.

75. Derrida, *Mal d'archive*, 96; *Archive Fever*, 60.

76. Derrida, *Mal d'archive*, 83.

77. The correspondence between the two authors, stored, according to Cixous, at her Paris apartment, is destined one day for the *fonds* Cixous at the BNF, though withheld from public access for an indeterminate duration. Hélène Cixous, personal interview, November 3, 2013.

78. Thomas Dutoit et al., "Guide to the Jacques Derrida Papers," Special Collections and Archives, UCI Libraries, Irvine, California, 2007, http://hydra.humanities.uci.edu/derrida/uci.html.

79. See the IMEC's finding aid to the *fonds* Derrida, at https://portail-collections.imec-archives.com/ark:/29414/a011433424761LQUFTQ.

80. Ann Laura Stoler, *Along the Archival Grain: Epistemic Anxieties and Colonial Common Sense* (Princeton, NJ: Princeton University Press, 2009), 17.

81. I evoke Greene and Meissner's call, in "More Product, Less Process: Revamping Traditional Archival Processing" (*American Archivist* 68 [2005]: 208–63), for a new model of efficiency in archival processing to account for new technological developments and the increase in born-digital materials.

82. Stoler, *Along the Archival Grain*, 1.

83. Anjali Arondekar, *For the Record: On Sexuality and the Colonial Archive in India* (Durham, NC: Duke University Press, 2009), 1–2.

84. Arlette Farge, *Le Goût de l'archive* (Paris: Seuil, 1989), 71, 79; *The Allure of the Archives*, trans. Thomas Scott-Railton (New Haven, CT: Yale University Press, 2013), 55, 62.

85. In the vein of the new and renewed claim to philology, see Stephen Nichols's introduction to "The New Philology" special issue of *Speculum* and his essay "Philology and Its Discontents"; Edward Said, "The Return to Philology"; and Werner Hamacher's "95 Theses on Philology."

86. Kate Eichhorn, *The Archival Turn in Feminism: Outrage in Order* (Philadelphia: Temple University Press, 2013), 19.

87. Ann Cvetkovich, *An Archive of Feelings* (Durham, NC: Duke University Press, 2003), 268.

88. Cvetkovich, *Archive of Feelings*, 243–44.

89. This is based on the sheer number of individual voices included: the Feminist Theory Archive's website lists over 150 donors as of October 2018; all have contributed to feminist thought and diverse understandings of gender, and the names range widely across academic disciplines. The FTA's archival significance comes in part from the vast number of contributors, not from any one figurehead. The inaugural donation of Naomi Schor's papers appears to serve as an exemplary impetus, not as the capstone of a hierarchy.

90. Joan W. Scott, *The Fantasy of Feminist History* (Durham, NC: Duke University Press, 2011), 143.

91. Scott, *Fantasy of Feminist History*, 148.

92. Scott, *Fantasy of Feminist History*, 148.

93. Jane Bennett, *Vibrant Matter: A Political Ecology of Things* (Durham, NC: Duke University Press, 2010), 23–24.

94. Bennett, *Vibrant Matter*, 23.

95. Within book history, the seminal work is Darnton's "What Is the History of Books?"; see also his "'What Is the History of Books?' Revisited." For manuscript study, see Cerquiglini's *Éloge de la variante*; and "The New Philology," a 1990 special issue of the journal *Speculum* with an introduction by Stephen Nichols. For a discussion of textual fluidity in literature of the modern period, a good example is John Bryant's *The Fluid Text*. Carolyn Dinshaw's *How Soon Is Now?* explores communities of readers across the centuries.

96. Martha Dana Rust, *Imaginary Worlds in Medieval Books: Exploring the Manuscript Matrix* (New York: Palgrave Macmillan, 2007), 9.

97. Hélène Cixous, *Double Oubli de l'Orang-Outang* (Paris: Galilée, 2010), 30; *Double Oblivion of the Ourang-Outang*, trans. Suzanne Dow (Cambridge: Polity, 2013), 27, 45.

98. Hélène Cixous, *Hyperrêve* (Paris: Galilée, 2006), 199; *Hyperdream*, trans. Beverley Bie Brahic (Cambridge: Polity, 2009), 151.

99. Johnson, *System and Writing*, 103–5.

100. Fleming, *Cultural Graphology*, 9.

101. Fleming, *Cultural Graphology*, 24.

102. Johnson, *System and Writing*, 11.

103. Johnson, *System and Writing*, 95–96.

104. Johnson, *System and Writing*, 106. Jacques Derrida, *L'Écriture et la différence* (Paris: Seuil, 1967), 313; *Writing and Difference*, trans. Alan Bass (London: Routledge, 2001), 265, quoted in Johnson, *System and Writing*, 106.

105. Catherine Malabou, *Plasticity at the Dusk of Writing*, trans. Carolyn Shread (New York: Columbia University Press, 2009), 11.

106. Malabou, *Plasticity at the Dusk of Writing*, 12.

107. This model of biographical analysis has affinities with François Dosse's *Le Pari biographique* and Vincent Kaufmann's *L'Équivoque épistolaire*.

108. On Plath's archive, see *The Haunting of Sylvia Plath* by Jacqueline Rose and *The Unraveling Archive* (ed. Helle). Dickinson's manuscripts have been collected in the high-resolution facsimile volumes *The Gorgeous Nothings: Emily Dickinson's Envelope Poems* (2013) and *Emily Dickinson's Poems: As She Preserved Them* (2016), which highlight the materiality of her work.

109. For an overview of genetic approaches to literary artifacts, see *Genetic Criticism: Texts and Avant-textes* (ed. Deppman et al.). See also Laurent Jenny's critical view in "Genetic Criticism and Its Myths."

Chapter 1

1. In Cixous's essay "Sans arrêt, non . . ." in *Repentirs* (Paris: Réunion des Musées Nationaux, 1991), 55; "Without End, no . . . ," trans. Catherine A. F. MacGillivray, *New Literary History* 24, no. 1 (1993): 91.

2. Hélène Cixous, ". . . de main en main jusqu'à un maintenant éphémère," in *Brouillons d'écrivains* (Paris: Bibliothèque nationale de France, 2001), 175.

3. Cixous, *Brouillons d'écrivains*, 175–76.

4. From "Propos d'Hélène Cixous recueillis," in *Chroniques de la Bibliothèque nationale de France*, 7; cited in Marie-Odile Germain, "Around *Tours Promises*: The Donation of Hélène Cixous's Manuscripts to the Bibliothèque Nationale de France," *parallax* 13, no. 3 (2007): 32.

5. Cixous, *Brouillons d'écrivains*, 175.

6. Cixous, *Brouillons d'écrivains*, 173.

7. Cited in Germain, "Around *Tours Promises*," 32.

8. Other examples of Cixous's focus on the materiality of the writing process, especially in the years leading up to the creation of her *fonds* at the BNF, include *L'Amour même dans la boîte aux lettres* and *Hyperrêve*—both examined in subsequent chapters.

9. Cixous, "Sans arrêt," 59.

10. Hélène Cixous, "Germes, gestes, restes," *Revue de la Bibliothèque nationale de France* 5 (June 2000): 81.

11. Hélène Cixous, *Hélène Cixous: The Writing Notebooks*, ed. Susan Sellers (New York: Continuum, 2004), 116.

12. Cixous, *The Writing Notebooks*, 117.

13. Cixous, "Germes, gestes, restes," 81.

14. For genetic criticism, according to Pierre-Marc de Biasi, the *avant-texte* is "le dossier de genèse rendu accessible et intelligible. L'avant-texte est une production critique. . . . L'avant-texte ne désigne donc pas la matérialité des manuscrits, mais leur redéploiement critique" (*Génétique des textes* [Paris: CNRS Éditions, 2011], 69). For an overview of genetic criticism, see de Biasi, *Génétique des textes* and the volume *Genetic Criticism: Texts and Avant-textes* (ed. Deppman et al.).

15. Cixous further discusses her interest in the traces of writing in "'Je suis d'abord une lisante': Entretien avec Daniel Ferrer, *Genèses* 17 (2001) ("'I am before all a reader': Interview with Daniel Ferrer"): "Je pense que le texte publié est un tour de passe-passe, il manque l'atelier. J'ai toujours eu besoin de l'atelier. . . . Je ne peux pas me passer de la forge" (56; "I think that the published text is a sleight of hand, missing the workshop. I have always needed the workshop. . . . I cannot do without the forge").

16. Hélène Cixous, *Manhattan: Lettres de la préhistoire* (Paris: Galilée, 2002), 111; *Manhattan: Letters from Prehistory*, trans. Beverley Bie Brahic (New York: Fordham University Press, 2007), 87.

17. Cixous, *Tours promises*, 15.

18. Cixous, "Sans arrêt," 55; "Without End," 91.

19. Germain, "Around *Tours Promises*," 34.

20. Cixous, *Double Oubli*, 51.

21. In the preparatory notes for *Double Oubli*, Cixous uses an even stronger religious vocabulary: the manuscript of *Le Prénom de Dieu* has been "repêché et baptisé par JD" (Chemise 3, f° 39, Fonds Cixous, BNF, France).

22. Derrida, *Mal d'archive*, 11; *Archive Fever*, 1.

23. The penciled marks—"on la garde," "Le lac," the number 7—are indeed present on the typescript at the BNF and seem unfaded by the decades. From my experience consulting Derrida's handwriting in his archival collections, I was immediately convinced that "Le lac" was written by him, but I did not have the same immediate reaction to "on la garde."

24. See "La Parole soufflée" and "Freud et la scène de l'écriture" in *L'Écriture et la différence* (1967), "La Double séance" in *La Dissémination* (1972), *Éperons: Les Styles de Nietzsche* (1978), *De la grammatologie* (1967), and "La Main de Heidegger (Geschlecht II)."

25. Johnson, *System and Writing*, 95–96.

26. Jacques Derrida, *La Carte postale: De Socrate à Freud et au-delà* (Paris: Flammarion, 1980), 7–10.

27. Jacques Derrida, "La Main de Heidegger (Geschlecht II)," in *Psyché: Inventions de l'autre II* (Paris: Galilée, 1987), 42–43; "*Geschlecht* II: Heidegger's Hand," trans. John P. Leavey, Jr., in *Deconstruction and Philosophy*, ed. John Sallis (Chicago: University of Chicago Press, 1987), 168–69, slightly modified.

28. Derrida, "La Main de Heidegger (Geschlecht II)," 53; "*Geschlecht* II: Heidegger's Hand," 179.

29. Derrida, "La Main de Heidegger (Geschlecht II)," 53; "*Geschlecht* II: Heidegger's Hand," 179.

30. Derrida, *Genèses, généalogies, genres*, 49–50; *Geneses, Genealogies, Genres*, 39.

31. Derrida, *Genèses, généalogies, genres*, 50; *Geneses, Genealogies, Genres*, 39–40.

32. Jacques Derrida, "Circonfession," in *Derrida*, by Geoffrey Bennington and Jacques Derrida (Paris: Seuil, 1991), 117; "Circumfession," in *Jacques Derrida*, by Geoffrey Bennington and Jacques Derrida, trans. Geoffrey Bennington (Chicago: University of Chicago Press, 1993), 134.

33. On "secrécitation," see Cixous, *Hyperrêve*, 103–4, discussed in chapter 5 of the present study.

34. In his 1967 triptych—*L'Écriture et la différence*, *La Voix et le phénomène*, and *De la grammatologie*—Derrida develops the notion of the trace as a means of exposing the logocentric tradition of Western philosophy. *Marges de la philosophie* expanded on textuality and foreshadowed Derrida's experimental works *Glas* and *La Carte postale*. Derrida's early remarks on understanding trace beyond human activity (in *De la grammatologie*) are taken up again in *L'Animal que donc je suis*, *La Bête et le souverain*, and other essays. Klapana Rahita Seshadri foregrounds this aspect of Derrida's thought in *HumAnimal: Race, Law, Language* (Minneapolis: University of Minnesota Press, 2012), noting in her introduction that for Derrida trace "is the mark of 'living in life' " (xiv).

35. Hélène Cixous, "Co-responding Voix You," in *Derrida and the Time of the Political* (Durham, NC: Duke University Press, 2009), 43. Quoted in "Thoughtprints," Anne Berger's and Marta Segarra's introduction to the volume *Demenageries: Thinking (of) Animals after Derrida* (Amsterdam: Rodopi, 2011).

36. See, in particular, Derrida's own assessment of his enduring engagement with animals in *L'Animal que donc je suis*, as well as the animal throughline in *La Bête et le souverain* (two volumes). Critical scholarship on the animal in Derrida and deconstruction, and inspired by Derrida's work, includes "Derridanimals," a special issue of the *Oxford Literary Review*; *Demenageries: Thinking (of) Animals after Derrida*, a collection of essays edited by Anne Berger and Marta Segarra; the collected volume *L'Animal autobiographique: Autour de Jacques Derrida*, edited by Marie-Louise Mallet; *The End of the World and Other Teachable Moments: Jacques Derrida's Final Seminar*, by Michael Naas; *HumAnimal: Race, Law, Language*, by Kalpana Rahita Seshadri; and *Derrida and Other Animals: The Boundaries of the Human*, by Judith Still.

37. Bennington and Derrida, *Jacques Derrida*, 11.

38. Derrida, "Circonfession," 59, 58, 83; "Circumfession," 59, 59, 89.

39. Bennington, "Derridabase," in *Jacques Derrida*, 7; "Derridabase," in *Jacques Derrida*, 1.

40. Derrida, "Circonfession," 34; "Circumfession," 28–30.

41. Derrida, "Circonfession," 33–34; "Circumfession," 30–31.

42. Derrida, "Circonfession," 19; "Circumfession," 12–13.

43. Derrida, "Circonfession," 133; "Circumfession," 154.

44. Derrida, "Circonfession," 32; "Circumfession," 26.

45. Derrida, "Circonfession," 22; "Circumfession," 15.

46. Derrida, "Circonfession," 18–19; "Circumfession," 10–12.

47. Derrida, "Circonfession," 16; "Circumfession," 6.

48. Derrida, "Circonfession," 16; "Circumfession," 6.

49. In "Contes de la différence sexuelle" (46), Cixous addresses Derrida's periods as menstruation "regulated" by the aleatoric rules of Derrida's word-processing software. See also "Chorégraphies," an interview with Christie MacDonald in which Derrida discusses his use of "female" bodily imagery in his work; and "Derrida's Gift," a special issue of *differences* (16, no. 3, December 2005), especially the essays by MacDonald and Berger.

50. Derrida, "Circonfession," 118; "Circumfession," 124.

51. Derrida, "Circonfession," 118; "Circumfession," 134–35, slightly modified.

52. Derrida, "Circonfession," 94; "Circumfession," 103.

53. Derrida's "Circonfession" notebooks have recently been added to his collection at the IMEC—too recently to be included in the research for this book (archival reference 219DRR/269/1–219DRR/269/3, IMEC).

54. Dossier "Travaux en cours été 2004," Jacques Derrida, 219DRR/201/18, IMEC. At the time of publication, the Derrida collection at the IMEC no longer includes a subseries of this title.

55. Carolyn Dinshaw, *How Soon Is Now? Medieval Texts, Amateur Readers, and the Queerness of Time* (Durham, NC: Duke University Press, 2012), 4–6.

Chapter 2

1. The BNF acquired Michel Foucault's papers in 2013.

2. Cixous, ". . . de main en main," 176.

3. See, for example, Sellers, *The Writing Notebooks*; Bennington, *Géographie et autres lectures*; Clément and Segarra, eds., *Rêver croire penser: Autour d'Hélène Cixous*; and Michaud, "Ombilic: L'Œuvre à l'insu de l'archive."

4. The Society of American Archivists' online glossary gives the following definitions of these terms: original order is "the organization and sequence of records established by the creator of the records"; and provenance is "the origin or source of something" or "information regarding the origins, custody, and ownership of an item or collection." See also Hensen, *Archives, Personal Papers, and Manuscripts.*

5. See Elizabeth Grosz, *Volatile Bodies.*

6. In *What Should We Do with Our Brain?* (New York: Fordham University Press, 2008), Catherine Malabou writes: "According to its etymology—from the Greek *plassein*, to mold—the word *plasticity* has two basic senses: it means at once to *receive form* (clay is called "plastic," for example) and the capacity to *give form* (as in the plastic arts or in plastic surgery). . . . But it must be remarked that plasticity is also the capacity to annihilate the very form it is able to receive or create. We should not forget that *plastique*, from which we get the words *plastiquage* and *plastiquer*, is an explosive substance made of nitroglycerine and nitrocellulose, capable of causing violent explosions. We thus note that plasticity is situated between two extremes: on the one side the sensible image of taking form (sculpture or plastic objects), and on the other side that of annihilation of all form (explosion)" (5). See also Malabou, *Plasticity at the Dusk of Writing*, 60–62.

7. Michel Contat, Denis Hollier, Jacques Neefs, and Alyson Waters, eds., "Drafts," special issue of *Yale French Studies* 89 (1996): 2.

8. Daniel Ferrer, *Logiques du brouillon: Modèles pour une critique génétique* (Paris: Seuil, 2011), 16.

9. Ferrer, *Logiques du brouillon*, 139.

10. Ferrer, *Logiques du brouillon*, 139.

11. Bernard Cerquiglini, *Éloge de la variante* (Paris: Seuil, 1989), 112–16.

12. See Derrida's use of the word *contretemps* in "L'Aphorisme à contretemps," in Derrida and Malabou, *La Contre-Allée* (Paris: Quinzaine Littéraire-Louis Vuitton, 1999), 15, 58; and in the *Cahiers de l'Herne* volume on Derrida (ed. Marie-Louise Mallet and Ginette Michaud [Paris: L'Herne, 2004] 32–34). Ginette Michaud's *Jacques Derrida et l'art du contretemps* reads Derrida's

oeuvre—from the concept of *différance* to *survie*—as an engagement with the idea of *contretemps*.

13. The term *Nachträglichkeit*, from a little-studied text by Freud, was taken up by Lacan and is usually translated as "afterwardness" in English and "l'après-coup" in French. It refers to the psychic process of giving meaning to a previous trauma. This must be done belatedly, with the traumatic event simultaneously named and reinforced by being revisited. In fact, the moment of "trauma" is only understood as such in this second phase. Understood as two distinct events in time, a "coup" must first occur for the meaning-making "après-coup" to function. Lacan's understanding of the temporality involved in the *après-coup* is similar to his formulation from Poe's "Purloined Letter": the letter is constituted as a letter in the event of its arrival, not in its sending. Hence Derrida's untimely response to Lacan in *La Carte postale*, and his revision of Lacan's formulation "la lettre arrive toujours à destination" in the concept of *destinerrance*. For Lacan's discussion of "l'après-coup," see *Les Quatre concepts fondamentaux de la psychanalyse*. For Freud on *nachträglichkeit*, see especially his "Wolf Man" ("From the History of an Infantile Neurosis"). Laplanche was also interested in the concept of *nachträglichkeit* for its temporal ambiguity, shuffling between past and present in a mixture of retrogressive and progressive directionality (see his "Notes on Afterwardness").

14. Derrida, "Le Futur antérieur de l'archive," 43.

15. Derrida, *Mal d'archive*, 83; *Archive Fever*, 51–52.

16. Jacques Derrida, *Spectres de Marx* (Paris: Galilée, 1993), 48.

17. Derrida, *Spectres of Marx*, 6.

18. Dinshaw, *How Soon Is Now?* 4–6.

19. Cixous, *OR: Les Lettres de mon père*, 110.

20. Hélène Cixous, *L'Amour même dans la boîte aux lettres* (Paris: Galilée, 2005), 110–11; *Love Itself in the Letterbox*, trans. Peggy Kamuf (Cambridge: Polity, 2008), 79.

21. Cixous, *L'Amour même*, 110; *Love Itself*, 79.

22. Some of these handwritten pages are reproduced in *Hélène Cixous: The Writing Notebooks*.

23. Dinshaw, *How Soon Is Now?* 4–6.

24. Manuscript of *OR: Les Lettres de mon père*, Preparatory notes. Folder 3, folio 1. Département des Manuscrits, Bibliothèque nationale de France.

25. Cixous, *OR: Les Lettres de mon père*, 186; translation by Laurent Milesi in Derrida, *H. C. for Life*, 62.

26. Both Derrida's "archive fever" and that of social scientists such as Anjali Arondekar and Carolyn Steedman (who discusses the literal fever caused by breathing in archival dust—a true inspiration) acknowledge the tension between creation and destruction at the heart of an archive's formation and its consultation. See Derrida's *Mal d'archive*; Arondekar, *For the Record*; and Steedman, *Dust: The Archive and Cultural History*.

27. Cixous, *L'Amour même*, 162; *Love Itself*, 119.

28. Cixous, *L'Amour même*, 162; *Love Itself*, 119.

29. Cixous, *L'Amour même*, 51; *Love Itself*, 34.

30. Cixous, *L'Amour même*, 127; *Love Itself*, 92.

31. Cixous, *L'Amour même*, 105–6, 138–44.

32. It is not clear why several of Cixous's manuscripts remain in the Derrida Library at Princeton, while other artifacts determined to have been written by her were transferred to the IMEC.

33. Per the notation "v.[ersement] 2013" and "v.[ersement] 2014" on Chemise 7 and Chemise 8 in the folder of "Correspondance Hélène Cixous" (219DRR/24/10). Prior to these additions, the folder had contained approximately 37 postcards, telegrams, and letters, as well as postmarked envelopes.

34. Derrida, *H. C. pour la vie*, 71, 74. Derrida quotes "injonction télégraphique" from Cixous's *OR: Les Lettres de mon père*, 21.

35. On the physical makeup of paper and ink, see Joyce Irene Whalley, *Writing Implements and Accessories* (Michigan: Gale Research, 1975): "The nineteenth century saw the complete mechanization of paper-making processes and also the substituting, for cheaper papers, of mechanical wood pulp, esparto grass, and similar materials instead of rags" (74); early recipes for ink called for wine, pomegranate bark, and hawthorn (78–79).

36. For the debated etymology of "ivy," see *An Analytic Dictionary of the English Etymology: An Introduction*, by Anatoly Liberman (Minneapolis: University of Minnesota Press, 2007), 117–23.

37. Derrida, *H. C. pour la vie*, 71; *H. C. for Life*, 79.

38. Cote 219DRR/24/10, "Lettres d'Hélène Cixous à Jacques Derrida," IMEC.

39. "Un fichu" is a scrap of fabric, such as a rag or a scarf, and the adjective "fichu" means doomed. On the "fichu" as a motif linking Derrida and Cixous, see Derrida, *Fichus* (Paris: Galilée, 2002); as well as chapter 5 of this book.

40. See Derrida's "Envois" (28, 73, 149) and "Le Facteur de la vérité" (517), both in *La Carte postale: De Socrate à Freud et au-delà* (Paris: Flammarion, 1980). See also Derrida and Malabou's *La Contre-Allée*, 26–30. In "Cixanalyses—Towards a Reading of *Anankè*," Laurent Milesi links Derrida's interest in destiny and *adestination* to Cixous's *Anankè*, published in 1979, one year before Derrida's *La Carte postale*, as Milesi points out. On the *clinamen*, see Lucretius, *On the Nature of Things*. J. Hillis Miller discusses the *clinamen* in relation to *destinerrance* in "Derrida's *Destinerrance*."

41. On *La Carte postale*, see the essays collected in the volume *Going Postcard: The Letter(s) of Jacques Derrida*, ed. Vincent W. J. Van Gerven Oei.

42. Mairéad Hanrahan also draws attention to the importance of chance and contingency in "Envois"—especially in relation to psychoanalysis and literature, both of which Derrida seeks to move beyond, according to Hanrahan—in "Writing Symptomatically," in "Cixous, Derrida, Psychoanalysis," special issue of *Paragraph* 36, no. 2 (2013): 212–16.

43. Derrida, *La Carte postale*, 472; *The Post Card*, trans. Alan Bass (Chicago: University of Chicago Press, 1987), 444.

44. Derrida, *La Carte postale*, 472; *The Post Card*, 444.

45. *La Carte postale* itself forms a kind of archive: this collection of texts written between 1975 and 1979 is arranged in reverse chronological order, with the newest material appearing first. If the book is read from cover to cover, the reader travels backwards through time, an experience that mimics the temporal logic Derrida explores in relation to Lacan, with whom the whole of *La Carte postale* is in dialogue. On the "round robin" of Derrida's and Lacan's readings of Poe, see Barbara Johnson's "The Frame of Reference: Poe, Lacan, Derrida," *Yale French*

Studies 55/56 (1977). According to Johnson, the "sins of omission" Derrida accuses Lacan of in fact amount to a "*transference of guilt* from a certain *reading* of Lacan onto Lacan's *text*" (480, 478). *La Carte postale* is above all about reading and the possible relationships between text, reader, and writer.

46. David Wills discusses "Envois" as a reflection on narrative in relation to the epistolary novel in "Post/Card/Match/Book/'Envois'/Derrida."

47. Derrida, *La Carte postale*, 32; *The Post Card*, 27.

48. Derrida, *La Carte postale*, 60; *The Post Card*, 53.

49. Derrida, *La Carte postale*, 46; *The Post Card*, 40.

50. Derrida, *La Carte postale*, 47; *The Post Card*, 40.

51. Derrida, *La Carte postale*, 185; *The Post Card*, 171.

52. The tactic of hiding in plain sight recalls the thief's strategy in Poe's story "The Purloined Letter": just as the best way to protect the letter is to keep it out in the open, the best way to destroy the correspondence is to save it.

53. Derrida, *La Carte postale*, 8–9; *The Post Card*, 4–5.

54. Benoît Peeters, *Trois ans avec Derrida: Les Carnets d'un biographe* (Paris: Flammarion, 2010), 215.

55. Peeters, *Trois ans avec Derrida*, 91.

56. Derrida, *La Carte postale*, 9–16.

57. F° 3, 16, and 17 of the correspondence dossier refer to "In prenostica S . . ." ("La Carte postale," Derrida Collection, UC Irvine).

58. Derrida, *La Carte postale*, 185; *The Post Card*, 171.

59. Dutoit et al., "Guide to the Jacques Derrida Papers," http://hydra.humanities.uci.edu/derrida/uci.html, p. 54.

60. "Guide to the Jacques Derrida Papers," 86.

61. Conversation with Alexandra Bisio, processing archivist for the Critical Theory Archive, June 25, 2014.

62. See Meissner and Greene, "More Product, Less Process: Revamping Traditional Archival Processing." "Series-level processing" is especially important now that technological developments have widened the scope of what is archivable, making archives potentially even more immense, and even seemingly infinite.

63. On contingency and the moving image related to the concept of the archive, see Mary Ann Doane, *The Emergence of Cinematic Time: Modernity, Contingency, the Archive*.

64. Derrida, *La Carte postale*, 193; *The Post Card*, 178, slightly modified.

65. Interview with Hélène Cixous, November 3, 2013.

Chapter 3

1. Cixous, *Hyperrêve*, 105; *Hyperdream*, 77, slightly modified.

2. Derrida, "Circonfession," 117; "Circumfession," 133.

3. Derrida, *H. C. pour la vie*, 59; *H. C. for Life*, 63.

4. Derrida, *H. C. pour la vie*, 59; *H. C. for Life*, 63.

5. Deleuze distinguishes between simulacrum and copy through difference: "The copy is an image endowed with resemblance, the simulacrum is an image without resemblance"; though it "produces an *effect* of resemblance . . . the simulacrum is built upon a disparity or upon a difference. It internalizes a dissimilarity. This is why we can no longer define it in relation to a model imposed on the copies, a model of the Same, from which the copies' resemblance derives"

(*The Logic of Sense*, trans. Mark Lester (New York: Columbia University Press, 1990) 256–58).

6. Buchanan, *A Dictionary of Critical Theory*.

7. Derrida, "Circonfssion," 118; "Circumfession," 134–35.

8. The transcription of this discussion, titled "Le Futur antérieur de l'archive," appears in the volume *Questions d'archives*.

9. Derrida, "Le Futur antérieur de l'archive," 48–49.

10. Derrida, "Le Futur antérieur de l'archive," 50.

11. I thank Olivier Corpet for authorization to quote from this letter. Letter from Olivier Corpet to Jacques Derrida, November 24, 2000, Dossier "Sur la question de l'archive," 219DRR/199/3, *fonds* Derrida, IMEC.

12. In November 2004, UC Irvine demanded that Derrida's executors (his widow and two sons) complete the university's collection by sending Derrida's papers from 2000 on. When the executors refused, maintaining that Derrida never intended to give all of his papers to UC Irvine, the latter sued. The lawsuit was dropped in May 2007. For a fuller account of these legal struggles, including what could be construed as Derrida's controversial withholding (and even threatened retraction) of his collection in retaliation for the punishment of a friend (then-Associate Professor Dragan Kujundzic) who'd been accused of having an inappropriate sexual relationship with a graduate student, see Thomas Bartlett, "Archive Fever," as well as documentation available at http://www.jacques-derrida.org/UCI%20Affair.html, a website created by Geoffrey Bennington and Peggy Kamuf, the literary executors of Derrida's papers at UC Irvine.

13. Dutoit et al., "Guide to the Jacques Derrida Papers," http://hydra.humanities.uci.edu/derrida/uci.html.

14. Stoler, *Along the Archival Grain*, 49, 53.

15. J. Mort, *The Anatomy of Xerography* (Jefferson, NC: McFarland, 1989), 55–58.

16. David Owen, *Copies in Seconds* (New York: Simon and Schuster, 2004), 44–47.

17. Owen, *Copies in Seconds*, 35–36.

18. Dani Cavallaro relates the twentieth-century interest in simulacra to the development of mechanical reproduction and "the electronic production of virtual worlds" ("Simulacrum," in *Critical and Cultural Theory* [London: Bloomsbury, 2001], 203). On the simulacrum in Derrida, see "La Pharmacie de Platon." See also Deleuze's *Logique du sens*.

19. In *Dust: The Archive and Cultural History*, cultural historian Carolyn Steedman expresses the "empirical doggedness" of historians who criticize Derrida for presenting an overly abstract portrait of the archive (10), and who feel a sense of confusion for having "assumed that 'Archive Fever' has something to do with archives" (9).

20. The word "dispositif" also belongs to the Foucauldian lexicon, e.g., *le dispositif de sexualité*, referring to the process or system through which the idea of the materiality of sex and sexuality emerges (in *Histoire de la sexualité*).

21. The "Derrida hexadécimal" project, hosted by the ITEM (Insitut des textes et mémoires modernes), maintains the website http://www.item.ens.fr/derrida-hexadecimal/. Aurèle Crasson, Jean-Louis Lebrave and Jérémy Pedrazzi give a

detailed account of the project in "Le 'Siliscrit' de Jacques Derrida: Exploration d'une archive nativement numérique" (published in *Genèses* 49, 2019).

22. Johnson, *System and Writing*, 105, 106.

23. Malabou, *Plasticity at the Dusk of Writing*, 59. Malabou's reading of Jean-Pierre Changeux's *Neuronal Man: The Biology of Mind* leads her to suggest other metaphors arising from neuronal plasticity: "the metaphor used to describe it is *not a graphic metaphor*. Instead, the metaphor used is the geographic or political metaphor of *assemblies*, *forms*, or *neuronal populations*" (*Plasticity*, 60).

24. Derrida, *Mal d'archive*, 101; *Archive Fever*, 63.

25. Derrida, *Mal d'archive*, 103; *Archive Fever*, 64.

26. Derrida, *Mal d'archive*, 103; *Archive Fever*, 64.

27. Derrida, *Mal d'archive*, 105; *Archive Fever*, 65–66.

28. Derrida, *Mal d'archive*, 106–7; *Archive Fever*, 66.

29. Derrida, *Mal d'archive*, 107; *Archive Fever*, 66–67.

30. Derrida, *Mal d'archive*, 100; *Archive Fever*, 62.

31. Derrida, *Mal d'archive*, 100; *Archive Fever*, 62.

32. Derrida, *Mal d'archive*, 100; *Archive Fever*, 62.

33. Derrida, *Spectres of Marx*, 10, 48.

34. Derrida, *Spectres de Marx*, 34–35; *Spectres of Marx*, 13.

35. Derrida, *Spectres de Marx*, 93; *Spectres of Marx*, 67.

36. Derrida, *Spectres of Marx*, 213.

37. Jacques Derrida, *L'Université sans condition* (Paris: Galilée, 2001), 56; "The University without Condition," in *Without Alibi*, trans. Peggy Kamuf (Stanford, CA: Stanford University Press, 2002), 225.

38. Derrida, *L'Université sans condition*, 17, 11; "The University without Condition," 208, 202.

39. Derrida, *Mal d'archive*, 12–13; *Archive Fever*, 3.

40. On the creation of the Collège international de philosophie, see Derrida, "Titles," in *Du droit à la philosophie* (1990), as well as Châtelet, *Le Rapport bleu*; and Peeters, *Derrida*, part III, chapter 1.

41. Jacques Derrida, *Eyes of the University: The Right to Philosophy II*, trans. Jan Plug et al. (Stanford, CA: Stanford University Press, 2004), 204.

42. Derrida, "Le Futur antérieur de l'archive," 48–49. Published in *Questions d'archives*, the transcription of this talk, as well as several preparatory notes for it, are included in the *fonds* Derrida at the IMEC (Dossier "Sur la question de l'archive," 219DRR/199/3).

43. Derrida, "Le Futur antérieur de l'archive," 50.

44. Derrida, "Circonfession," 118; "Circumfession," 134–35.

45. Derrida, "Circonfession," 118; "Circumfession," 134–35, slightly modified.

46. Derrida, "Circonfession," 117; "Circumfession," 133.

47. According to a description for this type of floppy disk, available for purchase on Amazon.com (https://www.amazon.com/Maxell-Double-Density-Tracks-Floppy/dp/B009KMVKAI).

48. Derrida, "Circonfession," 132–33; "Circumfession," 153.

49. According to the Museum of Obsolete Media (http://www.obsoletemedia.org/data/disk/).

50. Derrida, "Circonfession," 118; "Circumfession," 134.

51. See Derrida, "La Main de Heidegger" and "Le Papier ou moi, vous savez . . ."

52. Jacques Derrida, "La Machine à traitement de texte," in *Papier machine* (Paris: Galilée, 2001), 153; "The Word Processor," in *Paper Machine*, trans. Rachel Bowlby (Stanford, CA: Stanford University Press, 2005), 20.

53. Derrida, "Circonfession," 118; "Circumfession," 134–35, slightly modified.

54. Derrida, "Circonfession," 118; "Circumfession," 134–35.

55. Johanna Drucker explains how letters appear on the screen through the translation of binary code in "From A to Screen."

56. Derrida, "La Machine à traitement de texte," 155–56; "The Word Processor," 23.

57. Conversations with archivists at the IMEC in November 2013 and May 2014.

58. Crasson et al., "Le 'Siliscrit' de Jacques Derrida," 190.

59. Crasson et al., "Le 'Siliscrit' de Jacques Derrida," 196.

60. E-mail communication with Christine Kim, public services and archives assistant, Special Collections and Archives, UCI Libraries, January 20, 2015.

61. See, for example, Hal Foster's critique of "virtual" (i.e., digital) technology in "An Archival Impulse" and "The Archive without Museums"; or Friedrich Kittler's sometimes apocalyptic view of the digital in *Gramophone, Film, Typewriter*.

62. See Clement, Hagenmaier, and Kneis, "Toward a Notion of the Archive of the Future."

63. Geoffrey Yeo's essay "The Conceptual Fonds and the Physical Collection" provides a model for combining technological innovations with post-structuralist theory in archival practice. In 2004, Terry Cook advocated for a turn to postmodern theories of the archive, giving in "Archival Science and Postmodernism: New Formulations for Old Concepts" an extensive bibliography of "archivists now starting to explore the implications of these postmodern ideas for their profession" (*Archival Science* 1 [2001]: 10n13). These archivists include Brien Brothman and Richard Brown, Bernadine Dodge, Verne Harris, Eric Ketelaar, Tom Nesmith, Theresa Rowatt, and Joan Schwartz.

64. See Timothy Colburn, "Software, Abstraction, and Ontology," *The Monist* 82, no. 1 (January 1999): 3–19.

65. Examples of innovative projects providing access to digitized literary artifacts, available to consult online, include the Emily Dickinson Archive (https://www.edickinson.org/), the Walt Whitman Archive (https://whitmanarchive.org/), and Stendhal numérisé (https://www.bm-grenoble.fr/853-stendhal-numerise.htm).

66. See Matthew McKinley, "Imaging Digital Media for Preservation with LAMMP," in The Electronic Media Review, Volume 3 (2015), 89–96. Further illuminating the inventiveness of archivists working with limited resources, McKinley's system is an artisanal version of a much more expensive product called FRED (Forensic Recovery of Evidence Device, http://www.digitalintelligence.com/products/fred/), developed at Stanford (conversation with Alex Bisio, June 2014, and e-mail exchange June 30, 2014).

67. Matthew Kirschenbaum, "The .txtual Condition," in *Comparative Textual Media: Transforming the Humanities in the Postprint Era*, ed. N. Katherine Hayles and Jessica Pressman (Minneapolis: University of Minnesota Press, 2013), 58.

68. Kirschenbaum, "The .txtual Condition," 60.

69. McKinley, "Imaging Digital Media for Preservation with LAMMP," 89.

70. In "The .txtual Condition" Kirschenbaum discusses the Rushdie collection at Emory University Library, where researchers can consult one of Rushdie's four personal computers (53).

71. A little too close for some readers of Benjamin Moser's *New Yorker* article "In the Sontag Archives," judging from the comments left online in response to his article decrying such an invasion of Sontag's privacy. The comments section is unfortunately no longer accessible on the website—a limit of internet archivability! Moser's article describes the work of the archivist and digital humanist Gloria Gonzalez to preserve and maintain accessibility for Susan Sontag's two hard drives at the UCLA Special Collections. (The article was published January 30, 2014, in the *New Yorker*, and online at http://www.newyorker.com/books/page-turner/in-the-sontag-archives.)

72. Daniel Smith, "The Concept of the Simulacrum: Deleuze and the Overturning of Platonism," *Continental Philosophy Review* 38, no. 1–2 (2005): 101.

73. Smith, "Concept of the Simulacrum," 101.

74. Kirschenbaum, "The .txtual Condition," 60.

75. Cixous, *Hyperrêve*, 83; *Hyperdream*, 59–60.

76. Derrida, *H. C. pour la vie*, 57; *H. C. for Life*, 61.

77. Derrida, *H. C. pour la vie*, 65; *H. C. for Life*, 72.

78. Derrida, *H. C. pour la vie*, 75, 81, 71; *H. C. for Life*, 83.

79. Derrida, *H. C. pour la vie*, 59; *H. C. for Life*, 63.

80. Cixous, *Hyperrêve*, 104–5; *Hyperdream*, 76–77.

81. Cixous, *Hyperrêve*, 105; *Hyperdream*, 77.

82. Cixous, *Hyperrêve*, 106; *Hyperdream*, 77.

83. Cixous, *Hyperrêve*, 199; *Hyperdream*, 151.

84. Cixous, *Tours promises*, 63, 62–63.

85. Cixous, *Tours promises*, 68.

86. Cixous, *Tours promises*, 37.

87. Cixous, *Tours promises*, 73.

88. Cixous, *Tours promises*, 75.

89. Paula Amad, *Counter-Archive: Film, the Everyday, and Albert Kahn's Archives de la Planète* (New York: Columbia University Press, 2010), 4.

90. Amad, *Counter-Archive*, 4.

91. Hélène Cixous and Frédéric-Yves Jeannet, "Le Livre que Tu n'écriras pas," Remue.net (2007), 9.

92. Hélène Cixous, "Le Livre que je n'écris pas," in *Genèses Généalogies Genres* (Paris: Galilée, Bibliothèque nationale de France, 2006), 233.

93. Mallarmé's *Livre* is discussed in his "Quant au livre" and in *Le Livre de Mallarmé* by Jacques Schérer. Maurice Blanchot's *Le Livre à venir* (Paris: Gallimard, 1959) also discusses Mallarmé (303–32).

94. Cixous and Jeannet, "Le Livre que Tu n'écriras pas," 3; "The Book That You Will Not Write: An Interview with Hélène Cixous," trans. Thomas Dutoit, ed. Eric Prenowitz, *New Literary History* 37 (2006): 252.

95. See *Spectres de Marx* relating to Derrida's deconstruction of the messianic, "une messianicité sans messianisme" ("a messianic without messianism," 92), as well as the *à venir*, which is also discussed in *Mal d'archive* (109).

96. Cixous, *Tours promises*, 49, 20.

97. Cixous and Jeannet, "Le Livre que Tu n'écriras pas," 8.

98. Cixous makes note of this comment in the *prière d'insérer* to *Chapitre Los*, written in 2012.

99. Chapter 1 of the present study discusses the "avant d'un livre" that motivates Cixous.

100. Cixous, *Hyperrêve*, 105; Derrida, "Circonfession," 117. In "The Work of Art in the Age of Mechanical Reproduction," in *Illuminations* (New York: Schocken, 1968), Walter Benjamin argues that mechanical reproduction strips the work of art (particularly visual art) of its aura, which Benjamin characterizes through the unique existence of the art object in time and space, its authenticity, its distance from the spectator, and its use as a ritual instrument of magic (220–25).

101. Derrida, *H. C. pour la vie*, 59; *H. C. for Life*, 63.

Chapter 4

1. The first page of "Le Mythe d'Ars" (in *Le Prénom de Dieu*, MS. Boîte 1, 1.0, Fonds Hélène Cixous, Bibliothèque nationale de France).

2. Milesi, "Portraits of H. C. as J. D. and Back," 67.

3. The conference was in 1990, but its proceedings were published in 1994. In "Contes de la Différence Sexuelle" Cixous writes: "J'ai eu, parce que J. D., toi, me l'as communiqué tout récemment, entre les mains un texte extraordinaire: *Circonfession*" (38); "I have had, in my hands—because J.D., you, gave it to me recently—an extraordinary text: *Circonfession*" ("Tales of Sexual Difference," 50). In *Battements du secret littéraire* (23), Ginette Michaud draws attention to the fact that Cixous was referring to the manuscript of "Circonfession."

4. Derrida, "Fourmis," 35; "Ants," 35.

5. Proofs of this text are located at the IMEC (219DRR/194/13). At Irvine, the "Fourmis" dossier (Box 56, Folders 9–10) contains three versions and three pages of preliminary notes (with nearly illegible handwriting).

6. Cixous, *Insister à Jacques Derrida*, 49; *Insister of Jacques Derrida*, 62.

7. In *Insister*, the section "Le Manuscrit volant" ("The Flying Manuscript") discusses the rediscovery of the *Voiles* manuscript.

8. Cixous, *Insister à Jacques Derrida*, 50; *Insister of Jacques Derrida*, 63.

9. Cixous, *Insister à Jacques Derrida*, 54; *Insister of Jacques Derrida*, 69.

10. Cixous, *Insister à Jacques Derrida*, 50; *Insister of Jacques Derrida*, 64.

11. These are located in files labeled "Documents: Hélène Cixous" and include *Rêve je te dis* and *Tours promises* (Box 635/928: Folder 3, Fonds Cixous, BNF), *La Ville parjure* (Box 635/928: Folder 4), Fonds Cixous, BNF), and *OR: Les Lettres de mon père* (Box 636/929: Folder 10, Fonds Cixous, BNF).

12. Jacques Derrida, with Simon Hantaï and Jean-Luc Nancy, *La Connaissance des textes* (Paris: Galilée, 2001), 155. Derrida's practice of safeguarding works in progress is further described in his interview with Daniel Ferrer: "Entre le corps écrivant et l'écriture . . .": "Je ne quitte jamais ma maison sans avoir multiplié le texte en question . . . que je laisse en différents endroits . . . Cela, c'est la névrose qui se développe avec la technologie" (64–65; "I never leave my house without having multiplied the text in question . . . which I leave in several different places . . . That's a neurosis that develops with technology").

13. Derrida, *La Connaissance des textes*, 155. Presa's resulting piece, *Four Horizons of the Page* (Linden Gallery, Melbourne, 2000), can be viewed at https://archive.clivejames.com/gallery/horizons.htm. Dimitris Vardoluakis studies this

work and the relationship between Presa and Derrida in his article "Beside(s): Elizabeth Presa with Jacques Derrida."

14. Eve Kosovsky Sedgwick, *Touching Feeling* (Durham, NC: Duke University Press, 2003). On the "hermeneutics of suspicion," see Paul Ricoeur, *De l'interprétation.*

15. "The Way We Read Now," a special issue of *Representations*, suggests alternative methods of reading such as surface reading, and discusses Sedgwick's interest in reparative reading. In the introduction to this issue, editors Stephen Best and Sharon Marcus discuss Sedgwick's spatial metaphors for paranoid and reparative reading.

16. Arondekar, *For the Record*, 7–11.

17. Derrida, "Circonfession," 18; "Circumfession," 12–13.

18. Derrida, "Circonfession," 19; "Circumfession," 12.

19. In *Le Pacte autobiographique*, Philippe Lejeune proposes that autobiographical writing is defined by a pact between the author and the reader who can accurately identify the narrator and the author as the same person.

20. Derrida, "Circonfession," 94; "Circumfession," 103.

21. Derrida, "Circonfession," 132; "Circumfession," 153.

22. Derrida, "Circonfession," 132–33; "Circumfession," 154–55.

23. Derrida, "Circonfession," 132–33; "Circumfession," 154. This nostalgia for a readable handwriting reappears in Period 42: "'*Retrouver le goût (perdu) de tenir la plume, du bien écrire en un sens que j'ai maltraité, remachiné, . . . retrouver une écriture facile, offerte, lisible, détendue* (14-10-77),' oh, comme ses mains sont fines, ma survivante, elle avait une si belle écriture, cela peut se dire au passé, toute différente de la mienne, et très lisible, élancée, élégante . . . je demande encore ce qui a peu se passer quand mon écriture a changé, après trente ans, puis encore plus tard, quand les machines l'ont prise en mer" ("Circonfession," 185). "'*Rediscover the (lost) taste for holding the pen, for writing well in a sense I have mistreated, reworked, . . . rediscover an easy, offered, readable, relaxed writing*' (10-14-77), oh how fine her hands are, my survivress, she has such beautiful handwriting, that can be said in the past, quite different from mine, and very legible, stylish, elegant . . . I wonder again what can have happened when my writing changed, after thirty years, then again later, when machines took it over on the sea" ("Circumfession," 220–21).

24. Jacques Derrida, *Artaud le Moma* (Paris: Galilée, 2002), 72; *Artaud the Moma*, trans. Peggy Kamuf (New York: Columbia University Press, 2017), 49.

25. Derrida's fluidity in "Circonfession" should be read in light of Irigaray's text "La 'Mécanique' des fluides," which argues that physics has historically privileged solid over fluid mechanics, reinforcing a hierarchy of masculine over feminine.

26. Derrida, "Circonfession," 33–34; "Circumfession," 30–31.

27. Derrida, "Circonfession," 187–88; "Circumfession," 236.

28. Adeena Karasick analyzes the proximity to Talmudic reading in "Of Poetic Thinking: A 'Pataphysical Investigation of Cixous, Derrida, and the Kabbalah" (Ph.D. thesis, Concordia University, 1997).

29. Cixous, *Portrait de Jacques Derrida*, 14; *Portrait of Jacques Derrida*, 7.

30. Regard, "Faulty Burials," 280.

31. Hélène Cixous, *Portrait de Jacques Derrida en Jeune Saint Juif*, Manuscript, Box III.3, Fonds Cixous, Département des manuscrits, Bibliothèque nationale de France.

32. Cixous, *Portrait de Jacques Derrida*, 21; *Portrait of Jacques Derrida*, 14.

33. Cixous, *Portrait de Jacques Derrida*, 14; *Portrait of Jacques Derrida*, 7.

34. Cited by Ginette Michaud in "Circonfections: Les Lire en secret," in *L'Événement comme écriture: Cixous et Derrida se lisant* (Paris: CampagnePremière, 2007), 243n2.

35. Manuscript and typescript of "Circonfession," Box 33, folders 2–4, Jacques Derrida Collection, Langson Library, UC Irvine.

36. Cixous, *Portrait de Jacques Derrida*, 21; *Portrait of Jacques Derrida*, 14.

37. On the graft in Derrida, see *Glas* and "La Double séance" in *La Dissémination*.

38. Cixous, *Portrait de Jacques Derrida*, 21.

39. Frédéric Regard suggests that the color-coding of Cixous's reading, between the highlighting on the manuscript and the published text of *Portrait*, also evokes the technique of injection or infusion that Derrida dreams of in "Circonfession," and constitutes a "Portrait" of Derrida (Regard, "Derrida Un-Cut: Cixous's Art of Hearts," *Paragraph* 30, no. 2 [2007]: 14–15).

40. Derrida, "Circonfession," 197; "Circumfession," 236.

41. On Judaism in Derrida, see John D. Caputo, *The Prayers and Tears of Jacques Derrida*; Martin Hägglund, *Radical Atheism: Derrida and the Time of Life*; Gideon Olfrat, *The Jewish Derrida*; and *Judéités: Questions pour Jacques Derrida* (ed. Joseph Cohen and Raphael Zagury-Orly, with contributions by Catherine Malabou, Jean-Luc Nancy, and Hélène Cixous, whose text "Ce corps étranjuif" was an early version of *Portrait de Jacques Derrida en Jeune Saint Juif*).

42. Hélène Cixous, *Portrait de Jacques Derrida, prière d'insérer*; *Portrait of Jacques Derrida*, x.

43. Interview with Aliette Armel, "Du mot à la vie: Un dialogue entre Jacques Derrida et Hélène Cixous." On their experiences of growing up in, leaving, and returning to Algeria, see Cixous, "Mon Algérience" and *Si près*. For Derrida, see "Moi, l'Algérien," in *Le Monolinguisme de l'autre*; as well as the concept of the transplant (*la greffe*) in John D. Caputo, *The Prayers and Tears of Jacques Derrida* (Bloomington: Indiana University Press, 1997), 305 ff. Brigitte Weltman-Aron discusses Cixous's and Derrida's experiences of school in Algeria in "The Pedagogy of Colonial Algeria: Djebar, Cixous, Derrida." For the accusation of complicity, even if retrospective, leveled at Derrida, see Lynne Huffer, "Derrida's Nostalgeria." Amy Hubbell includes Cixous and Derrida, along with Leïla Sebbar, in her chapter "(Re)turning to Algeria: Nostalgia, Imagination, and Writing" in *Remembering French Algeria: Pieds-Noirs, Identity, and Exile* (Lincoln: University of Nebraska Press, 2015), although she acknowledges that "these authors are generally excluded from studies of the Pieds-Noirs" (35).

44. Mara Negrón, "À propos de greffes: Ce que l'on singe en écriture autobiographique," in *L'Événement comme écriture: Cixous et Derrida se lisant* (Paris: CampagnePremière, 2007), 270–71.

45. On the body as a surface for writing and mark-making, see the chapter "The Body as Inscriptive Surface" in Elizabeth Grosz, *Volatile Bodies*; as well as Anne Anlin Cheng's essay "Skins, Tattoos, and Susceptibility" in *The Way We*

Read Now and Sarah Kay's *Animal Skins and the Reading Self in Medieval Latin and French Bestiaries*.

46. Jacques Derrida with Hélène Cixous, "Un ver à soie," in *Voiles* (Paris: Galilée, 1998), 83; "A Silkworm of One's Own," in *Veils*, trans. Geoffrey Bennington (Stanford, CA: Stanford University Press, 2001), 89.

47. Derrida, "Un ver à soie," 85; "A Silkworm of One's Own," 91. Along with Derrida's autobiographical *périodes* in "Circonfession," the black dot of the silkworm's "tache" evokes menstruation, signifying sexual maturity in female mammals. Derrida responds to a question about his use of "female" anatomical terms (including his use of "hymen" and "invagination") in "Chorégraphies."

48. The phrase "coming to writing" also alludes to Cixous's text "La Venue à l'écriture," in *Entre l'écriture* (1986), first published in 1975 by Éditions 10/18 in the series "Féminin futur."

49. Derrida, "Un ver à soie," 25, 82; "A Silkworm of One's Own," 21, 87.

50. Derrida, "Un ver à soie," 82; "A Silkworm of One's Own," 87.

51. Derrida, "Un ver à soie," 82; "A Silkworm of One's Own," 87.

52. Derrida, "Un ver à soie," 81; "A Silkworm of One's Own," 86.

53. Derrida, "Un ver à soie," 78; "A Silkworm of One's Own," 82.

54. Derrida, "Un ver à soie," 83; "A Silkworm of One's Own," 89.

55. Claudia Simma discusses the transformation at the end of "Un ver à soie" in terms of movement *toward*, flagging the prepositional homonym of Derrida's title, in "*Ver(s)*: Toward a Spirituality of One's Own."

56. Derrida, "Un ver à soie," 44, 82; "A Silkworm of One's Own," 43, 87.

57. Derrida, "Un ver à soie," 66; "A Silkworm of One's Own," 69.

58. Derrida, "Un ver à soie," 66; "A Silkworm of One's Own," 69.

59. Derrida, "Un ver à soie," 63, 55; "A Silkworm of One's Own," 65, 57.

60. Luce Irigaray develops a different kind of *auto-affection* through the concept of the *se toucher des lèvres* as the essence of femininity and sexual difference: "L'auto-érotisme de la femme [est] très différent de celui de l'homme. Celui-ci a besoin d'un instrument pour se toucher: sa main, le sexe de la femme, le langage . . . Et cette auto-affection exige un minimum d'activité. La femme, elle, se touche d'elle-même et en elle-même sans la nécessité d'une médiation, et avant tout départage possible entre activité et passivité. La femme 'se touche' tout le temps, sans que l'on puisse d'ailleurs le lui interdire, car son sexe est fait de deux lèvres qui s'embrassent continûment. Ainsi, en elle, elle est déjà deux—mais non divisibles en un(e)s—qui s'affectent" (Irigaray, *Ce sexe qui n'en est pas un* [Paris: Minuit, 1977], 24). "Woman's autoeroticism is very different from man's. In order to touch himself, man needs an instrument: his hand, a woman's body, language . . . And this self-caressing requires at least a minimum of activity. As for woman, she touches herself in and of herself without any need for mediation, and before there is any way to distinguish activity from passivity. Woman 'touches herself' all the time, and moreover no one can forbid her to do so, for her genitals are formed of two lips in continuous contact. Thus, within herself, she is already two—but not divisible into one(s)—that caress each other" (*This Sex Which Is Not One*, trans. Catherine Porter [Ithaca, NY: Cornell University Press, 1985], 24).

61. Derrida, "Un ver à soie," 56; "A Silkworm of One's Own," 101. Though the V is not, in English or in French, technically a *bilabial* consonant, it would be in

Spanish (and it is worth noting that *ver* is a verb in Spanish—meaning "to see"). It is, however, considered by linguists to be a labial consonant, since it is formed by the bottom lip actively touching the teeth.

62. Derrida, "Un ver à soie," 56; "A Silkworm of One's Own," 101.

63. Derrida, "Un ver à soie," 84; "A Silkworm of One's Own," 91.

64. Derrida, "Un ver à soie," 56; "A Silkworm of One's Own," 101. The dream of a burned manuscript here finds a corollary in *La Carte postale*, where "des blancs de 57 signes" dispersed throughout "Envois" represent the burn marks of "un grand incendie holocaustique, un brûle-tout" (47; "a great holocaustic fire, a burn-everything," 40) intended to destroy the correspondence.

65. Jacques Derrida, Dossier "Un ver à soie" (IMEC reference 219DRR/198/3–216DRR/198/4).

66. Cixous, *Insister à Jacques Derrida*, 77; *Insister of Jacques Derrida*, 107.

67. Cixous, *Insister à Jacques Derrida*, 79; *Insister of Jacques Derrida*, 110.

68. Cixous, *Insister à Jacques Derrida*, 79; *Insister of Jacques Derrida*, 111.

69. Dossier "Un ver à soie" (IMEC reference 219DRR/198/3–216DRR/198/4).

70. Derrida, "Un ver à soie," 85; "A Silkworm of One's Own," 91, slightly modified.

71. Cixous, *Portrait de Jacques Derrida*, 21; *Portrait of Jacques Derrida*, 14.

72. Frédéric Regard, "Le Portrait biographique selon Hélène Cixous," in *Biographie et intimité des Lumières à nos jours*, ed. Daniel Madelénat (Clermont-Ferrand: Presses Universitaires Blaise Pascal, 2009), 244.

73. Cixous, *Insister à Jacques Derrida*, 54; *Insister of Jacques Derrida*, 69.

74. Cixous, *Insister à Jacques Derrida*, 55; *Insister of Jacques Derrida*, 71.

75. Derrida, *La Carte postale*, 472.

76. Cixous, *Portrait de Jacques Derrida*, 33; *Portrait of Jacques Derrida*, 26.

77. Cixous, *Insister à Jacques Derrida*, 71; *Insister of Jacques Derrida*, 97.

78. Cixous, *Portrait de Jacques Derrida*, 55; *Portrait of Jacques Derrida*, 56.

Chapter 5

1. Derrida, "Fourmis," 89; "Ants," 31.

2. Derrida, "Fourmis," 80; "Ants," 24.

3. Several essays in *L'Événement comme écriture* discuss Cixous and Derrida's telephonic relationship: see the essays by Peggy Kamuf and Eric Prenowitz, but especially Anne Berger's "Appels," which draws out the thematic richness of the telephone in the two writers' works, touching on voice, the call, names, pronouns, and the secret or the unsayable.

4. Derrida, "Fourmis," 71; "Ants," 18.

5. Derrida, "Fourmis," 94–95; "Ants," 35.

6. Derrida, "Fourmis," 94–95; "Ants," 35.

7. Derrida, "Fourmis," 71; "Ants," 18.

8. Derrida, "Fourmis," 72; "Ants," 19.

9. Derrida, "Fourmis," 71; "Ants," 18–19.

10. Hélène Cixous, *Rêve je te dis* (Paris: Galilée, 2003), 18–19; *Dream I Tell You*, trans. Beverley Bie Brahic (Edinburgh: Edinburgh University Press, 2006), 8–9.

11. Mairéad Hanrahan, "Rêver cru," in *Rêver croire penser*, ed. Bruno Clément and Marta Segarra (Paris: CampagnePremière, 2010), 227. Hanrahan

further develops this analysis of the status of dreams in Cixous's writing process in *Cixous's Semi-Fictions* (20–21).

12. Derrida, *Genèses, généalogies, genres*, 15; *Geneses, Genealogies, Genres*, 6.

13. Derrida, *Genèses, généalogies, genres*, 57; *Geneses, Genealogies, Genres*, 46.

14. In his seminars on "Hostilité/hospitalité" (1995, at the EHESS), Derrida draws out the two words' shared etymology, coining the term "hostipitalité."

15. Maria Yassa, "Nicolas Abraham and Maria Torok—The Inner Crypt," *Scandinavian Psychoanalytic Review* 25, no. 2 (2002): 8. See also Derrida's work on the concept of the crypt in "Fors: Les Mots Anglés de Nicolas Abraham et Maria Torok," discussed in Lynn Hughley Engelbert, "'Wild' Freudian Psycho-Analysis."

16. Frédéric Regard explores the consequences of "Faulty Burials," not all of which are negative, in his essay of the same title. See also Geoffrey Bennington on Derrida's resistance to mourning, favoring the half-mourning of melancholia, in *Not Half No End*.

17. This is not to say that psychoanalysis is not an important theoretical presence in Cixous's and Derrida's work. Cixous's texts are in a dense intertextual dialogue with Freud and Lacan; and Derrida engaged directly with texts by those figures and with others, including Abraham and Torok. See in particular his *Résistances—de la psychanalyse* (1996). The 2013 special issue of *Paragraph*, "Cixous, Derrida, Psychoanalysis," draws out the two writers' shared interest in and resistance to psychoanalysis.

18. Sigmund Freud, *The Interpretation of Dreams*, trans. and ed. James Strachey (New York: Avon, 1965), 143, 564.

19. Freud, *Interpretation of Dreams*, 143, 564. Freud's original German "der Nabel" is given as *navel* in Strachey's English translation; the standard French uses *ombilic* instead of *nombril*. The "ombilic" is an important archival figure in Ginette Michaud's essay "Ombilic: L'Œuvre à l'insu de l'archive," a first version of which was presented at the conference "Genèses Généalogies Genres" inaugurating Cixous's archives at the BNF. Derrida engages with the figure of the *ombilic* in *Résistances—de la psychanalyse*.

20. Freud, *Interpretation of Dreams*, 528.

21. Freud, *Interpretation of Dreams*, 528.

22. Cixous, *Hyperrêve*, 179; *Hyperdream*, 135–36.

23. Hélène Cixous and Frédéric-Yves Jeannet, *Rencontre terrestre* (Paris: Galilée, 2005), 131; *Encounters*, trans. Beverley Bie Brahic (Cambridge: Polity, 2013), 139; Cixous, *Three Steps on the Ladder of Writing*, 79, 80.

24. Derrida, *Genèses, généalogies, genres*, 57; *Geneses, Genealogies, Genres*, 46.

25. Cixous, *Insister à Jacques Derrida*, 49.

26. Cixous, *Hyperrêve*, 188; *Hyperdream*, 142.

27. Cixous, *Hyperrêve*, 188; *Hyperdream*, 142, slightly modified.

28. Cixous, *Hyperrêve*, 193; *Hyperdream*, 146.

29. Cixous, *Hyperrêve*, 193; *Hyperdream*, 146.

30. Cixous, *Hyperrêve*, 195; *Hyperdream*, 147.

31. Cixous, *Hyperrêve*, 199, 203; *Hyperdream*, 151, 154.

32. Cixous, *Hyperrêve*, 203; *Hyperdream*, 154, modified.

33. Cixous, *Hyperrêve*, 206; *Hyperdream*, 156.
34. Cixous, *Hyperrêve*, 211; *Hyperdream*, 160.
35. Cixous, *Hyperrêve*, 204, 195.
36. Cixous, *Insister à Jacques Derrida*, 50; *Insister of Jacques Derrida*, 64.
37. Cixous, *Insister à Jacques Derrida*, 50; *Insister of Jacques Derrida*, 63.
38. Cixous, *Insister à Jacques Derrida*, 50; *Insister of Jacques Derrida*, 63.
39. Cixous, *Double Oubli*, 53; *Double Oblivion*, 36.
40. Cixous, *Insister à Jacques Derrida*, 45; *Insister of Jacques Derrida*, 55.
41. Cixous, *Insister à Jacques Derrida*, 50, 71; *Insister of Jacques Derrida*, 64, 97, slightly modified.
42. Cixous, *Insister à Jacques Derrida*, 71; *Insister of Jacques Derrida*, 97.
43. Derrida, "Un ver à soie," 25; "A Silkworm of One's Own," 21.
44. Cixous, *Insister à Jacques Derrida*, 71; *Insister of Jacques Derrida*, 97.
45. For Geoffrey Bennington, reading *Hyperrêve* in his article "Teleanalysis," this node of contact flags the *coup* or the "cut" as that which separates and binds simultaneously.
46. Cixous, *Hyperrêve* 78; *Hyperdream*, 56.
47. Jacques Derrida, *Fichus*, 39; "Fichus," in *Paper Machine*, trans. Rachel Bowlby (Stanford, CA: Stanford University Press, 2005), 174.
48. Cixous, *Hyperrêve*, 101; *Hyperdream*, 74.
49. Cixous, *Hyperrêve*, 101, 105; *Hyperdream*, 74, 77.
50. Cixous, *Hyperrêve*, 103–4; *Hyperdream*, 75–76.
51. Regard, "Faulty Burials," 256.
52. Hélène Cixous, *Le Rire de la Méduse et autres ironies* (Paris: Galilée, 2010), 58–60.
53. Cixous, *Insister à Jacques Derrida*, 31, 33; *Insister of Jacques Derrida*, 35, 39.
54. As such, the intertextual method of linking up texts and reading them that we find in Cixous and Derrida recalls Barthes and Kristeva (in "Word, Dialogue, and Novel" [1966] and "The Bounded Text" [1967]), both of whom discussed intertextuality as a phenomenon that takes the text beyond a single author. In fact, Barthes's explanation of intertextuality in "Théorie du texte" is strikingly similar to what Cixous describes as *secrécitation*: "Any text is a new tissue of past citations. Bits of code, formulae, rhythmic models, fragments of social languages, etc., pass into the text and are redistributed within it, for there is always language before and around the text. Intertextuality, the condition of any text whatsoever, cannot, of course, be reduced to a problem of sources or influences; the intertext is a general field of anonymous formulae whose origin can scarcely ever be located; of unconscious or automatic quotations, given without quotation marks." Roland Barthes, "Théorie du texte," in *Œuvres completes,* vol. 4, ed. Éric Marty (Paris: Seuil, 2002), 39.
55. Derrida, "Fourmis," 76; "Ants," 22.
56. Cixous, *Insister à Jacques Derrida*, 86–87; *Insister of Jacques Derrida*, 128–30, slightly modified.
57. Cixous, *Insister à Jacques Derrida*, 96; *Insister of Jacques Derrida*, 145.
58. Cixous, *Insister à Jacques Derrida*, 89; *Insister of Jacques Derrida*, 134.
59. Cixous, *Insister à Jacques Derrida*, 109; *Insister of Jacques Derrida*, 166.
60. Derrida, "Un ver à soie," 82; "A Silkworm of One's Own," 87.

61. Cixous, *Insister à Jacques Derrida*, 71; *Insister of Jacques Derrida*, 97.

62. See Derrida's "Tympan" in *Marges de la philosophie* and "La Double Séance" in *La Dissémination*.

63. Jacques Derrida, "Chorégraphies," in *Points de suspension: Entretiens* (Paris: Galilée, 1982), 114; "Choreographies: Interview," in *Feminist Interpretations of Jacques Derrida*, ed. Nancy J. Holland (University Park: Pennsylvania State University Press, 1997), 40.

64. Derrida, "Chorégraphies," 114–15; "Choreographies: Interview," 40, slightly modified.

65. Derrida, *Genèses, généalogies, genres*, 53; *Geneses, Genealogies, Genres*, 43.

66. Derrida, *H. C. pour la vie*, 65; *H. C. for Life*, 71–72.

67. Derrida, *H. C. pour la vie*, 75; *H. C. for Life*, 81.

68. Derrida, *H. C. pour la vie*, 57; *H. C. for Life*, 61.

69. Gilles Deleuze also commented on the necessary speed of Cixous's writing, calling it "l'écriture stroboscopique" in his review of *Neutre*, titled "Héléne Cixous ou l'écriture stroboscopique" (*Le Monde*, August 11, 1972). Like Derrida's use of "injonction télégraphique," Deleuze borrows Cixous's own term from *Neutre* to describe her style of writing.

70. Derrida, *H. C. pour la vie*, 57–58; *H. C. for Life*, 62.

71. Cixous, *Three Steps on the Ladder of Writing*, 80.

72. Derrida quotes Cixous's "puissance d'impuissance" from *Jours de l'an* (in *H. C. pour la vie*, 68; 75 in *H. C. for Life*).

73. Derrida, *H. C. pour la vie*, 67; *H. C. for Life*, 74.

74. Derrida, *H. C. pour la vie*, 61; *H. C. for Life*, 66.

75. Derrida, *H. C. pour la vie*, 31; *H. C. for Life*, 29.

76. Derrida, *Genèses, généalogies, genres*, 54; *Geneses, Genealogies, Genres*, 44.

77. Derrida, *Genèses, généalogies, genres*, 54; *Geneses, Genealogies, Genres*, 43–44.

78. Derrida, *Genèses, généalogies, genres*, 56–57; *Geneses, Genealogies, Genres*, 46. "Vigilance" is a watchword associated with the dream in several of Derrida's texts, including "Chorégraphies," *H. C. pour la vie*, *Genèses*, and *Fichus*. In "Fourmis," he attributes the virtuosity of Cixous's writing to "sa vigilance travaillant au rêve, écriture inspirée au réveil, c'est la plus matinale invention de la plus vieille langue" (97; "her vigilance working in dream, inspired writing on waking, it is the earliest morning invention of the oldest language," 37). In *H. C. pour la vie*, he comments that "la veille de la plus impeccable vigilance fait de son écriture la plus surveillée, la plus savante, la plus composée" (68; "the most impeccably wakeful vigil causes her writing to be the most closely watched, the most accomplished, the most skillfully composed," 75). Derrida is careful to insist that the dream he speaks of is not a phantasmatic, idealistic imagining, but a clarity of thought and a hyperawareness borrowed from dreaming—a prime example of which he locates in Cixous's writing. He also does so in *Fichus*, the acceptance speech for the Adorno Prize he received on September 22, 2001. Alluding specifically to the New York attacks of September 11, *Fichus* was written as a call for political "vigilance," a warning against terrorism and tyranny of all kinds.

79. Derrida, "Fourmis," 100; "Ants," 39.

Chapter 6

1. Interview with Manuel Irniger and Claudia Simma, June 28, 2015. "La Phrase début" was presented at the conference "Cixéminaire: Le Séminaire d'Hélène Cixous en Études féminines" on May 22, 2014.

2. For example, Kittler's representation of technology in *Gramophone, Film, Typewriter* is often characterized by homogeneity and totality.

3. Roland Barthes, "Au séminaire," in *Le Bruissement de la langue: Essais Critiques IV* (Paris: Seuil, 1984), 508; "To the Seminar," in *The Rustle of Language*, trans. Richard Howard (Berkeley: University of California Press, 1989), 339.

4. Jacques Derrida, *La Bête et le souverain: Tome 1, 2001–2002*, ed. Michel Lisse, Marie-Louise Mallet, and Ginette Michaud (Paris: Galilée, 2008), 11, 9.

5. Derrida, *La Bête et le souverain: Tome 1, 2001–2002,* 11; *The Beast and the Sovereign, Volume 1 (2001–2002)*, trans. Geoffrey Bennington (Chicago: The University of Chicago Press, 2008), xi.

6. See also the website of the Derrida Seminars Translation Project, at http://derridaseminars.org/.

7. In her introduction to the first published volume of Cixous's seminars, *Lettres de fuite: Séminaire 2001–2004* (Paris: Gallimard, 2020), Marta Segarra details the history of Cixous's seminar and its material form.

8. As of summer 2020, the recordings had only very recently come to the BNF. Because of this timing, they fell beyond the scope of this study's research.

9. The ongoing project of transcribing, editing, and publishing Cixous's seminars, directed by Marta Segarra, produced a first volume in 2020 covering the years 2001–2002, 2002–2003, and 2003–2004. A second volume is in preparation.

10. Verena A. Conley, "Introduction," in *Readings: The Poetics of Blanchot, Joyce, Kafka, Kleist, Lispector, and Tsvetayeva*, by Hélène Cixous (Minneapolis: University of Minnesota Press, 1991), ix.

11. Conley, "Introduction," ix–x.

12. Conley, "Introduction," ix.

13. Cixous, *Lettres de fuite*, ed. Segarra, 13–14.

14. Lucy O'Meara, *Roland Barthes at the Collège de France* (Liverpool: University of Liverpool Press, 2012), 5–6.

15. O'Meara, *Roland Barthes*, 4, 5–6.

16. Barthes, "Au séminaire," 506; "To the Seminar," 337.

17. Barthes, "Au séminaire," 506; "To the Seminar," 337.

18. Hélène Cixous, *Writing Differences: Readings from the Seminar of Hélène Cixous*, ed. Susan Sellers (New York: St. Martin's Press, 1988), 141.

19. Derrida, *Spectres de Marx*, 15; *Spectres of Marx,* xviii.

20. Jacques Derrida, *Échographies de la television*, with Bernard Stiegler (Paris: Galilée, 1996), 133 (my translation).

21. From the collection guide: "This collection comprises video recordings made by Safaa Fathy to document selected public lectures and other activities of the French philosopher and critical theorist Jacques Derrida between 2000 and 2004. Events include public lectures, panel discussions, conferences, and ceremonies. Some events contain recordings of additional participants, including theorists such as Jürgen Habermas, Hélène Cixous, and Axel Honneth" (http://www.oac.cdlib.org/findaid/ark:/13030/kt0n39q6th/). The timeline provided by

the collection guide is striking, indicating that the recordings were made after Derrida's contribution to UC Irvine had ended (in 2000).

22. Derrida, *L'Université sans condition*, 15; "The University without Condition," 204.

23. On knowledge and *savoir absolu* elsewhere in Derrida's work, see especially *Glas*, "Un ver à soie," and *Foi et savoir*.

24. Jacques Derrida, "*Mochlos*: L'Œil de l'université," in *Du droit à la philosophie* (Paris: Galilée, 1990), 421–22; "Mochlos, or the Conflict of Faculties," in *Eyes of the University: Right to Philosophy 2*, trans. Jan Plug et al. (Stanford, CA: Stanford University Press, 2004), 100–101. "Le concept de la communauté scientifique et de l'Université . . . doit être lisible dans chaque phrase de cours ou de séminaire, dans chaque acte d'écriture, de lecture ou d'interprétation" (421–22). "The concept of the scientific community and the university that ought to be legible in every sentence of a course or seminar, in every act of writing, reading, or interpretation" (100).

25. Derrida, *H. C. pour la vie*, 14; *H. C. for Life*, 7.

26. Derrida, *H. C. pour la vie*, 126; *H. C. for Life*, 147.

27. Eric Prenowitz's reading of this scene in "Introduction: Cracking the Book—Readings of Hélène Cixous," *New Literary History* 37 (2006), suggests that Derrida portrays himself as a "dutiful young philosopher" in order to carry out this "performative" proclamation of Cixous's writing as unidentifiable (xix). In their introduction to "Unidentifiable Literary Objects" (special issue of *parallax* 25, no. 3 [2019]), Camilla Bostock and Sarah Jackson trace Derrida's questioning of how to read to Cixous's disorientation in *Insister* as she encounters the manuscript of *Voiles* (104). On the Derrida-Cixous ULO, see the essays by Garnier, Milesi, and Royle in the same issue.

28. On mastery and prophecy in Derrida's approach to Cixous as a novel and monstrous literary event, see Laurent Milesi, "De-monstrating Monsters: Unmastering (in) Derrida and Cixous."

29. In "Les Écritures du 'comme si' " (in *Enduring Resistance: Cultural Theory after Derrida* [Amsterdam: Rodopi, 2010), Mireille Calle-Gruber explains that, for Derrida, the event is a virtual element that "intervient comme performatif interrupteur de performatif, fait trembler *et* la faculté performative *et* le souverain savoir" (290; ("intervenes as a performative interrupter of performative, shakes up *both* the performative faculty *and* sovereign knowledge").

30. Derrida, *H. C. pour la vie*, 20; *H. C. for Life*, 15.

31. Derrida, *H. C. pour la vie*, 116–17; *H. C. for Life*, 134–35.

32. On the constative and performative in speech act theory, see Derrida's "Signature événement contexte" and *Limited Inc*.

33. Derrida, *H. C. pour la vie*, 34, 81; *H. C. for Life*, 33, 91.

34. Derrida, *H. C. pour la vie*, 117; *H. C. for Life*, 135.

35. Barthes, "Au seminaire," 506; "To the Seminar," 337.

36. Filmed interview with Hélène Cixous at the Maison Française of New York University, New York City, September 2010, in *Philosofemmes* (A. Brancky, I. Brey, L. Hughes, Y. Kwak, V. Lauret).

37. Folio 1, January 6, 2001, seminar session (Fonds Cixous, Bibliothèque nationale de France).

38. This tradition was restaged in "Lengua por venir / Langue à venir: Seminario de Barcelona" organized by Marta Segarra (2004).

39. Cixous, *Writing Differences*, 141.

40. Barthes, "Au séminaire," 506; "To the Seminar," 336, modified.

41. Barthes, "Au séminaire," 506; "To the Seminar," 336, modified.

42. Cixous was assisted by a *conseil consultatif*, as recounted in the bio-bibliographic chronology in *Hélène Cixous: Photos de racines* (Paris: Éditions des femmes, 1994).

43. Jean-Louis Boissier, "L'Illumination de Vincennes," Arts des nouveaux médias, http://www.arpla.fr/canal20/adnm/?p=716.

44. Boissier, "L'Illumination de Vincennes."

45. Boissier, "L'Illumination de Vincennes."

46. In "L'Amitié, la trahison, la traduction," Marta Segarra presents spectrality as an essential aspect of friendship in her reading of Derrida's *Politiques de l'amitié* (184).

47. bell hooks also advocates for the use of passion as a pedagogical tool in "Eros, Eroticism, and the Pedagogical Process" and "Ecstasy: Teaching and Learning without Limits," the last two chapters in *Teaching to Transgress* (New York: Routledge, 1994): "The quest for knowledge that enables us to unite theory and practice is one such passion. To the extent that professors bring this passion, which has to be fundamentally rooted in a love for the ideas we are able to inspire, the classroom becomes a dynamic place where transformations in social relations are concretely actualized and the false dichotomy between the world outside and the inside world of the academy disappears" (195).

48. Pierre Nora's concept of the *lieux de mémoire* catalogs the significance of geographical and historical locations, monuments, and concepts charged with cultural and affective memory.

49. Cixous's work with the Théâtre du Soleil, directed by Ariane Mnouchkine, known for its collective, non-hierarchical process, adds another layer to the virtual archive of Vincennes. As a *lieu de mémoire* channeling a specific cultural history, "Vincennes" signifies for Cixous the relinquishing of authority and the powerful ephemerality of shared experience—both in the Université expérimentale de Vincennes and in the Théâtre du Soleil, based in the Cartoucherie de Vincennes. Cixous's documentation of her work with the troupe constitutes its own section of the *fonds* Cixous at the BNF, giving Vincennes a presence in the archive where it does not exist in seminars. The Théâtre du Soleil is another community that can be glimpsed through its own archives (stored on-site and at the BNF) and in the archives of Cixous, since Cixous's role as a co-writer within the Théâtre du Soleil sheds light on the collaborative process of the troupe. On Cixous's theatrical writing, see Julia Dobson (*Hélène Cixous and the Theater: The Scene of Writing*), Judith Miller ("The Theatre of Hélène Cixous: Re-memberings, Re-fashionings, and Revenants"), Eric Prenowitz (*The Selected Plays of Hélène Cixous*), and Morag Shiach (*Hélène Cixous: A Politics of Writing*).

50. Volume 2 of Pierre Nora's *Les Lieux de mémoire* includes an article on "La Forêt" by Andrée Corvol as part of the section "Partages de l'espace-temps."

51. Robert Harrison discusses the psychic charge of this etymology in *Forests: The Shadow of Civilization*.

52. Derrida, *Mal d'archive*, 36; *Archive Fever*, 18.
53. Derrida, *Mal d'archive*, 100; *Archive Fever*, 62.
54. Derrida, "Le Futur antérieur de l'archive," 43; *Spectres of Marx*, 16, 62–64.
55. Derrida, *Spectres of Marx*, 37.

Conclusion

1. This interview with Jean Birnbaum was first published in *Le Monde* under the title "Je suis en guerre contre moi-même."
2. Derrida, *Apprendre à vivre enfin*, 27, 30; *Learning to Live Finally*, 27, 30.
3. Derrida, *Apprendre à vivre enfin*, 27; *Learning to Live Finally*, 27.
4. Derrida, *Apprendre à vivre enfin*, 34; *Learning to Live Finally*, 33.
5. François Cusset gives an account of the invention and evolution of "Theory" in *French Theory* (2003).
6. But see Rancière, *Le Maître ignorant*; Barthes, "Au séminaire" (in *L'Arc*); and Pierre Bourdieu, *La Reproduction: Éléments pour une théorie du système d'enseignement*, *Homo Academicus*, and *Les Héritiers: Les Étudiants et la culture*.
7. As discussed by Benoît Peeters in *Derrida* (370).
8. See in particular the introduction to the "Critical Archival Studies" special issue of *Journal of Critical Library and Information Studies* (1, no. 2 [2017]) by Michelle Caswell, Ricardo Punzalan, and T-Kay Sangwand, and the essays that follow.
9. Rosalind Krauss, "Poststructuralism and the 'Paraliterary,'" *October* 13 (1980): 37.
10. Interview with Benoît Peeters, "Sur les archives de Jacques Derrida," at http://www.imec-archives.com/les-collections/les-archives-jacques-derrida/
11. I paraphrase Derrida's formulation in the film *Derrida*.
12. When Cixous decided to bequeath her papers to the BNF around 2000, the Barthes, Derrida, and Foucault collections were all at the IMEC; Foucault's and Barthes' collections have since moved to the BNF.
13. Cixous, *Insister à Jacques Derrida*, 42; *Insister of Jacques Derrida*, 52.

BIBLIOGRAPHY

Works by Hélène Cixous

Lettres d'Hélène Cixous à Jacques Derrida. 219DRR/24/10. Fonds Jacques Derrida. Institut Mémoires de l'édition contemporaine. Normandy, France.

Correspondance. Fonds Hélène Cixous (NAF 28080). Département des manuscrits, Bibliothèque nationale de France.

Le Prénom de Dieu. Manuscript. Fonds Hélène Cixous (NAF 28080). Département des manuscrits, Bibliothèque nationale de France.

Le Prénom de Dieu. Paris: Grasset, 1967.

Tombe. Paris: Seuil, 1973.

Cixous, Hélène, Madeleine Gagnon, and Annie Leclerc. *La Venue à l'écriture*. Paris: Éditions 10/18, 1977.

Entre l'écriture. Paris: Éditions des femmes, 1986.

Jours de l'an. Paris: Éditions des femmes, 1990.

Readings: The Poetics of Blanchot, Joyce, Kafka, Kleist, Lispector, and Tsvetayeva. Ed. and trans. Verena Andermatt Conley. Minneapolis: University of Minnesota Press, 1991.

"Sans arrêt, non . . ." In *Repentirs*. Paris: Réunion des musées nationaux, 1991. English translation: "Without End, no / State of Drawingness / no, rather: The Executioner's Taking off." Trans. Catherine A. F. MacGillivray. *New Literary History* 24, no. 1 (1993): 91–103.

Three Steps on the Ladder of Writing. New York: Columbia University Press, 1993.

"Contes de la différence sexuelle." In *Lectures de la différence sexuelle*, ed. Anne Berger and Mara Negrón, 31–68. Paris: Éditions des femmes, 1994. English translation: "Tales of Sexual Difference," trans. Eric Prenowitz, in *The Portable Cixous*, ed. Marta Segarra, 48–60. New York: Columbia University Press, 2010.

"Quelle heure est-il, ou la porte (celle qu'on ne passe pas)." In *Le Passage des frontières: Autour du travail de Jacques Derrida*, 83–98. Paris: Galilée, 1994.

"Mon Algériance." *Les Inrockuptibles* 115 (August 20–September 1997): 71–74.

OR: Les Lettres de mon père. Manuscript. Preparatory notes. Folder 3, folio 1. Fonds Hélène Cixous (NAF 28080). Département des manuscrits, Bibliothèque nationale de France.

OR: Les Lettres de mon père. Paris: Éditions des femmes, 1997.

Séminaires 1998–1999, 1999–2000, 2000–2001, 2001–2002. Fonds Hélène Cixous. Département des manuscrits, Bibliothèque nationale de France.

"Savoir." In *Voiles*, with Jacques Derrida, 11–19. Paris: Galilée, 1998. English translation: *Veils*, trans. Geoffrey Bennington. Stanford, CA: Stanford University Press, 2001.

"Germes, gestes, restes." *Revue de la Bibliothèque nationale de France* 5 (June 2000): 81–84.

Benjamin à Montaigne: Il ne faut pas le dire. Paris: Galilée, 2001.

". . . de main en main jusqu'à un maintenant éphémère." In *Brouillons d'écrivains*, 172–76. Paris: Bibliothèque nationale de France, 2001.

"'Je suis d'abord une lisante': Entretien avec Daniel Ferrer." *Genèses* 17 (2001): 45–57.

Portrait de Jacques Derrida en Jeune Saint Juif. Manuscript. Box III.3. Fonds Hélène Cixous (NAF 28080). Département des manuscrits, Bibliothèque nationale de France.

Portrait de Jacques Derrida en Jeune Saint Juif. Paris: Galilée, 2001. English translation: *Portrait of Jacques Derrida as a Young Jewish Saint*, trans. Beverley Bie Brahic. New York: Columbia University Press, 2004.

Manhattan: Lettres de la préhistoire. Paris: Galilée, 2002. English translation: *Manhattan: Letters from Prehistory*, trans. Beverley Bie Brahic. New York: Fordham University Press, 2007.

Rêve je te dis. Paris: Galilée, 2003. English translation: *Dream I Tell You*, trans. Beverley Bie Brahic. Edinburgh: Edinburgh University Press, 2006.

Hélène Cixous: The Writing Notebooks. Ed. Susan Sellers. New York: Continuum, 2004.

Tours promises. Paris: Galilée, 2004.

L'Amour même dans la boîte aux lettres. Paris: Galilée, 2005. English translation: *Love Itself in the Letterbox*, trans. Peggy Kamuf. Cambridge: Polity, 2008.

Hyperrêve. Paris: Galilée, 2006. English translation: *Hyperdream*, trans. Beverley Bie Brahic. Cambridge: Polity, 2009.

Insister à Jacques Derrida. Paris: Galilée, 2006. English translation: *Insister of Jacques Derrida*, trans. Peggy Kamuf. Edinburgh: Edinburgh University Press: 2007.

"Le Livre que je n'écris pas." In *Genèses Généalogies Genres: Autour de l'œuvre d'Hélène Cixous*, 229–63. Paris: Galilée, Bibliothèque nationale de France, 2006.

Si près. Paris: Galilée, 2007.

Ciguë: Vieilles femmes en fleurs. Paris: Galilée, 2008.

"Co-responding Voix You." In *Derrida and the Time of the Political*, ed. Suzanne Guerlac and Pheng Cheah, 41–53. Durham, NC: Duke University Press, 2009.

Ève s'évade. Paris: Galilée, 2009.

Philippines: Prédelles. Paris: Galilée, 2009.

Double Oubli de l'Orang-Outang. Paris: Galilée, 2010. English translation: *Double Oblivion of the Ourang-Outang*, trans. Suzanne Dow. Cambridge: Polity, 2013.

Le Rire de la Méduse et autres ironies. Paris: Galilée, 2010.

Interview at New York University. September 2010. Conducted and filmed by A. Brancky, I. Brey, L. Hughes, Y. Kwak, and V. Lauret.

Revirements. Paris: Galilée, 2011.

Chapitre Los (Abstracts et brèves chroniques du Temps I). Paris: Galilée, 2012.

"A Kind of Magic." In "Cixous, Derrida, Psychoanalysis," special issue of *Paragraph* 36, no. 2 (2013): 161–88.
Personal interview. November 3, 2013, Paris, France.
Homère est morte Paris: Galilée, 2014.
Le Détronement de la mort. Paris: Galilée, 2014.
Gare d'Osnabrück à Jerusalem. Paris: Galilée, 2016.
Une autobiographie allemande. Paris: Galilée, 2016.
"Documents: Hélène Cixous." Firestone Library. Princeton University. Princeton, New Jersey.
Lettres de fuite: Séminaire 2001–2004. Ed. Marta Segarra. Paris: Gallimard, 2020.
Cixous, Hélène, and Mireille Calle-Gruber. *Hélène Cixous, Photos de racines*. Paris: Éditions des femmes, 1994.
Cixous, Hélène, and Catherine Clément. *La Jeune Née*. Paris: Christian Bourgois, 1975.
Cixous, Hélène, and Jacques Derrida. *Lengua por venir / Langue à venir: Seminario de Barcelona*. Ed. Marta Segarra. Barcelona: Icaria, 2004.
Cixous, Hélène, and Jacques Derrida. "Du mot à la vie: Un dialogue entre Jacques Derrida et Hélène Cixous." With Aliette Armel. *Magazine Littéraire* 430 (2004): 22–29.
Cixous, Hélène, and Frédéric-Yves Jeannet. "Le Livre que Tu n'écriras pas." Remue.net, 2007. English translation: "The Book That You Will Not Write: An Interview with Hélène Cixous," trans. Thomas Dutoit, ed. Eric Prenowitz. In "Hélène Cixous," special issue of *New Literary History* 37, no. 1 (2006) : 249–61.
Cixous, Hélène, and Frédéric-Yves Jeannet. *Rencontre terrestre*. Paris: Galilée, 2005. English translation: *Encounters*, trans. Beverley Bie Brahic. Cambridge: Polity, 2013.

Works by Jacques Derrida

"Collections: Fonds Jacques Derrida (1930–2004)." Institut Mémoires de l'édition contemporaine. n.d. http://www.imec-archives.com/fonds/derrida-jacques/.
"Notecards." Box 74, Folders 1–6. Jacques Derrida Papers. Special Collections and Archives, University of California at Irvine.
De la grammatologie. Paris: Minuit, 1967.
L'Écriture et la différence. Paris: Seuil, 1967. English translation: *Writing and Difference*, trans. Alan Bass. London: Routledge, 2001.
La Dissémination. Paris: Seuil, 1972.
Marges de la philosophie. Paris: Minuit, 1972.
"Signature événement contexte." In *Marges de la philosophie*, 365–93. Paris: Minuit, 1972.
Positions. Paris: Minuit, 1972.
"Fors: Les Mots anglés de Nicolas Abraham and Maria Torok." In *Le Verbier de l'Homme aux loups: Cryptonymie*, by Nicolas Abraham and Maria Torok, 12–76. Paris: Flammarion, 1976.
Éperons: Les Styles de Nietzsche. Paris: Flammarion, 1978.

La Carte postale. Manuscript. Boxes 27–31. Jacques Derrida Papers. Special Collections and Archives, University of California at Irvine.

La Carte postale: De Socrate à Freud et au-delà. Paris: Flammarion, 1980. English translation: *The Post Card*, trans. Alan Bass. Chicago: University of Chicago Press, 1987.

"Chorégraphies." In *Points de suspension: Entretiens*, 95–115. Paris: Galilée, 1982. English translation: "Choreographies: Interview," in *Feminist Interpretations of Jacques Derrida*, ed. Nancy J. Holland, 23–41. University Park: Pennsylvania State University Press, 1997.

"My Chances/Mes Chances: A Rendezvous with Some Epicurean Stereophonies." In *Taking Chances: Derrida, Psychoanalysis, and Literature*. Baltimore, MD: Johns Hopkins University Press, 1984.

"La Loi du genre." In *Parages*, 250–87. Paris: Galilée, 1986.

"Survivre." In *Parages*, 109–203. Paris: Galilée, 1986.

"Aphorisme à contretemps." In *Psyché: Inventions de l'autre I*, 519–33. Paris: Galilée, 1987.

"Télépathie." In *Psyché: Inventions de l'autre I*, 237–70. Paris: Galilée, 1987.

"Geschlecht: Différence sexuelle, différence ontologique." In *Psyché: Inventions de l'autre I*, 395–414. Paris: Galilée, 1987.

"La Main de Heidegger (Geschlecht II)." In *Psyché: Inventions de l'autre II*, 35–68. Paris: Galilée, 1987. English translation: "*Geschlecht* II: Heidegger's Hand," trans. John P. Leavey, Jr. In *Deconstruction and Philosophy*, ed. John Sallis. Chicago: University of Chicago Press, 1987.

"Mochlos ou le conflit des facultés." In *Du droit a la philosophie*, 397–438. Paris: Galilée, 1990. English translation: "Mochlos, or the Conflict of Faculties." In *Eyes of the University: Right to Philosophy 2*, trans. Jan Plug et al., 83–112. Stanford, CA: Stanford University Press, 2004.

Limited Inc. Paris: Galilée, 1990.

Mémoires d'aveugles: L'Autoportrait et autres ruines. Paris: Musée du Louvre, 1990.

"*Mochlos*: L'Œil de l'université." In *Du droit à la philosophie*. Paris: Galilée, 1990.

"Circonfession." In *Derrida*, by Geoffrey Bennington and Jacques Derrida. Paris: Seuil, 1991. English translation: "Circumfession," in *Jacques Derrida*, by Geoffrey Bennington and Jacques Derrida, trans. Geoffrey Bennington. Chicago: University of Chicago Press, 1993.

Donner le temps: La Fausse monnaie. Paris: Galilée, 1991.

Spectres de Marx. Paris: Galilée, 1993. English translation: *Spectres of Marx*, trans. Peggy Kamuf. New York: Routledge, 2006.

"Fourmis." In *Lectures de la différence sexuelle*, 69–102. Paris: Éditions des femmes, 1994. English translation: "Ants," trans. Eric Prenowitz, *Oxford Literary Review* 24 (2002): 17–42.

Politiques de l'amitié. Paris: Galilée, 1994. English translation: *The Politics of Friendship*, trans. George Collins. New York: Verso, 2005.

"Lettre au ministre de l'Éducation nationale en appui du DEA d'études féminines. 20 mars 1995." 219DRR/23/2. Fonds Derrida. Institut Mémoires de l'édition contemporaine. Normandy, France.

Mal d'archive: Une impression freudienne. Paris: Galilée, 1995. English translation: *Archive Fever*, trans. Eric Prenowitz. Chicago: University of Chicago Press, 1998.

Échographies de la télévision. With Bernard Stiegler. Paris: Galilée, 1996.

Le Monolinguisme de l'autre, ou la prothèse de l'origine. Paris: Galilée, 1996.

Résistances—de la psychanalyse. Paris: Galilée, 1996.

"Archive et brouillon: Table ronde du 17 juin 1995." In *Pourquoi la critique génétique?* ed. Michel Contat and Daniel Ferrer. Paris: CNRS Éditions, 1998.

"Un ver à soie." Manuscript. 219DRR/198/3–216DRR/198/4. Fonds Derrida. Institut Mémoires de l'édition contemporaine. Normandy, France.

"Un ver à soie: Points de vue piqués sur l'autre voile." In *Voiles*, with Hélène Cixous, 25–85. Paris: Galilée, 1998. English translation: "A Silkworm of One's Own," in *Veils*, trans. Geoffrey Bennington, 17–92. Stanford, CA: Stanford University Press, 2001.

Donner la mort. Paris: Galilée, 1999. English translation: *The Gift of Death*, trans. David Wills. Chicago: University of Chicago Press, 2008.

"Hostipitalité." In "Pera Peras Poros," ed. Ferda. Keskin and Önay Sözer. Special issue of *Cogito* 85 (1999): 17–44.

Le Toucher, Jean-Luc Nancy. Paris: Galilée, 2000.

"'Entre le corps écrivant et l'écriture': Entretien avec Daniel Ferrer." *Geneses* 17 (2001): 59–72.

Foi et savoir. Paris: Points, 2001.

"La Machine à traitement de texte." In *Papier machine*. Paris: Galilée, 2001. English translation: "The Word Processor," in *Paper Machine*, trans. Rachel Bowlby. Stanford, CA: Stanford University Press, 2005.

L'Université sans condition. Paris: Galilée, 2001. English translation: "The University without Condition," in *Without Alibi*, trans. Peggy Kamuf. Stanford, CA: Stanford University Press, 2002.

Eyes of the University: The Right to Philosophy II. Trans. Jan Plug et al. Stanford, CA: Stanford University Press, 2004.

Artaud le Moma. Paris: Galilée, 2002. English translation: *Artaud the Moma*, trans. Peggy Kamuf. New York: Columbia University Press, 2017.

Fichus. Paris: Galilée, 2002. English translation: "Fichus," in *Paper Machine*, trans. Rachel Bowlby, 164–81. Stanford, CA: Stanford University Press, 2005.

"Le Futur antérieur de l'archive." In *Questions d'archives*, ed. Nathalie Léger, 41–50. Paris: Institut Mémoires de l'édition contemporaine, 2002.

H. C. pour la vie, c'est à dire . . . Paris: Galilée, 2002. English translation: *H. C. for Life, That Is to Say . . .* trans. Laurent Milesi and Stefan Herbrechter. Stanford, CA: Stanford University Press, 2006.

Béliers: Le Dialogue ininterrompu: Entre deux infinis, le poème. Paris: Galilée, 2003. English translation: "Rams: Uninterrupted Dialogue—Between Two Infinities, the Poem," trans. Thomas Dutoit and Philippe Romanski. In *Sovereignties in Question: The Poetics of Paul Celan*, ed. Thomas Dutoit and Outi Pasanen, 135–63. New York: Fordham University Press, 2005.

Chaque fois unique, la fin du monde. Paris: Galilée, 2003. English translation: *The Work of Mourning*, ed. Pascale-Anne Brault and Michael Naas. Chicago: University of Chicago Press, 2001.

Genèses, généalogies, genres . . . et le génie: Les Secrets de l'archive. Paris: Galilée, 2003. English translation: *Geneses, Genealogies, Genres, and Genius: The Secrets of the Archive*, trans. Beverley Bie Brahic. New York: Columbia University Press, 2008.
"Travaux en cours été 2004." 219DRR/201/18. Fonds Derrida. Institut Mémoires de l'édition contemporaine. Normandy, France.
"Jacques n'a voulu [. . .]." *Rue Descartes* 48 (2005): 6–7.
L'Animal que donc je suis. Paris: Galilée, 2006.
"Moi, l'Algérien." Interview with Mustafa Chérif. *Le Nouvel Observateur* 2192 (November 9, 2006).
La Bête et le souverain: Tome 1, 2001–2002. Paris: Galilée, 2008.
La Bête et le souverain: Tome 2, 2002–2003. Paris: Galilée, 2010.
Copy, Archive, Signature: A Conversation on Photography. Stanford, CA: Stanford University Press, 2010.
Trace et archive, image et art. Paris: Institut national de l'audiovisuel éditions, 2014.
Library of Jacques Derrida. Finding Aid. Princeton University Library. http://arks.princeton.edu/ark:/88435/vq27zr16f.
Derrida, Jacques, et al. *Pour Nelson Mandela*. Paris: Gallimard, 1986.
Derrida, Jacques, and Jean Birnbaum. *Apprendre à vivre enfin*. Paris: Galilée, 2005. English translation: *Learning to Live Finally*, trans. Pascale-Anne Brault. Hoboken, NJ: Melville House, 2007.
Derrida, Jacques, and Anne Dufourmantelle. *De l'hospitalité*. Paris: Calmann-Lévy, 1997.
Derrida, Jacques, and Safaa Fathy. *Tourner les mots: Au bord d'un film*. Paris: Galilée, 2000.
Derrida, Jacques, and Maurizio Ferraris. *Il gusto del segreto*. Rome: Laterza, 1997.
Derrida, Jacques, Simon Hantaï, and Jean-Luc Nancy. *La Connaissance des textes: Lecture d'un manuscrit illisible*. Paris: Galilée, 2001.
Derrida, Jacques, and Catherine Malabou. *La Contre-Allée*. Paris: Quinzaine Littéraire-Louis Vuitton, 1999.

Other Sources

Amad, Paula. *Counter-Archive: Film, the Everyday, and Albert Kahn's Archives de la Planète*. New York: Columbia University Press, 2010.
Anlin Cheng, Anne. "Skins, Tattoos, and Susceptibility." In "The Way We Read Now," special issue of *Representations* 108, no. 1 (2009): 98–119.
Appadurai, Arjun, ed. *The Social Life of Things: Commodities in Cultural Perspective*. Cambridge: Cambridge University Press, 1986.
Appelbaum, David. *Jacques Derrida's Ghost: A Conjuration*. Albany: State University of New York Press, 2009.
Apter, Emily, and Elaine Freedgood. "Afterword." In "The Way We Read Now," special issue of *Representations* 108, no. 1 (2009): 139–46.

Arendt, Hannah, and Martin Heidegger. *Briefe 1925 bis 1975: Und andere Zeugnisse*. Frankfurt: Klostermann, 1998.

Arondekar, Anjali. *For the Record: On Sexuality and the Colonial Archive in India*. Durham, NC: Duke University Press, 2009.

Artous-Bouvet, Guillaume. "Le Supplément de fiction: Derrida et l'autobiographie." *Littérature* 162, no. 2 (2011): 100–114.

Assouline, Pierre. "Roland Barthes fait ses cartons." *Le Monde,* July 10, 2010.

Azoulay, Ariella. "Archive." Political Concepts: A Critical Lexicon, issue 1. http://www.politicalconcepts.org/issue1/archive/ 16.

Badmington, Niel, ed. "Derridanimals." Special issue of *Oxford Literary Review* 29 (2007).

Bal, Mieke. "Telling Objects: A Narrative Perspective on Collecting." In *The Cultures of Collecting*, ed. Roger Cardinal and John Elsner, 97–116. London: Reaktion, 1994.

Balcázar Moreno, Melina, and Sarah-Anaïs Crevier Goulet. *Pensées du corps: La Matérialité et l'organique vus par les sciences humaines*. Paris: Presses Sorbonne Nouvelle, 2011.

Barthes, Roland. "Au séminaire." [1974]. In *Le Bruissement de la langue: Essais critiques IV*, 393–404. Paris: Seuil, 1984. English translation: "To the Seminar." In *The Rustle of Language*, trans. Richard Howard, 332–42. Berkeley: University of California Press, 1989.

———. *Comment vivre ensemble: Simulations romanesques de quelques espaces quotidiens: Notes de cours et de séminaires au Collège de France, 1976–1977*. Paris: Seuil/IMEC, 2002.

———. "La Mort de l'auteur." In *Le Bruissement de la langue*, 63–69. Paris: Seuil, 1984.

———. *La Préparation du roman*. Paris: Seuil/IMEC, 2003.

———. *Roland Barthes par Roland Barthes*. Paris: Seuil, 2010.

———. *S/Z*. Paris: Seuil, 1976.

———. "Théorie du texte." In *Œuvres completes,* vol. 4, ed. Éric Marty. Paris: Seuil, 2002.

Bartlett, Thomas. "Archive Fever." *Chronicle of Higher Education* 53, no. 46 (2007): A8–A13.

Bataille, Laurence. *L'Ombilic du rêve*. Paris: Seuil, 1987.

Benjamin, Walter. "The Work of Art in the Age of Mechanical Reproduction." In *Illuminations*, 217–42. New York: Schocken, 1968.

Bennett, Jane. *Vibrant Matter: A Political Ecology of Things*. Durham, NC: Duke University Press, 2010.

Bennington, Geoffrey. "Derridabase." In *Derrida*, by Geoffrey Bennington and Jacques Derrida. Paris: Seuil, 1991. English translation: "Derridabase," in *Jacques Derrida*, by Geoffrey Bennington and Jacques Derrida, trans. Geoffrey Bennington. Chicago: University of Chicago Press, 1993.

———. *Géographie et autres lectures*. Paris: Hermann, 2011.

———. *Not Half No End*. Edinburgh: Edinburgh University Press, 2010.

———. Personal interview. January 23, 2015, New York City.

———. "Teleanalysis." In "Cixous, Derrida, Psychoanalysis," special issue of *Paragraph* 36, no. 2 (2013): 270–85.

Bennington, Geoffrey, and Peggy Kamuf, eds. "These Web pages aim to help correct misleading and inaccurate press reports . . ." http://www.jacques-derrida.org/UCI%20Affair.html.

Benstock, Shari. "Letters: The Post Card in the Epistolary Genre." In *Textualizing the Feminine: On the Limits of Genre*, ed. Shari Benstock et al., 86–122. Norman: University of Oklahoma Press, 1991.

Benveniste, Émile. *Problèmes de linguistique générale*. Paris: Gallimard, 1966.

Berger, Anne. "Appels." In *L'Événement comme écriture: Cixous et Derrida se lisant*, 85–107. Paris: CampagnePremière, 2007.

———. "Sexing Differances." In "Derrida's Gift," special issue of *differences: A Journal of Feminist Cultural Studies* 16, no. 3 (2005): 52–67.

Berger, Anne, and Marta Segarra. *Demenageries: Thinking (of) Animals after Derrida*. Amsterdam: Rodopi, 2011.

Berglund Hall, Elizabeth, et al. *Cixous after/depuis 2000*. London: Brill, 2017.

Bergson, Henri. *Duration and Simultaneity*. Manchester, UK: Clinamen, 1999.

Bervin, Jen, and Marta Werner. *The Gorgeous Nothings: Emily Dickinson's Envelope Poems*. New York: New Directions, 2013.

Best, Stephen, and Sharon Marcus. "Surface Reading: An Introduction." In "The Way We Read Now," special issue of *Representations* 108, no. 1 (2009): 1–21.

Bisio, Alexandra. Personal interview. June 26, 2014, Irvine, California.

Blanchot, Maurice. *Le Livre à venir*. Paris: Gallimard, 1959.

Blyth, Ian, and Susan Sellers. *Hélène Cixous: Live Theory*. New York: Continuum, 2004.

Boissier, Jean-Louis. "L'Illumination de Vincennes." Arts des nouveaux médias. http://www.arpla.fr/canal20/adnm/?p=716.

Bostock, Camilla, and Sarah Jackson, eds. "Unidentifiable Literary Objects." Special issue of *parallax* 25, no. 3 (2019).

Bourdieu, Pierre. *Homo Academicus*. Paris: Les Éditions de Minuit, 1984.

———. *La Reproduction: Éléments pour une théorie du système d'enseignement*. Paris: Les Éditions de Minuit, 1970.

———. *Les Héritiers: Les Étudiants et la culture*. Paris: Les Éditions de Minuit, 1964.

Breton, Mahité. "Rêve qui peut: La Pensée du rêve dans *Fichus*." *Mosaic* 40, no. 2 (2007): 199.

Brown, Bill. *A Sense of Things: The Object Matter of American Literature*. Chicago: University of Chicago Press, 2003.

Bryant, John. *The Fluid Text: A Theory of Revision and Editing for Book and Screen*. Ann Arbor: University of Michigan Press, 2002.

Buchanan, Ian. *A Dictionary of Critical Theory*. Oxford: Oxford University Press, 2010. doi: 10.1093/acref/9780199532919.001.0001.

Butler, Judith. "How Can I Deny That These Hands and This Body Are Mine?" In *Material Events: Paul de Man and the Afterlife of Theory*, 254–73. Minneapolis: University of Minnesota Press, 2001.

———. "On Never Having Learned How to Live." In "Derrida's Gift," special issue of *differences: A Journal of Feminist Cultural Studies* 16, no. 3 (2005): 27–34.

Calle-Gruber, Mireille. "Les Écritures du 'comme si': Héritage de Derrida." In *Enduring Resistance: Cultural Theory after Derrida*, 281–94. Amsterdam: Rodopi, 2010.

———. "Périodes." In *Jacques Derrida*, 335–41. Ed. Marie-Louise Mallet and Ginette Michaud. Paris: L'Herne, 2004.

Calle-Gruber, Mireille, and Marie-Odile Germain, eds. *Genèses Généalogies Genres: Autour de l'œuvre d'Hélène Cixous*. Paris: Galilée, Bibliothèque nationale de France, 2006.

Caputo, John D. *The Prayers and Tears of Jacques Derrida: Religion without Religion*. Bloomington: Indiana University Press, 1997.

Casey, Edward. *The Fate of Place*. Oakland: University of California Press, 2013.

Cavallaro, Dani. "Simulacrum." In *Critical and Cultural Theory*. London: Bloomsbury, 2001.

Cerquiglini, Bernard. *Éloge de la variante*. Paris: Seuil, 1989.

Chadwick, Whitney, and Isabelle de Courtivron. *Significant Others: Creativity and Intimate Partnership*. New York: Thames and Hudson, 1996.

Chartier, Roger. "Labourers and Voyagers: From the Text to the Reader." In *The Book History Reader*, ed. David Finkelstein and Alistair McCleery, 87–98. London: Routledge, 2006.

Châtelet, François. *Le Rapport bleu: Les Sources historiques et théoriques du Collège international de philosophie*. Paris: Presses Universitaires de France, 1998.

Cifor, Marika, and Stacy Wood. "Critical Feminism in the Archives." In "Critical Archival Studies," ed. Michelle Caswell, Ricardo Punzalan, and T-Kay Sangwand. Special issue of *Journal of Critical Library and Information Studies* 1, no. 2 (2017).

Clément, Bruno, and Marta Segarra, eds. *Rêver croire penser: Autour d'Hélène Cixous*. Paris: CampagnePremière, 2010.

Clément, Catherine. *Martin et Hannah: Roman*. Paris: Calmann-Lévy, 1999.

Clement, Tanya, Wendy Hagenmaier, and Jennie Levine Knies. "Toward a Notion of the Archive of the Future: Impressions of Practice by Librarians, Archivists, and Digital Humanities Scholars." *Library Quarterly* 83, no. 2 (2013): 112–30.

Clough, Patricia T. "The Affective Turn: Political Economy, Biomedia, and Bodies." In *The Affect Theory Reader*, ed. Melissa Gregg and Gregory J. Seigworth, 206–27. Durham, NC: Duke University Press, 2010.

Cohen, Joseph, and Raphaël Zagury-Orly, eds. *Judéités: Questions pour Jacques Derrida*. Paris: Galilée, 2003.

Cohen, Tom, et al., eds. *Material Events: Paul de Man and the Afterlife of Theory*. Minneapolis: University of Minnesota Press, 2001.

Colburn, Timothy. "Software, Abstraction, and Ontology." *The Monist* 82, no. 1 (January 1999): 3–19.

Colebrook, Claire. "Friendship, Seduction, and Text: Cixous and Derrida." *Angelaki: Journal of Theoretical Humanities* 13, no. 2 (2008): 109–24.

———. "Matter without Bodies." *Derrida Today* 4, no. 1 (2011): 1–20.

———. *New Literary Histories: Theory after Poststructuralism*. Manchester, UK: Manchester University Press, 1997.

Colonnello, Pio. *Martin Heidegger à Hannah Arendt: Lettre jamais écrite*. Paris: Mimésis, 2014.

Conley, Tom. "Tours de force." In *L'Événement comme écriture: Cixous et Derrida se lisant*, 153–65. Paris: CampagnePremière, 2007.

Conley, Verena Andermatt. *Hélène Cixous*. Toronto: University of Toronto Press, 1992.

Contat, Michel. *L'Auteur et le manuscrit*. Paris: Presses Universitaires de France, 1991.

Contat, Michel, Denis Hollier, Jacques Neefs, and Alyson Waters, eds. "Drafts." Special issue of *Yale French Studies* 89 (1996).

Cook, Terry. "Archival Science and Postmodernism: New Formulations for Old Concepts." *Archival Science* 1 (2001): 3–24.

Corbman, Rachel F. "A Genealogy of the Lesbian Herstory Archives, 1974–2014." *Journal of Contemporary Archival Studies* 1, no. 1 (2014): 1–16.

Corpet, Oliver. "Letter to Jacques Derrida, November 24, 2000." Dossier "Sur la question de l'archive." 219DRR/199/3. Fonds Derrida. Institut Mémoires de l'édition contemporaine. Normandy, France.

Crasson, Aurèle, et al. "Le 'Siliscrit' de Jacques Derrida: Exploration d'une archive nativement numérique." *Genèses* 49 (2019): 189–96.

Craven, Louise, ed. *What Are Archives? Cultural and Theoretical Perspectives: A Reader*. Aldershot, UK: Ashgate, 2008.

Critchley, Simon. "Il y a—A Dying Stronger Than Death (Blanchot with Levinas)." *Oxford Literary Review* 15, no. 1/2 (1993): 81–131.

Cusset, François. *French Theory*. Paris: La Découverte, 2005.

Cvetkovich, Ann. *An Archive of Feelings*. Durham, NC: Duke University Press, 2003.

Daigle, Christine, and Jacob Golomb, eds. *Beauvoir and Sartre: The Riddle of Influence*. Bloomington: Indiana University Press, 2009.

D'ailleurs, Derrida. Dir. Safaa Fathy. 1999.

Darnton, Robert. "'What Is the History of Books?' Revisited." *Modern Intellectual History* 4, no. 3 (2007): 495–508.

Dawson, Mark, Mairéad Hanrahan, and Eric Prenowitz, eds. "Cixous, Derrida, Psychoanalysis." Special issue of *Paragraph* 36, no. 2 (2013).

de Biasi, Pierre-Marc. *Génétique des textes*. Paris: CNRS Éditions, 2011.

de Certeau, Michel. "L'Espace de l'archive, ou la perversion du temps." *Traverses* 36 (1986): 4–6.

Deleuze, Gilles. *Différence et répétition*. Paris: Presses Universitaires de France, 1968.

———. "Hélène Cixous or Stroboscopic Writing," trans. Martin McQuillan. *Oxford Literary Review* 24 (2002): 203–5.

———. *Logique du sens*. Paris: Éditions de Minuit, 1966. English translation: *The Logic of Sense*. Trans. Mark Lester. New York: Columbia University Press, 1990.

Deleuze, Gilles, and Félix Guattari. "Introduction: Rhizome." In *Mille plateaux*, 9–37. Paris: Minuit, 1980.

———. *Qu'est-ce que la philosophie?* Paris: Minuit, 1991. English translation: *What Is Philosophy?* Trans. Hugh Tomlinson and Graham Burchell. New York: Columbia University Press, 1994.

de Man, Paul. *The Resistance to Theory*. Minneapolis: University of Minnesota Press, 1986.

Deppman, Jed, Daniel Ferrer, and Michael Groden, eds. *Genetic Criticism: Texts and Avant-textes*. Philadelphia: University of Pennsylvania Press, 2004.

Derrida. Dir. Kirby Dick and Amy Ziering Kofman. 2002.

"Derrida hexadécimal." Institut des textes et mémoires modernes. http://www.item.ens.fr/derrida-hexadecimal/.
Derrida Seminars Translation Project. http://derridaseminars.org/.
"Derrida's Margins: Inside the Personal Library of Jacques Derrida." Project dir. Katie Chenoweth. Princeton University. https://derridas-margins.princeton.edu/.
Dever, Mary Anne, Ann Vickery, and Sally Newman. *The Intimate Archive: Journeys through Private Papers*. Canberra: National Library of Australia, 2009.
Di Leo, Jeffrey R., ed. *Dead Theory: Derrida, Death, and the Afterlife of Theory*. New York: Bloomsbury, 2016.
Dinshaw, Carolyn. *Getting Medieval: Sexualities and Communities, Pre- and Postmodern*. Durham, NC: Duke University Press, 1999.
———. *How Soon Is Now? Medieval Texts, Amateur Readers, and the Queerness of Time*. Durham, NC: Duke University Press, 2012.
Doane, Mary Ann. *The Emergence of Cinematic Time: Modernity, Contingency, the Archive*. Cambridge, MA: Harvard University Press, 2002.
Dobson, Julia. "Revisiting the Scene of Writing: New Readings of Cixous." *Paragraph* 23, no. 3 (2000): 243–352.
Doon, Ellen, Susan Pyzynski, et al. "Connecting the Dots: Using EAC-CPF to Reunite Samuel Johnson and His Circle." Harvard University, Yale University, 2014–15. https://wiki.harvard.edu/confluence/display/connectingdots/Connecting+the+Dots%3A+Using+EAC-CPF+to+Reunite+Samuel+Johnson+and+His+Circle.
Dosse, François. *Gilles Deleuze, Félix Guattari: Biographie croisée*. Paris: La Découverte, 2009.
———. *Le Pari biographique*. Paris: La Découverte, 2011.
Drucker, Johanna. "From A to Screen." In *Comparative Textual Media: Transforming the Humanities in the Postprint Era*, ed. N. Katherine Hayles and Jessica Pressman, 71–96. Minneapolis: University of Minnesota Press, 2013.
Dubreuil, Laurent. "Leur biographies d'auteurs." In *L'Événement comme écriture: Cixous et Derrida se lisant*, 213–30. Paris: CampagnePremière, 2007.
———. "The Presences of Deconstruction." *New Literary History* 37, no. 1 (2006): 107–17.
Dutoit, Thomas. "Il s'agit." In *L'Événement comme écriture: Cixous et Derrida se lisant*, 135–51. Paris: CampagnePremière, 2007.
Dutoit, Thomas, et al. "Guide to the Derrida Papers." UC Irvine Libraries. 2009. http://www.oac.cdlib.org/findaid/ark:/13030/tf3q2nb26c/.
Edwards, Brent. "The Taste of the Archive." *Callaloo* 35, no. 4 (2002): 944–72.
Eichhorn, Kate. *The Archival Turn in Feminism: Outrage in Order*. Philadelphia: Temple University Press, 2013.
———. "Archiving the Movement." In *Make Your Own History: Documenting Feminist and Queer Activism in the 21st Century*, ed. Lyz Bly and Kelly Wooten. Los Angeles: Litwin Books, 2012.
Emily Dickinson Archive. http://www.edickinson.org.
Enwezor, Okwui. *Archive Fever: Uses of the Document in Contemporary Art*. New York: International Center of Photography, 2008.
Farge, Arlette. *Le Goût de l'archive*. Paris: Seuil, 1989. English translation: *The Allure of the Archives*, trans. Thomas Scott-Railton. New Haven, CT: Yale University Press, 2013.

New Haven, CT: Yale University Press, 2013.
Farge, Arlette, and Natalie Zemon Davis. *History of Women in the West, Vol. III*. Cambridge, MA: Harvard University Press, 2000.
Ferrer, Daniel. *Logiques du brouillon: Modèles pour une critique génétique*. Paris: Seuil, 2011.
Fiorini, Monica. "Départs donnés." In *L'Événement comme écriture: Cixous et Derrida se lisant*, 315–26. Paris: CampagnePremière, 2007.
Fleischacker, Samuel. *Heidegger's Jewish Followers: Essays on Hannah Arendt, Leo Strauss, Hans Jonas, and Emmanuel Levinas*. Pittsburgh, PA: Duquesne University Press, 2008.
Fleming, Juliet. *Cultural Graphology: Writing after Derrida*. Chicago: University of Chicago Press, 2016.
———. "Curtains." Presentation at "Artefactualities: Derrida and the Hauntology of Media." Conference at New York University, October 16, 2014.
Forrester, John. "Psychoanalysis: Gossip, Telepathy, and/or Science?" In *The Seductions of Psychoanalysis: Freud, Lacan and Derrida*, 243–59. Cambridge: Cambridge University Press, 1990.
Foster, Hal. "An Archival Impulse." *October* 110 (2004): 3–22.
———. "The Archive without Museums." *October* 77 (1996): 97–119.
Foucault, Michel. *Histoire de la sexualité*, vol. 1: *La Volonté de savoir*. Paris: Gallimard, 1994.
———. *L'Archéologie du savoir*. Paris: Gallimard, 1969.
———. *Subjectivité et vérité: Cours au Collège de France (1980–81)*. Paris: Seuil, 2014.
Freeman, Elizabeth, ed. "Queer Temporalities." Special issue of *GLQ* 13, no. 2–3 (2007).
———. *Time Binds: Queer Temporalities*. Durham, NC: Duke University Press, 2010.
Freud, Sigmund. "Dreams and Telepathy." In *The Standard Edition of the Complete Psychological Works of Sigmund Freud*, vol. 18, ed. and trans. James Strachey, 197–220. London: Hogarth, 1955.
———. "From the History of an Infantile Neurosis." In *The Freud Reader*, ed. Peter Gay, 400–426. London: Vintage, 1995.
———. *The Interpretation of Dreams*, ed. and trans. James Strachey. New York: Avon, 1965.
———. "Mourning and Melancholia." In *The Standard Edition of the Complete Psychological Works of Sigmund Freud*, vol. 14, ed. and trans. James Strachey. London: Hogarth, 1957.
———. "A Note Upon the 'Mystic Writing-Pad'" [1925]. In *The Standard Edition of the Complete Psychological Works of Sigmund Freud*, vol. 19, ed. and trans. James Strachey, 227–32. London: Hogarth, 1961.
———. "Psychoanalysis and Telepathy." In *The Standard Edition of the Complete Psychological Works of Sigmund Freud*, vol. 18, ed. and trans. James Strachey, 175–93. London: Hogarth, 1955.
Furet, François. "L'Histoire quantitative et la construction du fait historique." *Annales, Économies, Sociétés, Civilisations* 26, no. 1 (1971): 63–75.
Gallop, Jane. "The Ethics of Reading: Close Encounters." *Journal of Curriculum Theorizing* 16, no. 3 (2000): 7–18.

Gelber, Hester Goodenough. *It Could Have Been Otherwise: Contingency and Necessity in Dominican Theology at Oxford, 1300–1350*. Studien und Texte zur Geistesgeshichte des Mittelalters, no. 81. Leiden: Brill, 2004.

Germain, Marie-Odile. "Around *Tours Promises*: The Donation of Hélène Cixous's Manuscripts to the Bibliothèque nationale de France." *parallax* 13, no. 3 (2007): 31–36.

———. "Fonds Cixous." Inventory list (NAF 28080). Bibliothèque nationale de France.

———. Personal interview. May 23, 2014, Paris, France.

Ghost Dance. Dir. Ken McMullen. 1983.

Ginzburg, Carlo. *Myths, Emblems, Clues*, trans. John Tedeschi and Anne C. Tedeschi. London: Hutchinson, 1990.

Greene, Mark, and Dennis Meissner. "More Product, Less Process: Revamping Traditional Archival Processing." *American Archivist* 68 (2005): 208–63.

Grosz, Elizabeth. *Sexual Subversions*. Crows Nest, Australia: Allen and Unwin, 1989.

———. *Volatile Bodies: Toward a Corporeal Feminism*. Bloomington: Indiana University Press, 1994.

Guattari, Félix. *The Anti-Oedipus Papers*, ed. Stéphane Nadaud, trans. Kélina Gotman. Cambridge, MA: MIT Press, 2006.

Gumbrecht, Hans Ulrich. "Aesthetic Experience in Everyday Worlds: Reclaiming an Unredeemed Utopian Motif." *New Literary History* 37, no. 2 (2006): 299–318.

Hägglund, Martin. *Radical Atheism: Derrida and the Time of Life*. Stanford, CA: Stanford University Press, 2008.

Hamilton, Carolyn, ed. *Refiguring the Archive*. Dordrecht: Kluwer Academic and David Philip Publishers, 2002.

Hanrahan, Mairéad. *Cixous's Semi-Fictions: Thinking at the Borders of Fiction*. Edinburgh: Edinburgh University Press, 2014.

———. "Rêver cru." In *Rêver croire penser*, ed. Bruno Clément and Marta Segarra, 226–38. Paris: CampagnePremière, 2010.

———. "Survivre." In *L'Événement comme écriture: Cixous et Derrida se lisant*, 195–211. Paris: CampagnePremière, 2007.

———. "Writing Symptomatically." In "Cixous, Derrida, Psychoanalysis," special issue of *Paragraph* 36, no. 2 (2013): 206–22.

Harrison, Robert. *Forests: The Shadow of Civilization*. Chicago: University of Chicago Press, 1992.

Helle, Anita, ed. *The Unraveling Archive: Essays on Sylvia Plath*. Ann Arbor: University of Michigan Press, 2007.

Hemmings, Clare. *Why Stories Matter: The Political Grammar of Feminist Theory*. Durham, NC: Duke University Press, 2010.

Hensen, Steven. *Archives, Personal Papers, and Manuscripts*. Chicago: Society of American Archivists, 1989.

———. *Describing Archives: A Content Standard*. Chicago: Society of American Archivists, 2007.

Hildenbrand, Suzanne, ed. *Women's Collections: Libraries, Archives, and Consciousness*. New York: Haworth, 1986.

Hill, Jennie, and Will Slocombe. "An Interdisciplinary Dialogue." *English Language Notes* 45, no. 1 (2007): 21–31.

Hirsch, David, and Frank Moore. "The Archive Project." Visual Aids. https://www.visualaids.org.

Hollier, Denis. *Le Collège de sociologie*. Paris: Folio, 1995.

———. "The Use-Value of the Impossible." *October* 60 (1992): 3–24.

hooks, bell. *Feminist Theory: From Margin to Center*. New York: Routledge, 2015.

———. *Teaching to Transgress*. New York: Routledge, 1994.

Hubbell, Amy. *Remembering French Algeria: Pieds-Noirs, Identity, and Exile*. Lincoln: University of Nebraska Press, 2015.

Huffer, Lynne. "Derrida's Nostalgeria." In *Algeria and France, 1800–2000: Identity, Memory, Nostalgia*, ed. Patricia M. E. Lorcin, 228–46. Syracuse, NY: Syracuse University Press, 2006.

Hughey Engelbert, Lynn. "'Wild' Freudian Psycho-Analysis: Ingestion, Incorporation, and Mourning in Derrida and Deleuze and Guattari." *Mosaic* 44, no. 4 (2011): 161–76.

Institut Mémoires de l'édition contemporaine. Fonds Derrida Finding Aid. https://portail-collections.imec-archives.com/ark:/29414/a011433424761LQUFTQ.

Irigaray, Luce. *Ce sexe qui n'en est pas un*. Paris: Minuit. 1977. English translation: *This Sex Which Is Not One*, trans. Catherine Porter. Ithaca, NY: Cornell University Press, 1985.

Irniger, Manuel. "La Phrase début." Presentation at the conference "Cixéminaire: Le Séminaire d'Hélène Cixous en Études Féminines," May 22, 2014.

Irniger, Manuel, and Claudia Simma. Personal interview. June 28, 2015, Chelles, France.

Jenny, Laurent. "Genetic Criticism and Its Myths." *Yale French Studies* 97 (2000): 198–214.

Jimerson, Randall. *American Archival Studies: Readings in Theory and Practice*. Chicago: Society of American Archivists, 2000.

Johnson, Barbara. "The Frame of Reference: Poe, Lacan, Derrida." In "Literature and Psychoanalysis: The Question of Reading: Otherwise," special issue of *Yale French Studies* 55/56: 457–505.

Johnson, Christopher. *System and Writing in the Philosophy of Jacques Derrida*. Cambridge: Cambridge University Press, 1993.

Kamuf, Peggy. "Aller à la ligne." In *L'Événement comme écriture: Cixous et Derrida se lisant*, 73–84. Paris: CampagnePremière, 2007.

Karasick, Adeena. "Of Poetic Thinking: A 'Pataphysical Investigation of Cixous, Derrida, and the Kabbalah." PhD thesis, Concordia University, 1997.

Kaufmann, Vincent. *L'Équivoque épistolaire*. Paris: Minuit, 1990.

Kay, Sarah. *Animal Skins and the Reading Self in Medieval Latin and French Bestiaries*. Chicago: University of Chicago Press, 2017.

———. "Surface and Symptom on a Bestiary Page." *Exemplaria* 26, no. 2–3 (2014): 125–45.

———. "Surface Reading and the Symptom That Is Only Skin-Deep." *Paragraph* 35, no. 3 (2012): 451–59.

Keilty, Patrick, and Rebecca Dean, eds. *Feminist and Queer Information Studies Reader*. Sacramento, CA: Litwin Books, 2013.

Kim, Christine. E-mail communication, January 20, 2015.

Kirschenbaum, Matthew. "The .txtual Condition." In *Comparative Textual Media: Transforming the Humanities in the Postprint Era*, ed. N. Katherine Hayles and Jessica Pressman, 53–70. Minneapolis: University of Minnesota Press, 2013.

Kittler, Friedrich. *Gramophone, Film, Typewriter*. Stanford, CA: Stanford University Press, 1999.

Krauss, Rosalind. "Poststructuralism and the 'Paraliterary.'" *October* 13 (1980): 36–40.

Kristeva, Julia. *Recherches pour une sémanalyse*. Paris: Seuil, 1969.

Kumbier, Alana. *Ephemeral Material: Queering the Archive*. Los Angeles: Litwin, 2014.

Lacan, Jacques. "Le Séminaire sur la lettre volée." In *Écrits*, 11–61. Paris: Seuil, 1966.

Lafon, Michel, and Benoît Peeters. *Nous est un autre: Enquête sur les duos d'écrivains*. Paris: Flammarion, 2006.

Laplanche, Jean. "Notes on Afterwardness." In *Jean Laplanche: Seduction, Translation, Drives*, ed. John Fletcher and Martin Stanton, trans. Martin Stanton, 217–24. London: Institute of Contemporary Arts, 1992.

Lejeune, Philippe. *Le Pacte autobiographique*. Paris: Seuil, 1996.

———. *Les Brouillons de soi*. Paris: Seuil, 1998.

Lernout, Geert. *The French Joyce*. Ann Arbor: University of Michigan Press, 1990.

Lesbian Herstory Archives. http://www.lesbianherstoryarchives.org/.

Levinas, Emmanuel. *Entre nous: Essais sur le penser-à-autre*. Paris: Grasset, 1991.

Liberman, Anatoly. *An Analytic Dictionary of the English Etymology: An Introduction*. Minneapolis: University of Minnesota Press, 2007.

Loeffelholz, M. "Networking Dickinson: Some Thought Experiments in Digital Humanities." *Emily Dickinson Journal* 23, no. 1 (2014): 106–19.

Lucretius, *On the Nature of Things*. Loeb Classical Library no. 181. Cambridge, MA: Harvard University Press, 1924.

Lukacher, Ned. "Introduction: Mourning Becomes Telepathy." In *Cinders*, by Jacques Derrida, 1–18. Lincoln: University of Nebraska Press, 1991.

Maier-Katkin, Daniel. *Stranger from Abroad: Hannah Arendt, Martin Heidegger, Friendship and Forgiveness*. New York: W. W. Norton, 2010.

Malabou, Catherine. *Plasticity at the Dusk of Writing*, trans. Carolyn Shread. New York: Columbia University Press, 2009.

———. *What Should We Do with Our Brain?* trans. Sebastian Rand. New York: Fordham University Press, 2008.

Mallarmé, Stéphane. "Quant au livre." In *Igitur—Divagations—Un coup de dés*. Paris: Gallimard, 2003.

Mallet, Marie-Louise, ed. *L'Animal autobiographique: Autour de Jacques Derrida*. Paris: Galilée, 1999.

Manoff, Marlene. "Theories of the Archive from across the Disciplines." *Portal: Libraries and the Academy* 4, no. 1 (2004): 9–25.

Margel, Serge. *Les Archives fantômes*. Paris: Lignes, 2012.

Masó, Joana. "De l'écriture et du corps chez Jacques Derrida." In *Pensées du corps: La Matérialité et l'organique vus par les sciences humaines*, ed. Balcázar Moreno and Crevier Goulet, 49–57. Paris: Presses Sorbonne Nouvelle, 2011.

Mauss, Marcel. *Essai sur le don*. Paris: Presses Universitaires de France, 2012.

McGann, Jerome. "The Socialization of Texts." In *The Book History Reader*, ed. David Finkelstein and Alistair McCleery, 66–73. New York: Routledge, 2006.

McGrady, Deborah. *Controlling Readers: Guillaume de Machaut and His Late Medieval Audience*. Toronto: University of Toronto Press, 2006.

McKinley, Michael. "Imaging Digital Media for Preservation with LAMMP." In *The Electronic Media Review* 3 (2015): 89–96.

McQuillan, Martin. "Tele-Techno-Theology." In *Deconstruction after 9/11*, 47–64. New York: Routledge, 2001.

Merewether, Charles, ed. *The Archive*. Documents of Contemporary Art. London and Cambridge, MA: Whitechapel Gallery and MIT Press, 2006.

Merleau-Ponty, Maurice. *Phénoménologie de la perception*. Paris: Gallimard, 1945.

Michaud, Ginette. *Battements du secret littéraire: Lire Jacques Derrida et Hélène Cixous*, vol. 1. 2 vols. Paris: Hermann, 2010.

———. "Circonfections: Les lire en secret." In *L'Événement comme écriture: Cixous et Derrida se lisant*, 231–58. Paris: CampagnePremière, 2007.

———. *"Comme en rêve . . .": Lire Jacques Derrida et Hélène Cixous*, vol. 2. 2 vols. Paris: Hermann, 2010.

———. "Derrida & Cixous: Between and Beyond, or 'What to the Letter Has Happened.' " *New Literary History* 37, no. 1 (2006): 85–106.

———. *Jacques Derrida: L'Art du contretemps*. Montréal: Nota Bene, 2014.

———. "Ombilic: L'Œuvre à l'insu de l'archive." In *Genèses Généalogies Genres: Autour de l'œuvre d'Hélène Cixous*, ed. Mireille Calle-Gruber and Marie-Odile Germain. Paris: Galilée, 2006. 275–99.

———. *Tenir au secret (Derrida, Blanchot)*. Paris: Galilée, 2006.

Mikics, David. *Who Was Jacques Derrida? An Intellectual Biography*. New Haven, CT: Yale University Press, 2009.

Milesi, Laurent. "Cixanalyses—Towards a Reading of *Anankè*." In "Cixous, Derrida, Psychoanalysis," special issue of *Paragraph* 36, no. 2 (2013): 286–302.

———. "De-monstrating Monsters: Unmastering (in) Derrida and Cixous." In "Unidentifiable Literary Objects," special issue of *parallax* 25, no. 3 (2019): 269–87.

———. "Entre eux deux: Le Traductor." In *L'Événement comme écriture: Cixous et Derrida se lisant*, 303–14. Paris: CampagnePremière, 2007.

———. "Portraits of H. C. as J. D. and Back." *New Literary History* 37, no. 1 (2006): 65–84.

Miller, Christianne. *Emily Dickinson's Poems as She Preserved Them*. Cambridge, MA: Harvard University Press, 2016.

Miller, J. Hillis. "Derrida's Destinerrance." *MLN* 121, no. 4 (2006): 893–910.

Miller, Judith. "The Theatre of Hélène Cixous: Re-memberings, Re-fashionings, and Revenants." In *The Portable Cixous*, ed. Marta Segarra, 215–78. New York: Columbia University Press, 2010.

Mitchell, W. J. Thomas, and Arnold Ira Davidson, eds. *The Late Derrida*. Chicago: University of Chicago Press, 2007.

Moi, Toril. "Helene Cixous: An Imaginary Utopia." In *Sexual/Textual Politics: Feminist Literary Theory*, 102–26. London: Methuen, 1985.
Mort, J. *The Anatomy of Xerography*. Jefferson, NC: McFarland, 1989.
Moser, Benjamin. "In the Sontag Archives." *The New Yorker*, January 30, 2014. http://www.newyorker.com/books/page-turner/in-the-sontag-archives.
Naas, Michael. *The End of the World and Other Teachable Moments: Jacques Derrida's Final Seminar*. New York: Fordham University Press, 2014.
Negrón, Mara. "À propos de greffes: Ce que l'on singe en écriture autobiographique." In *L'Événement comme écriture: Cixous et Derrida se lisant*, 259–75. Paris: CampagnePremière, 2007.
Nichols, Stephen. "Introduction: Philology in a Manuscript Culture." *Speculum* 65 (1990): 1–9.
———. "Philology and Its Discontents." In *The Future of the Middle Ages: Medieval Literature in the 1990s*, ed. W. D. Paden, 113–41. Gainesville: University of Florida Press, 1994.
Nora, Pierre. *Les Lieux de mémoire*. Paris: Gallimard, 1984.
Ofrat, Gideon. *The Jewish Derrida*. Syracuse, NY: Syracuse University Press, 2001.
O'Meara, Lucy. *Roland Barthes at the Collège de France*. Liverpool: University of Liverpool Press, 2012.
Osborne, Peter. "Guattareuze?" *New Left Review* 69 (2011): 139–51.
Osborne, Thomas. "The Ordinariness of the Archive." *History of the Human Sciences* 12, no. 2 (1999): 51–64.
Owen, David. *Copies in Seconds*. New York: Simon and Schuster, 2004.
Peeters, Benoît. *Derrida*. Paris: Flammarion, 2010.
———. "Sur les archives de Jacques Derrida." Institut Mémoires de l'édition contemporaine. http://www.imec-archives.com/les-collections/les-archives-jacques-derrida/.
———. *Trois ans avec Derrida: Les Carnets d'un biographe*. Paris: Flammarion, 2010.
Pembroke Center. Feminist Theory Archive. Brown University. https://pembroke.brown.edu/archives/feminist-theory-archive/.
Piégay-Gros, Nathalie. *Le Futur antérieur de l'archive*. Rimouski, Québec: Tangence, 2012.
Prenowitz, Eric. "Foreword: Modernepic Theatre." In *The Selected Plays of Hélène Cixous*, vii–ix. New York: Routledge, 2003.
———. "Introduction: Cracking the Book—Readings of Hélène Cixous." *New Literary History* 37 (2006): ix–xxvii.
———. "'Je t.'" In *L'Événement comme écriture: Cixous et Derrida se lisant*, 109–33. Paris: CampagnePremière, 2007.
Presa, Elizabeth. *Four Horizons of the Page*. Linden Gallery, Melbourne, Australia, 2000.
Rancière, Jacques. *Le Maître ignorant*. Paris: Éditions 10/18, 2004.
Rapaport, Herman. *Later Derrida: Reading the Recent Work*. London: Routledge, 2003.
———. *The Theory Mess*. New York: Columbia University Press, 2001.
Regard, Frédéric. "Autobiography as Linguistic Incompetence: Notes on Derrida's Readings of Joyce and Cixous." *Textual Practice* 19, no. 2 (2005): 283–95.

———. "Derrida *in time*: Critique et contemporaneité dans le rituel de surlignement chez Hélène Cixous." In *L'Événement comme écriture: Cixous et Derrida se lisant*, 277–88. Paris: CampagnePremière, 2007.

———. "Derrida Un-Cut: Cixous's Art of Hearts." *Paragraph* 30, no. 2 (2007): 1–16.

———. "Faulty Burials." In "Cixous, Derrida, Psychoanalysis," special issue of *Paragraph* 36, no. 2 (2013): 255–69.

———. "Le Portrait biographique selon Hélène Cixous." In *Biographie et intimité des Lumières à nos jours*, ed. Daniel Madelénat, 203–19. Clermont-Ferrand: Presses Universitaires Blaise Pascal, 2009.

Ricoeur, Paul. *De l'interprétation: Essai sur Sigmund Freud*. Paris: Seuil, 1965.

———. *La Mémoire, l'histoire, l'oubli*. Paris: Seuil, 2000.

Roe, Kathleen. *Arranging and Describing Archives and Manuscripts*. Chicago: Society of American Archivists, 2005.

Ronell, Avital. *Dictations: On Haunted Writing*. Champaign: University of Illinois Press, 2006.

———. *Fighting Theory*, trans. Catherine Porter. Champaign: University of Illinois Press, 2010.

———. *The Telephone Book: Technology, Schizophrenia, Electric Speech*. Lincoln: University of Nebraska Press, 1989.

Rooney, Ellen, and Elizabeth Weed, eds. "Derrida's Gift." Special issue of *differences: A Journal of Feminist Cultural Studies* 16, no. 3 (2005).

Rose, Jacqueline. *The Haunting of Sylvia Plath*. London: Virago, 1991.

Royle, Nicholas. "The Remains of Psychoanalysis (I): Telepathy." In *After Derrida*. Manchester, UK: Manchester University Press, 1994.

———. *Telepathy and Literature: Essays on the Reading Mind*. Oxford: Blackwell, 1990.

Rust, Martha. *Imaginary Worlds in Medieval Books: Exploring the Manuscript Matrix*. New York: Palgrave Macmillan, 2007.

Said, Edward. "The Return to Philology." In *Humanism and Democratic Criticism*, 67–84. New York: Columbia University Press, 2004.

Scherer, Jacques. *Le "Livre" de Mallarmé*. Paris: Gallimard, 1957.

Scott, Joan. "Epilogue: A Feminist Theory Archive." In *The Fantasy of Feminist History*. Durham, NC: Duke University Press, 2011.

———. "The Evidence of Experience." *Critical Inquiry* 17 (1991): 773–97.

Sedgwick, Eve Kosovsky. *A Dialogue on Love*. Boston: Beacon, 1999.

———. *Touching Feeling*. Durham, NC: Duke University Press, 2003.

Segarra, Marta. "Cixous, Derrida and Psychoanalysis: The Principle of Intermittence, or Dwelling on the Angle." In "Cixous, Derrida, Psychoanalysis," special issue of *Paragraph* 36, no. 2 (2013): 240–54.

———. "Hélène Cixous's Other Animal: The Half-Sunken Dog." *New Literary History* 37, no. 1 (2006): 119–34.

———. "L'Amitié, la trahison, la traduction." In *L'Événement comme écriture: Cixous et Derrida se lisant*, 181–93. Paris: CampagnePremière, 2007.

———, ed. *L'Événement comme écriture: Cixous et Derrida se lisant*. Paris: CampagnePremière, 2007.

Sekula, Allan. "The Body and the Archive." *October* 39 (1986): 3–64.

Sellers, Susan, ed. *Hélène Cixous: Authorship, Autobiography, and Love*. Cambridge: Polity, 1996.

———, ed. *Writing Differences: Readings from the Seminar of Hélène Cixous*. New York: St. Martin's Press, 1988.

Seltzer, Sara Renée, Alexandra Bisio, and Shu Liu. "Deconstructing the Critical Theory Archive at UCI: An Experiment with EAC-CPF and Linked Open Data." *Journal of Western Archives* 5, no. 1 (2014). http://digitalcommons.usu.edu/westernarchives/vol5/iss1/8.

Seshadri, Kalpana Rahita. *HumAnimal: Race, Law, Language*. Minneapolis: University of Minnesota Press, 2012.

Shiach, Morag. *Hélène Cixous: A Politics of Writing*. London: Routledge, 1991.

Shrewsbury, Carolyn M. "What Is Feminist Pedagogy?" *Women's Studies Quarterly* 15, no. 3–4 (1978): 6–14.

Simma, Claudia. "*Ver(s)*: Toward a Spirituality of One's Own." In *Demenageries: Thinking (of) Animals after Derrida*, 73–96. New York: Rodopi, 2011.

Simondon, Georges. *L'Individuation psychique et collective*. Paris: Aubier, 2007.

Smith, Daniel. "The Concept of the Simulacrum: Deleuze and the Overturning of Platonism." *Continental Philosophy Review* 38, no. 1–2 (2005): 89–123.

Smith, Robert. *Derrida and Autobiography*. Cambridge: Cambridge University Press, 1995.

Sontag, Susan. "Against Interpretation." In *Against Interpretation and Other Essays*, 3–14. New York: Picador, 1966.

Sprinkler, Michael, ed. *Ghostly Demarcations: A Symposium on Jacques Derrida's Spectres of Marx*. London: Verso, 2008.

Steedman, Carolyn. *Dust: The Archive and Cultural History*. New Brunswick, NJ: Rutgers University Press, 2002.

Stevens, Christa. "La Première fois plus d'une fois: Autour de *Manhattan*." In *L'Événement comme écriture: Cixous et Derrida se lisant*, 167–80. Paris: CampagnePremière, 2007.

Stiegler, Bernard. *La Technique et le temps*. Paris: Galilée, 1994.

Still, Judith. *Derrida and Hospitality: Theory and Practice*. Edinburgh: Edinburgh University Press, 2010.

———. *Derrida and Other Animals: The Boundaries of the Human*. Edinburgh: Edinburgh University Press, 2017.

Stoler, Ann Laura. *Along the Archival Grain: Epistemic Anxieties and Colonial Common Sense*. Princeton, NJ: Princeton University Press, 2009.

Taylor, Diana. *The Archive and the Repertoire: Performing Cultural Memory in the Americas*. Durham, NC: Duke University Press, 2003.

Terada, Rei. "Imaginary Seductions: Derrida and Emotion Theory." *Comparative Literature* 51, no. 3 (1999): 193–216.

Thomas, Marcel. "Manuscripts." In *The Book History Reader*, ed. David Finkelstein and Alistair McCleery, 147–56. London: Routledge, 2006.

Thompson, Ashley. "Voir à lire." In *L'Événement comme écriture: Cixous et Derrida se lisant*, 327–42. Paris: CampagnePremière, 2007.

Torok, Maria. "Afterword: What Is Occult in Occultism?" In *The Wolf Man's Magic Word: A Cryptonomy*, by Nicholas Abraham and Maria Torok, trans. Nicholas Rand, 84–106. Minneapolis: University of Minnesota Press, 1986.

Trifonas, Peter Pericles. *The Ethics of Writing: Derrida, Deconstruction, and Pedagogy*. Lanham, MD: Rowman and Littlefield, 2000.

Vadrot, Claude-Marie. "Naissance d'une université," and "Quand Vincennes déménage à Saint-Denis." *Politis* 30 (2008).

Van Gerven Oei, Vincent W. J., ed. *Going Postcard: The Letter(s) of Jacques Derrida*. Punctum Books, 2017.

Vardoluakis, Dimitris. "Beside(s): Elizabeth Presa with Jacques Derrida." *Derrida Today* 2, no. 2 (2009): 200–209.

Voss, Paul J., and Martin Werner. "Towards a Poetics of the Archive." *Studies in the Literary Imagination* 32, no. 1 (1999): i–vii.

Walt Whitman Archive, ed. Ed Folsom and Kenneth M. Price. http://www.whitmanarchive.org.

Weed, Elizabeth. "Notes on Pembroke Center's History: 1981–2011." Pembroke Center, Brown University. https://pembroke.brown.edu/about/history/documenting-browns-history.

Weed, Elizabeth, and Ellen Rooney, eds. "Derrida's Gift." *differences: A Journal of Feminist Cultural Studies* 16, no. 3 (2005).

Weltman-Aron, Brigitte. "The Pedagogy of Colonial Algeria: Djebar, Cixous, Derrida." *Yale French Studies* 113 (2008): 132–46.

Whalley, Joyce Irene. *Writing Implements and Accessories: From the Roman Stylus to the Typewriter.* Michigan: Gale Research, 1975.

Wills, David. "Post/Card/Match/Book/'Envois'/Derrida." *SubStance* 13, no. 2 (1984): 19–38.

Wolfreys, Julian. "A Note on a Post Card: Derrida, Deronda, Deguy." In *Applying: To Derrida*, ed. John Brannigan, Ruth Robbins, and Julian Wolfreys, 71–95. New York: St. Martin's Press, 1996.

Yassa, Maria. "Nicolas Abraham and Maria Torok—The Inner Crypt." *Scandinavian Psychoanalytic Review* 25, no. 2 (2002): 1–14.

Yeo, Geoffrey. "The Conceptual Fonds and the Physical Collection." *Archivaria* 73 (2012): 43–80.

Zemon Davis, Natalie. *Women on the Margins*. Cambridge, MA: Harvard University Press, 1995.

Žižek, Slavoj. "Why Does a *Letter* Always Arrive at Its Destination?" In *Enjoy Your Symptom!* 1–30. New York: Routledge, 1992.

INDEX